Managing Through Incentives

Managing Through Incentives

How to Develop a More Collaborative,
Productive, and Profitable Organization

Richard B. McKenzie
Dwight R. Lee

New York   Oxford
OXFORD UNIVERSITY PRESS
1998

Oxford University Press

Oxford   New York

Athens   Auckland   Bangkok   Bogotá   Bombay
Buenos Aires   Calcutta   Cape Town   Dar es Salaam   Delhi
Florence   Hong Kong   Istanbul   Karachi
Kuala Lumpur   Madras   Madrid   Melbourne
Mexico City   Nairobi   Paris   Singapore
Taipei   Tokyo   Toronto   Warsaw

and associated companies in
Berlin   Ibadan

Published by Oxford University Press, Inc.
198 Madison Avenue, New York, New York 10016

Oxford is a registered trademark of Oxford University Press

Library of Congress Cataloging-in-Publication Data
McKenzie, Richard B.
Managing through incentives : how to develop a more
collaborative, productive, and profitable organization /
Richard B. McKenzie and Dwight R. Lee.
p.   cm.
Includes bibliographical references (p.) and index.
ISBN 0-19-511901-0
1. Incentives in industry. 2. Employee motivation.
3. Industrial management. 4. Incentives (Psychology).
5. Motivation (Psychology). I. Lee, Dwight R. II. Title.
HF5549.5.I5M393   1998   658.3'14—dc21   98-14526

1 3 5 7 9 8 6 4 2
Printed in the United States of America
on acid-free paper

Contents

Preface

This book is concerned with the most fundamental of problems facing owners and managers—the one that can cause them to lose sleep or can drive them to sell out—*getting people within a firm to cooperate for long stretches of time in pursuit of agreed-upon common objectives*.

Getting agreement on a common objective is not always easy. All too frequently people's focus starts with some variant of "what's best for *me*," not what's best for the *firm* (much less for stockholders). And cooperation does not always follow naturally once general consent on the common objective is achieved. If cooperation were innate in the human condition, surely the jobs of many managers would be far easier. In fact, fewer managers would be needed overall. Managers' job security comes in part from the fact that many people cooperate only reluctantly.

In one way or another, all management practices seek to deal with the difficulty managers face when they try to advance their own and their workers' agreed-upon collective interests by acting cooperatively and synergistically within the context of a single business organization.

In firms, the common, overarching objective—the one dearest to the hearts of stockholders—is typically straightforward—increasing profitability. Certainly, managers and line workers would prefer working for a more, rather than less, profitable firm. Higher profits spell greater long-run job security and higher lifetime incomes for workers. But the mere identification of the firm's objective—to maximize profits or anything else—does little to guarantee that anyone in the firm will work effectively and cooperatively to achieve it. Establishing a well-defined mission for the company and equally clear, measurable, and potentially achievable firm goals and objectives that can be derived from the firm's mission can be a big help in eliciting cooperation within firms. Goals and objectives can focus workers' attention and possibly even inspire cooperation, at least to a limited extent.

Firms must be managed by objectives in one way or another. People need to know what they and others are supposed to be doing. But "management by objectives," as important as those touchstone words have become in management circles, cannot be expected to be a complete guiding management philosophy and practice. The simple fact remains that workers cannot always be expected to appropriately use the information, resources, and authority at their disposal in the pursuit of the firm's goals unless they have a personal motivation to do so.

And the *profitability* of the firm is seldom a sufficient motivation for most workers. Indeed, firm profitability, in and of itself, is likely to inspire only limited cooperation among many workers, who will surely wonder why they should work harder and smarter for the benefit of far-removed stockholders. In large firms especially, each person knows that any extra effort is likely to make little difference to the firm's bottom line *without similar effort on the part of many others*. Many workers can be expected to wonder why they should make the extra effort. They will want assurance that others are doing their part, which means that they will want assurance that others will have some personal motivation to make the requisite extra effort.

The job of managers is relatively simple: to provide the information, resources, and personal motivation workers need in order to do their jobs and to pull together in productive and profitable ways. This means that managers cannot avoid the creative use of incentives. Incentives are the various money and nonmoney ways managers use to incite action within firms, namely, work and cooperation. They are what breath life into any system of "management by objectives." Incentives are necessarily ubiquitous in any firm, since without the motivation they provide, there would be little hope of getting the vast majority of workers to make the needed extra effort and to take the requisite risks that every successful enterprise requires.

Incentives do more than provide worker drive, however. When they become part and parcel of the firm's policy structure, they are also an important means of communicating the firm's mission and most valued goals and objectives to everyone. Incentives, in effect, tell workers loud and clear, "This is what counts here." And the message is not like a policy memorandum that is periodically passed down to workers to remind them of what they are supposed to do. The message in incentives is ever present, relentless, something that is a constant reference point for workers: "This is how I can improve my well-being."

As readers will quickly discover, we strongly believe that incentives are necessary and that they do in fact work. The central problem managers face is making sure that the incentives are consistent with patterns of behavior that promote the general goals of the firm. Otherwise, incentives can work perversely. Getting incentives wrong can be the deathblow of firms just as surely as producing the wrong combination of products.

In our view, managers must manage *through* incentives, which involves not just putting incentives in place but getting those incentives right. Managers have to recognize that their success depends on more than the simple listing of the firm's goals and objectives. It involves establishing mechanisms—the *right* incentives—for ensuring that those goals and objectives are cooperatively sought and met.

However, managers must also realize that they, too, must be willing to submit themselves to the right set of incentives to ensure that they, the managers, come up with the right set of goals and objectives and with the right set of incentives for those they are managing. This is an intriguing problem. Some might see it as a Catch-22, with no obvious solution, given that we must wonder about the incentives managers have to select the right incentives for themselves. But read on. In this book we propose a way of thinking about incentives that will help you demystify the problems of getting incentives right.

We hasten to add, however, that current interest in incentives— revealed in the trend of tying the pay of top executives and line workers to firm performance—does not spring completely from the hearts and minds of management experts. Greater use of incentives should be expected in a world of growing production sophistication and of flattening organizational structures in which direct supervision of workers is limited by the reduction in the number of management layers and by the spread of employees across the globe. The interest springs also from competitive market pressures. Firms must use incentives as never before because their competitors are using them, and they must get them right in order to become more cost effective in a highly competitive global economy. Firms must get more output from their workers for the benefit of their workers and must offer their investors a higher return on their money. Those firms that don't will have a tough time attracting and holding the labor and capital they need to remain competitive on a world scale. In essence, firms' very survival depends on how incentives are used.

Most business people know how to *do* business. Throughout this book, we are concerned with providing a better way of *thinking* about doing business, specifically with reference to the incentives that are employed. Our expectation is that the methods of thinking provided will enable managers to develop more cooperative, productive, and profitable business ventures. Such dedicated and directed thought will help managers get incentives right and, in the process, cut the waste of firm resources.

Managing Through Incentives is the result of several years of writing that has been affected by the many valuable discussions we have had with our colleagues in our respective schools of business. We are indebted to them and to others for the considerable help they provided. We are especially indebted, however, to our MBA students who used early drafts of this book in the classes on incentives that we taught (and one of our students, through a passing e-mail comment, helped us with the title). Our student critics—especially the executives in our classes—have made valuable criticisms and suggestions for improvement, an outgrowth of the years they have spent actually trying to come to grips with the problem of getting incentives right within their firms. We are indebted to anonymous referees for their advice. However, we were also very pleased with the suggestions for reorganization and focus provided by Herb Addison, our editor at Oxford University Press. Karen McKenzie's editorial suggestions improved greatly the flow of the discussion.

Richard B. McKenzie
Graduate School of Management
University of California, Irvine
mckenzie@uci.edu

Dwight R. Lee
Terry College of Business
University of Georgia
dlee@cbacc.cba.uga.edu

I

INTRODUCTION

1

Why Incentives Matter

Key Insight: Incentives matter because information is dispersed throughout the firm and those who have the information do not always have an interest in using it for the benefit of the firm as a whole and its owners.

INCENTIVES ARE IN! News reports constantly remind us of this contemporary fact of American business.

American executives have come under increasing attacks in the media for accepting huge compensation deals that can run into tens of millions of dollars a year in salary, bonuses, and stock options—all justified as incentives for running more efficient and profitable firms. The total compensation of many executives now rivals the pay of successful rock, sports, and movie stars, and executive compensation packages continue to outpace the rate of inflation by a substantial margin.

The average salary of the CEOs at the 365 largest corporations in the country hit $2.3 million 1996, up 39 percent over the average CEO salary for the previous year. But salary represented less than half of the average CEO's total compensation, which was $5.8 million for the year, 54 percent higher than the year before.[1]

But the "average" doesn't come close to the maximum. Al Dunlap made over $100 million in salary, bonus, stock options, and stock appreciation during his eighteen-month tenure as CEO of Scott Paper Company, and he minces few words in explaining why he deserved every nickel he got.[2] Les McCraw, the former chairman and CEO of Fluor Daniel, one of the world's largest construction companies, received 15 percent more in annual salary, bonus, stock, and stock options in 1996 than he did the previous year, making his compensation package for the year worth about $5.3 million.[3] But McCraw's compensation was a pittance compared with the compensation received by Andrew Grove, CEO of Intel, that same year. Grove earned *only* $425,000 in salary, but he was granted a bonus of $2.6 million and then was able to exercise stock options worth $95 million.[4]

The trend is evident. More and more companies have begun to use stock options as incentives for their CEOs. In 1992, only about 6 percent of the companies surveyed by *Executive Compensation Reports* provided "mega options," or options of more than 250,000 shares to their top executives. In 1996, nearly 25 percent of the surveyed companies doled out "mega options."[5] Understandably, pay experts and stockholders alike have begun to worry if the exorbitant pay has resulted in higher performance levels for corporations.

Workers' pay is a pittance compared to the pay of company heads, averaging less than one-half of 1 percent of CEO pay. Still, worker pay is increasingly being tied to production through commission, bonuses, and employee stock option plans. Safelite Glass Corporation of Columbus, Ohio, a nationwide company that installs automobile glass, has followed what has become a well-worn pattern in employee compensation. In the mid-1990s, it moved its production workers from compensation based on hours of work (under which the minimum wage was $11 an hour) to a fixed amount ($20) for each glass unit installed. Average productivity per worker rose 20 percent, with the percentage gain evenly split between workers and the company. Moreover, the company's output surged 36 percent as the growth in worker productivity per hour was accompanied by a lower rate of absenteeism and, therefore, an increase in hours worked.[6]

And consumers are being encouraged to become loyal customers by creative incentive programs that go beyond simply lowering the price of products. Through its frequent flyer program, American Airlines has long encouraged repeat business among its flying customers. General Motors has also attempted to "incentivize" customers by giving credit on purchases of GM cars when they use the GM-backed credit card, a topic we cover later in the book.

Incentives are growing in importance as a tool of management for several important reasons that are explored in detail in this book but can be stated briefly:

- Production of goods and services in many industries has become unbelievably sophisticated and complex, which has required managers to draw on the creativity, skills, and human capital of line workers who often have local information about their work—what can and cannot be done—that is not, and cannot be, available to their supervising managers.

- Production processes for many goods and services have become global in scope, which necessarily means that many workers must work far removed from their supervisors, who have no way of monitoring what the workers are doing each day.

- Firms have, to a growing extent, relied on "outsourcing," which means firms are buying more and more of their inputs—from parts to human resources services—from outside suppliers whose business goals are not always in line with the business goals of the buyers.
- The hierarchical organizational structures of many firms have been "flattened," which implies fewer layers of managers and super-visors.
- The pace of technological and organizational innovations and change has speeded up, increasing the extent to which decision making has devolved to lower and lower levels within firms' organizational structures.

These ongoing and far-reaching changes in the economy have long been documented. What has not been fully appreciated is that fact these changes mean that a growing number of workers must work without the direct supervision of their bosses. Because managers are less able to directly monitor the workers under them, old command-and-control methods of management have begun to wane. Managers have become less able to tell their employees what to do simply because the managers, in highly sophisticated and complex production processes, don't have the skills and the knowledge to do what their employees can do or even to figure out exactly what their workers should do with a substantial share of their time. Production has truly become "participatory," which means that higher managers must rely on their underlings to do what they are supposed to do.

Under the circumstances, managers must find ways to entice workers to use their creativity, skills, and human capital to pursue the firm's goals. In short, managers must use *incentives*. They can no longer manage by commands, at least not to the extent that they once could. The count of firms that tie managers and worker incomes to performance is not known, but few observers doubt that it is growing rapidly. In 1945, there were only 2,113 firms in the United States that had deferred compensation or profit-sharing plans for their workforces. In 1991, the count of firms with such group incentive plans had risen to nearly 500,000.[7] One researcher predicted in the late 1980s that, by the turn of the century, a quarter of all firms listed on the American, New York, and NASDAQ stock exchanges will, because of distribution of shares of stock and stock options to workers, have more than 15 percent of their shares owned by their workers.[8] We submit that incentives are a popular solution for today's management dilemmas for a simple reason: *Incentives work and always have, often with dramatic effect.*

In the late nineteenth century, British boat captains were paid to carry prisoners from England to the wilds of Australia, to solve England's crime problem and to reduce the cost of housing criminals. The captains were paid a flat fee for each prisoner who boarded at an English port, which meant that the captains had a strong incentive to board as many prisoners as they could but only a weak incentive to deliver them to Australia alive. In other words, the incentive system was perverse. If prisoners died along the way from lack of food and care, the cost of the trips was lowered, but the captain's pay was unchanged. And the survival rate was a miserable 40 percent, a fact that outraged humanitarians then, as it would now! But despite the moral outrage at the time, the survival rate of the prisoners didn't budge until the incentive was changed. Edwin Chadwich, the government official in charge of the deportation of criminals in the 1860s, had a bright idea for restructuring the incentive system: pay the captains not by the count of prisoners who boarded the boats in England, but by the number of prisoners who disembarked in Australia. The survival rate rose quickly and dramatically to 98.5 percent—all because the captains then had a strong incentive to take care of their charges.[9]

Under the former Soviet Union, there was more than an ounce of truth in the widely circulated Soviet witticism "We pretend to work, and they pretend to pay us." In the new economy, the pretense of work is not rewarded. The former (and the last) premier of the Soviet Union Mikhail Gorbachev made much the same point when he wrote that "amazing things happen when people take responsibility for everything themselves. The results are quite different, and at times people are unrecognizable. Work changes and attitudes to it, too."[10] Many world leaders worry that the Russian people have become accustomed to being communists and will not make the transition to market thinking without grave difficulty and that instituting property rights and the attendant incentives may not have all the beneficial effects that they have had in the West. After all, the Russian citizens need to rebuild their economy, and the rebuilding process has imposed a major disruption on economic activity.

We also harbored such grave concerns until we heard an American diplomat talk about the resale of burned-out light bulbs in the black (or even the gray) markets of Moscow. Light bulbs were scarce in Moscow under the communist regime, partly because of the inefficiency of the Russian light-bulb producers and partly because light bulbs were underpriced and producers had only weak incentives to meet customer needs. To get light bulbs, Russians had to wait in long lines, possibly two or three hours. Reducing the shortage was impeded by the fact that many producers did not have the right to own, buy, and sell all of the materials that go into light bulbs and the light bulbs themselves.

The planners, however, forgot about imposing such restrictions on the ownership and resale of burned-out light bulbs, which were of no use to anyone, or so it might have been thought. Russian consumers found a use for them, however. They could buy the burned-out light bulbs, take them to work, and install them in place of good bulbs in their work places. They could then call the maintenance department to have the bulbs replaced. The bulbs were typically replaced with unusual quickness. Why? Because the maintenance people knew that they could claim ownership of the used bulbs once they replaced them with good bulbs, and they could then sell the used bulbs back to the Moscow black market. The diplomat reported that used bulbs had a life cycle of approximately twenty-four hours. Within that time, the used bulbs would be back for resale again. To paraphrase Gorbachev, amazing, unexpected things happen when people are given meaningful incentives to lay claims to the benefits of their actions.

Like most other universities, the University of California, Irvine, has graduate student apartments that are heavily subsidized. That is to say, the rents charged for on-campus apartments are several hundred dollars lower than the rents charged for comparable off-campus, privately owned apartments close to campus. The university claims that the apartments must be underpriced in order that "good" but "poor" graduate students can afford to follow their degree programs at the university. The university also argues that if it were to raise the rents, the quality of the graduate students the university could attract would fall unless a graduate student assistantship and fellowships payments were raised.

Naturally, the incentives in the subsidized rents have led to consequences that undermine the "official line" on the subsidies. First, students likely use the subsidies to rent apartments that are larger than those they would have chosen to rent if they had to pay market prices, soaking up space that could be used by other students. Second, the quality of the apartments has deteriorated because maintenance has been deferred, a result of the low rents. Third, and perhaps most important, the graduate students tend to stay much longer than you would think graduate students would need in order to finish their degree programs. Indeed, many of the student-residents have been in their apartments for more than a decade, using all sorts of means to prolong their graduations (for example, sending spouses to school, taking years off in the middle of their programs, and pursuing postdoctoral research). In extending their stays, they deny the spaces to other students who might otherwise choose UC-Irvine.

Moreover, we must question the official argument—"they can't afford higher rents"—for maintaining the low rents. Of course, the students could afford higher rents. If there is a problem, the university could raise the rent and hand the additional revenue back to the graduate students in the form of cash. If the rent were raised by $400 and the students were given the $400 back, then they could clearly afford what they had. The question is whether they would actually continue to rent the same apartments. Not likely. Many students would take the cash and run to buy other things, after accepting a smaller place to live (because the price of space would then be higher).

Instead of increasing the quality of the university's graduate students, the rent subsidies are very likely lowering the quality. If the rent were raised by $400 and the revenue were transferred to departments for distribution as assistantships and fellowships, potential graduate students would surely be happier to have the $400 in cash rather than as a rent subsidy. With the cash, the students could still rent apartments at the higher rents, but then they could do other, more valuable things with the cash. When the subsidy is in the form of a reduction in the price of a particular good, then it is locked in, limited to the good in question, a point that has escaped the thinking of the university officials. This is one general reason why businesses—not just universities—should think seriously before they give their workers in-kind work-related benefits in lieu of salary.

Of course, incentives have been found to be important for more mundane, everyday business reasons. Tying compensation to some objective measure of firm performance can cause the affected workers' productivity to rise substantially, a point covered in detail later. As would be expected, appropriately structured incentive pay can increase a firm's rate of return and stock price, as well as the income of the affected workers. One study of thousands of managers of large corporations found that adding a 10 percent bonus for good performance could be expected to add .3 to .9 percent to the companies' after-tax rate of return on stockholder investment. If managerial bonuses are tied to the market prices of the companies' stock, share prices can be expected to rise by 4 to 12 percent. The study also found that the greater the sensitivity of management pay to company performance, the better the performance.[11] Another study found that firms don't have to wait around for the incentives to have an impact on the firms' bottom line to get a jump in their stock prices; all they have to do is *announce* that executives' compensation over the long haul is going to be more closely tied (through stock options or bonuses) to performance measures, and the stock will, within days, go up several percentage points, increasing shareholder wealth by tens, if not hundreds, of millions of dollars (depending on the firm's size).[12]

Naturally, if managers are paid only a straight salary, they have little reason to take on risky investments. They gain nothing from the higher rates of return associated with risky investments, which is why they may shy away from them. Accordingly, it should surprise no one to learn that when managers are given bonuses based on performance, they tend to undertake riskier, higher-paying investments.[13] But then, if the bonuses are based on some short-term goal—say, this year's earnings—instead of some longer-term goal—say, some level for the stock price—you can bet that managers will tend to sacrifice investments with higher longer-term payoffs in favor of smaller payoffs that will be received within the performance periods. The managers' time horizons can be lengthened by tying their compensation to the firm's stock value by requiring that they hold the firm's stock until some later date, for example, retirement.[14]

While incentives have always mattered, they probably have never been more important to businesses interested in competing aggressively on a global scale. Greater global competition means that producers everywhere must meet the best production standards anywhere on the globe, which requires having the best incentive systems anywhere. Incentives will continue to grow in importance in business as the economy becomes more complex, more global, and more competitive. While incentives are both positive and negative, incentives, when structured properly, can ensure that managers, workers, and consumers prosper.

Like it or not, businesspeople will have to learn to think about incentives with the same rigor that they now contemplate their balance sheets and marketing plans. They will need to justify the incentive structures they devise, which means they will have to understand why they do what they do. High pay and golden parachutes for executives and stock options for workers need to be used judiciously. They can't be employed just because they seem like a nice idea, or because everyone else is using them. Investors who find it easier and easier to move their investment funds anywhere in the world will not allow their capital to be used for "nice ideas." Unless well thought out, "nice ideas" can spell wasted investments. The multitude of ways that incentives can matter in business must be incredibly large, which makes a study of them mandatory—if managers want to get them right.

Unless policies are carefully thought out, perverse incentives can be an inadvertent consequence, mainly because people can be very creative in responding to policies. Lincoln Electric is known for achieving high productivity levels among its production workers by tying their pay to measures of how much they produce. But they went too far. When they tied the pay of secretaries to "production," with counters installed on typewriters to measure how much was typed, the secretaries responded by spending their lunch hours typing useless pages of manuscript to increase their pay; as a result, that incentive was quickly abandoned.[15] In seeking to reduce the number of "bugs" in its programs, a software company began paying programmers to find and fix bugs. The goal was noble, but the response wasn't. Programmers began creating bugs so that they could find and fix them, with one programmer increasing his pay $1,700 through essentially fraudulent means. The company eliminated the incentive pay scheme within a week of its introduction.[16] Incentives always work, but they don't always work well or in the way that's expected (a fact that has led to harsh criticisms of even attempts to use incentives, punishments, or rewards[17]).

In the twenty-first-century world economy, business incentives will be commonplace; getting them right will be an abiding and taxing concern of managers. This book has one overarching goal: *helping you with the difficult managerial assignment of getting the incentives within your organization right!*

Some firms prosper, while other firms fail. Why? An easy answer is that some firms produce a better product or provide a better service. The fortunes of many fast-food restaurants have depended on the quality of their burgers and the cleanliness of their rest rooms.

Some firms have failed not because they have done anything "wrong" but because they have not done as much "right" as have their competitors. Many textile firms in the southeastern part of the country have folded over the past two decades in spite of their substantial efforts to improve their productivity and to increase quality. The failing firms closed their doors simply because they were not able meet the competition from lower-priced textile imports and from textiles produced by even more aggressive (and successful) domestic textile firms.[18]

Many firms have failed because they did not pay attention to their costs or because their managers were not very smart in setting their firms' product and service strategies to meet the changes in their markets. Several major airlines (and scores of smaller ones) have folded their wings over the past two decades because their planes and personnel were too expensive relative to the value of the service they provided and therefore relative to the prices the airlines could charge in deregulated skies.

A lot of things are important to success in business, not the least of which are the leadership of managers, worker skills and character, firm strategies, and cost-control methods. However, the title of our book, *Managing Through Incentives*, gives away our principal concern—the crucial role *incentives* play in the control and development of any successful firm. One of the more important points managers must remember is that incentives can be very powerful forces within a firm—for good or bad! This means managers must pay attention to the art and logic of getting incentives *right*. In this book, we examine a large number of different questions related to the organization of production within firms: *How large should firms be? Do workers want tough bosses? Why don't more firms pay piece rate? What difference does debt make? What good are corporate raiders?* At the most obvious level, these questions are concerned with widely different problems firms have to face. But underneath all that is written about firm structure or piece-rate pay or corporate raiders is our central theme: *developing incentives so that everyone in your firm or connected to it—owners, executives, managers, workers, suppliers, and customers—wins from your firm's operation.*

It is all too common for people to think that the only way for one group of "stakeholders" in a firm to gain is for some other group to lose. The search is all too frequently for ways to cut costs for one group of stakeholders (owners or managers) by skewering another group (line workers or customers). In this book we seek incentive arrangements by which everyone profits. That means that we seek incentives that are *mutually* beneficial, incentives that promote cooperation among all those with an interest in the firm. Devising mutually beneficial incentives is a tough order, but we think it is the only way to ensure a viable business. Business arrangements that do not benefit all parties involved are arrangements that are not likely to survive for long.

As noted, we typically think of firms competing with each other by producing better products at lower costs and making them more conveniently available to consumers at lower prices. But underlying this competition, which we can observe in the marketplace, is a more fundamental struggle taking place *within* firms to organize production in the most efficient manner, which necessarily requires an understanding of the incentives that face firm stakeholders—owners, managers, workers, and suppliers. This book has been written with one central proposition in mind: *in the competitive marketplace, the firms that survive and thrive are the ones that recognize that incentives matter—and they matter a great deal.* Successful firms play to the power of smart incentives (those that drive firm and worker incomes upward) and avoid perverse incentives (ones that undermine firm and worker incomes). And managers have good reason to make incentives a major focus for their firms: they can reduce their chances of being replaced.[19]

But such facts beg a critical question: Why are incentives important? Why do they work? The answers are many. One of the more important reasons incentives matter within firms is that firms are collections of workers whose interests are not always aligned with the interests of the people who employ them, that is, the owners. The principal problem facing the owners is how to get the workers to do what the owners want them to do. The owners could just issue directives, but without some incentive to obey the directives, nothing may happen. Directives may have some value in themselves; people do feel a sense of obligation to do what they were hired to do, and one of the things they may have been hired to do is obey orders (within limits). However, directives can be costly. Firms may use incentives simply as a cheaper substitute for giving out orders that can go unheeded unless the workers have some reason to heed them.

Firms may also use incentives to clarify firm goals, to spell out in concrete terms to workers what the owners want to accomplish. As every manager knows all too well, it's difficult to establish and write out the firm's strategy that will be used to achieve its stated goals, and it is an even more difficult task to get workers to appreciate, understand, and work toward those goals. The communication problem typically escalates with the size of the organization. Goals are always imperfectly communicated, especially when they are disseminated by memoranda or employment manuals that may be read once and tossed. Workers don't always know how serious the owners and upper managers are; they can remember any number of times when widely circulated memos were nothing but window dressing. Incentives are a means by which owners and upper managers can validate overall company goals and strategies. They can, in effect, say through incentives, "This is what we think is important. This is what we will be working toward. This is what we will be trying to get everyone else to do. And this is where we will put our money." Even if workers were not sensitive to the pecuniary benefits of work but were interested only in doing what their companies want them to do, incentives, because of the messages they convey, can have a valued and direct impact on what workers do and how long and hard they work.[20]

But there is a far more fundamental reason that incentives matter: *managers don't always know what orders or directives to give*. No matter how intelligent, hard working and well informed managers are, they seldom know as much about particular jobs as those who are actually doing those jobs. Knowing about the peculiarities of a machine, the difficulties a fellow worker on the production line is experiencing at home, or the personality quirks of a customer are just a few examples of the innumerable particular bits of localized knowledge that are crucial to the success of a firm. And this knowledge is spread among everyone in the firm without the possibility of being fully communicated to, and effectively utilized by, those who are primarily responsible for managerial oversight. The only way a firm can fully benefit from such localized knowledge is to allow those who possess the knowledge—the firm's employees—the freedom to use what they know.

Management theorists are increasingly recognizing this simple fact—that a great deal of knowledge is widely dispersed throughout the firm. In doing so, they are turning away from the approach to management recommended by Frederick Taylor.[21] At the beginning of the twentieth century, Taylor had popularized the time-and-motion approach to management in which experts, or managers, determined the most efficient way to do particular jobs and then required employees to work accordingly. Instead of the top-down or command style recommended by Taylor, the management profession is now sympathetic to a more participatory managerial approach, under which the management hierarchy is flatter, with authority for particular decisions dispersed throughout the firm and residing with those who are in the best position to exercise it. As noted, in varying degrees, all firms are necessarily involved in *participatory management*, with practically everyone having some management authority over some firm resources. The principal difference between those workers at the top of the firm hierarchy and those at the bottom is the scope of their authority over resources.

But the benefits from participatory management can be realized only if employees have not only the freedom but also the motivation to use their special knowledge in productive cooperation. The crucial ingredient for bringing about the requisite coordination is incentives that align the otherwise conflicting interests of individual employees with the collective interests of all members of the firm. Without such incentives, there can be no hope that the knowledge dispersed throughout the firm will be used in a cooperative and coordinated way. The only practical alternative to a functioning system of incentives is, again, a top-down, command-and-control approach that, unfortunately, can never allow the full potential of a firm's employees to be realized.

Managers must heed the words of the social philosopher Frederick Hayek: "The more men know, the smaller the share of knowledge becomes that any one mind [the planner's mind included] can absorb. The more civilized we become, the more relatively ignorant must each individual be of the facts on which the working of civilization depends. The very division of knowledge increases the necessary ignorance of the individual of most of this knowledge."[22] That insight applies within the firm. With the growing complexity and sophistication of production, knowledge is becoming ever more widely dispersed among a growing number of workers. Hence, the importance of incentives has grown with modern-day leaps in the technological sophistication of products and production processes. Incentives will continue to grow in importance as production and distribution processes become ever more complex.

Seen in this light, the problems facing firms are the same as those facing the general economy. Like Hayek, economists have argued for years that no group of government planners, no matter how intelligent and dedicated, can acquire all the localized knowledge necessary to allocate resources intelligently. The long and painful experiments with socialism and its extreme variant, communism, have confirmed that this is one argument that economists got right. But the freedom for people to use the knowledge that only they individually have has to be coupled with incentives that motivate people to use that knowledge in socially cooperative ways— meaning that the best way for individuals to pursue their own objectives is by making decisions that improve the opportunities for others to pursue their objectives. In a market economy, these incentives are found primarily in the form of prices that emerge out of the rules of private property and voluntary exchange. Market prices provide the incentive people need to productively coordinate their decisions with each other, thus making it not only possible but desirable for people to have a large measure of freedom to make use of the localized information and know-how they have.

A perfect incentive system would ensure that everyone could be given complete freedom because it would be in the interest of each person to advance the interests of all. No such perfect incentive system exists, neither within any firm nor within any economy. In every economy there is always some appropriate mix of market incentives and government controls that achieves the best overall results. The argument over just what the right mix is will no doubt continue indefinitely, but few deny that both incentives and controls are needed. Similarly, for any firm made up of more than one person there is some mix of incentives and direct managerial control that best promotes the objectives of the firm, that is, the general interests of its members. In this volume, we focus on how incentives matter simply because incentives are our area of expertise and because incentives have not been given their due in the management literature.

Incentives may not seem to matter much at any point in time, but even so, the power of incentives can accumulate over time. For example, suppose that without improved incentives firm profits will grow in real-dollar terms by 2 percent a year. Suppose that with more effective incentives firm profits can grow by 2.5 percent a year. The difference is not much, just a half of a percentage point per year. However, the compound impact of the higher growth rate means that after thirty years, real profits will be 33 percent higher with the improved incentives (a fact that is likely to be reflected in the firm's stock prices). Furthermore, the firm may be able to achieve the relatively higher profits with little or no cost. "Good" incentives may be no more expensive than "bad" incentives. Good incentives are the proverbial "free lunch" that economists typically dismiss.

Of course, if a firm doesn't pay attention to its incentives, it may lose more than its lunch; it may be forced out of business by those firms that do recognize the importance of incentives. Seen from this perspective, incentives can be a critical component of firm survival, perhaps just as critical as product development or technological sophistication.

The problem is in getting the incentives right and using the full range of potential incentives. Unfortunately, we can't say exactly what incentives your firm should employ. The exact incentives chosen depend on local conditions that can vary greatly across firms. You would not want us to write about *particular incentives* for your particular circumstances mainly because we can be assured of only one constant fact about business: particular circumstances will change with time and markets. Here, we offer a *way of thinking* about incentives that, if employed with diligence, will enable managers and owners to get their firms' incentives more in line with their desire for increased productivity and profits.

Incentives matter in a host of contexts, from personal to business. In fact, seeing the application of incentives to personal decisions can illuminate their value in business decisions. A few years ago, McKenzie's college-age daughter, Susan, indicated in late fall that she needed a new jacket. On the way to the shopping center, she told her father that she also needed a pair of slacks and would like to add shoes. McKenzie knew then that they might end up with a long shopping spree if the trip were not restricted to a search for a jacket.

Once in the department store, Susan headed, without hesitation, straight for the most expensive section of clothes for young adults. She quickly picked out a trendy jeans jacket. At the time, the brand name did not ring a bell with her father, but its price tag did, more than $125 (in 1996 dollars) for what was nothing more than denim. McKenzie protested in a fatherly way, suggesting that she look a little longer and try to find something that would be warmer and possibly cheaper. Susan insisted that she "loved" this one jacket.

Fortunately, just as her irritation was becoming evident, McKenzie had an inspired thought. He took out his wallet and gave her $125 in cash, noting as he handed it to her that she could do anything with the money that she wanted. Her eyes lit up, and she took off immediately for the men's section in which she found a generic jeans jacket on sale for $48. She bought it and had money left over to buy a pair of pants.

The change in her attitude before and after McKenzie gave her the money was as remarkable as the change in the purchases she made. Why the change in attitude and purchases?

The most obvious explanation is that *before* Susan got the money, her expenditures were a drain on her *father's* finances—*his* property, to which she had no direct rights. The cost of her expenditures was all *his*, not *hers*. Naturally, she began to think differently after receiving the money because she then understood that she would bear the cost of her own expenditures *and* that she would receive the benefits of any change in her choices. By acquiring what amounted to property rights to a portion of her father's bank account, Susan became what economists call a *residual claimant*, someone who has rights to what is left or garnered from the choices made.

This is a nonbusiness example, but its underlying truth is clearly evident in your day-to-day work. How many times have employees professed that they needed some valuable piece of equipment only because they knew the cost would be covered by the firm? The obvious moral for business from this personal example is that many employees may make what appear to be silly spending decisions simply because they have no incentive—receive no benefit—for doing otherwise. The advice is equally obvious: if employees benefit from making good decisions, as would a residual claimant, better decisions will be made.

The way residual claimacy changes people's incentives can be seen in the least likely circumstances—wartime. Wars are typically brutal affairs; there is a long history of mistreatment and killing of prisoners of war by their captors. But not all wars have been equally brutal to the prisoners that have been taken, and the differences can be explained by differences in incentives. Consider the three types of property rights systems that can be adapted to prisoners of war:

1. The individual soldier (or platoon of soldiers) who captures a prisoner can be given a form of "property rights" to the prisoner.
2. The property right over a prisoner can belong to the government that finances the military unit that captures the prisoner.
3. The property right over a prisoner can be transferred to a supranational organization.

Two economists cite historical examples suggesting that under condition 1, prisoners were more likely not only to be allowed to live but to be treated humanely.[23] A prisoner was often, though not always, a valuable asset that could be traded to those to whom he was worth most. Indeed, there is some indication that the incentives created by the "ownership" of prisoners led not only to better treatment of prisoners but also to less bloody battles. For example, at the end of the sixteenth century some battles were rather harmless affairs. When two opposing armies met in the field, the number of soldiers in each army was counted and the side with the smallest number simply surrendered to the other side.

When long-range firing weapons became available, it became less likely that individual soldiers would capture a prisoner from an opposing army. As a result, wars became more brutal, not only because of improvements in the technology of slaughter but also because the ownership of prisoners of war shifted to the state. Since there is far less individual incentive to take care of state property than of private property, it became more common for prisoners to be mistreated and killed than to be cared for and exchanged.

In response to many mass atrocities, international rules and organizations (the Geneva conventions and the Red Cross) were established to promote more humanitarian treatment of war prisoners. Most would agree that these efforts, as well intended as they are, have been only partially successful. Appeals to moral conduct are usually an incomplete substitute for material incentives when it comes to increasing moral behavior.

The lesson of the power of being a residual claimant that is evident in the author's handling of his daughter's purchases and in the wartime treatment of prisoners was also fully borne out in a change in the departmental budgeting process at Clemson University in South Carolina. Clemson, like all other colleges and universities, has limited funds for long-distance telephone calls, faculty travel, and supplies. Rex Cottle, who eventually became president of Lamar University in Texas, started his tenure as an academic administrator as chairman of the Clemson economics department in the late 1970s with the usual rules for expenditures on long-distance telephone calls (ones that are also used in many nonacademic businesses). Faculty members were permitted to make long-distance calls only if they were "business-related," but they were free to make as many calls as they liked. The system didn't work well, given that the department's total monthly phone bill always exceeded the department's monthly budget.

Cottle first complained about the calls and then pleaded with department members to curb their calls, because, he attested, the department would run out of funds in a couple of months. His plea went unheeded.

By late fall, the problem underlying the excessive telephone calls was self-evident. The department's phone budget was, in scholarly parlance, a "common-access resource," or common property, which means that no one "owned" it. No one was a residual claimant. Hence, all department members used and overused the budget. When Cottle warned the members that the budget might be depleted, he gave them all the more reason to make calls *then*, as soon as possible, not later when the budget might be gone. The result was, predictably, that more calls were made.

As McKenzie did with his daughter, Cottle changed the system and, in the process, radically restructured incentives. He gave the department members property rights, in effect, to a portion of the departmental budget, providing each professor with a given dollar amount that could be spent on supplies, travel, and phone calls. In doing so, he set limits on the behavior of faculty members *and* changed the way they thought about their calls. This happened because, after the budget change, each faculty member incurred a cost for making calls. More calls by individual faculty members meant less money for postage, pens, and travel. Accordingly, the budget change encouraged each faculty member to weigh more carefully the relative value of different purchases with an eye toward picking the more valuable options, whether calls or pens. One month after the new budget rules took effect, total expenditures on long-distance telephone calls fell by 25 percent.

The former CEO of Scott Paper, Al Dunlap, who is known as "Chainsaw Al" for his slashing of company payrolls when he takes charge of a company with the intent of restructuring it, recounts how, before his arrival, Scott had the usual inventory policy of buying its supplies from a number of vendors, all of whom had an incentive to maximize Scott's inventories of whatever they were selling. Of course, the vendors were happy to see Scott "overstock," as it tended to do, and were not at all concerned if the inventories were not where they were needed. Dunlap solved the overstocking problem by negotiating "consignment inventories," which meant that the inventories, when they were in Scott's warehouses, belonged to the vendors, not to Scott. The cost of overstocking went up for the suppliers who had to cover the carrying cost of Scott's excessive inventories. No one should be surprised that, as a consequence, the vendors immediately cut their shipments to Scott. "By the same token," Dunlap adds, "they [the vendors] made sure we didn't run out."[24]

A few years back, garbage was collected (and managed) in a small Mississippi town in the usual way. Workers were paid by the hour to go house to house emptying cans. If they worked harder and faster, they might finish their rounds in less time, but that would mean only that their routes would be lengthened or that other tasks would be assigned. They were not residual claimants to their time. Hence, they did what was generally expected of hourly workers—they took as long to complete their routes as their supervisors would allow. The more time they were able to squeeze into their jobs, the more they were rewarded, and the more taxpayers were squeezed.

The city manager had a bright idea and changed the town's garbage-collection procedures. He gave the garbage workers fixed routes and paid them by the route, not by the hour. In shifting to the new system, the city manager effectively gave workers back the rights to their time, making them residual claimants in the process. Any time saved was now "owned" by the workers, not by the city. As a consequence, the pace of garbage collection speeded up dramatically. Indeed, soon after the new route and pay system were instituted, the garbage workers could be seen on the job early in the morning almost running through their routes. And, furthermore, crew members began showing less tolerance for slack work by coworkers, because they all bore the cost of the slacking off. As a consequence, a route that once took eight hours to complete now took three. Many of the workers used the extra time to which they then had claim to take on additional jobs. Both city taxpayers and workers gained. Taxpayers developed a more efficient and punctual garbage collection system, while the incomes of the garbage workers from all jobs undertaken rose.

Care has to be exercised in using incentives *because they are so powerful*. Again, unless they are carefully thought through, incentive systems can have perverse effects—dramatically so. Consider the experience of the city government of Los Angeles when it also attempted to motivate trash collectors to work faster by changing the incentives.[25] Because city trash collectors were thought to be working too slowly, they were told that they could leave work as soon as they had finished their designated routes. As expected, trash collection speeded up, but at a cost that had not been anticipated. Trash collectors responded to the new incentive by disabling the speed controls on the mechanical arm that lifts the trashcans and dumpsters. This had the intended effect of speeding things up as dumpsters were practically catapulted into the trash trucks. Unfortunately, the excessive speed of the mechanical lifting arm caused the arms to break down more frequently. Also, in their rush to finish, the L.A. trash collectors quit cleaning their trucks thoroughly and undertaking the prescribed inspections at the end of their routes, leading to damage and breakdowns. In short order, the new incentive scheme put as many as 30 percent of the city's 900 trash trucks out of commission and in the repair shop, as opposed to only about 5 percent before the new incentive was put in place.

There is no way that managers can ever know for sure what the best set of incentives is. The problems of determining the proper incentives are many. And one of the main problems is not the dearth but the great variety of incentives that can be used. In this book, we necessarily focus on monetary incentives. We do so mainly because such incentives have been well tested but also because monetary incentives should be expected to be effective for the broad sweep of managers and workers: most people can usually find some reason to want more money, given that it can be used to buy so many things that people want. But our emphasis on monetary incentives doesn't mean that money is all that matters to people at work, and managers should realize that simple fact. Managers need to know what counts. We *know* money should count for most people at work. But what attributes of work can count? That's not always easy to answer. But not recognizing the question, and not looking for answers, can have incentive consequences that are not expected.

To see this point, we take a sports example that involves people at work, albeit baseball players. Starting in 1973, the American League allowed "designated hitters" to bat for pitchers (who are generally poor at batting). What would you expect to be the consequence of such a workplace change? Three economists have reasoned that, given that American League pitchers would not come up to bat, we should expect more batters to be hit by errant pitches in the American League than in the National League, because the American League pitchers would not have to fear being hit themselves in retaliation. Hence, American League pitchers could be expected to take more chances of brushing back batters than would be the case in the National League. Using sophisticated statistical methods, the economists found what they expected: since 1973 (after adjusting for other relevant factors that might affect hit batters), 10 to 15 percent more batters in the American League have been hit than in the National League.[76]

In the following chapters, we remind readers that "hits" and "pats" on the back can be important ways of increasing firm profits. However, there is a problem in talking about "hits" and "pats," or any other nonmoney attribute of the work environment, that must be kept in mind: Are "hits" and "pats" *goods* (something workers want) or *bads* (something they don't want)? Most people might want to avoid being hit by a baseball going ninety miles an hour, but what about "hits" that come close to being "pats"? Some workers might consider a "pat" on the back as a valued form of encouragement, while others might consider it to be an unwanted form of patronization or sexual overture (depending on exactly how the "pat" is given and where).

As complicated as these issues are, we can't avoid them, and managers would not get the pay they do if all such problems of "what counts" in the workplace were easily and readily solved. Psychology will always be a part of management precisely because it helps identify workers' likes and dislikes. Economics will always be a part of management because it can guide managers in making money by instituting and adjusting on the margin the combination of money and nonmoney incentives set out for workers. You can bet that we also show how the workers' willingness to trade off money for other attributes of the work environment (for example, common courtesies and respect) can increase firm profits and, at the same time, enhance worker welfare. That means that an unheralded job of managers is to stay attuned to what their workers want and then try to figure out how much they are willing to pay for what they want.

Another problem in the management of incentives is that no set of incentives is ever perfect, nor could it be. But even if managers knew the best incentive structure and how best to implement it, a serious incentive problem would remain: *What incentive should managers have to find the* best *set of incentives?* That's a tough but interesting question. Chapters throughout the book are either directly or indirectly concerned with this basic, difficult-to-handle problem. An understanding of the structure of firms requires that we recognize the need to subject managers, as well as other employees, to the proper incentives. The need to impose the proper set of incentives on managers is also necessary for understanding firms' financial structure. For example, the question of what combination of debt and equity instruments is best for financing a firm cannot be answered properly without a consideration of managerial incentives.

As is the case in any enterprise, we do have a strategy for unraveling the power and mystery of incentives. In the introductory section we consider the pervasive role of incentives in all dimensions of human interaction, but especially business. The importance of business as a "game" and the constant tension between cooperative and noncooperative behavior within firms, which incentives are intended to modify, are considered. In that short section we cover the limited list of elementary concepts and principles that are needed to use incentives creatively in a variety of business contexts. In the second section we examine the way incentives can be (and should not be) used to motivate worker behavior. The emphasis in this section is how incentives can enhance worker productivity, resulting in higher pay for workers at a lower cost to the firm.

Throughout the book, we concentrate not on those incentives that benefit one party at the expense of the other but rather on those incentives that harbor opportunities for *mutual* gains for all parties in business—for workers and managers on the one hand and stockholders and customers on the other. We do this because of our simple, underlying conviction: any set of incentives that benefits only a single "stakeholder" (for example, stockholders) at the expense of some other "stakeholder" (for example, managers or workers) is not likely to be a set of incentives that will be enduring.

Executive incentives are covered in the third section. As is true throughout the book, we are willing to deal with controversial issues, and in this section we consider head-on the widely discussed issues of executive "overcompensation." We stress a general point—executives cannot be expected to creatively manage through incentives unless they have the incentive to do so. The fourth section explores the incentive foundations of why firms are organized the way they are—why, for example, they buy some parts and make others that they use in production. You will not, by then, be surprised to learn that "make-or-buy decisions" are determined largely by the extant incentives. In addition, several business issues—such as profitable ways to "mistreat" customers, creative pricing strategies, and how to motivate a long-run perspective in the face of short-run temptations—are also considered as examples of the power of managing through incentives. In the penultimate chapter we consider the case against the use of incentives in business.

Our message in this book, repeated and reinforced with analysis and anecdotes, is simple: *incentives are important.* They are worthy of serious reflection. But that doesn't mean to suggest that incentives are *all* that matter. Many things matter. As noted earlier, leadership, product design, and customer service, as well as company adaptability, culture, and goals, also matter. However, we suspect that all of those good things in business might not matter very much or for long if the incentives are not right. We hope our discussion of the importance of incentives in understanding the organization and performance of firms serves as an *incentive* to continue reading.

2

An Economic Look at Incentives Within Firms

Key Insight: Firms matter in the economy only because they are less costly to use than markets.

IN CONVENTIONAL ECONOMIC DISCUSSIONS of how firms are managed, incentives are nowhere considered. This is the case because the "firm" is little more than a theoretical "black box" in which things happen somewhat mysteriously. Economists typically acknowledge that the "firm" is the basic production unit, but little or nothing is said of why the firm ever came into existence or, for that matter, what the firm is. As a consequence, we are told little about why firms do what they do (and don't do). There is nothing in conventional discussions that tells us about the role of real people in a firm.

How are firms to be distinguished from the markets they inhabit, especially in terms of the incentives people in firms and markets face? That question is seldom addressed (other than, perhaps, by specifying that firms can take one of several legal forms, for example, proprietorships, partnerships, professional associations, or corporations). In conventional discussions of the "theory of the firm," it is said that firms maximize their profits, which is their only noted *raison d'être*. But students of conventional theory are never told how firms do what they are supposed to do. The owners, presumably, devise ways to ensure that everyone in the organization follows instructions, all of which are intent on squeezing every ounce of profit from every opportunity. Students are never told what the instructions are or what is done to ensure that workers follow them. The structure of incentives inside the firm never comes up because their purpose is effectively assumed away: people do what they are supposed to do, naturally or by some unspecified mysterious process. For people in business, the economist's approach to the "firm" must appear strange indeed, given that business people spend much of their working day trying to coax people to do what they are supposed to do. Nothing is less automatic in business than getting people to pay attention to their firms' profits (as distinguished from the workers' more personal concerns).

In this chapter, we address the issue of why firms exist, not because it is an interesting philosophical question. Rather, we are concerned with that question because its answer can help us understand why the existence of firms and incentives go hand in hand. There is more than an ounce of truth to the refrain, "You cannot have one without the other." In this chapter, we lay out the limited economic propositions that undergird the analysis of much of the book. These propositions are as powerful as they are simple.

Why is it that firms add to the efficiency of the markets? That's an intriguing question, especially given how standard theories trumpet the superior efficiency of markets. Students of conventional theory might rightfully wonder, If markets are so efficient, why do entrepreneurs ever go to the trouble of organizing firms? Why not just have everything done by way of markets, with little or nothing actually done (in the sense that things are "made") inside firms? All of the firm's inputs could be bought by individuals, with each individual adding value to the inputs he or she purchases and then selling this result to another individual who adds more value, and so on, until a final product is produced and a final market is reached, at which point the completed product is sold to consumers. The various independent suppliers may be at the same general location, even in the same building, but everyone, at all times, could be up for contracting with all other suppliers or some centralized buyer of the inputs. By keeping everything on a market basis, the benefits of competition could be constantly reaped. Entrepreneurs could always look for competitive bids from alternative suppliers for everything used, whether parts to be assembled, accounting and computer services to be used, or executive talent to be employed.

Individuals, as producers relying exclusively on markets, could always take the least costly bid. They could also keep their options open, including retaining the option to switch to new suppliers that propose better deals. No one would be tied down to internal sources of supply to meet production needs. Producers would not have to incur the considerable costs of organizing themselves into production teams and departments and various levels of management. They would not have to incur the costs of internal management. They could, so to speak, maintain a great deal of freedom.

Then why do firms exist? What is the incentive, the driving force, behind firms? For that matter, what is a *firm* in the first place? The University of Chicago law and economics professor Ronald Coase, whose classic work "The Nature of the Firm" is the basis for much of this chapter and the source of many of the particular arguments drawn, proposed a substantially new but deceptively simple explanation.[1] He reasoned that the *firm* is any organization that supersedes the pricing system, in which hierarchy and methods of command and control, is substituted for exchanges. To use his exact words: "A firm, therefore, consists of the system of relationships which comes into existence when the direction of resources is dependent on an entrepreneur."[2]

Good answers to the question of why firms exist are more complicated and longer in the making than might be thought, but space limitations require us to be brief. Some economists have speculated that firms exist because of the *economies of specialization* of resources, a key one being labor. Clearly, Adam Smith and many of his followers were correct when they observed that when tasks are divided among a number of workers, the workers become more proficient at what they do. Smith began his economic classic *The Wealth of Nations* by writing about how specialization of labor increased "pin" (really nail) production.[3] By specializing, workers can become more proficient at what they do, which means they can produce more in their time at work. They also don't have to waste time changing tasks, which means that more time can be spent directly on production.

While efficiency improvements can certainly be had from specialization of any resource, especially labor, Smith was wrong to conclude that firms were needed to coordinate the workers' separate tasks. As economists have long recognized, those separate tasks could be coordinated by the pricing system within markets.

Markets could, conceivably, exist even within the stages of production that are held together by, say, assembly lines. Workers at the various stages could simply buy what is produced before them. The person who produces soles in a shoe factory could buy the leather and then sell the completed soles to the shoe assemblers; the bookkeeping services provided a shoe factory by its accounting department could easily be bought on the market. Similarly, all of the intermediate goods involved in Smith's pin production could be bought and sold until the completed pins were sold to those who wanted them.

Why, then, do we observe *firms* as such, which organize activities by hierarchies and directions that are not based on changing prices (which distinguishes them from markets)? In terms of our examples, why are there shoe and pin companies? Over the years, economists have given various answers.[4]

Many of the reasons people might come up with to explain the existence of firms are dismissed by Coase as wrongheaded or not important.[5] What Coase was interested in was not a catalogue of "small" explanations for this or that firm but an explanation for the existence of firms that, to one degree or another, is applicable to virtually all firms. He was seeking a unifying theme, a common basis. In his 1937 article, he came upon an unbelievably simple answer to his puzzle, an explanation that earned him the Nobel Prize in Economics—more than half a century later!

What did he say? How did he justify the firm's existence? Simply put, he observed that there are costs of dealing in markets. He dubbed these costs *marketing costs*, but most economists now call them *transaction costs*. Whatever they are called, these costs include the time and resources that must be devoted to organizing economic activity through markets. Transaction costs include the particular real economic costs (whether or not measured in money) of discovering the best deals in terms of prices and attributes of products, negotiating contracts, and ensuring that the resulting terms of the contract are followed. When we were going through our explanation of how work on an assembly line could be viewed as passing through various markets, most readers probably imagined that the whole process could be terribly time consuming, especially if the suppliers and producers at the various stages were constantly subject to replacement by competitors.

Once the costs of market activity are recognized, the reason for the emergence of the firm is transparent: *Firms, which substitute internal direction for markets, arise because they reduce the need for making market transactions. Firms thus lower the costs that go with market transactions.* If internal direction were not, at times and up to some point, more cost-effective than markets, then firms would never exist—would have no reason for being, meaning that no one would have the required incentive to go to the trouble of creating them. However, while firms will never eliminate the costs of market transactions, they must surely reduce them.

Entrepreneurs and their hired workers essentially substitute one long-term contract for a series of short-term contracts: the workers agree to accept directions from the entrepreneurs (or their agents, or managers) within certain broad limits (with the exact limits subject to variation) in exchange for security and a level of welfare (including pay) that is higher than the workers would be able to achieve in the market in the absence of firms. Similarly, the entrepreneurs (or their agents) agree to share with the workers some of the efficiency gains obtained from reducing transaction costs.[6]

The firm is a viable economic institution because both sides to the contract—owners and workers—gain. Firms can be expected to proliferate in markets simply because of the mutually beneficial deals that can be made. Those entrepreneurs who refuse to operate within firms and stick solely to market-based contracts, when in fact a firm's hierarchical organization is more cost-effective than market-based organizations, will simply be outcompeted for resources by the firms that do form and achieve the efficiency-improving deals with workers (and owners of other resources).

If firms reduce transaction costs, does it follow that one giant firm should span the entire economy, as, say, Lenin and his followers thought possible for the Soviet Union? Our intuition says, "No!" But there are also good reasons for expecting firms to be limited in size.

First, by organizing activities under the umbrella of firms, entrepreneurs give up some of the benefits of markets, which provide competitively delivered goods and services. Managers suffer from their own limited organizational skills, and skilled managers are scarce, as evidenced by the relatively high salaries many of them command. Communication problems within firms expand as firms grow, encompassing more activities, more levels of production, and more diverse products. Because many people may not like to take directions, as the firm expands to include more people it may have to pay progressively higher prices to workers and other resource owners in order to draw them into the firm and then direct them.

There are, in short, limits to what can be done through organizations. These limits can't always be overcome, except at greater costs, even with the application of the best organizational techniques, whether the establishment of teams, the empowerment of employees, or the creation of new business and departmental structures (for example, reliance on top-down, bottom-up, or participatory decision making). Even the best industrial psychology theories and practices have their limits when applied to human relationships.

Second, firms might be restricted in size because they suffer from a major problem—the so-called *agency problem* (or, alternately, the *principal-agent problem*), which is considered and reconsidered throughout this book. This problem is easily understood as a conflict of interests between identifiable groups within firms. The entrepreneurs or owners of firms (the *principals*) organize firms to pursue their own interests, which are often (but not always) greater profits. To pursue profits, however, the entrepreneurs must hire managers who then hire workers (all of whom are *agents*). However, the goals of the worker-agents are not always compatible with the goals of the owner-principals. Indeed, they are often in direct conflict. Both groups want to get as much as they can from the resources assembled in the firms.

The problem the principals face is getting the agents to work diligently at their behest and with the principals' interests in mind, a core problem that the venerable Adam Smith recognized more than two centuries ago.[7] Needless to say, agents often resist doing the principals' bidding, a fact that makes it difficult—that is, costly—for the principals to achieve their goals.

It might be thought that most, if not all, of these conflicts can be resolved through contracts, and many can. However, like all business arrangements, contracts have serious limitations, not the least of which is that they can't be all-inclusive or cover all aspects of even "simple" business relationships (which are all more or less complex). Contracts simply cannot anticipate and cover all possible ways the parties to the contract, if they are so inclined, can get around specific provisions. The cost of enforcing the contracts can also be a problem and present an added cost, even when both parties know that provisions have been violated. Each party will recognize the enforcement costs and may be tempted to exploit them, and will figure that the other may be equally tempted. Each will seek some means by which the contract will be self-enforcing or will encourage each party to live up to the letter and the spirit of the contract because it is in the interest of each party to do so. This is where incentives come in, because they help make contracts self-enforcing. Incentives can encourage the parties to more closely follow the intent and letter of contracts.

Competition is a powerful force toward minimizing agency costs. Firms in competitive markets that are not able to control agency costs are firms that are not likely to survive for long, mainly because of what has been dubbed the "market for corporate control."[8] Firms that allow agency costs to get out of hand risk either failure or takeover (by way of proxy fights, tender offers, or mergers). In this book, we discuss at length how managers can solve their own agency problems, including controlling their own behavior as agents for shareholders. At the same time, we would be remiss if we didn't repeatedly point out the market pressures on managers to solve such problems, even if they are not naturally inclined to do so. If corporations are not able to adequately solve their agency problems, we can imagine that the corporate form of doing business will be (according to one esteemed financial analyst[9]) "eclipsed" as new forms of business emerge. Of course, this means that obstruction in the market for corporate control (for example, legal impediments to takeovers) can translate into greater agency costs and less efficient corporate governance.

Why are firms the sizes they are? When economists in or out of business usually address that question, the answer most often given relates in one way or another to *economies of scale*. By economies of scale, we mean something very specific—the cost savings that emerge when all resource inputs (e.g., labor, land, and capital) are increased together. In some industries, it is true that as more and more of all resources are added to production within a given firm, output expands by more than the use of resources. That is, if resource use expands by 10 percent and output expands by 15 percent, then the firm experiences economies of scale. Its (long-run) average cost of production declines. Why does that happen? The answer is almost always "technology," which is another way of saying that it "just happens," given what is known about combining inputs and getting output. This is not the most satisfying explanation, but it is nonetheless true that economies of scale are available in some industries (automobile) but not in others (crafts).

The standard approach toward explaining firm size is instructive. We have spent long hours at our classroom boards with chalk in hand developing and describing scale economies in the typical fashion of professors, using (long-run) average cost curves and pointing out when firms in the expansion process contemplate starting a new plant. We think the standard approach is useful, but we also believe it leaves out a lot of interesting forces at work on managers within firms. This is understandable, given that standard economic theory totally assumes away the roles of managers, which we intend to discuss at length.

Coase and his followers have taken a dramatically different tack in explaining why firms are the sizes they are in terms of scale of operations and scope of products delivered to market. The new breed of theorists pays special attention to the difficulties managers face as they seek to expand the scale and scope of the firm. As a firm expands, agency costs mount, primarily because workers have more and more opportunities to engage in what can only be tagged *opportunistic behavior*—taking advantage of their positions by misusing and abusing firm resources. *Shirking*, or not working with due diligence, is one form of opportunistic behavior that is known to all employees. Theft of firm resources is another form. As the firm grows, the contributions of the individual worker become less detectable, which means workers have progressively fewer incentives to work diligently on behalf of firm objectives or to do what they are told by their superiors. They can more easily hide.

The tendency for larger firm size to undercut the incentives available to participants in any group is not just theoretical speculation. It has been observed in closely monitored experiments. In an experiment conducted more than a half century ago, a German scientist asked workers to pull on a rope connected to a meter that would measure the effort expended. Total effort for all workers combined increased as workers were added to the group doing the pulling at the same time that the individual efforts of the workers declined. When three workers pulled on the rope, the individual effort averaged 84 percent of the effort expended by one worker. When eight workers pulled, the average individual effort was one-half the effort of the one worker.[10] Hence, group size and individual effort were inversely related—as they are in most group circumstances.

The problem evident in the experiment is not that the workers become any more corrupt or inclined to take advantage of their situation as their number increases. The problem is that their incentive to expend effort deteriorates as the group expands. Each person's effort counts for less in the context of the larger group, a point upon which the late University of Maryland economist Mancur Olson elaborated decades ago.[11] The "common objectives" of the group become less and less compelling in directing individual efforts. As more workers are added to the group, the inclination of each worker to "free ride"—or to not make the expected contribution—increases. When some workers begin to free ride, others should be expected to follow suit, given that they don't want to be the patsy for the rest of the group, since they learn quickly from what the others do that free riding has benefits. Hence, free riding should be expected to escalate as the work process continues, unless otherwise abated by managerial policies. Researchers have indeed found that free riding can be pervasive and can increase with time, even within even small groups (of four and ten members).[12]

Such research findings mean that if the work group size is expanded and if each worker added to the group must be paid the same as all others, the cost of additional production will rise with the size of the working group. The finding also implies that to get a constant increase in effort as additional workers are added, all workers must be given greater incentives to hold to their previous levels of effort.[13]

How large should a firm be? Incentives are just as important as technology in answering this question. Technology determines what *might* be possible, but it doesn't determine what *will* happen. And what happens depends on policies that minimize shirking and maximize the use of the technology by workers. This means that scale economies depend as much on what happens within any given firm as they do on what is technologically possible, and perhaps more. The size of the firm depends on the extent to which owners must incur greater monitoring costs as they lose control as a result of increases in the size of the firm and additional layers of hierarchy, a point well developed by Oliver Williamson in his classic article written more than thirty years ago.[14] However, the size of the firm also depends on the cost of using the market.

The management information professors Vijay Gurbaxani and Seungjin Whang have devised a graphical means of illustrating the "optimal firm size" as the consequence of two forces: "internal coordinating costs" and "external coordinating costs."[15] As a firm expands, its internal coordinating costs are likely to increase, because the firm's hierarchical pyramid will likely become larger, with more and more decisions made at the top by managers who are further and further removed from the local information available to workers at the bottom of the pyramid. There is a need to process information up and down the pyramid. When the information goes up, there are unavoidable problems and costs: costs of communication, costs of miscommunication, and opportunity costs associated with delays in communication, all of which can lead to suboptimal decisions. These "decision information costs" become progressively greater as the decision rights are moved up the pyramid.

Attempts to rectify the decision costs by delegating decision making to the lower ranks may help, but this can—and *will*—also introduce another form of costs, which we previously have called *agency costs*. These include the cost of monitoring (managers actually watching employees as they work or checking their production) and bonding (workers providing assurance that the tasks or services will be done as the agreement requires) and the loss of the residual gains (or profits) through worker shirking, which we covered in chapter 1.

The basic problem managers face is one of balancing the decision information costs with agency costs and finding that location for decision rights
that minimizes the two forms of costs. From this perspective, where the
decision rights are located will depend heavily on the amount of information flow per unit of time. When upward flow of information is high, the
decision rights will tend to be located toward the floor of the firm, mainly
because the costs of suboptimal decisions made high up the hierarchy will
be high. The firm, in other words, can afford to tolerate agency costs
because the costs of avoiding them, by opting for centralized decisions,
can be higher.

Nevertheless, as the firm expands, we should expect that the internal
coordinating costs, as well as the cost of operations, will increase. The
upward sloping line in Figure 2.1A depicts this relationship.

But internal costs are not all that matter to a firm contemplating an

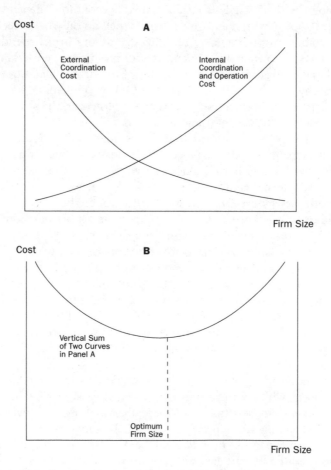

Figure 2.1 Coordination Costs and the Optimum Size Firm

expansion. It must also consider the cost of the market, or what Gurbaxani and Whang call "external coordination costs." If the firm remains "small" and buys many of its parts, supplies, and services (such as accounting, legal, and advertising services) from outside vendors, then it must cover a number of what we have called "transaction costs." These include the costs of transportation, inventory holding, communication, contract writing, and contract enforcing. As the firm expands in size, these transaction costs should be expected to diminish. After all, a larger firm seeks to supplant market transactions. The downward sloping line in Figure 2.1A depicts this inverse relationship between firm size and transaction costs.

Again, how large should a firm be? If a firm vertically integrates, it will engage in fewer market transactions, lowering its transaction costs. It can also benefit from economies of scale, the technical kind mentioned earlier. However, in the process of expanding, it will confront growing internal coordination costs, or the problems of trying to move information up the decision-making chain, getting the "right" decisions, and then preventing people from exploiting their decision-making authority to their own advantage.

The firm should stop expanding in scale and scope when the total of the two types of costs—external and internal coordinating costs—are minimized. This minimum can be shown graphically by summing the two curves in Figure 2.1A to obtain the U-shaped curve in Figure 2.1B. The *optimal* (or most efficient/cost-effective) firm size is at the bottom of the U.

This way of thinking about firm size would have only limited interest if it did not lend itself to a couple of additional observations that permit thinking about the location, shape, and changes in the curve. First, the exact location of the bottom will, of course, vary for different firms in different industries. Different firms have different capacities to coordinate activities through markets and hierarchies. Second, firm size will also vary according to the changing abilities of firms to coordinate activities internally and externally.

A firm that is efficient at processing information will be larger, everything else equal, than one that isn't so able. If a firm is able to improve the efficiency of its upward information flow and reduce the number of wrong decisions, then the upward sloping curve in Figure 2.1A will move down and to the right, causing the sum of the two curves in the bottom panel of the figure to move to the right, for a greater optimal size firm. If the costs of using markets go down, the firm size can be expected to decline, not because the firm has become less efficient internally (it may have become more efficient) but because markets are now relatively more cost effective. Again, from this perspective, the size of the firm changes for reasons other than those related to the technology of actual production. It depends on the ability of managers to take full advantage of the possible scale economies with the help of their workers.

Of course, knowing that owners will always worry that their manager-agents will exploit their positions for their own benefit at the expense of the owners, managers will want to "bond" themselves against exploitation of their positions. (We don't use the term "bond" in the modern pop-psychology sense of developing warm and fuzzy relationships; rather, we use it in the same sense that is common when accused criminals post a bond or give some assurance that they will appear in court if released from jail.) That is to say, managers have an interest in letting the owners know that they, the managers, will suffer some loss when exploitation occurs. Devices such as audits of the company are clearly in the interest of stockholders. But they are also in the interest of managers because they reduce the scope for managerial misdeeds, thus increasing the market value of the company—and the value of its managers. By buying their companies' stock, manager-agents can also bond themselves, assuring stockholders that they will incur at least some losses from agency costs. To the extent manager-agents can bond themselves convincingly, the firm can grow from expanded sources of external investment funds. By bonding themselves, manager-agents can also demand higher compensation. Firms can be expected to expand and contract with reductions and increases in the costs of developing effective managerial bonds.[16]

Finally, we can observe that the size of the firm can be expected to change with changes in the relative costs of organizing a given set of activities by way of markets and hierarchies. For example, suppose that the costs of engaging in market transactions are lowered, meaning that markets become relatively more economical vis-à-vis firms. Entrepreneurs should be expected to organize more of their activities through markets and fewer through firms. In that case, those firms that more fully exploit markets and rely less on internal directions should be able to increase the payments provided to workers and other resources that they buy through markets, collectively leaving fewer resources to expand their market share relative to those firms that make less use of markets. Accordingly, firms should be expected to *downsize*, to use a popular expression.

An old, well-worn, and widely appreciated explanation for downsizing is that modern technology has enabled firms to produce more with less. Personal computers, with their ever-escalating power, have enabled firms to lay off workers (or hire fewer workers). Banks no longer need as many tellers, for example, given the advent of the ATMs.

One not so widely appreciated explanation is that markets have become cheaper, which means that firms have less incentive to use hierarchical structures and more incentive to use markets. And one good reason firms have found markets relatively more attractive is the rapid development of computer and communication technology, which has reduced the costs to entrepreneurs of operating in markets. The new technology has lowered the costs of locating suitable trading partners and suppliers, as well as negotiating, consummating, and monitoring market-based deals (and the contracts that go with them). In terms of Figure 2.1, the downward sloping transaction-costs curve has dropped down and to the left, causing the bottom of the U to move leftward.

"Outsourcing" became a management buzzword in the 1980s because the growing efficiency of markets, through technology, made it economical. Outsourcing continued apace in the 1990s. Of twenty-six major companies surveyed, 86 percent said they outsourced some activity in 1995, up from 58 percent who gave the same response in 1992, with the budding outsourcing industry generating $100 billion in annual revenues by 1996.[17] For all practical purposes, airlines now outsource the acquisition of their reservations through independent contractors called travel agents, given that more than 70 percent of all airline reservations are now taken by such agents, working through computerized markets, not through the hierarchical structures within the airlines.

Modern technology has also improved the monitoring of employees, reducing agency costs, which has been a force for the expansion of firms. Firms have been able to use the technology to garner more of the gains from economies of scale and scope. The optical scanners at grocery store checkout counters are valuable because they can speed up the flow of customers through the checkout counters, but they can also be used for other purposes, such as inventory control and restocking. Each sale is immediately transmitted to warehouse computers that determine the daily shipments to stores. The scanners can also be used to monitor the work of the clerks, a factor that can diminish agency costs and increase the size of the firm. (We are told that even "Employee of the Month Awards" are made based on reports from scanners.) Books on Tape, a firm that rents audio versions of books, tracks its production of tapes by using scanners, not so much to reward and punish workers but to be able to identify problem areas. In terms of Figure 2.1, the upward sloping curve moves down and to the right, while the U-shaped curve in the lower panel moves to the right.

Frito-Lay has issued its salespeople hand scanners, in part to increase the reliability of the flow of information back to company distribution centers but also to track the work of the salespeople. The company can obtain reports on when each employee starts and stops work, the time spent on trips between stores, and the number of returns. The sales people can be asked to account for more of their time and activities while they are on the job.

Obviously, we have not covered the full spectrum of explanations for the rich variety of sizes of firms that exists in the "real world" of business. We have also left the net impact of technology somewhat up in the air; in reality, it is pressing some firms to expand and others to downsize. The reason is simple: technology is having a multitude of impacts that can be exploited in different ways by firms in different situations.

The discussion to this point reduces to a relatively simple message: Firms exist to bring about cost savings, and they generate the cost savings through cooperation. However, cooperation is not always and everywhere "natural"; people have an incentive to "cheat," or not do what they are supposed to do or have agreed to do. This may be the case because of powerful incentives toward noncooperation built into many business environments.

An illustration of the tendency toward noncooperative behavior, despite the general advantage from cooperation, is a classic so-called "conditional-sum game" known as the *prisoners' dilemma*.[18] This is a dilemma, commonly found in business, that takes its name from a particular situation involving the decision two prisoners have to make about whether or not to confess to a crime they committed. But the dilemma is also evident whenever two or more people find themselves in a situation where the best decision from the perspective of each leads to the worst outcome from the perspective of all.

Consider a situation in which the police have two people in custody who are known to be guilty of a serious crime but who, in the absence of a confession by one of them, can be convicted only of a relatively minor crime. How can the police (humanely) encourage the needed confession? One effective approach is to separate the two prisoners and present each with the same set of choices and consequences. Each is told that if one confesses to the serious crime and the other does not, then the one who confesses will receive a light sentence of one year, while the one who does not confess will receive the maximum sentence of fifteen years. If they both confess, then both will receive the standard sentence of ten years. And if both refuse to confess, then each will be sentenced to two years for the minor crime.

The choices and consequences facing the prisoners are presented in the "payoff" matrix in Figure 2.2, where the first number in each parenthesis is the sentence in years received by prisoner A and the second number is the sentence received by prisoner B.

From the perspective of both prisoners, the best outcome occurs if neither one confesses (they serve a total of four years), and the worst outcome occurs if both confess (they serve a total of 20 years). In other words, if both prisoners cooperate with each other by keeping their mouths shut, they will both be far better off than if they act noncooperatively with each

		Prisoner B	
		Don't Confess	Confess
	Don't Confess	(2 2)	(15 1)
Prisoner A			
	Confess	(1 15)	(10 10)

Figure 2.2. Prisoners' Dilemma

other by confessing. However, from the perspective of each prisoner, the best choice is the noncooperative one of confession.

Consider the situation from prisoner A's vantage point. If A believes that B will refuse to confess, then he receives two years in prison if he also refuses to confess but only one year if he does confess. His best choice is to confess. On the other hand, if A believes that B will confess, then he will receive fifteen years in prison if he does not confess and only ten years if he does. Again, his best choice is to confess. No matter what A believes B will do, it is in A's best interest to confess. And the incentives are exactly the same for B. So while it is rational from their individual perspectives for both A and B to make the noncooperative choice, the result is the worst possible outcome from their collective perspective.

When, as in our example, only two people are in a prisoners' dilemma setting, it is quite possible for them to avoid the worst outcome by choosing the cooperative option of not confessing. The two prisoners may be good friends and have genuine regard for the well-being of each other, in which case each will feel confident that the other will not betray him with a confession and will refuse to betray his friend. But if the number of prisoners grows and becomes quite large, then it becomes much less likely that any one of them can reasonably trust everyone else to keep quiet. This means that as the number grows. it becomes increasingly irrational for any one of them to keep quiet.

Overcoming a large-number prisoners' dilemma by motivating cooperative behavior is obviously difficult, but not impossible. *The best hope for those who are in a prisoners' dilemma situation is to agree ahead of time to certain rules, restrictions, or arrangements that will punish those who choose the noncooperative option* For example, those who are jointly engaging in criminal activity will see advantages in forming gangs whose members are committed to punishing noncooperative behavior. The gang members who are confronted with the prisoners' dilemma will seriously consider the possibility that the shorter sentence received for confessing will hasten the time when a far more harsh punishment for "squealing" on a fellow gang member will be imposed by the gang.

The problem illustrated by the prisoners' dilemma is a very general one that is encountered in many different guises, most of which have nothing to do with prisoners. Excessive pollution, for example, can be described as a prisoners' dilemma in which citizens—meaning, typically, a very large number of people—would be better off collectively if everyone polluted less; yet, from the perspective of each individual, the greatest payoff comes from continuing to engage in polluting activities no matter what others are expected to do. A major part of the problem in stopping pollution, without some form of government intervention, is that the costs of pollution control are "private"—that is, borne by the person or firm incurring the costs of pollution control—while the benefits are "external"—that is, received by people other than the person or firm incurring the costs of pollution control. As another example, while there may be wide agreement that we would be better off with less government spending, each interest group is better off lobbying for more government spending on its favorite program. People are tempted by the noncooperative solution in polluting and lobbying because they benefit individually and have only limited and costly ways of ensuring that others resist the noncooperative solution.

Many areas of business are fertile grounds for the conditional-sum game situations represented by the prisoners' dilemma. Lojack, a firm that sells systems to retrieve stolen cars by use of a beacon that can lead the police to the car and the thieves, must overcome the so-called "externality problem" associated with its antitheft system. The person who pays for a Lojack system gains from the purchase, since his or her stolen car may be returned. However, most of the benefits from the purchase are external, since a stolen car with a Lojack system in it can lead the police to the dens of the professional car thieves and to "chop shops," thus potentially eliminating a large number of car thefts.[19] Indeed, researchers have found that the systems are so effective that car thefts go down by one for every three Lojack-equipped cars in high-crime areas. Lojack has a sales problem because the buyers pay the entire cost of the systems while other people get the overwhelming majority of the benefits. If the buyers could garner more of the benefits, they would be more willing to pay more for a larger number of installed systems. One way Lojack might overcome buyer resistance, the researchers suggest, is to require insurers to give buyers a major break on their car insurance premiums.

This is just one of a large number of examples of business-related prisoners' dilemmas. Others are discussed in some detail in subsequent chapters. An important task of managers is to identify and resolve these dilemmas as they arise, both within the firm and with suppliers and customers of the firm. Indeed, we see "management" as concerned with finding resolutions of prisoners' dilemmas. Good managers constantly seek to remind members of the firm of the benefits of cooperation and of the costs that can be imposed on people who insist on taking the noncooperative course.

Consider, for example, the issue of corporate travel, which is a major business expense, estimated at more than $130 billion in 1994.[20] If a business were able to economize on travel costs, it would realize significant gains. And much of this gain would be captured by the firms' traveling employees, who, if they were able to travel at less cost, would earn higher incomes as their net value to the firm increased. So all the traveling employees in a firm could be better off if they all cut back on unnecessary travel expenses. But the employees are in a prisoners' dilemma with respect to reducing travel costs, because each recognizes that he or she is personally better off by flying first-class, staying at hotels with multiple stars, and dining at elegant restaurants (behaving noncooperatively), instead of making the least expensive travel plans (behaving cooperatively) regardless of what the other employees do. Each individual employee would be best off if all other employees economized, which would allow her salary to be higher as she continued to take luxury trips. But if the others also make the more expensive travel arrangements, she would be foolish not to do so herself since her sacrifice would not noticeably increase her salary.

Airlines have recognized the "games" people play with their bosses and other workers and have played along by making the travel game more rewarding to business travelers, more costly to the travelers' firms, and more profitable to the airlines—all through their "frequent-flyer" programs. You can bet managers are more than incidentally concerned about the use of frequent-flyer programs by employees. When American Airlines initiated its AAdvantage frequent-flier program in 1981, the company was intent on staving off the fierce price competition that had broken out among established and new airlines after fares and routes were deregulated in 1978. As other writers have noted, American was seeking to enhance "customer loyalty" by offering their best, most regular customers free or reduced-price flights after they built up their mileage accounts. Greater customer loyalty can mean that customers are less responsive to price increases, which could translate into actual higher prices.[21]

At the same time, there is more to the issue than customer loyalty. American figured that it could benefit from the obvious prisoners' dilemma their customers, especially business travelers, are in. By setting up the frequent-flier program, American (and all other airlines that followed suit) increased the individual payoff to business travelers for noncooperative behavior. American did this under its frequent-flier program by allowing travelers to earn more free flights and first-class upgrades if they chose more expensive, and often less direct, flights. They encouraged business people to act opportunistically, to use their discretion for their own benefit at the expense of everyone else in their firms.

For example, a business traveler who is on the verge of having enough miles in his American account to qualify for elite status (additional upgrades of travel perks) might choose a more expensive American flight over a comparable Southwest Airline flight just to get additional AAdvantage miles. The company would in effect, pick up the cost of the traveler's vacation flight. Business travelers are also encouraged to book their flights later than absolutely necessary, which requires paying full fare, so that they can use their frequent-flier upgrades to first class (these upgrades are typically not allowed with discount tickets). Businesspeople can also take circuitous routes to their destinations to qualify for more frequent-flier miles than could be gotten from a direct trip. The prisoners' dilemma problem for workers and their companies has, of course, prompted a host of other nonairline firms—rental car companies, hotels, and restaurants—to begin granting frequent-flier miles with selected airlines for travel services people buy with them, once again encouraging higher than necessary travel costs. The company incurs the cost of the added miles plus the lost time.

Use of frequent-flier miles might actually lower worker wages (because of the added cost to their firms, which can reduce the demand for workers, and the benefit of the miles to workers, which can increase worker supply and lower wages, topics to be covered later), but, still, workers have an incentive to exploit the program. Again, they are in prisoners' dilemma under which the cooperative strategy might be best for all but the noncooperative strategy dominates the choice each individual faces.

The problems created by frequent-flier programs are not trivial for many businesses, and we would expect that the bigger the firm, the greater the problem (given the greater opportunity for opportunistic behavior in large firms). Thirty percent of business travelers working for Mitsubishi Electronics America wait until the last few days before booking their flights, according to the corporate travel manager, John Fazio. Fazio adds, "We have people who need to travel at the last minute, but it's not 30 percent."[22] Corporate travel managers complain that the frequent-flier programs have resulted in excessive air fares (a problem for 87 percent of the firms surveyed), wasted employee time (a problem for 68 percent of the surveyed firms), use of more expensive hotels (a problems for 67 percent of the surveyed firms), and unnecessary travel (a problem for 59 percent of the surveyed firms).[23] The corporate travel managers interviewed felt that the frequent-flier programs resulted in an average "waste" equaling about 8 percent of all of the companies' travel expenditures.[24]

Frequent-flier programs put business travelers in a game situation that benefits the airlines at the expense of business travelers and their firms by encouraging noncooperative behavior. Recognizing this game, and the noncooperative incentives built into it, is important for managers who are trying to cut travel costs. In the effort to cut these costs, managers are also in a game with the airlines, which respond to cost-cutting measures with new wrinkles designed to intensify the prisoners' dilemma faced by business travelers. For example, USAirways announced plans to provide a Business Select class (featuring roomier seats and better meals) for those business travelers who pay full fare for their coach tickets.[25] Of course, when all airlines have frequent-flier programs, the problems for firms may be compounded by the fact that all airlines have more "loyal" customer bases and all are less likely to cut prices (another topic to be addressed on pp. 246–47).

Much of our analysis throughout the book is grounded in the *principal-agent problem*, or the tendency of workers and managers to pursue their own private goals at the expense of the goals of the firm and its owners. We do that for a simple reason: We want to understand how employees *might* behave in order that managers can draw up policies and incentives that can protect the firm and its owners from agency costs.

We do not by any means wish to suggest that people are not at all driven by an innate sense of duty or obligation to do what they are supposed to do as employees in a team or firm. On the contrary, people do seem to have a built-in tendency to cooperate—to a degree. The UCLA business professor James Q. Wilson has shown, through casual observation and a host of psychological experiments, that most people do have a "moral sense," which can show up in their willingness to forgo individual advantage (or opportunities to shirk) for the good of the group, which can be a firm.[26]

Moreover, a variety of factors, including considerations of equity and fairness, influence people's willingness to cooperate. As organizational behaviorists have shown, "culture" has an impact on the extent of cooperation. People from "collectivistic" societies like China may be more inclined to cooperate than people from "individualistic" societies like the United States.[27] Training in "group values" can affect the extent of cooperation. Experiments have shown that people are more cooperative when they have equal shares of whatever it is that is being divided (and women are more inclined to favor "equal shares" than men). They are willing to extend favors in cooperative ventures when they know that the favor will be returned. They work harder when they believe they are not underpaid. They are more likely to cooperate with close family members and friends than with strangers, and they are less likely to cooperate with others, whether close at hand or far removed, when the cost of cooperating is high. They work harder, in other words, when they believe they are among members of their relevant "in-group." Even training can be more effective in raising worker productivity when it is provided within in-groups, regardless of whether the workers come from collectivistic or individualistic societies.

Why is it that people are inclined to cooperate more or less naturally? Wilson repeats a favorite example of game theorists to explain why "cooperativeness" might be partially explained as an outcome of natural selection. Consider two people in early times, Trog and Helga, who are subject to attack by saber-toothed tigers. The "game" they must play in the woods is a variant of the prisoner's dilemma game. If they both run, then the tiger will kill and eat the slowest runner. If they both stand their ground—and cooperate in their struggle—then perhaps they can defeat the tiger. However, each has an incentive to run when the other stands his or her ground, leaving the brave soul who stands firm to be eaten.

What do people do? What *should* they do? Better yet, what do we *expect* them to do—eventually? We suspect that different twosomes caught in the woods by saber-toothed tigers over the millennia have tried a number of strategies. However, running is, over the long run, a strategy for possible extinction, given that the tiger can pick off the runners one by one. We should not be surprised that human society has come to be dominated by people who have a "natural" tendency to cooperate or who have found ways to inculcate cooperation in their colleagues. Moreover, parents spend a lot of family resources trying to ensure that children see the benefits of cooperation, and schoolteachers and coaches reinforce those values, emphasizing the benefits of sharing and doing what one is supposed to do or has agreed to do vis-à-vis people beyond the reach of the family. Managers do much the same.

Those societies that have found ways of cooperating have prospered and survived. Those that haven't have languished or retrogressed into economic oblivion, leaving the current generation with a disproportionate representation from groups that have been cooperative. Those who didn't cooperate long ago when confronted with attacks by saber-toothed tigers were eaten; those who did cooperate with greater frequency lived to propagate future generations.

What we are saying here is that human society is complex, driven by a variety of forces, based in both psychology and economics, that vary in intensity with respect to one another and that are at times conflicting. However, there are evolutionary reasons, if nothing else, to expect that people who cooperate will be disproportionately represented in societies that survive. Organizations can exploit—and, given the forces of competition, must exploit—people's limited but inherent desire or tendency to work together, to be a part of something that is bigger and better than they are individually. Organizations should be expected to try to reap the synergetic consequences of their individual and collective efforts.

However, if that were the whole story—if all that mattered were people's tendencies to cooperate—then management would hardly be a discipline worthy of much professional reflection. There would be little or no need or role for managers, other than that of cheerleader. The problem is that firms are also beset with the very incentive problems that we have stressed. The evolutionary process is far from perfect. Moreover, as the evolutionary biologist Richard Hawkins has argued, we are all beset with "selfish genes" intent on using "survival machines" (living organisms such as human beings) to increase their chances (the genes' individual chances, not so much the species' chances) of survival.[28] "Selfish genes" are willing to cooperate, if that's what is needed (or, rather, is what works), but the fundamental goal is survival. To the extent that Hawkins is right, what he is saying is, in essence, that we have to work very hard to override basic, self-centered drives at the core of our being.

It may well be that two people can work together "naturally," fully capturing their synergetic potential. The same may be said of groups of three and four people, maybe ten or even thirty. The point that emerges from the "logic of collective action" is that as the group size—team or firm—gets progressively larger, the consequences of impaired incentives mount, giving rise to the growing prospects that people will shirk or in other ways take advantage of the fact that they and others cannot properly assess what they contribute to the group's output.

Economists concerned with the economics of politics have long recognized how the "logic of choice" within groups applies to politics. The infamous "special-interest" groups, which are relatively small and have long been the whipping boys of commentators, tend to have political clout that is disproportionate to their numbers. Indeed, special-interest groups often get benefits from governments, with the high costs of their programs diffused over a much larger number of a more politically latent group, the general population of voters. Mancur Olson cites farmers as the classic case of an interest group that constitutes a minor fraction (less than 3 percent) of the population but that has persuaded Congress to pass a variety of programs over the years that benefit farmers and their families, programs paid for by higher prices on consumers and higher taxes on taxpayers.[29]

The political economist James Buchanan points out that honor codes, which, when they work, can be valuable to all students, tend to break down as universities grow in size. For that matter, crime, which is a violation of the cooperative tendency of a community, if not a nation, tends to rise disproportionately to the population. Buchanan's explanation is that the probability that criminals will be detected, arrested, and prosecuted falls with the growth in the populations of cities.[30]

James Wilson also stresses that experimental evidence shows that people in small towns are, indeed, more helpful than people in larger cities; the more densely packed the city population, the less helpful people will be. Presumably, people in smaller cities believe that their assistance is more detectable. People in larger cities are also less inclined to make eye contact with passersby and to walk faster, presumably to reduce their chances of being assaulted from people who are more likely to commit crimes.[31]

In his survey of the literature on the contribution of individuals to team output, Gary Miller reports that when people think that their contribution to group goals, for example, pulling on a rope, cannot be measured, they will reduce their effort.[32] When members of a team pulling on a rope were blindfolded and then told that others were pulling with them, the individual members exerted 90 percent of their best individual effort when one other person was supposed to be pulling. The effort fell to 85 percent when two to six other players were pulling. The shirking that occurs in large groups is now so well documented that it has a name—"social loafing."

A central point of this discussion is not that managers can never expect workers to cooperate. They will—but only *to a degree, given normal circumstances*. However, there are countervailing incentive forces, which, unless attention is given to the details of firm organization, can undercut the power of people's natural tendencies to cooperate and achieve their synergetic potential.

More on Games

Earlier in this chapter, we discussed one widely played game in business, the prisoners' dilemma game. This is not the only game encountered in business. What can be described as a "commitment" game is often encountered by managers. Consider the problem faced by firms that attempt to sell high-quality products for which customers would be willing to pay premium prices except for the fact that it is hard for them (the customers) to determine the quality. In Figure 2.3, the first figure in each pair of parentheses gives the payoff to the seller, and the second figure gives the payoff to the buyer for the joint choice indicated. The best joint choice is for the seller to provide a high-quality product and for the buyer to trust the seller's claim that it is indeed of high quality, in which case the buyer will be willing to pay the premium price warranted by the superior quality. In this case both receive a payoff of 100 (a completely arbitrary number useful only as a concrete example of the gain experienced). But notice that the buyer is not likely to believe the seller's claim that the product is of high quality. If the seller thinks that the buyer believes the high-quality claim, then he captures a bigger payoff of 150 by reducing production cost and providing a low-quality product, in which case the buyer pays an excess price and receives a payoff -50. On the other hand, if the seller thinks the buyer does not believe the high-quality claim, then the seller will provide a low-quality product (and sell it at a lower price, leaving both parties with a payoff of 40), since a high-quality product would go unsold at a price that covered cost, leaving him with a payoff of -50 and the buyer (nonbuyer in this case) with a zero payoff.

Unlike in the prisoners' dilemma, in this case the best solution can be reached if the seller produces a high-quality product and then somehow conveys that he or she has done so. In this scenario, the relevant possibilities for the buyer are restricted to the top row of the payoff matrix in Figure 2.3, and it then pays the buyer to trust the high-quality claim and buy at the high-quality price. The question is, How does the seller make a credible commitment to high quality when the buyer cannot easily verify the claim? This is a crucial question for managers, and it is discussed later in this book. But our point now is that business commonly involves knowing how to best make decisions in a game situation, one in which your best

		BUYER	
		Trust	Don't Trust
	High Quality	(100, 100)	(-50, 0)
SELLER			
	Low Quality	(150, -50)	(40, 40)

Figure 2.3 Commitment Game

decision depends on the decisions you believe others are making and the decisions that others are making depend on what they believe your decision will be.

Being able to make credible commitments is useful to managers in many situations. Consider another commitment game that describes circumstances often encountered in business activity. The game is often referred to as the battle of the sexes.[33] The name comes from considering a situation in which two people who enjoy each other's company are deciding on the movie to see one evening. Sally prefers the action-packed *True Lies* with Arnold Schwarzenegger, while John much prefers to see the sentimental *Sleepless in Seattle* with Meg Ryan. However, each would rather go together and see the other's choice than see his or her choice alone. This situation can be represented in the "payoff" matrix in Figure 2.4, where the first number in each set of parentheses is the value attached to the joint choice by John, and the second number is the value attached to the joint choice by Sally. If both see *True Lies*, Sally realizes a payoff of 100 and John realizes a payoff of 50, with the payoffs exactly reversed if both see *Sleepless in Seattle*. On the other hand, if each goes to his or her first choice alone, each receives a payoff of only 25 (and each would get a payoff of 0 from going to the second choice alone, which is obviously an irrelevant possibility).

The battle of the sexes game creates a set of incentives different from those set up by the prisoners' dilemma. If one participant commits himself beforehand in a prisoners' dilemma situation, then he is sure to be taken advantage of by the other.[34] But in the battle of the sexes, the advantage goes to the one who is the first to make a commitment. For example, assume Sally calls John while he is out of his office and leaves the following message on his voice mail: "Hi, Sally here. I'm out of the office for the rest of the day and you won't be able to reach me. So I'll meet you at the Savoy Theater [which just happens to be where *True Lies* is showing] at 7 tonight." Sally has probably won this game. By committing herself to go to her favorite movie, Sally has narrowed the relevant payoff possibilities for John to the second column in Figure 2.4, which makes his best choice *True Lies*.

The difference between the prisoners' dilemma and the battle of the sexes has important implications when the participants are faced with the

		SALLY	
		S. in S.	T. L.
	S. in S.	(100, 50)	(25, 25)
JOHN			
	T. L.	(0, 0)	(50, 100)

Figure 2.4. Battle of the Sexes

prospects of repeated play of the game. If two people, for example, are going to interact with each other in a repeated series of prisoners' dilemmas, then each has a strong motivation to establish a reputation for behaving cooperatively as long as the other participant does the same. When there are a large number of repeated plays, the long-run payoff to each participant when both play cooperatively is so large compared to the long-run payoff from mutual noncooperation that cooperation will be the preferred choice for each as long as the other reciprocates.

Good business managers recognize the cooperative benefits that can be realized through long-term associations when negotiating with suppliers, customers, and employees. On the other hand, the prospects of interacting within a long series of situations described by the battle of the sexes can reduce the motivation to cooperate with the other.

If you are going to deal with another person only once in a battle of the sexes situation, there is not much to be gained by developing a reputation for making credible commitments through stubbornness. When going out on a first date, for example, with little anticipation of a long-term relationship, you will probably be quite accommodating to your date's movie preference. Almost no one is as nice as he or she seems to be on a first date. But once it looks as if a relationship may last a while, a reputation for being inflexible becomes worth more. If you can convince your long-term partner that you are unyielding and are prepared to stick with a choice no matter what the cost, then you are in a position to realize a long series of preferred outcomes by making accommodation to your preferences the best choice for your partner. So if John really likes Sally and expects to keep seeing her, before going to see *Sleepless in Seattle* he will likely leave the following message on her voice mail, even though he knows she won't hear it until late that night: "Hi Sunshine, I got your message, but I'll be damned if I am going to see one of those violent movies. I'll see you tomorrow."

Of course, the other partner also sees the same advantage in establishing a reputation for stubbornness. This helps explain why two people who get along extremely well on the first few dates may soon have major-league disagreements over completely trivial matters, like what movies to see. The individual matters may be trivial, but it's power that the two are really fighting over, and that is not a trivial matter (because the power can be exercised over a series of future decisions). Several possibilities exist. One, the couple will split up, with each looking for another relationship. Second, one partner will become the dominant decision maker, with the other party willing to go along. Third, through the early disagreements, each partner will carve out separate areas of control based on the relative intensity of preferences. For example, the man might make the decisions on automobiles and vacations, with the woman making the decisions on investments and house furnishings.

These kinds of situations come, just like prisoners' dilemmas, in many different forms, and they commonly arise in business interactions. A good business manager needs to be able to recognize when a situation conforms to the battle of the sexes and to be prepared to respond appropriately. Many bargaining situations are the same as battles of the sexes, in that both parties are better off reaching an agreement (going to a movie together) than not, but each is even better off if the agreement is on—or close to—his or her terms. So a reputation for being a tough bargainer can be extremely valuable, *but within limits*. An attempt to be too tough by capturing all the benefits from an agreement may cause a breakup between you and your trading partners. The best reputation is one of toughness *and* fairness.

One of the most important things a good manager can do is to help those he or she manages overcome some of the problems of these power struggles. Consider the fact that often the choices made on such things as computer software, production schedules, and office procedures are far less important than is making sure that everyone agrees to those choices. It is less important, for example, whether people in the office use Word Perfect, Microsoft Word, or something else than that they all use the same word-processing package. Yet, workers have different preferences on such matters, and, if the decision were left up to the group, many of them would attempt to hold out for the choice that best suited them. The result could easily be a protracted and messy bargaining process in which only the level of hostility exceeds the level of stubbornness. Everyone can benefit from letting a strong but fair-minded manager eliminate the need for such bargaining by making key decisions and imposing them on everyone. Each worker will "lose" on some decisions but will "win" on others, and everyone will gain overall by being able to avoid the costs of reaching agreement on issues that are less important than is the fact that an agreement is reached.

There are an unlimited number of games that are played in business, and they all have features that distinguish them from others. But most of the games can be usefully assigned to a few broad categories that have important features in common. While in this chapter we have not come close to exhausting the categories of games that are relevant to business, we have considered two that illustrate situations that managers constantly must face and to which they must respond appropriately.[35] As we continue through the subsequent chapters, examples of the types of game situations highlighted here will be encountered frequently. And in recognizing the game people are playing, as in so much a good manager has to do, the key to acheiving productive cooperation is an understanding of the importance of incentives within the firm.

II

WORKER INCENTIVES

3

The Value of Tough Bosses

Key Insight: Tough bosses raise workers' wages. Owners hire workers, and not vice versa, because owners have incentives to be the tough bosses workers want.

BEING (OR HAVING) A TOUGH BOSS is tough, but a boss who isn't tough isn't worth much. And because tough bosses are valuable and lenient bosses are not, there is a reason for believing that existing organizational arrangements serve to impose the discipline on bosses necessary to ensure that they do a good job imposing discipline on the workforce. Competition presses firms to hire tough bosses, and, as we show in this chapter, the owners of the firm, or their manager-agents, not the workers, tend to the bosses. That is to say, owners or their agents tend to boss workers, not the other way around, for the simple reason that worker-bosses will not likely survive in competitive markets. Workers may not like tough bosses, but we explain that, if given the option, workers would choose to hire tough bosses.[1]

Everyone recognizes that firms compete with each other by providing better products at lower prices in a constant effort to capture the consumer dollar. This competition takes place on a number of fronts, including innovative new products, cost-cutting production techniques, clever and informative advertising, and the right pricing policy. But a continuing theme of this book is that none of these competitive efforts can be successful unless a firm backs them up with an organizational structure that is competitive—one that motivates its employees to work diligently and cooperatively. Those firms that do the best job in this organizational competition are the most likely to survive and thrive.

The organizational arrangements used by the most successful firms are most likely to be adopted by other firms, because of the force of profit maximization and market competition. So we should expect business firms to be organized in ways that motivate bosses to work diligently at motivating workers to work diligently and at the least cost. We should expect that the choice between workers and owners of capital as bosses will depend on who can be expected to press the other to work the most diligently or at the least cost. We have already given away the answer: owners (or their manager-agents) tend to boss the workers, a perfectly acceptable outcome for the owners, of course, but also for the workers, which is less predictable. To understand that point, we must first appreciate why workers would want tough bosses.

Though probably overstated, common wisdom has it that workers do not like their bosses, much less tough bosses. The sentiment expressed in the well-known country song "Take This Job and Shove It" could only be directed at a boss. Bosses are also the butts of much humor. There is the old quip that boss spelled backward is "Double SOB."

And there is the story about the fellow who went to the president of a major university and offered his services as a full professor. Noticing that the fellow had no advanced degree, the president informed him that he was unqualified. The fellow then offered his services as an associate professor and received the same response. After offering his services as an assistant professor and hearing that he was still unqualified, the fellow muttered, "I'll be a son-of-a-bitch," at which point the president said, "Why didn't you tell me earlier? I'm looking for someone to be dean of the business school."

If it were not for an element of truth contained in them, such jokes would be hopelessly unfunny. Bosses are often unpopular with those they boss. But tough bosses are much like foul-tasting medicines are to the sick; you don't like them, but you want them anyway because they are good for you. Workers may not like tough bosses, but they willingly put up with them because tough bosses mean higher productivity, more job security, and better wages.

The productivity of workers is an important factor in determining wages.[2] More productive workers receive higher wages than less productive workers. Firms would soon go bankrupt if they paid workers more than their productivity justified, but firms would soon lose their workers if they paid them less than their productivity warranted.

Many things, of course, determine how productive workers are. The amount of physical capital they work with and the amount of experience and education (human capital) the workers bring to their jobs are two extremely important, and commonly discussed, factors in worker productivity. But how well the workers in a firm work together as a team is also important. An individual worker can have all the training, capital, and diligence needed to be highly productive, but overall productivity will suffer unless other workers pull their weight by properly performing their duties. The productivity of each worker is crucially dependent on the efforts of *all* workers in the vast majority of firms.

So *all* workers are better off if they *all* work conscientiously on their *individual* tasks and as part of a team. In other words, it is collectively rational for everyone to work responsibly. But there is little individual motivation to work hard to promote the collective interest of the group, or firm.[3]

While each worker wants other workers to work hard to maintain the general productivity of the firm, each worker recognizes that her contribution to the general productivity is small. By shirking some responsibilities, she receives all of the benefits from the extra leisure but suffers from only a very small portion of the resulting productivity loss, which is spread over everyone in the firm. She suffers, of course, from some of the productivity loss when other workers choose to loaf on the job, but she knows that the decisions others make are independent of whether or not she shirks. And if everyone else shirks, little good will result for her, or for the firm, from diligent effort on her part. So no matter what she believes other workers will do, the rational thing for her to do is to capture the private benefits from shirking at practically every opportunity. With all other workers facing the same incentives, the strong tendency is for shirking on the job to reduce the productivity, and the wages, of all workers in the firm, and quite possibly to threaten their jobs by threatening the firm's viability.

The situation just described is another example of the general problem of the prisoners' dilemma discussed in chapter 2. Consider the matrix in Figure 3.1, which shows the payoff to Jane for different combinations of shirking on her part and shirking on the part of her fellow workers.[4] No matter what Jane believes others will do, the biggest payoff to her (in term of the value of her expected financial compensation and leisure time) comes from shirking. Clearly, she hopes everyone else works responsibly so that general labor productivity and the firm's profits are high despite her lack of effort, in which case she receives the payoff of 125, the highest that any one individual can receive.[5] Unfortunately for Jane, all workers face payoff possibilities similar to the ones she faces (and, to simplify the discussion, we assume everyone faces the same payoffs). So everyone will shirk, which means that everyone ends up with a payoff of 50, which is the lowest possible collective payoff for workers.[6]

| | | | Other Workers | |
		None shirk	Some shirk	All shirk
	Don't shirk	100	75	25
Jane				
	Shirk	125	100	50

Figure 3.1 Jane's Payoff

Workers are faced with self-destructive incentives when their work environment is described by the shirking version of the prisoners' dilemma. It is clearly desirable for workers to extricate themselves from this prisoners' dilemma. They can double their gain. But how?

In an abstract sense, the only way to escape this prisoners' dilemma is to somehow alter the payoffs for shirking. This requires workers to agree to collectively subject themselves to tough penalties that no one individual would be willing to accept unilaterally. While no one likes being subjected to tough penalties, everyone will be willing to accept the discipline those penalties impose in return for having that discipline applied to everyone else.

The situation here is analogous to many other situations we find ourselves in. For example, consider the problem of controlling pollution, which was mentioned briefly in chapter 2. While each person would find it convenient to be able to pollute the environment freely, when everyone is free to do so we each lose more from the pollution of others than we gain from our own freedom to pollute. So we accept restrictions on our own polluting behavior in return for having restrictions imposed on the polluting behavior of others. Littering and shirking may not often be thought of as analogous, but they are. One pollutes the outside environment, and the other pollutes the work environment.

An even better analogy is that between workers and college students. The "productivity" of a college from the student's perspective depends on its reputation for turning out well-educated graduates with high grades, a reliable indication that a student has worked hard and learned a lot. But students are tempted to take courses from professors who let them spend more time at parties than in the library and still give high grades. But if all professors curried favor with their students with lax grading policies, all students would be harmed as the value of their degrees decrease. While students may not like the discipline imposed on them by tough professors, they want tough professors to help them maintain the reputation of their college and the value of their diplomas. (The ideal situation for each student is for the professor to go easy on him or her alone and to be demanding of all other students.[7])

Similarly, workers may not like bosses who carefully monitor their behavior, spot the shirkers, and ruthlessly penalize them, but they want such bosses. We mean penalties sufficiently harsh to change the payoffs in Figure 3.1 and eliminate the prisoners' dilemma. As shown in Figure 3.1, the representative worker Jane captures 25 units of benefits from shirking no matter what other workers do. If she had a boss tough enough to impose more than 25 units of suffering, say, 35 units, on Jane if she engaged in shirking, her relevant payoff matrix would be transformed into the one shown in Figure 3.2. Jane might not like her new boss, but she would cease to find advantages in shirking. And with a tough boss monitoring all workers and unmercifully penalizing those who dare shirk, Jane

		Other Workers		
		None shirk	Some shirk	All shirk
	Don't shirk	100	75	25
Jane				
	Shirk	90	65	15

Figure 3.2 An Alternative Outcome

will find that she is more than compensated, because her fellow workers have also quit shirking. Instead of being in an unproductive firm, surrounded by a bunch of other unproductive workers, each receiving a payoff of 50, she will find herself as part of a hard-working, cooperative team of workers, each receiving a payoff of 100.

The common perception is that bosses hire workers, and in most situations this is what appears to happen. Bosses see benefits that can be realized only by having workers, and so they hire them. But since it is also true that workers see benefits that can be realized only from having a boss, it is reasonable to think of workers hiring a boss, and preferably a tough one.

The idea of workers hiring a tough boss is illustrated by an interesting, though probably apocryphal, story of a missionary in nineteenth-century China. Soon after arriving in China, the missionary, who was then full of enthusiasm for doing good, came upon a group of men pulling a heavily loaded barge up a river. Each man was holding onto a rope attached to the barge as he struggled forward against the river's current, while on the barge was a large man with a long whip with which he lashed the back of anyone who let his rope go slack. Upon seeing this, the missionary experienced a surge of indignation and rushed up to the group of men to inform them that he would put an end to such outrageous abuse. Instead of appreciating the missionary's concern, however, the men told him to butt out. They said that they owned the barge and that they earned more money the faster they got the cargo up the river. They had therefore hired the brute with the whip to eliminate the temptation each would otherwise have to slack off.

The missionary story may be doubted, but the point shouldn't be. Even highly skilled and disciplined workers can benefit from having a "boss" help them overcome the shirking that can be motivated by the prisoners' dilemma. Consider the experience related by Gordon E. Moore, a highly regarded scientist and one of the founders of Intel, Inc. Before Intel, Moore and seven other scientists entered a business venture that failed because of what Moore described as "chaos." Because of the inability of the group of scientists to act as an effective team in this initial venture, before they embarked on their next venture, according to Moore, "the first thing we had to do was to hire our own boss—essentially hire someone to run the company."[8]

Pointing to stories and actual cases in which the workers hire their boss is instructive in emphasizing the importance of tough bosses to workers. But the typical situation finds the boss hiring the workers, not the other way around. We explain later in the chapter why this is the case, but we can lay the groundwork for such an explanation by recognizing that our discussion of the advantages of having tough bosses has left an important question unanswered. An important job of bosses is to monitor workers and impose penalties on those who shirk, but how do we make sure that the bosses don't shirk themselves? How can you organize a firm to make sure that bosses are tough?

The work of a boss is not easy or pleasant. It requires serious effort to keep close tabs on a group of workers. It is not always easy to know when a worker is really shirking or just taking a justifiable break. A certain amount of what appears to be shirking at the moment has to be allowed for workers to be fully productive over the long run. There is always some tension between reasonable flexibility and credible predictability in enforcing the rules, and it is difficult to strike the best balance. Too much flexibility can lead to an undisciplined workforce, and too much rigidity can destroy worker morale. Also, quite distinct from the difficulty of knowing when to impose tough penalties on a worker is the unpleasantness of doing so. Few people enjoy disciplining those they work with by giving them unsatisfactory progress reports, reducing their pay, or dismissing them. The easiest thing for a boss to do is not to be tough on shirkers. But the boss who is not tough on shirkers is also a shirker.

A boss can also be tempted to form an alliance with a group of workers who provide favors in return for letting them shirk more than other workers. Such a group improves its well-being at the expense of the firm's productivity, but most of this cost can be shifted to those outside the alliance.

Of course, you could always have someone whose job it is to monitor the boss and to penalize him when he shirks on his responsibility to penalize workers who are shirking. But two problems with this solution immediately come to mind. One, the second boss will be even more removed from workers than the first boss and so will have an even more difficult time knowing whether the workers are being properly disciplined. Second, and even more important, who is going to monitor the second boss and penalize him or her for shirking? Who is going to monitor the monitor? This approach leads to an infinite regression, which means it leads nowhere. The solution to the problem is the one workers should want—making sure that the boss has some incentive to be tough. The workers should want their bosses to be "incentivized" to remain tough in spite of all the temptations to concede in particular circumstances for particular workers.

Every good boss understands that he or she has to be more than just "tough." A boss needs to be a good "leader," a good "coach," and a good "nursemaid," as well as many other things. The good boss inspires allegiance to the firm and the commonly shared corporate goals. Every good boss wants workers to seek the cooperative solutions in the various prisoners' dilemmas that invariably arise in the workplace. Having said that, however, it is also true that a good boss will invariably be called on to make some pretty tough decisions, mainly because the boss usually straddles the interests of the owners above and the workers below. The lesson of the chapter to this point should not be forgotten: "Woe be to the boss who simply seeks to be a nice guy to all claims." But firms must structure themselves so that bosses will *want* to be tough. How can that be done?

In many firms the boss is also the owner. The owner-boss is someone who owns the physical capital (such as the building, the land, the machinery, and the office furniture), provides the raw materials and other supplies used in the business, and hires and supervises the workers necessary to convert those factors of production into goods and services. In return for assuming the responsibility of paying for all of the productive inputs, including labor, the owner earns the right to all of the revenue generated by those inputs.

Throughout this volume, we (like other economists) refer to the owners as *residual claimants*, since they are the ones who claim any residual (commonly referred to as profits) that remains from the sales revenue after all the expenses have been paid. As the boss, the owner is responsible for monitoring the workers to see if each one of them is properly performing his or her job, and for applying the appropriate penalties (or encouragement) if they aren't. Combining the roles of ownership and boss in the same individual creates a boss who, as a residual claimant, has a powerful incentive to work hard at being a tough boss.

The employees who have the toughest bosses are likely to be those who work for residual claimants. But the residual claimants probably have the toughest boss of all—themselves. There is a lot of truth to the old saying that when you run your own business, you are the toughest boss you will ever have. Small-business owners commonly work long and hard since there is a very direct and immediate connection between their efforts and their income.[9] When they are able to obtain more output from their workers, they increase the residual they are able to claim for themselves. A residual-claimant boss may be uncomfortable disciplining those who work for her or dismissing someone who is not doing the job and indeed may choose to ignore some shirking. But in this case the cost of the shirking is concentrated on the boss who allows it, rather than diffused over a large number of people who individually have little control over the shirking and little motivation to do anything about it even if they did. So with a boss who is also a residual claimant, there is little danger that shirking on the part of workers will be allowed to get out of hand.

When productive activity is organized by a residual claimant, all resources—not just labor—tend to be employed more productively than when those who make the management decisions are not residual claimants. The contrast between government agencies and private firms managed by owner-bosses, or proprietors, is instructive. Examples abound of the panic that seizes the managers of public agencies at the end of the budget year if their agencies have not spent all of the year's appropriations. The managers of public agencies are not claimants to the difference between the value their agency creates and the cost of creating the value. This does not mean that public agencies have no incentive to economize on sources, only that their incentives to do so are impaired by the absence of direct, close-at-hand residual claimants.[10]

If, for example, a public agency managed to perform the same service for a hundred thousand dollars a year less than in previous years, the agency administrator would not benefit by being able to put the savings in her pocket. In fact, she would find herself worse off, since her budget would probably be cut and she would be left in charge of an agency with a smaller budget and therefore one with less prestige in the political pecking order. She would also realize that the money she saved by her diligence would be captured by an overbudgeted agency, enhancing the prestige of its less efficient administrator.

The clever public administrator is one who makes sure every last cent, and more, of the budget is spent by the end of the budget year, regardless of whether it is spent on anything that actually improves productivity. Can you imagine a proprietor of a private firm responding to the news that production costs are less than expected by urging his employees to buy more computers and office furniture and attend more conferences before the end of the year?[11]

To make the point differently, assume that as a result of your management training you become an expert on maximizing the efficiency of trash pickup services. In one nearby town the trash is picked up by the municipal sanitation department, financed out of tax revenue and headed by a public-spirited, bureaucratic sanitation professional. In another nearby town the trash is picked up by a private firm, financed by direct consumer charges and owned by a local businessperson who is proud of her loyal workers and her impressive fleet of trash trucks. By applying linear programming techniques to the routing pattern, you discover that each trash service can continue to provide the same pickup with half the number of trucks and personnel currently being used.

Who is going to be most receptive to your consulting proposal to streamline the trash pickup operation, the bureaucratic manager who never misses an opportunity to tell of his devotion to the taxpaying public or the proprietor who is devoted to her workers and treasures her trash trucks? Bet on this—the bureaucrat will show you the door as soon as he becomes convinced that your idea really would save a lot of taxpayer dollars by reducing his budget by 50 percent.

On the other hand, the proprietor will hire you as a consultant as soon as she becomes convinced that your ideas will allow her to lay off half her workers and sell half her trucks. The manager who is also a residual claimant can be depended on to economize on resources, despite his or her other concerns. The manager who is not a residual claimant can be depended on to waste resources, despite his or her statements to the contrary.[12]

No matter how cheaply a service is produced, resources have to be employed that could have otherwise been used to produce other things of value. The value of the sacrificed alternative has to be known and taken into account to make sure that the right amount of the service is produced. As a residual claimant, a proprietor not only has a strong motivation to produce a service as cheaply as possible but also has the information and motivation to increase the output of the service only as long as the additional value generated is greater than the value forgone elsewhere in the economy.

The prices of labor and other productive inputs are the best indicators of the value of those resources in their best alternative uses. So the total wage and input expense of a firm reflects quite well the value sacrificed elsewhere in the economy to manufacture that firm's product. Similarly, the revenue obtained from selling the product is a reasonable reflection of the product's value. So proprietors of businesses receive a constant flow of information on the net value their firm is contributing to the economy, and self-interest motivates a constant effort to produce any given level of output, and produce it in the way that maximizes firms' contributions.

When the one controlling the firm can claim a firm's profits, those profits serve a very useful function in guiding resources into their most valuable uses. If, for example, consumers increase the value they place on musical earrings (if such were ever made) relative to the value they place on other products, the price of musical earrings will increase in response to increased demand, as will the profits of the firms producing them. The increased profit will give the proprietors of these firms the financial ability, and the motivation, to obtain additional inputs to expand output of this dual-purpose fashion accessory of which consumers now want more. Also, some proprietors of firms making other products will now experience declining profits and find advantages in shifting into production of musical earrings. This redirection of labor and other productive resources will continue, driving down prices and profits in musical earring production, until the return in this productive activity is no greater than the return in other productive activities. At this point there is no way to further redirect resources to increase the net value they generate.[13]

The incentives created by residual-claimant business arrangements do a reasonable job of lining up the interests of bosses with the interests of their workers, their customers, and the general goal of economic efficiency—

using scarce resources to create as much wealth as possible. This alignment of interests is a crucial factor in getting large numbers of people with
diverse objectives and limited concern for the objectives of others to cooperate with one another in ways that promote their general well-being.
Having the residual claimant direct resources is, understandably, an organizational arrangement that workers should applaud. The residual
claimant can be expected to press all workers to work diligently, so that
wages, fringes, and job security can be enhanced. Indeed, the workers
would be willing to pay the residual claimants to force all workers to apply
themselves diligently (which is what they effectively do); both workers and
residual claimants can share in the added productivity from added diligence.

Certainly this ability to productively harmonize a diversity of interests
is a major reason for the emergence and sustainability of residual-claimant
business arrangements. But there is another reason why firms are commonly owned and managed by the same person, a reason that helps explain
why the typical situation finds the boss hiring the workers instead of the
workers hiring the boss.

People differ in a host of ways, and many of their differences have
important implications for the type of productive efforts for which they
are best suited. For example, both of the authors would have liked to have
been successful movie stars, but because we have slightly less charisma
than baking soda, we became economists instead. More relevant to the
current discussion, however, is the fact that people differ in their willingness to accept risk. Most people are what economists call *risk averse;* they
shy away from activities whose outcomes are not known with reasonable
certitude. Such people might, for example, prefer a sure $500 than a 50
percent chance of receiving $1,500 with a 50 percent chance of losing
$500 (which has an expected value of $500).[14] But some people are more
risk averse than others, as measured by how much less than $500 a sure
payoff would have to be before they would no longer prefer it to a gamble
with a $500 expected value. And people who are highly risk averse will
make career choices very different from the choices of those who are not.

Consider the choice between becoming a residual claimant by starting
your own business and taking a job offered by a residual claimant. The
choice to become a residual claimant is a risky one, requiring the purchase
of productive capital and the hiring of workers (thereby obligating yourself to fixed payments) with no guarantee that the revenue generated will
cover those costs. The person who starts a firm can lose a tremendous
amount of money. Of course, in return for accepting this risk, a residual
claimant who combines keen foresight, hard work, and a certain amount of
luck may end up claiming a lot of residual and becoming quite wealthy.
Clearly, those willing to accept risks will tend to be attracted to careers of
owning and managing businesses as residual claimants.

Those people who are more risk averse will tend to avoid the financial perils of entrepreneurship. They will find it more attractive to accept a job with a fixed and *relatively* secure wage, even though the return from such a job is less than the expected return from riskier entrepreneurial activity.

So business arrangements that put management control in the hands of residual claimants not only create strong incentives for efficient decisions; they also allow people to sort themselves out occupationally in accordance with important differences in their productive attributes and their attitude toward risk. Not only will people who are not very risk averse be more comfortable as residual claimants than most people; they will generally be more competent at dealing with the risks that are inherent in organizing production in order to best respond to the constantly changing prefer-ences of consumers. At the same time, those who are not averse to taking risk are likely less reliable at the relatively routine and predictable activity typically associated with earning a fixed wage than are those who are high-ly averse to risk.

By having people sort themselves into jobs according to their willing-ness to assume risk, the risk cost of doing business is minimized. And remember that when firms face competition in either their resource or product markets, they must look to lower all costs as much as possible. Otherwise, the firms' very existence can be threatened by those firms that pay attention to costs, including costs that are as hard to define as risk costs. If the firms that don't pay attention to costs avoid outright closure from being underpriced by competitors, they will be taken over by investors who detect an unexploited opportunity—who buy the firms (or their stock) at a low price and sell them at a higher price after restructuring the firms to lower their costs.

Consider the prospect that more risk-averse workers own their firms and hire the less risk-averse owners of capital (as well as other resources) who would be paid a fixed return on their investments (with the fixed return having all the guarantees that are usually accorded worker wages).[15] Workers would then, in effect, be the residual claimants, and worker wages would then tend to vary (as do profits in the usual capitalist-owned firm) in less than predictable ways with the shifts in market forces and gen-eral economic conditions. Such a firm would not likely be a durable arrangement for even moderately large firms in which fixed investments are important. It's not hard to see why.[16]

The workers *might* be spurred to work harder and smarter because of the sense of ownership, which the proponents of worker ownership argue would be the case. But then, maybe not. Workers might be more inclined to shirk once they are no longer pushed to work harder and smarter by owner-capitalists. And each worker can reason that his or her contribution to profits is very little (especially in large firms), so little that the power of residual claimacy is lost in the dispersion of ownership among workers.

For this reason alone, we would expect most worker-owned firms to be relatively small.

Risk-averse worker-owners would require a "risk premium" built into their expected incomes, and their risk premium would be greater than the risk premium that the less averse owners of capital would require. Hence, the cost of doing business for the worker-owned firm would be higher than for the capitalist-owned firm, which means that the worker-owned firms would tend to fail in competition with capitalist-owned firms. Instead of outright failure, we might expect many worker-owned firms to be converted to capitalist-owned firms simply because the workers would want to sell their ownership rights to the less risk-averse capitalists who, because of their lower risk aversion, can pay a higher price for ownership rights than other workers. The net income stream would be higher under the capitalist-owned firm, which means that the capital owners can pay more for the firm than it is worth to the workers. (The worker-owned firms would continue only if the workers were not allowed to sell their supposed ownership rights, which was true in the former Soviet Union and in Yugoslavia.)

However, the worker-owned firm would be fraught with other competitive difficulties. Because of their risk aversion, workers would demand higher rates of return on their investments, a fact that would likely restrict their investments and lower their competitiveness and viability over the long run. Moreover, with workers in control over the flow of payments to the capitalists after they, the capitalists, have made the fixed investment, the capitalists would have a serious worry. The capitalists must fear that the workers would tend to use their controlling position to appropriate the capital through noncompetitive wages and fringe benefit payments to themselves, a fear that is not so prominent among workers when capitalists own the fixed assets and pay the workers a fixed wage.[17] Therefore, even the capitalists would require a risk premium before they invested in worker-owned firms.

Of course, the workers could make the requisite investment, but we must wonder where they would obtain the investment funds. Out of their own pockets? Would they not want to put their own funds in secure investments? We must also wonder whether workers would be interested in investing in their own worker-run firms. Like capitalists, workers can understand the threat to their investments from other workers, given the limited competitiveness of their worker-owned firm and the tendency of workers to restrict investment and drain the capital stock through over-payments in wages and fringes. Workers, however, would face an additional problem: if they were to invest their financial resources in their own firms, then they would have a very narrow range of personal investments. By their work for their firms, they already plan to invest a great deal of their resources in their jobs just by spending time at work. Adding a financial investment means they would restrict the scope of assets in their personal portfolio of investments. That fact alone would increase their aversion to risky investments by their firm, and the longer the term of the investment, the greater the risk. Accordingly, we would expect the investments of worker-owned firms to be for shorter periods than would be the case in capitalist-owned firms, which implies that worker-owned firms would tend to lag in the development and application of new technologies. Such a tendency would once again make worker-owned firms less competitive, especially over the long run.

We are not suggesting that no firms are worker-owned and managed. After all, some are. Instead, the analysis explains why there are relatively few such firms, and why they are typically small firms, relying primarily on human capital of the owner-workers rather than physical capital. When large firms, such as Weirton Steel and United Airlines, are worker-owned, they are not worker-managed. The worker-owners of such firms immediately hire bosses to make the tough decisions that have to be made to keep a firm viable, but then there are the inevitable tensions that come with worker ownership.

Weirton Steel Company was taken over by employees in 1983. For a while it was a big success as workers put in long hours, helped each other outside their narrow work rule responsibilities, and did what it took so they could say, "We kept the job moving," as maintenance worker Frank Slanchik said. But soon distrust built between workers and their managers (they still hire managers). The two big issues were money and management control. Slanchik notes, "These two issues are especially likely to crop up in capital-intensive industries such as steel and airlines, which constantly require huge capital expenditures that can be viewed as draining money away from potential wage increases."[18]

In July 1994, United Airline workers took an average pay cut of 15 percent in return for a 55 percent interest in the company and three of the twelve seats on the airline's board of directors. According to *Business Week*, worker ownership of United Airlines has worked surprisingly well.[19] But even in the case of United, some problems that should have been expected are now evident. The 20,000 United flight attendants never joined the buyout and are still unhappy with the management. And, according to *Business Week*, "Many other employees still resent the pay cuts they took and suspect the ESOP [Employee Stock Ownership Plan] was foisted on them by greedy corporate executives and investment bankers who walked off with millions."[20] Moreover, the company offended many employees when it announced bonuses for 600 managers under a long-standing incentive-compensation plan. Investors have been reluctant to infuse additional capital into the airline, fearing that the employees would "revolt against cost-cutting decisions."[21]

This fear has so far been unfounded, but the worker-ownership arrangement took place at the beginning of a very profitable period for airlines, United included. Part of the carrier's postbuyout success stems from a surge in air travel that generated a record $2 billion in profits for the industry in 1996. Investors have to worry that when times get tougher in the future, United's newfound cooperative spirit might be seriously challenged, in view of the strains already evident among the different worker groups. The 21,000 United Airlines flight attendants, who (at the time this book was being finalized) had been working without a contract for more than a year, were thinking about an attack against United with a tactic known as "Create Havoc Around Our System"—or "Chaos."[22] The tactic consisted of unannounced strikes against individual flights, which can disrupt the entire schedule of an airline. The flight attendants' union, the Association of Flight Attendants, says it does not want to invoke Chaos, but in view of United's "record profits," United attendants were "angry" and ready to strike, or so claims Kevin Lum, president of the association.[23]

Understandably, investors can't be sure just how tough United's workers will be on each other. They also have to fear that the workers will not add their share to the company's capital stock by depleting retained earnings with wage increases and will be tempted to drain the firm of any capital added by outside investors through wage increases. The workers have to worry about the inclination of each worker group to corral firm profits at the expense of other groups and the investors. The workers also have to worry that they have taken over the role of the investors, which is accepting the risk that comes from being residual claimants. The workers' insecurities may be heightened by the fact that the company's future will be jeopardized by the absence of the capital that it will need to remain competitive with investor-owned airlines that don't have the problems and fears that United may face.

We should not be surprised if, at some later date, the workers effectively try to "buy back" some security by selling their stake in their company, giving the investors the right to be tough bosses in exchange for more investment funds and a more certain income stream for workers (with more of their income coming from wages, salaries, and fringe benefits and less of it coming from dividends).

Technology has given workers a chance to loaf on the job while they appear busy at their desk. All workers have to do is surf the World Wide Web for entertainment, shopping, and sex sites on their office computers while giving passersby (including their bosses) the impression that they, the workers, couldn't be more focused on company business. And workers are often good at acting busy and engaged.

At the same, technology is coming to the rescue of manager-monitors—or bosses who want to be really tough, if not oppressive. Programs such NetNanny, SurfWatch, and CyberPatrol enable managers to block worker access to web sites with certain words on the site, for example, "sex." However, with the aid of a program called com.Policy from SilverStone Software, managers now can, from their own desktop computers, go much further and check out what workers have on their computer screens. The software can take a snapshot of the worker's computer screen and send it, via the local area network, to the boss's screen. If a worker visits an XXX-rated web site or writes a love note to a coworker or someone across the country, managers can know it and, depending on how tough they want to be, can penalize or dismiss the worker for using company equipment for personal use. Presumably, the managers can, with the aid of the software, increase worker productivity, given that the penalties or threat of penalties can eliminate worker shirking.

The real question is whether managers should use technology that allows them to "snoop" (to use the characterization of the technology's critics). Would workers want them to use it? Clearly, there are good reasons managers and workers alike would not want to use the software; it represents an invasion of worker privacy. Many managers and, we suppose, almost all workers find "snooping" distasteful. But, as in all other business matters, the worker problems must be weighed against the benefits to the firm *and* its workers.

Workers might not want their privacy invaded at the whim of their bosses, but the workers can understand the now familiar prisoners' dilemma they are in—one in which many of the workers might be inclined to misuse their office computers for private gain (entertainment, maintenance of love affairs, and sexual stimulation). In large offices, the workers can reason that all other employees are misusing (at least to some extent) their computers, that their individual misuse will have an inconsequential impact on the firm's profitability or survivability, and that each worker should do what everyone else is doing, take advantage of the opportunity to misuse their computers—even though long-run firm profits and worker wages will suffer as a result of what the workers do (or, rather, don't do).

Accordingly, workers could welcome the invasion of their privacy, primarily because the gain in income and long-term job security is of greater value than the loss of privacy. Managers can use the software simply because they are doing what their stockholders *and* their workers want them to do—make mutually beneficial trades with their workers, in this case, to ask them to give up some privacy in exchange for the prospects of higher wages and security.

At the same time, we should not expect that this reasoning will apply in every worker group. Some worker groups will value their privacy very highly, so highly, in fact, that in some instances the managers would have to add more to worker wages than the firm could gain in greater productivity from the use of the monitoring software. In such cases, use of the software would be nonsensical: it would hurt both the workers and the firm's bottom line. Put another way, some bosses aren't as tough as they might want to be simply because, beyond some point, toughness—added "snooping"—doesn't pay; it can be a net drain on the company.

Critics of the snooping software often characterize it as "intrusive," if not "Orwellian." One such critic was reported to have reacted to the software's introduction with the comment, "It worries me that with the assistance of a variety of tools that every moment of a person's workday can be monitored. Workers are not robots that work twenty-four hours a day without ceasing."[24] We simply don't see the matter in such black-and-white terms. The old quip "different strokes for different folks" has much to recommend it, especially in business. We see nothing wrong with employers warning their employees, "The computers are the firm's, and we reserve the right to snoop on what you are doing with the firm's equipment as we see fit." To the extent that the (potential) snooping is seen as a threat to workers, the firm will have to pay in higher wages for the snooping bosses might do. If it does not pay a higher wage in return for the announcement, workers can be expected to go to firms where snooping is explicitly ruled out. What is understandably objectionable to employees is snooping when it is not announced or, worse yet, when managers profess, or just intimate, that they will not use the available technology to snoop. Such managers not only violate the privacy and trust of their workers; they engage in a form of fraud. They effectively ask their workers to take a lower rate of pay than they would otherwise demand while not giving their workers what they pay for—privacy. Moreover, such after-the-fact snooping doesn't do what the firm wants, which is to increase the incentive workers have to apply themselves.

Unannounced snooping is just poor management policy on virtually all scores. Where announced snooping policies exist, workers can decide for themselves their stance. Those workers who value privacy or on-the-job entertainment highly can work for firms that don't snoop. Those workers who value their privacy very little can work for firms that announce that they might snoop. "Different strokes for different folks" can be a means of elevating on-the-job satisfaction.

What firms would be most likely to use the monitoring software (or any other technology that permits close scrutiny of worker behavior)? We can't give a totally satisfactory answer. Workplace conditions and worker preferences are bound to vary across industries. But we can say with conviction that there is no "one size fits all" monitoring policy. We can only imagine that different firms will announce different levels of snooping, with some firms ruling it out, other firms adopting close snooping, and still others announcing occasional snooping. And many firms with the same level of snooping can be expected to impose penalties of different degrees of severity.

Although we can't say much in theory about what firms should do, we can note that the snooping software, and similar technologies, are more likely be used in "large" firms, where the output of individual workers is hard to detect, measure, and monitor, than in "small" firms, where output is relatively easy to detect, measure, and monitor precisely because each worker's contribution to the firm's output is such a large share of the total. The snooping technology is not likely to be used among workers whose incomes are tied strongly to measures of their performance, for example, salespeople who are on commission and physically far removed from the company headquarters. Such workers suffer a personal cost if they spend their work time surfing the Web or writing love notes. Managers should be little more concerned with such workers' misuse of their company computers than they are concerned about how their workers use their paychecks at the mall. If such workers are not performing (because they are "spending" too much of their "pay" on Net surfing), then the firm should consider whether they need to increase the cost of wasted time by more strongly tying pay to performance (a subject to which we return in chapter 5).

By implication, managers are not likely to use the software to monitor employees who are highly creative. "Creativity" does not always happen when workers diligently apply themselves, and it often occurs precisely because workers are relaxed, with the ability to do as they please without fear of being penalized for goofing off. Firms may be more inclined to use the software to check on employees who are paid by the hour and who derive little or no personal payoff from working hard and smart. It should go without saying that the more workers value their privacy, the less likely it is that monitoring software will be used, simply because the more workers value their privacy, the more managers would have to pay in higher wages to invade that privacy.

Competition determines which business arrangements will survive and which will not. The prevalence of single proprietorship is explained by the advantage of this business form in producing those products the consumers want as inexpensively as possible. But changing circumstances can reduce the competitive advantage of a business arrangement as new arrangements are found to do a better job of organizing productive activity. Technological advances that took place during the late nineteenth century made it possible to realize huge economies from large-scale production in many manufacturing industries. These technological advances shifted the advantage to business organizations that were far too large to be owned and managed by one proprietor, or even by a few. But the advantage of large business firms is reduced by the fact that they make it impossible to concentrate the motivation created by ownership entirely in the hands of those making management decisions.

Those manufacturing firms that developed organizational arrangements that did the best job of reducing the disconnection between the owners' incentives and the managers' control were best able to take advantage of economies from large-scale production. The result was a competition that resulted in the development of the modern corporation, the business form that today accounts for most of the value produced in the United States economy, even though small, owner-managed firms still make up, by far, the largest number of firms in the economy.

However, it must be remembered (contrary to what is often taught in business books) that the corporation (an organization under which investors have limited liability) was not a creation of the state.[25] The corporation emerged before states got into the incorporating business. Groups of private investors formed corporations because they believed that there were economies to be had if they all agreed to create a business in which outside parties could not hold the individual investors liable for more than their investment in the corporation (that is, the investors' personal fortunes would not be at risk from the operation of the firm, as was and remains true of proprietorships and partnerships). Clearly, such a public announcement of limited liability (made evident by the appendage "Inc." on the end of the corporate name) may make lenders wary and cause them to demand higher interest rates on loans. However, corporations have the offsetting advantage of being able to attract more funds from more investors, increasing firm equity, a force that not only increases the firm's ability to achieve scale economies grounded in technology but lowers risk costs to lenders. Of course, the outside investors can be hard taskmasters, since they can shift their investments away from firms that were not yielding acceptable profits. But that doesn't mean the workers will find the corporate form unattractive. On the contrary, given the potential scale economies and the risk reductions, corporations may provide more secure employment than small proprietorships.

We have stressed that the growth in the size of a firm can cause a deterioration in the motivation people have to work productively. We have also stressed the need for tough bosses. As a firm grows, it must be concerned with the languishing motivation bosses might have to remain tough. This means that in order to continue to grow, firms must find means of fortifying incentives for bosses. In chapters that follow, we examine some of the arrangements large corporations have developed to motivate managers to behave like residual claimants. Large corporations can never perfectly synchronize the interests of owners, managers, workers, and consumers as closely as a firm managed by a hands-on residual claimant—owner, but that is the ideal that all business arrangements strive for. Firms that don't voluntarily seek to achieve that ideal will either soon have to change their ways or struggle to implement cost-effective business arrangements to match what their competitors do.

In all firms, an important factor behind the organizational structure is the often unrecognized desire workers have for tough bosses. As will become clear in later chapters, we are talking about all workers, including the top managers of the largest corporations. Managers and workers may not like tough bosses, but the evidence from the way that firms are organized certainly indicates that they want them.

Jack Welch, the chief executive officer of General Electric, has played out the central point of this chapter because he surely qualifies as a tough boss. Indeed, Fortune once named Welch "America's toughest boss."[26] Welch earned his reputation by cutting payrolls, closing plants, and demanding more from those that remained open. Needless to say, these decisions were not always popular with workers at GE. But today GE is one of America's most profitable companies, creating far more wealth to the economy and far more opportunities for its workers than it would have if the tough and unpopular decisions had not been made. In Welch's words, "Now people come to work with a different agenda: They want to win against the competition, because they know that . . . customers are their only source of job security. They don't like weak managers, because they know that the weak managers of the 1970s and 1980s cost millions of people their jobs."[27]

4

The Value of "Teams"

Key Insight: The economies of "team production" are a major reason for the existence of firms. However, the tendency of workers to shirk on their obligations as "team players" is a major reason for the existence of managers.

THE CENTRAL REASON firms exist is that people are often more productive when they work together—in "teams"—than when they work in isolation from one another but are tied together by markets. "Teams" are no passing and empty management fad. Firms have always utilized them. What seems to be new is the emphasis within management circles on the economies that can be garnered from assigning complex sets of tasks to relatively small teams of workers, both within departments and, for larger projects, across departments.

At its defense avionics plant, Honeywell reports that its on-time delivery went from 40 percent in the late 1980s to 99 percent at the start of 1996, when it substituted teams in which workers' contributions are regulated by the members for assembly-line production in which workers' contributions are regulated extensively by the speed of the motors that drive the conveyor belts. Dell Computer is convinced that its team-based production has improved quality in made-to-order mail-order sales. Within twelve months of switching to teams in its battery production, Electrosource found its output per worker doubled (while its workforce dropped from 300 to 80 workers).[1]

If people could not increase their joint productivity by cooperating, individual proprietorships (with no employees other than the owners) would be the most common form of business organization and also the form that contributed most to national production. As it is, while proprietorships outnumber other business forms (for example, partnerships and corporations) by a wide margin, they account for only a minor fraction of the nation's output. Even then, many proprietorships can't get along without a few employees. Single-worker firms tend to be associated with the arts. Few artists have employees. Even we are writing this book as a partnership in the expectation that our joint efforts will pay off in a better book than either of us could write alone. We are a "team" of a sort. But notice there are only two of us, and we aren't about to write a book with a number of others, for reasons explained later in this chapter. As important as teams can be in business, managers must recognize inherent incentive problems that limit the size of productive teams.

What do we mean by "team production"? If Mary and Jim could each produce 100 widgets independent of one another and could together produce only 200 widgets, there would be no basis for team production, and no basis for the two to form a firm with all of the trappings of a hierarchy. The added cost of their organization would, no doubt, make them uncompetitive vis-à-vis other producers like themselves who worked independent of one another. However, if Mary and Jim could produce 250 widgets when working together, then team production might be profitable (depending on the exact costs associated with operating their two-person organization).

Hence, we define "team production" as those forms of work in which results are highly interactive: the output of any one member of the group is dependent on what the other group members do. The simplest and clearest form of "team work" is that which occurs when Mary and Jim (and any number of other people) move objects that neither can handle alone from one place to another. The work of people on an assembly line or on a television-advertising project is a more complicated form of teamwork.

Finding business endeavors that have the potential of expanding output by more than the growth in the number of employees is a major problem businesses face, but it is not the only problem and may not be the most pressing day-to-day problem when groups of people are required to do the work. The truly pressing problem facing managers on a daily basis is making sure that the synergetic potential of the workers who are brought together into a team is actually realized, that is, that production is carried out in a cost-effective manner so that the cost of organization does not dissipate the expanded output of, in our simple Mary/Jim example, fifty widgets.[2]

We often think of firms as failing for purely financial reasons. They don't make a profit, or they incur losses. Firms are said to be illiquid and insolvent when they fail. That view of failure is instructive, but the matter can also be seen in a different light, as an organizational problem *and* as a failure in organizational incentives. A poorly run organization can mean that all of the fifty "extra" widgets that Mary and Jim can produce together are lost in unnecessary expenditures and impaired productivity. If the organizational costs exceed the equivalent of fifty widgets, then we can say that Mary and Jim have incurred a loss, which will force them to adjust their practices as a firm or to part ways.

Many firms do fail and break apart, not because the *potential* for expanded output does not exist but because the potential is not realized when it could be. The people who are organized in the firm can do better apart, or in other organizations, than they can together.

Why can't people always realize their collective potential? There is a multitude of reasons. Firms may not have the requisite product design or a well thought out business strategy to promote the products. Some people just can't get along; they rub each other the wrong way when they try to cooperate. Nasty conflicts, which deflect people's energies at work to interpersonal defensive and predatory actions, can be so frequent that the production potentials are missed.

While recognizing many noneconomic explanations for organizational problems, we, however, reiterate our recurring theme, that incentives always matter a great deal and can become problematic within firms. Our general answer to the question of why firms' potential can go unrealized is that frequently firms do not find ways to properly align the interests of some groups of workers with the interests of other groups of workers and of the owners. They don't cooperate as they should.

In our simple firm example, involving only two people, Mary and Jim, each party has a strong *personal* incentive (quite apart from an altruistic motivation) to work with the other. After all, Mary's contribution to firm output is easily detected by her *and* by Jim. The same is true for Jim. Moreover, each can readily tell when the other person is not contributing what is expected (or agreed upon). Each might like to sit on his or her hands and let the other person carry the full workload. However, the potential is not then likely to be realized, given that the active participation of both Mary and Jim is what generates the added production and is the basis for their becoming a firm (or team) in the first place.

Furthermore, Jim can tell when Mary is shirking her duties, and vice versa, just by looking at the output figures and knowing that there is only one other person to blame. Accordingly, when Mary shirks, Jim can "punish" Mary by shirking also, and vice versa, ensuring that they both will be worse off than they would have been had they never sought to cooperate. The agreement Mary and Jim might have to work together can be, in this way and to this extent, self-enforcing, with each checking the other—and each effectively threatening the other with reprisal in kind. The threat of added cost is especially powerful when Mary and Jim are also the owners of the firm. The cost of the shirking and any "tit for tat" consequences are fully borne by the two of them. There is no prospect for cost shifting.

Two-person firms are, conceptually, the easiest business ventures to organize and manage because the incentives are so obvious and strong and properly aligned. Organizational and management problems can begin to mount, however, as the number of people in the firm or "team" begins to mount.

Everyone who joins a firm may have the same objective as Mary and Jim—to make as much money as possible, or to reap the full synergetic potential of their cooperative efforts. At the same time, a number of things can happen as the number of employees in the firm or on the "team" grows. Clearly, communication becomes more and more problematic. What the boss says can become muffled and lose clarity and force as the message is spread through more and more people within the firm.

Also, and probably more important, as we have recognized in earlier chapters, incentives begin to change as groups increase in size. First, each individual's contribution to the totality of the firm's output becomes less and less obvious as the number of people grows. This is especially true when the firm is organized to take advantage of people's specialties. Employees often don't know what their colleagues do and, therefore, are not able to assess their work.

When Mary is one of two people in a firm, then she is responsible for half of the output (assuming equal contributions, of course), but when she is one of a thousand people, her contribution is down to one-tenth of one percent of total output. If she is a clerk in the advertising department assigned to mailing checks for ads, she might not even be able to tell that she is responsible for one-tenth of a percent of output, income, and profits.

If Mary works for a firm with several hundred thousand workers, you can bet that she has a hard time identifying just how much she contributes to the firm. She can't tell that she is contributing anything at all, and neither can anyone else. She can literally get lost in the company. If she doesn't contribute, she and others will have an equally difficult time figuring out what exactly was lost to the firm. Her firm's survival is not likely to be materially affected by what she does or does not do. She is the proverbial "drop in the bucket," and the bigger the bucket, the less consequential each drop is. Of course, the same could be said of Jim and everyone else in the firm.

Now, it might be said that all of the "drops" add up to a "bucket." The problem is that each person must look at what he or she can do, given what all the others do. And drops, taken individually, don't really matter, so long as there are a lot of other drops around. If one else contributes anything to production (there are no other drops in the bucket), the contribution of any one person is material—in fact, everything. The point is that in large groups and as output expands, each worker has an *impaired* incentive to do that which is in all of their interests to do—that is, to make her small contribution to the sum total of what the firm does. All workers may want the bucket to get filled, but to do so takes more than wishful thinking, which often comes in the form of assuming that people will dutifully do that which they were hired to do. Large-number prisoners' dilemmas are more troublesome than small-number prisoners' dilemmas.

A central lesson of this discussion is, as stressed before, not that managers can never expect workers to cooperate. Most people do have—very likely because of genetics and the way they were reared—a "moral sense," or a capacity to do what they have committed to doing, to cooperate—but only *to a degree, under normal circumstances.* However, there are countervailing incentive forces embedded in the way groups or teams of people work that, unless attention is given to the details of firm organization, can undercut the power of people's natural tendencies to cooperate and achieve their synergetic potential. If people were total angels, always inclined to do as they are told or as they promised to do, then the role of managers would be seriously contracted. Even if almost everyone were inclined to do as he was told or had committed to doing, managers would still want to have in place policies and an organizational structure that would prevent the few "bad" people from doing real damage to the firm— which, if left unchecked, they certainly can do.

The arguments presented also help us answer several questions:

- *Why are there so many small firms?* Many commentators give answers based in technology: economies of scale (relating strictly to production techniques and equipment) are highly limited in many industries. One very good organizational reason is that many firms have not been able to overcome the disincentives of size, making expansion too costly and uncompetitive.

- *Why are large firms broken into departments?* While it might be thought that the administrative overhead of department structures, which require that each department have a manager and an office with all the trappings of departmental power, is "unnecessary," departments are a means that firms use to reduce the size of the relevant group within the firm. The purpose is to make sure not only that the actions of individuals can be monitored more closely by bosses but also that the individuals in any given department can more easily recognize their own and others' contributions to "output."

- *Why do workers have departmental bosses?* One reason is that the owners want their instructions to be carried out. Another explanation, one favored by the UCLA economists Armen Alchian and Harold Demsetz, is that the workers themselves want someone who is capable of monitoring the output of their coworkers, to prevent than from shirking and to increase the incomes and job security of all workers.[3] Workers want someone who is given the authority to fire members who shirk. As we have noted, if owners didn't create bosses, then the workers probably would want them created in many situations for many of the same reasons and from much the same mold as do owners.

- *Why is there so much current interest in "teams"?* We suspect that the concept of teams in industry has always been around and has been used for a long time. After all, we, the authors, have worked as members of "teams" (mainly, departments of business and economics professors) for all of our careers. However, it is also probably true that in recent decades, managers have probably become far too enamored of the dictates of "scientific management," which focuses on controlling workers with punishments and rewards that come from bosses who are outside (and above) the workers' immediate working group. Managers have tried, with some success, to reduce shirking by installing assembly lines, where the speed of the assembly-line belt determined how fast workers worked (with the presumption that workers would not have much leeway to adjust behavior, which might have controlled the pace of the work done but not the quality). In the past, many managers overlooked the impact of team size on member incentives. They have now begun to realize that they can increase worker productivity by reducing the size of the relevant group, to ensure that workers, who know most about what needs to be done in many firms, can monitor each other. Workers in appropriately sized teams can monitor and direct each other's work. Team members can impose peer pressure (through the creation of shame and guilt for shirking), which is a way of increasing the cost of shirking and increasing output.[4] Such close-at-hand monitoring can become even more important when consumers begin to demand more emphasis on quality, as has happened.

    We also suspect that the modern interest in "teams" is driven by newfound global competition and by the growing sophistication of work in many industries. Those firms, domestic and foreign, that have employed teams successfully have forced other firms with traditional top-down management control structures to also consider teams to keep up with the competition. Technology has greatly elevated the sophistication of production, increasing the specialization of work so that much of the knowledge of what can be done in production is known only by the people who actually do the jobs. Bosses can know a lot, but they can't possibly know many of the things that their workers know. Managers must delegate decision-making authority to those who have the detailed knowledge to make the most cost-effective decisions, which, when production is interdependent or done jointly by a number of people, means that decisions must be made by teams of workers.

As a consequence of the benefits of team production, we should not be surprised that at Motorola's Arlington Heights cellular phone plant, team members participate in the hiring and firing of coworkers, determine training, and set work schedules. At Nucor Steel, teams can discipline their members. At both companies, the team-based plants are remarkably productive.

At the same time the team members are delegated decision-making authority, they must also shoulder responsibility for the decisions they make. That necessarily means that team members must share the rewards from good decisions and the costs from bad ones. Often, this can mean that production bonuses are tied to what the team *as a whole* accomplishes, not what individual members do. Often, it also means that when the decisions are systematically bad, then the entire team must be dismissed, not just individuals. If individuals can be chosen as scapegoats for the actions taken by their team, then all individuals will have an incentive to "game" the process, trying to shirk and then pinning the blame on others. Team members will then have less incentive to work together and more incentive for political intrigue, possibly corrupting the working relationship of all.

A natural question that is bound to puzzle business managers interested in maximizing firm output is, How large should teams be? How many members should they have? We obviously can't say exactly, given the many factors that affect the great variety of firms in the country. (If we could formulate a pat answer, this book would surely sell zillions of copies!) However, we can make several general observations, the most important of which is that managers must acknowledge that shirking (or "social loafing") tends to rise along with the size of the group, everything else held constant.

In addition, we suggest that since people who are alike tend to cooperate, the more alike the members, the larger the team can be.[5] The more training team members are given in cooperation, the larger the teams can be. Training, in other words, can pay not only because it makes workers more productive but also because it can reduce the added overhead of a larger number of smaller departments.

However, a lot depends on the type of training given workers. Apparently, economists, using their maximizing models (and the firmly held belief that everyone will shirk whenever possible), are inclined to play whatever margins are available to their own personal advantage, or to shirk when feasible, to a degree not true of other professionals.[6] As a consequence, it probably follows that the more economists (and other people with similar conceptual leanings) employed, the smaller the team should be. Although we may never have intended it, we must fear that the people who read this book may be less disposed to cooperate than they were before they picked it up.

The more workers are imbued with a corporate culture and accept the firm's goals, the larger the team can be. The money spent by corporate leaders as they try to define the firm's purpose can be self-financing, since the resulting larger departments can release financial and real resources.

The more detectable or measurable the outputs of individual team members by other team members, the larger the team can be. Firms, therefore, have an economic interest in developing ways to make work, or what is produced, objective. Finally, the greater the importance of quality, the more important team production should be, and the smaller teams will tend to be.

The size of the teams within a firm can affect the overall size of the firm. Firms with teams that are "too large" or "too small" can have unnecessarily high cost structures that can restrict market share and overall size, as well as depress the incomes of the workers and owners.

Recognizing that teams can add to firm output is only half the struggle to achieve greater output by getting workers to perform as they should. A question that all too often undercuts the value of teams is, How are the workers to be paid? If workers are rewarded only for the output of the team, then individual workers once again have incentives to "free ride" on the work of others (to the extent that they can get away with it), which can play out not only in slack work but also in absenteeism. If team members are rewarded exclusively for their own individual contributions, then the incentive for actual teamwork is reduced.

As a rule, managers effectively "punt" on compensation issues, not knowing exactly how to structure rewards. They compromise by offering compensation that is based partly on team output and partly on individual contributions to the team. Team output is generally the easier of the two compensation variables to measure, given that the teams are organized along functional lines, with some measurable objective in mind. Individual contributions are often determined partially by peer evaluation, since team members are the ones who have localized knowledge of who is contributing how much to team output. But this does not completely solve the compensation problem. Team members can reason that how they work and how they and their cohorts are evaluated can affect their slice of the compensation pie. The better the evaluation of others, the lower their own evaluation, a consideration that can lead team members to underrate the work of other team members. The result can be team discord, as has been the experience at the jean manufacturer Levi-Strauss, where supervisors reportedly spend a nontrivial amount of time refereeing team-member conflicts. To ameliorate (but not totally quell) the discord, Levi-Strauss has resorted to giving employees training in group dynamics and methods of getting along.[7]

One of the questions our conceptual discussion cannot answer totally satisfactorily is, How can managers best motivate workers to contribute to team output? There are four identifiable pay methods worth considering:

1. The workers can simply share in the revenues generated by the

team (or firm). We can call this reward system *revenue sharing*. The gain to each worker is the added revenue received minus the cost of the added effort expended. Under this method reward, each worker has maximum incentive to free ride, especially when the "team" is large.

2. The workers can be assigned target production or revenue levels and be given what are called *forcing contracts*, or a guarantee of one high wage level (significantly above their market wage) if the target is achieved and another, lower (penalty) wage if the target is not achieved. Under this system, each worker suffers a personal income loss from the failure of the team to work effectively to meet the target.

3. The workers can also be given an opportunity to share in the team or firm profits. Profit sharing (or sometimes called "gainsharing") is, basically, another form of a forcing contract, since the worker will get one income if the firm makes a profit (above some target level) and a lower income if the profit (above a target level) is zero.

4. The workers within different teams can also be rewarded according to how well they do relative to other teams. They can be asked to participate in *tournaments*, in which the members of the "wining team" are given higher incomes—and, very likely, higher rates of pay by the hour or month—than the members of other teams. We say "very likely" because the winning team members may work harder, longer, and smarter in order to win the tournament "prize." Hence, the "winners' " pay per hour (or any other unit of time) could be lower than that of the "losers."[8]

All of the pay systems may have a positive impact on worker input and, as a consequence, on worker output. For example, a number of studies reveal that profit sharing and worker stock ownership plans do seem to have an impact on worker productivity.[9] One study of fifty-two firms in the engineering industry in the United Kingdom (40 percent of which had some form of profit-sharing plans and the rest did not) found that profit sharing could add between 3 and 8 percent to firm productivity.[10] And it has also been shown that the more "participatory" the decision-making process, the more the information-sharing the communication process, the more flexible the job assignment, and the greater the extent of profit sharing, the greater the worker performance relative to more traditional organizational structures.[11] But the question that has been addressed all too infrequently is which method of rewarding workers and their teams is *most* effective in overcoming shirking and causing workers to apply themselves.

One of the more interesting studies that addresses that question uses an experimental or laboratory approach to develop a tentative assessment of the absolute and relative value of the different pay methods on worker effort. The experimental economists Haig Nalbantian and Andrew Schotter used two groups of six university economics students in a highly stylized experiment in which the students' pay for their participation in the experiment was determined by how "profitable" their respective teams were in achieving maximum "output."[12]

The students did their "work" on computers that were isolated from one another. The students indicated how much "work" they would do in the twenty-five rounds of the experiment by selecting a number from 0 to 100 that had a cost tied to it; each higher number had a higher cost to the student, just as rising effort tends to impose an escalating cost on workers. The students in each of the two teams always knew two pieces of important information—how much they "worked" (or the number they submitted) in each round and how much the "team" as a total "worked." They did not know the individual "effort levels" of the other students.

There is much left to be desired in this experiment, a point the authors fully concede. The experimental setting did not reflect the full complexity of the typical workplace. Direct communication among workers can have an important impact on the effort levels of individual workers, but the complexity of the workplace makes it difficult to determine how pay systems affect worker performance, especially relative to alternative compensation schemes.

Nonetheless, the researchers were able to draw conclusions that generally confirm expectations derived from the theory at the heart of this book. They found that when the revenue-sharing method of pay was employed, the median "effort level" for each of the two teams started at a mere 30 (with a maximum effort level of 100), but since the students were then told how little effort other team members were expending in total, the students began to cut their own effort in each of the successive rounds. The median effort level in both teams trended down until the twenty-fifth round, when the median effort level was under 13. That finding caused the researchers to assert: "Shirking happens."[13] They were also able to deduce that the history of the team performance matters: the higher the team performance at the start, the greater the team performance thereafter (although the effort level may decline over the rounds, it will still be higher at any given round if it started at a high level).

Nalbantian and Schotter found that forcing contracts and profit sharing could increase the initial level of effort to 40 or above, a third higher than the initial effort level under revenue sharing, but the effort level under forcing contracts and profit sharing still trended down with succeeding rounds of the experiment. Nalbantian and Schotter also found that the tournaments that were tried, which forced the team members to think competitively, yielded median initial effort levels on a par with the initial effort levels observed under forcing contracts. However, the effort level tended to increase in the first few rounds and then held more or less constant through the rest of the twenty-five rounds. At the end of the twenty-five rounds, the teams had a median effort level of 40 to 50, or up to four times the ending effort level under the revenue-sharing incentive system. Understandably, the authors conclude that "a little competition goes a very long, long way."[14]

Finally, the authors conclude that monitoring works, which is no surprise, but the extent which monitoring hiked the effort level does grab the attention. No monitoring system works perfectly, so the authors evaluated how the teams would perform with a competitive team pay system under two experimental conditions, one in which the probability that shirking team members would be caught was 70 percent and one in which the probability of being caught was 30 percent, with the penalty being stiff—loss of their "jobs." The median effort for one team level started about at 75 (the predicted effort level from the theory) and stayed there until the last round, at which point the effort level fell markedly (a finding that will be understandable after our discussion of the "last-period problem" in chapter 15). The median effort level for the other team started at about 50, rose quickly to 70, and stayed there through the rest of the rounds (with one very large drop in effort in the middle of the rounds).

When the probability of being caught shirking dropped to 30 percent, the effort level of one team started at 70 and fluctuated wildly between zero and 80 for the next twenty rounds, only to approach zero during the last five rounds. The effort level of the other team started close to zero and stayed very close to zero for most of the following rounds (exceeding 10 only twice).

Obviously, monitoring of team members can have a dramatic impact on team performance, but, as in all matters, the cost of the monitoring system can be high. The researchers have not yet been able to say, from the experimental evidence, whether the improvement team performance is worth the cost of the monitoring system that is required. However, managers can't wait for the experimental findings. They must find ways of minimizing the monitoring costs. One of the great cost-saving advantages of teams, which is not reflected in the way the experiments were run, is that teamwork tends to be self-monitoring, with team members monitoring one another. In the experiment, the team members could not do this. When the experimental work is extended, we would not be surprised if the effort level increases when the team members are able to monitor and penalize one another.

Should all firms adopt the competitive team approach? The evidence suggests a firm yes. But we hasten to add that greater effort to produce more output is desirable only so long as it does not come with a sacrifice in quality (or some other important dimension of production). Competitive team production may be shunned in firms in industries like pharmaceuticals and banking that can't tolerate concessions in their quality standards because of the risk of liability suits. The competition in the tournaments drives up output but can drive down quality, so firms in these industries may choose to use reward systems that keep the competition under control and the quality standards up. They may also want to rely on close monitoring; the cost would be justified, given the costs that they might suffer if their products were defective. This leads to an obvious conclusion—the greater the cost of mistakes, the greater the cost that can be endured from relaxed competition and from monitoring.

Committees are special forms of teams that are the subject of much business abuse, both in terms of the number of meetings held and in terms of what businesspeople think of most meetings. Indeed, businesspeople often chafe when the subject of committee meetings is aired. "People talk too much, and too little is accomplished," harried managers often fret. By the standards of university faculty meetings, however, business people have nothing to complain about. Indeed, they can thank their lucky stars that they do not have to suffer many of the meetings we've had to suffer throughout our academic careers. Now, we have something to complain about! Businesspeople may talk a lot, but faculty members have made "hot air" an entitlement.

Why are committee meetings so boring, as well as so frequently unproductive? We suspect that the problem is partly that the people who call the meetings do not necessarily suffer the costs that are incurred. We once heard a business executive give a talk in which he crystallized his point, and ours, by asking the audience for a show of hands in response to the question "How many people in this room can sign a purchase order for some piece of equipment worth $10,000 without having someone else in the organization approve the purchase and cosign the order?" No more than a half dozen in the crowd of more than a hundred raised their hands. He then asked, "How many in this room can organize a series of meetings of fifteen or twenty people without having anyone approve the meetings?" The room was full of hands.

The speaker then prodded those in the group: "Is there any difference?" Of course, there is one obvious difference. The purchase order involves *money*; the meetings involve *time*. But every businessperson (and professor) understands and appreciates the old aphorism "*Time* is *money*." Nevertheless, people everywhere all too often seem to forget that truism when it comes to meetings—which is understandable, given that the costs of meetings are rarely computed and, when they are considered, are "externalized" (or imposed on others).

Again, we submit that the problem with boring meetings is the incentive structure in the committees. The person calling the meeting will consider whether the meeting is worth his or her own time cost, apart from the costs suffered by others, but the cost suffered by each person is only a minor part of the total cost, and the greater the number of attendees at the meetings, the greater the cost.

The committee problem is similar to the problem of pollution, which we have already mentioned. The meeting organizer may determine whether to call a meeting on the basis of some rough comparison between the costs *he* or *she* incurs (but not all committee members incur) and the benefits *he* or *she* receives. However, since the organizer does not incur all of the costs, the meeting is called when there may be few overall benefits. Others, following the same logic, also call meetings; the net effect is that there can be too many meetings, with many of them lasting longer than their economics (costs and benefits) justify.

Also, every person at the meeting may want it to be short and productive, with every comment well thought out and to the point (just as every polluter may want a pond with no detectable waste in it). However, once in the meeting, each committee member can also think like the polluter: "If I make my comment, the meeting will not be extended by long. And the cost to me of my comments is surely lower than the benefits to everyone else of hearing my golden words. Besides, if I don't talk, then someone else will. The meeting will be no shorter if I hold back." If everyone thinks that way, then the meeting can easily be filled with frivolous comments (or "comment pollution"), and meeting length can seem interminable, or, more accurately, far too long, given the total costs and benefits to *everyone* for the issues considered and the comments made.

This does not mean that all meetings are completely worthless. Meetings do accomplish something of value (or else, we should think, no meetings would ever be called). The problem is that there is an incentive for people, when considering only the costs and benefits of their own situations (their willingness to shirk their duty to restrain themselves and to engage in opportunism), to diminish the meetings' net value by making a good thing go on for too long.

What's too long? It is when the additional value of a comment made on an additional issue resulting in an additional minute spent in the meeting is less than the cost to all involved. "Too long" means that everyone there would pay all others to keep their mouths shut—if they could somehow organize themselves to do just that.

The problem of overly long meetings is likely to increase as the number of people in the meeting increases, because the cost an individual incurs when making a comment, which is what the individual can be expected to focus on, stays more or less constant, regardless of how many people join the meeting. However, the total cost to the group—the "social cost"— escalates as more members join the meeting. There are simply more people to throw more "waste" into the meeting, increasing the likelihood that the meeting will be overly long—and boring and even unproductive, since many people may decide to tune out.

As the number of committee members escalates, each member can reason that the impact of his or her votes and comments on committee decisions is likely to diminish. As a consequence, each can conclude that there is less reason to prepare for the meetings, which can mean that comments made may be less well grounded in facts and less well thought out. Each person in a very large meeting may think, "Well, heck, my voice and vote will not affect the outcome of the meeting, so why should I prepare?"

We would be the first to admit that our arguments press the limits of economic reasoning, in that we have implicitly assumed that many people in meetings are never considerate of others and never try to assess the costs of the meetings they call or the comments they make in terms of their impact on others. We recognize that people, at times and to a degree, consider the feelings and costs that they may impose on others. We talk in terms of the logic of the extreme individualist because some people, in and out of business and in and out of meetings, no doubt will think that way. They simply don't consider the costs to others.

However, we also lay out the logic of people consumed by their own private interests because it reveals a force that affects even people who are considerate of others. That force can grow as the committee size grows, neutralizing, at some point, their best intentions and leading to some of the perverse consequences developed from highly strident thinking. Again, we suggest that managers must consider how people will behave in the extreme, not because that is the way everyone behaves all the time in every situation but because self-serving actions are the type of behavior many human beings exhibit and from which managers must protect themselves through appropriate organizational structures and policies.

More to the point, we suggest that managers consider our way of thinking because it leads to suggestions for improving the performance of all meetings and committees:

- First, managers ought to find ways of making sure that people who call meetings consider the cost of all involved. We cannot make concrete suggestions, because that requires knowledge of the details of particular work environments. What we do know is that potential committee members have an interest in managers who are tough on the issue of meetings, who are willing to call people to task for unproductive and overly long meetings. Someone, in other words, needs to take charge.

- Second, managers should appoint tough people as chairpersons. These are people who should be willing to cut others off when it is clear they are unprepared and are just sounding off. Managers should recognize that while individuals might prefer meetings in which they can say what they please for as long as they want at the same time everyone else is constrained, the group can still have an interest in tight controls on every member. People will give up some of their own freedom to sound off *if everyone else will, too.*

- Third, managers should be careful about organizing "large" meetings. The productivity of meetings tends to decline as the group size goes up. As a general rule, small groups should be organized when *action* is required. Large groups should be assembled for the purpose of *reaction* to proposals that have been devised by much smaller groups. If a large committee has been formed and little progress has been made, then the committee should be broken down into smaller working groups, with each subcommittee given a specific assignment that can be presented to the larger committee for final action.

• Fourth, on the other hand, if managers want to give people some sense of participation in the decision-making process without enabling them to actually do anything, then they should make the meetings as large as possible. The participants can be expected to talk without any decisive end, leaving the person who organized the meeting with the authority to take action when something needs to be done.

We suspect that business people are more constrained in meetings than faculty members are by a six-letter word: *profit*. The goals of a university education are far less clear, far more elusive and imprecise, because they cannot be relegated to a single bottom-line figure (a fact that, because it works to their advantage, is nurtured by professors). Universities are organized to produce "educated people," which covers a multitude of virtues and sins. This means that the performance of people on committees is hard to assess, and many meetings get bogged down in wrestling with the reasons that the meeting was called in the first place, with competing factions seeking to elevate their own personal goals above the goals for the committee, if not the university. Businesspeople can, with greater ease, ask a very forceful question that tends to focus the committee process: "What does this (or that) action do for the bottom line?"

In addition, state university budgets are typically determined by their far-removed state legislatures. Unproductive meetings can easily go undetected within the university bureaucracies, much less by legislators who have little incentive to monitor what the universities do at the committee level. The future welfare of people in the decision-making process is unaffected, one way or the other, by what does or does not go on in any particular meeting. There are simply no close-at-hand residual claimants.

Although taxpayers can be thought of as residual claimants, given that efficiency improvement in state university committee processes *can* translate into lower taxes, each taxpayer has precious little incentive to monitor universities. The monitoring costs can easily exceed the benefits that the individual taxpayer can realize from his or her monitoring, and the probability that the monitoring will have an impact on university efficiency is very close to zero. As we have explained, taxpayers are all too often the proverbial "free riders" when it comes to monitoring what governments generally do. And when most taxpayers attempt to free ride, they end up getting taken for a ride.

In many regards, faculty members who believe expelling hot air is virtue can thank their lucky stars for *rationally ignorant taxpayers*. Businesspeople must worry that wasteful meetings will affect their jobs and livelihoods. If firms hold too many meetings and the bottom line is materially affected, some wise investors will do what cannot be done with universities; the investors will buy the company, eliminate the unproductive meetings, increase the bottom line, and sell the reinvigorated company at a price higher than the purchase price to someone who, because of the price paid, will have an incentive to control meetings.

Managers often spend many of their waking hours trying to figure out how they can make more money by selling more of their product. The lesson of this chapter is that they can also make money by adjusting their internal structures to account for the impact of numbers on incentives. In short, more than what is produced counts in a firm's profitability. Relatively small teams have become increasingly important to business for a number of reasons, but the most important reason is that small teams are a means by which the actions of individual members become meaningful and more easily monitored by others. Teams are a means of discouraging free riding and encouraging everyone to contribute to the value of the whole. Teams are self-enforcing units. Businesspeople would be well advised to apply the principles of teams to the organizations of committees.

5

Paying for Performance

Key Insight: Many firms don't pay for performance in the most straightforward way—by the piece or "piece rate"—because their workers cannot trust
their managers. Two-part payments—salary plus commission—are a way by
which the two parties to a deal are able to share the risk while providing the
proper motivation for each party to continue to help the other.

ONE OF THE MOST FUNDAMENTAL RULES of economics, and the raison d'être
of this book, is that if you offer people a greater reward, then they will do
more of whatever is being rewarded, everything else being equal. Many
people find this proposition to be objectionable, because it implies that
people can, to one degree or another, be "bought." Admittedly, incentives
may not matter in all forms of behavior; some people will sacrifice their
lives rather than forsake a strongly held principle. However, the proposition that incentives matter does seem to be applicable to a sufficiently wide
range of behavior to be considered a "rule" that managers are well advised
to keep in mind: pay people a higher wage—such as time and a half—and
they will work overtime. Pay them double time, and they will even work
holidays. There is some rate of pay at which a lot of people will work
almost any time of the day or night on any day of the year.

This rule for incentives is not applicable only to the workplace. Parents
know that one of the best ways to get their children to take out the garbage
is to tie their allowance to that chore. Moreover, patients in psychiatric
hospitals, many of whom have literally lost virtually all capacity for rational discourse, appear to respond to incentives. According to research, if
mentally ill institutionalized patients are paid for the simple tasks they are
assigned (for example, sweeping a room or picking up trash), they perform
them with greater regularity.[1]

Even pigeons, well known for having the lowest form of birdbrains,
respond to incentives. Granted, pigeons may never be able to grasp the

concept of monetary rewards (offering them a dollar won't enlist much of a response), but pigeons apparently know how to respond to food rewards (offer a nut in the palm of your outstretched hand and a whole flock will descend, and maybe leave their mark, on your shoulder). From research, we also know that pigeons are willing to work—measured by how many times they peck colored levers in their cages—to get food pellets, and they will work harder if the reward for pecking is raised. Researchers have also been able to get pigeons to loaf on the job just like humans. How? Simply lower their rate of "pay."[2]

It may appear that knowledge of these rules would lead managers every-where to ensure that workers have the right incentives by always tying pay to some measure of performance. Clearly, the lone worker in a single pro-prietorship has the "right" incentive. His or her reward is the same as the reward for the whole firm. The full cost of any shirking is borne by the worker-owner. However, such a congruence between the rewards of the owners and workers is nowhere else duplicated. There are always gaps between the goals of the owners and those of the workers, and the greater the number of workers, typically, the greater the gap in incentives. In very large firms, workers have greatly impaired incentives to pursue the goals of the owners. The workers are far removed from the owners by layers of bureaucracy, communications on the firm's goals are often imperfect, and each worker at the bottom of the firm's pyramid can reason that his or her contributions to firm revenues and goals, or the lack of them, can easily go undetected. A reoccurring theme of this book is that when monitoring is difficult, one can expect many workers to exploit whatever opportunities for shirking are at their disposal.

And the opportunities taken can result in substantial losses in worker output. The management specialist Edward Lawler reported that during a strike at a manufacturing firm, a secretary was asked to take over a factory job and was paid on a piece-rate basis. Despite having no previous experi-ence, within days she was turning out 375 percent more output than the regular workers who had spent ten years on the job and were constantly complaining that the work standards were too demanding.[3] Obviously, the striking workers had been doing something other than working on the job.

How can managers improve incentives, reduce shirking, and increase worker productivity? At the turn of the century, the great management guru Frederick Taylor strongly recommended piece-rate pay as a means of partially solving what he termed the "labor problem," but he was largely ignored in his own time by both management and labor, and for the good reasons discussed in this chapter.[4]

There is a multitude of ways of getting workers to perform that don't involve money pay, many of which are studied in disciplines like organiza-tional behavior, which draws on the principles of psychology. Managers do need to think about patting workers on the back once in a while, clearly defining corporate goals, communicating goals in a clear and forceful manner, and exerting leadership.

Southwest Airlines, one of the more aggressive, cost-conscious, and profitable airlines, motivates its workers by creating what one analyst called a "community . . . resembling a seventeenth-century New England town more than a twentieth-century corporation." The airline *bonds* its workers with such shared values as integrity, trust, and altruism.[5] But a company with a productive corporate culture is almost surely a company with strong incentives in place to reward productivity. Without taking anything away from the corporate culture at Southwest Airlines, we should point out that one reason it has the lowest cost in the business is that its pilots and flight attendants are paid by the trip. This, along with a strong corporate culture, explains why Southwest's pilots and flight attendants hustle when the planes are on the ground. Indeed, Southwest has the shortest turn-around time in the industry. It pays the crews to do what they can to get their planes back in the air.[6] Motorola organizes its workers into teams and allows them to hire and fire their cohorts, determine training procedures, and set schedules. Federal Express's corporate culture includes giving workers the right to evaluate their bosses and to appeal their own evaluations all the way to the chairman. It's understandable that Federal Express delivery people move at least twice as fast as U.S. postal workers: FedEx workers have incentives to do so, whereas postal workers do not.[7]

We don't want to criticize the traditional, nonincentive methods for getting things done in business. Indeed, we have taken up the issue of "teams" in chapter 4, and we discuss the importance of virtues like "trust" in this chapter. At the same time, we wish to stress a fairly general and straightforward rule for organizing much production: *give workers a direct detectable stake in firm revenues or profits in order to raise revenues and profits, and pay for performance.* One means of doing that is to make workers' pay conditional on their output: the greater the output from each worker, the greater the individual worker's pay.

Ideally, we should dispense with salaries, which are paid by the week or year, and always pay by the "piece"—or "piece rate." Many firms—for example, hosiery mills—do pay piece rate; they pay by the number of socks completed (or even the number of toes closed). Piece rate can be expected to raise wages of covered workers for two reasons: First, the incentives can be expected to induce workers to work harder for more minutes of each hour and for more hours during the workday. Second, because piece-rate workers are asked to assume some of the risk of production, which is influenced by factors beyond their control (for example, how much each worker produces will be determined by what the employer does to provide workers with a productive work environment and what other workers are willing to do), they can be expected to demand and receive a *risk premium* in their paychecks. One study has, in fact, shown that a significant majority of workers covered under "output-related contracts" in the nonferrous foundries industry earn between 5 percent and 12 percent more than their counterparts who are paid strictly by their time at work, depending on the occupation. Of that pay differential, about a fifth has been attributable to risk bearing by workers, which means that a substantial share of the pay advantage for incentive workers is attributable to the greater effort expended by the covered workers.[8]

However, such a rule—paying by the piece—is hardly universally adopted. Indeed, piece-rate workers probably make up a minor portion of the total workforce (we have not been able to determine precisely how prevalent piece-pay systems are). Many automobile salespeople, of course, are paid by the cars sold. Many lawyers are paid by the hours billed (and presumably services provided). Musicians are often paid by the concert.

But there are relatively few workers in manufacturing and service industries whose pay is directly tied to each item or service produced. Professors are not paid by the number of students they teach. Office workers are not paid by the number of forms processed or memos sent. Fast-food workers are not paid by the number of burgers flipped. Most people's pay is, for the most part, directly and explicitly tied to time on the job. They are generally paid by the hour or month or even year.

Admittedly, the pay of most workers has some indirect and implicit connection to production. Many workers know that if they don't eventually add more to the revenues of their companies than they take in pay, their jobs will be in considerable jeopardy. The question we find interesting is why "piece rate," or "pay for performance," is not a more widely employed pay system, given the positive incentives it potentially provides.

Many explanations for the absence of a piece-rate pay system are obvious and widely recognized.[9] The output of many workers cannot be reduced to "pieces." In such cases, no one should expect pay to be tied to that which cannot be measured with tolerable objectivity. Our work as university professors is hard to define and measure. In fact, observers might find it hard to determine when we are working, given that while at work, we may be doing nothing more than staring at a computer screen or talking with students in the hallways. Measuring the "pieces" of what secretaries and executives do is equally, if not more, difficult.

If a measure of "output" is defined when the assigned tasks are complex, the measure will not likely be all-inclusive. Some dimensions of the assigned tasks will not be measured, which means that workers' incentives may be grossly distorted. They may work only to do those things that are defined and measured—and related to pay—at the expense of other parts of their assignments. If workers are paid by the number of parts produced, with the quality of individual parts not considered, some workers can be expected to sacrifice quality in order to increase their production count. If professors were paid by the number of students in their classes, you can bet they would spend less time at research and in committee meetings (which

would not be all bad). If middle managers were paid solely by units produced, they would produce a lot of units with little attention to costs.
There is an old story from the days before the fall of communism in the
former Soviet Union. According to the story, the managers of a shoe factory were given production quotas for the number of shoes they had to
make, and they were paid according to how much they exceeded their
quota. What did they do? They produced lots of shoes, *but only left ones!*
They could more easily exceed their quota by not having to switch production to right shoes.

Much work is the product of "teams" or groups of workers that can
extend to include the entire plant or office. Pay is often not related to output because it may be difficult to determine which individuals are responsible for the "pieces" that are produced. Because we took up the problems
of forming and paying teams in chapter 4, we here only remind readers
that team production creates special incentive problems. Making the
teams "small" is one way to enhance incentives by making the contributions, or lack thereof, of each team member noticeable to others on the
team.

When workers are paid by salary, they are given some assurance that
their incomes will not vary with the firm's output, which can go up and
down for many reasons not under their control. For example, how many
socks a worker can stitch at the toe is dependent upon the flow of socks
through the plant, over which the workers who do the stitching may have
no control. When workers are paid by the piece, they are, in effect, asked
to assume a greater risk that shows up in the variability of the income they
take home. Piece rate may give the workers a higher *average* income.
However, in order for the piece-rate system to work—and be profitable
for the firm—the increase in expected worker productivity has to exceed
the *risk premium* that risk-averse workers would demand. *Piece rate (or any
other form of incentive compensation) is not employed in many firms simply
because the risk premium workers demand is greater than their expected increase
in productivity.* This is often the case because workers tend to be risk averse
(reluctant to take chances, or to assume the costs associated with an uncertain and variable income stream).

If paid by the work done, workers also have to worry about how
changes in the general economy will affect their workloads and production
levels. A downturn in the economy, due to forces that are global in scope,
can undermine worker pay when pay is tied to output. When Du Pont
introduced its incentive compensation scheme for its fibers division in
1988—under which a portion of the workers' incomes could be lost if
profit goals were not achieved and could be multiplied if profit goals were
exceeded—the managers and employees expected, or were told to expect,
substantial income gains. [10] However, when the economy turned sour in
1990, employee morale suffered as profits fell and workers were threatened with reduced incomes. The incentive program was canceled before

the announced three-year trial period was up.[11] Du Pont obviously concluded that it could buy back worker morale and production by not subjecting worker pay to factors that were beyond worker control. Each individual employee could reason that there was absolutely nothing he could do about the national economy or, for that matter, about the work effort expended by the 20,000 other Du Pont workers who were covered by the incentive program. Workers could rightfully fear that their incomes were being put at risk by the free riding of all other workers.

This line of analysis leads to the conclusion that piece-rate (and other forms of incentive) pay schemes are most likely to be used in firms where the risk to workers is relatively low (relative to the benefits of the improved incentives). This means that they tend to be used where production is not highly variable and where, in the absence of piece-rate pay, workers can easily exploit opportunities to shirk—that is, where workers cannot be easily monitored. For example, salespeople who are always on the road (which necessarily means that no one at the home office knows much about what they do on a daily basis) tend to be paid, at least in part, by the "piece" in some form or another, say, by the sale.

Piece-rate pay systems may also be avoided because employers are likely to be in a better position to assume the risk of production variability than their employees are. This is true because much of the variability in the output of *individual* workers is "smoothed out" within a whole *group* of employees. When one worker's output is down, another worker's output will be up. Workers are, in effect, able to buy themselves out of the risk. If each of the workers sees the risk cost of the piece-rate system at $500 and the employer sees the risk cost at $100, then each worker can agree to give up, say, $110 in pay for the rights to a constant income. The worker gains, on balance, $390 in nonmoney income ($500 in risk cost reduction minus the $110 reduction in money wages). The employer gives up the piece-rate system simply because he or she can make a profit—$10 in this example—for each worker ($110 reduction in worker money wages minus the $100 increase in risk cost). *One would therefore expect that, other things equal, piece-rate pay schemes will be more prevalent in small firms than in large ones.*

Also, piece-rate pay systems can be used only when and where employers can make credible commitments to their workers to abide by the pay system that they establish and not to cut the *rate* in the *piece rate* when the desired results are achieved. Unfortunately, all too often managers are unable to make the credible commitment for the same reason that they might find, in theory, the piece-rate system to be an attractive way, in terms of worker productivity and firm profits, to pay workers. The basic problem is that both workers *and* managers have incentives to engage in opportunistic behavior to the detriment of the other group.

Managers understand that many workers have a natural inclination to shirk their responsibilities, to loaf on the job, and to misuse and abuse company resources with the intent of padding their own pockets.

Managers also know that if they tie their workers' pay to output, then output may be expected to expand, as fewer workers exploit their positions and loaf on the job. At the same time, the workers can reason that incentives also matter to managers. Like workers, managers are not always angels and they can be expected, to one degree or another, to exploit their positions, achieving greater personal and corporate gains at the expense of their workers.

Hence, workers can reason that if they respond to the incentives built into the piece-rate system and produce more for more pay, then managers can change the deal, raising the number of pieces that the workers must produce in order to get the previously established pay or dumping what will then be excess workers. To clarify this point, suppose a worker is initially paid $500 a week, and during the course of the typical week, he or she produces 100 pieces, for an average pay of $5 per piece. Management figures that the worker is spending some time goofing off on the job and that the worker's output can be raised if he or she is paid $5 for each piece produced.

If the worker responds by increasing output to 150 pieces, management can simply lower the rate to $3.50 per piece, which would give the worker $525 a week and would mean that the firm would take the overwhelming share of the gains from the worker's—not management's—greater efforts. The worker would, in effect, be working harder and more diligently with little to show for the effort. By heeding the piece-rate incentive, the worker could be inadvertently establishing a higher production standard.

These threats are real. Managers at a General Motors panel stamping plant in Flint, Michigan, announced that the company would allow workers to leave after they had satisfied daily production targets. Workers were soon leaving by noon. Management responded by increasing production targets. The result was a bitter workforce.[12]

In summary, one reason piece-rate systems aren't more widely used is that the systems can be abused by managers, which means that workers will not buy into them at reasonable rates of pay.

Another way of explaining the lack of use of piece-rate pay is that they often don't work as expected. Incentives do matter. The problem is that the workers don't believe that the much talked about incentives are there, because they don't—or can't—believe that their managers will resist the temptation to gain at their—the workers'—expense. Managers are unable to make what we have, in other contexts, called *a credible commitment* (a position on which workers can rely), meaning they have not been able to convince their workers that they will not take advantage of them (just as the workers may have been taking advantage of their managers).

Indeed, the piece-rate system can have an effect the exact opposite of the one intended. We have noted that workers can reason that their managers will increase the output demands if the workers produce more for any given rate. However, the implied relationship between output and production demands should also be expected to run the other way; that is, *the workers can reason that if managers will raise the production requirements when they produce more in response to any established rate, then managers should be willing to lower the production requirements when the workers lower their production after the piece-rate system is established.* Hence, the establishment of the piece-rate system can lead to a reduction in output as workers cut back on production. The purpose of the incentive pay may be to increase production, but the result can be to induce lower production standards for the same rate of pay. The workers' expectation can be that the rate of pay will be raised.

How? Suppose that a worker making $500 a week responds to the rate of $5 per piece by cutting back his or her total production from 100 to seventy-five pieces per week. Then management might be expected to increase the rate to, say, $6.50 per piece, leaving the worker with $487.50 for the week, or a 2.5 percent reduction in pay for a 25 percent reduction in effort.

The lesson of this discussion is not that piece-rate pay incentives can't work. Rather, the lesson is that getting them right can be tricky. Managers must convincingly *commit* themselves to holding to the established piece rate and not exploiting the workers. The best way for managers to be believable is to create a history of living up to their commitments, which means creating a valuable reputation with their workers.

Lincoln Electric, a major producer of arc-welding equipment in Cleveland, makes heavy use of piece-rate pay. The system has resulted in worker productivity almost double that of its competitors. There are several reasons for this success:

- First, the company has a target rate of return for shareholders. Deviations from that target either add to or subtract from their workers' year-end bonuses, with the bonus often amounting to 100 percent of workers' base pay.

- Second, employees largely own the firm, a fact that reduces the likelihood that piece rates will be changed.

- Third, management understands the need for credible commitments. According to one manager, "When we set a piecework price, that price cannot be changed just because, in management's opinion, the worker is making too much money. . . . Piecework prices can only be changed when management has made a change in the method of doing that particular job and under no other conditions. If this is not carried out 100 percent, piecework cannot work."[13]

- Fourth, Lincoln pursues a permanent employment policy. Permanent employees are guaranteed only 75 percent of normal hours, and management can move workers into different jobs in response to demand changes. Also, workers have agreed to mandatory overtime when demand is high (meaning that the firm doesn't have to hire workers in peak demand periods). In other words, workers and management have agreed to share some of the risk.

- Fifth, to combat quality problems, each unit produced is stenciled with the initials of the workers who produced it. If a unit fails after delivery because of flaws in production, the responsible worker can lose as much as 10 percent of his annual bonus.

- Sixth, large inventories are maintained to smooth out differences in the production rates of different workers.

Does this mean that managers can never raise the production standard for any given pay rate? Of course not. Workers should be concerned only if the standard is changed because of something *they*—the workers—did. If management in some way increases the productivity of workers (for example, by introducing computerized equipment or rearranging the flow of the materials through the plant), independent of how much effort workers apply, then the standard can be raised. Workers should not object. They are still getting their value for their effort. They are not being made worse off. What managers must avoid doing is changing the foundations of the work and then taking more in terms of lower *pay rate* than they are due, which effectively means violating the contract or commitment with their workers.

As the Lincoln Electric manager said, "Piecework prices can only be changed when management has made a change in the method of doing that particular job and under no other conditions."[14] Otherwise, piece-rate pay can have an effect the exact opposite of the one intended.

There are innumerable ways of paying people to encourage performance. The two-part pay contract—salary plus commission—is obviously a compromise between straight salary and straight commission pay structures. For example, a worker for a job placement service can be paid a salary of $1,500 a month, plus 10 percent of the fees received for any placement. If the recruiter can be expected to place one worker a month and the placement fee is $10,000, the worker's expected monthly income is $2,500 ($1,500 plus 10 percent of $10,000).

This form of payment can be mutually attractive to the placement firm and its recruiters because it accomplishes a couple of important objectives. First, the system can be a way by which workers and their employers can share the risks to reflect the way the actual placements depend on the actions of both the workers and their employers. While each worker understands that his or her placements are greatly affected by how hard and smart he or she personally works, each also knows that often, to a nontrivial degree, the placements are related to what all other workers and the employer do. Worker income is dependent on, for example, how much the employer advertises, seeks to maintain a good image for the firm, and develops the right incentives for *all* workers to apply themselves.

Workers have an interest in having everyone in the firm work as a team, just as the employer does. Productive work by all can increase firm output, worker pay, and job security. As a consequence, while each worker may, in one sense, "prefer" all income in the form of a guaranteed fixed monthly check, the worker also has an interest in commission pay—*if everyone else is paid commission and if perverse incentives are avoided.* Often each worker's income is dependent on how hard others work. Individual recruiters, to carry forward our example, often benefit from the attempts of other recruiters to make successful, quality placements. Such efforts can spread and enhance the name of the firm, making it easier for all other recruiters to make placements.

Hence, a pay system that is based, to a degree, on commission can raise the incomes of all recruiters. Put another way, to the extent that one worker's income is dependent on other workers' efforts, we should expect workers to favor a pay system that incorporates strong production incentives for all workers.

Of course, workers want an employer who can be trusted. They don't want to be caught in a situation in which the incentive system undercuts production, as we have suggested can be the case. As a consequence, workers favor bosses who are paid a premium because they can be trusted. They certainly do not want bosses who engage in opportunism by cutting the *rate* of pay when workers respond to incentive pay by working harder and increasing output.

Some combination of straight salary and piece-rate pay can achieve *optimum* incentives and, therefore, can maximize firm output, worker pay, and job security. We should not expect that maximum incentives are always achieved with pay tied strictly to production. Unfortunately, we can't say exactly what the combination should be. There is no one ideal pay combination, mainly because conditions of production—including the actual contributions by different workers and the degree of trust—vary so greatly across firms and industries. Our central point is that the two-part, or salary-plus-commission, pay systems can help workers by aligning their interests to those of their fellow workers and of their employers, and can do so without exposing workers to excessive risk.

With the two-part pay system, workers are given some security in that they can count on, for some undetermined amount of time, a minimum income level—$1,500 in our example. The workers shift some of their risk to their employer, but the risk assumed by the employer need not equal the sum of the risk that the workers avoid. This is because, as noted earlier, the employer usually hires a number of people, and the variability of the income of the employer is, therefore, not likely to be as great as the variability of the individual workers' income.

The workers, in other words, may want to give up something in straight commission income in order that their employer will assume some of the risk but, possibly just as important, the employer will have an interest in facilitating (to the extent possible) the placement process. After all, with the monthly salary hanging over the employer's head, the employer will want to work to make sure that the workers can earn their monthly keep. Each month *some* workers might do poorly, but other workers can have offsetting experiences. Moreover, with the employer assuming some of the risk, the employer can be expected to work harder in the interest of the workers, reducing some of the remaining risk that the workers must assume. The net effect of the two-part pay system should be that both parties gain precisely because each party is motivated to contribute to the success of the other.

Workers will also understand that if everyone has an incentive to work harder, there will be greater production from their "team" effort, resulting in greater production, more profits, and greater job security (as well as more pay and fringe benefits). Workers can also reason that some incentive pay can reduce the risk cost that the firm must incur, thus, once again, potentially improving everyone's well-being.

Also, workers can surely understand the press of market competition. If their firm doesn't find ways of sharing and reducing risk and increasing worker output, then other firms in their markets surely will. That fact can spell market failure for firms and their workers who fail to adopt two-part pay systems, if they are mutually beneficial.

Firms can expect that incentive schemes that enhance firm profits do not come free of charge. According to one early study, the nearly 200 punch-press operators in Chicago who were paid piece rate (so much per unit produced) earned, on average, 7 percent more than workers who did much the same jobs but who were paid a straight salary (so much per unit of time, for example, hour, week, or month).[15] According to another study involving more than 100,000 workers in 500 manufacturing firms within two industries, the incomes of the footwear workers on some form of piece-rate or salary-plus-commission pay averaged slightly more than 14 percent more than those of workers on salaries (with the differential ranging up to 31 percent for certain types of jobs). The workers in the men's coats and suits industry on piece rate averaged between 15 and 16 percent more than the salaried workers.[16] And the best evidence available suggests that the more workers' incomes are based on incentive pay, the greater the income differential between those who are earn piece-rate pay (or any other form of incentive pay) and those who don't.

Of course, it may be that the income differential between incentive-paid and salaried workers reflects the difference in the demands of the jobs incentive-paid workers and salaried workers take. Incentive-paid jobs may pay more because they are the jobs the most competent workers are most eager to take. However, the studies cited either have attempted to look at incentive-paid and salaried workers in comparable jobs or have adjusted (by statistical, econometric means) the pay gaps for differences in the "quality" of the different jobs.[17]

One of the more obvious explanations for why incentive-paid workers earn more than salaried workers is that the incentive-paid workers accept more risk. After all, the incomes of the incentive-paid workers can vary not only with the workers' effort but also with the promotional efforts of their firms and with general economic conditions in the market, among a host of other factors. A firm's ad campaigns can complement a worker's efforts to sell a product or service. A downturn in the national economy can make selling more difficult, effectively dropping the workers' rates of pay per hour (albeit for a long or short period of time). The incentive-paid workers' greater average pay amounts to a risk premium intended to account for the possibility that income may not always match expectations.

The business lesson is simple: to get workers to accept incentive pay, employers have to raise the pay. If both incentive-paid and salaried jobs were paid the same, workers would crowd into the salaried jobs, increasing the number of workers available to work for salaries and reducing the number of workers available to work on commission. The incomes of the salaried workers, everything else being equal, would tend to fall, while the incomes of the incentive-paid workers would tend to rise. If there were no considerations other than risk under the different pay schemes, the wage differential would continue to widen until the income difference was about equal to the difference in the added "risk cost" the incentive-paid workers suffered. That is to say, if the risk cost (or premium) were deducted from the pay of incentive-paid workers, the resulting net pay of the incentive-paid workers would be about the same as the pay of salaried workers.

But risk doesn't explain the entire differential (and would not ever likely do so). One of the studies mentioned found that the "risk premium" accounted for only a little more than 3 percent of the pay differential in the footwear industry and only 6 percent of the difference in the men's clothing industry (with a great deal of variance reported across occupational categories).[18] Another important portion of the differential can be explained by the dictum that is central to this volume: incentives matter! Incentive-paid workers simply gain more from extra work than do their salaried counterparts. A salaried worker is no doubt required to apply a given, minimal level of effort on the job. Salaried workers can choose to work more and produce more for the company. Their extra work might have some reward, a future raise or promotion, but such prospects are never certain. Many workers believe, with justification, that their raises are more directly tied to the number of years they survive at their firms than to how hard they work and how much they produce.

By way of contrast, the rewards of incentive-paid workers are much more immediate, direct, and contractual. Incentive-paid workers know that if they produce or sell more for their firms, their incomes will rise immediately and by a known amount. Accordingly, they have a greater incentive to apply themselves. One study in the early 1960s found that incentive pay improved worker productivity by as much as 40 percent, not all of which, as will be argued, is necessarily due to extra effort.[19]

Incentive pay does more than just motivate greater effort. Different methods of pay are likely to attract different workers. Workers who are relatively unproductive, or who just don't want to compete aggressively, are likely to opt out of incentive-paid work. They will tend to crowd into salaried jobs, where many other relatively unproductive and less aggressive workers are. In short, workers who tend to be more productive than average can be expected to self-select into jobs with incentive pay. We should expect some firms to use incentive pay elements in many jobs simply to cull out the unproductive workers. Incentive pay allows job applicants who know that they are willing to work hard to convincingly communicate this willingness to prospective employers by their willingness to accept the challenge of incentive pay.

Of course, it should follow that the demands of the incentive-paid work—and the resulting curb in the supply of incentive-paid workers—will press the output and wages of incentive-paid workers up. At the same time, the crowding of less aggressive workers into salaried jobs will tend to increase the supply of salaried workers and lower their wages (if not absolutely, then certainly in relation to those of incentive-paid workers).

If business becomes more uncertain, less predictable—as many seem to think it has over the past couple of decades, with the growing complexity and globalization of business—we would expect the income gap between incentive-paid and salaried workers to widen. Employers will want to increase their competitive positions by giving their workers a greater incentive to work harder and smarter. Employers will want to shift a share of the growing business risk to their workers, at a price, of course, through greater reliance on commissions. At the same time, relatively speaking, more workers might seek to avoid the greater risk by trying to move to salaried jobs. However, their efforts will simply hold salaries down, widening the gap between incentive-paid and salaried jobs.

Those who have been willing to accept and cope with risks have seen their incomes rise. Those who have sought to stay on salaries have probably had to accept relatively (if not absolutely) lower wages. Growing business risk is surely not the only source of the expanding pay gap, but it is certainly one that has played a role.

To this point in the chapter, one of our more important conclusions has been that one of the reasons employers should pay workers in two parts—in part by salary and in part by some form of tie to performance—is that both employer and employee can gain. The employer can accept the risk associated with having to meet a regular, contracted salary payment, and the employee can want the salary because it reduces his or her risk and, at the same time, motivates the employer to work hard at keeping the work going in order that the salary can be met with relative ease. By adding to the fixed salary, the employer may curb the incentive the employer has to work hard and smart, but the salary component can still be a paying proposition for the employer because the overall compensation demands of the employee can fall by more than performance does. Similarly, the employee gains more from reducing "risk cost" than he or she loses in total compensation. Everyone can be happy, which is the sort of outcome managers should always seek.

However, for all its elegance, our discussion sidesteps a problem that managers must face when they are thinking about paying for performance: getting the workers to deal honestly when their pay is at stake. For example, consider the manager who has to deal with a salesforce that works out in the field, far removed from headquarters. The salespeople are hard to monitor. They know a great deal more about the sales potential in their territories than do the managers back at headquarters. How do the managers get the salespeople to reveal the sales potential of their districts? This question is especially troublesome when the salespeople know that the information they reveal will affect their sales performance criteria and the combination of the salary and commission components of their compensation package. If the manager at headquarters simply asks the salespeople how much they can sell in their areas, there's a good chance the salespeople will understate the sales potential. After all, some understatement harbors the potential of raising the salary and commission rate.

There is a simple solution that will encourage the salespeople to deal honestly. The manager should offer the salespeople a menu of combinations of salary and commission rates. Consider the set of three salary-commission rate combinations illustrated in Figure 5.1, with pay on the vertical axis and sales on the horizontal axis. One pay package has a high salary, S_1, and a low commission rate, which is described by the low slope of the straight upward sloping compensation line that emerges from S_1 on the vertical axis. Another pay package has a salary component of S_2 and a higher commission rate; a third has an even lower salary, S_3, and an even higher commission rate.

What's a salesperson to do? Lying about the sales potential of his or her territory won't help. Indeed, the salesperson isn't even asked to lie. All he or she must do is choose from among the compensation packages in a way that he or she, not the manager, believes will maximize total pay. The salesperson who sees little prospect for sales will choose the package with the salary of S_1, which compensates the salesperson for the limited sales potential by providing a high salary. The salesperson who believes the sales potential will be greater than SP_1 (on the horizontal axis) but less

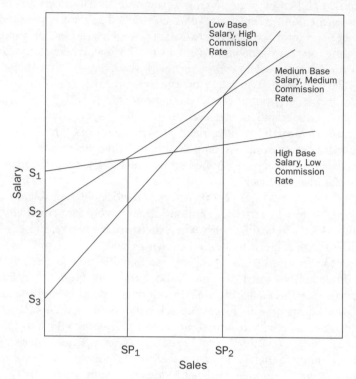

Low Base
Salary, High
Commission
Rate

Medium Base
Salary, Medium
Commission
Rate

High Base
Salary, Low
Commission
Rate

Salary

S_1

S_2

S_3

SP_1 SP_2

Sales

Figure 5.1 Menu of Two-Part Pay Packages

than SP_2 will choose the package with a salary of S_2. The salesperson who believes that the "sky is the limit" (meaning a sales potential of greater than SP_2) will choose the package with the low salary of S_3. This is the approach used in establishing salary-commission rate pay contracts at IBM.[20] It's not a sure-fire way of making salespeople totally honest, but it can help, and that's all real-world managers should strive to achieve.

Because risk-sharing and risk-reducing contracts can be mutually benefi-cial, we should not expect two-part payment schemes to be restricted to payments by employers to workers. They can also be a part of the pay-ments made by tenants to landlords. Rental agreements may not appear to involve "paying for performance," but surely they include performance pay. Both the landlord and tenant are intent on having an agreement that will ensure that the other will "perform" as specified. The landlord wants the rent. The tenant wants a nice living environment or, in the case of retail space, a profitable business environment. Each wants to get as much as possible from the other.

Consider the nature of rental payments within and near the city of

Irvine, California, which is situated along the coast south of Los Angeles. Irvine is a totally planned community with 110,000 residents and 140,000 jobs within an area of approximately 180,000 acres, or forty-two square miles. It has been planned and developed not by the usual government planning boards but by a private wealth-maximizing firm, the Irvine Company, which was once the Irvine Ranch.

One of the more interesting features of the city is that much of the commercial property continues to be owned and managed by the Irvine Company, which has an unusual contract with its commercial tenants. The contract requires that tenants make a three-part payment: a fixed monthly rental payment; a fixed monthly payment for upkeep of the common areas within the community shopping areas; and a payment based on a percentage of their profits. We are told that these payments can be quite stiff. For example, for a 1,000-square-foot store in a shopping center called Fashion Island, an upscale mall (actually in the adjoining city of Newport Beach), we are told that the rent can be several thousand dollars a month, plus several percentage points of the store's profits, plus several hundred dollars a month in maintenance fees.[21]

How can the Irvine Company charge so much and then take a part of the store's profits? It is all too tempting to conclude, as many have, that the contract is "exploitive," reflecting the monopoly power of the Irvine Company. Maybe so. The owners and executives of the Irvine Company are wealthy. But, at the same time, there are good reasons to believe that the stores also benefit from the contract, especially a provision that gives the Irvine Company a stake in the profit of the stores in their shopping centers.

Naturally, any store owner would love to retain the benefits of being in Fashion Island (or any other of the two dozen Irvine shopping centers) and, at the same time, pay no rent whatsoever. On reflection, however, the store owner could easily see that such a deal would be a loser, unless he or she was virtually the only owner to get such a deal. Each store owner can reason that the payment for the upkeep of the grounds can clearly be in his or her best interests, given that the upkeep payments can make the whole center attractive to customers, increasing the traffic in all stores. These mandatory payments override the inclination of each store owner to shirk on upkeep. The store owners are, in effect, employing the Irvine Company to overcome the prisoners' dilemma they would otherwise face and that has been at the heart of so many other management problems considered to this point. They want the Irvine Company to perform with the interests of the stores, as well as the interest of the Irvine company's stockholders, in mind. (Of course, there is a clear tie-in between the store owners' interests and those of the Irvine stockholders. The better the store owners do, the better the Irvine Company does, and that's the kind of performance tie-in that the store owners should seek.)

The store owners can also reason that the high rental payments accomplish a couple of objectives. They ensure that all stores are high-value stores, with a focused appeal to upscale shoppers. Low-value stores are not likely to be able to meet the stiff rental payments. The high payments also ensure that prices will be somewhat higher at Fashion Island than at other shopping centers, thus causing downscale shoppers to go elsewhere (permitting upscale shoppers freer access to the stores). The high rental payments also reflect the fact that the demand for the space at Fashion Island is high, and it is high simply because the Irvine Company has done a good job of enabling the store owners to make high profits. Stores, in other words, don't always want low rents, because low rents usually go hand in hand with low profits.

But why would the stores ever *want* to sign a contract that enables the Irvine Company to share in their profits? Even this provision has an advantage for the merchants, given the conditions of the area. Store owners understand that the Irvine Company controls much of the commercial space in the Fashion Island/Irvine area. The Irvine Company greatly influences the overall order of things in the area, including the income levels of residents, the distribution of various shopping centers within the Irvine area, and the distribution of stores within and across the shopping centers. The company has a terrific impact on the look and feel of the community, which means the company can greatly influence the degree of success of individual store owners. (In many respects, the entire Irvine area can be viewed as one big shopping mall.)

We should not be surprised that the Irvine Company takes a share of the stores' profits and that the store owners collectively *want* it to do just that. The percentage take gives the Irvine Company a direct incentive to operate in the interests of the store owners. If the Irvine Company allows the community to deteriorate or allows too many direct (or even indirect) competitors into their shopping centers, then the company will suffer an income and wealth loss (given that the value of their shopping centers are a function of the stores' profitability). Hence, we would imagine that the standard contract is one that the store owners like as much as the Irvine Company does, at least in terms of its basic features. The profit percentage is a way the store owners can "pay for performance" on the Irvine Company's part.

We also should not be surprised that in many other areas of the country landlords do not include the percentage take. In many other areas, property ownership is fragmented among a number of owners, with no one dominant property owner who is capable of determining, to a significant degree, the look and feel and the profitability of individual store owners. As a consequence, store owners are unlikely to give a percentage of their profits to their landlord when, in fact, the landlord can do little to earn the take. The landlord is unlikely to demand a percentage take because then the landlord would have to accept a lower fixed rental payment and would be at the mercy of the store owner, who has complete control over the store's profitability. There are simply no mutual gains to be divided.

Put another, perhaps more instructive way, we should expect percentage takes to be a part of lease contracts where the landlords have a significant impact on store sales, for example, in shopping malls and other planned communities. The more fragmented the property, the less likely (or the lower) the percentage take.

We should only infrequently expect rents to be determined totally by a percentage take. The reason is the same as the one given earlier for the two-part performance pay system for workers: both the landlords and tenants have an interest in sharing the risk. They both have an interest in a contract that reflects, to some degree, the influence that one party can have on the success of the other.

Business is full of risks, and it is full of risk sharing among owners, workers, suppliers, and even customers. Here, we have stressed that pay systems can be seen as a means by which employers and employees alike seek to share and spread the risk costs that are endemic to business. At its heart, the sharing will be a mutually beneficial exchange, with both parties accepting risk so long as the gains are greater than the risk costs incurred (or else the agreement will not last long). In addition, the pay system chosen is a means of inducing one party to act more effectively with the interest of the other party in mind. In a two-part pay system, the straight salary component (which can reduce the risk cost felt by the worker by more than the amount his or her pay is cut) can encourage employers to ensure that there is work for employees. The piece-rate or commission component can encourage workers to work hard and smart.

How much should workers be paid in salary and commission? The answer is a disappointing "It depends." The exact combination of pay components depends on such factors as the risk aversion of workers and how much the actual production levels in given work environments are under the control of workers and employers. The more risk averse workers are, the greater the salary component. This is true because there is more profit to the firm if it lowers its wage bill and accepts more risk of variations in worker incomes. The more output is dependent on the actions of the workers, the greater the commission component. How should employers determine the combination? A good start would be for the employers to see whether workers are willing to accept a reduction in their overall pay, with more of their income coming from guaranteed hourly or monthly payments. Of course, the firm will want to ensure that the reduction in compensation is greater than the added cost the firm calculates it will have to incur because of the reduction in production. The firm should continue to lower its overall wage bill that way so long as the reduction in overall pay is greater than the increase in the loss from slack output. It should, in other words, do what economists have long recommended—"equate at the margins," or balance the marginal gain with the marginal pain. In so doing, the firm can not only achieve maximum profits; it can actually improve the welfare of its workers.

Most books on economics rarely, if ever, mention concepts like "integrity," "commitment," "credibility," or "bonding" in their discussions of how well the economy works. We give those concepts special attention because their importance far exceeds their notice. Managers depend on such basic notions. The competitiveness of firms depends on them. The efficiency of the economy depends on them. Managers and firms fail when they do not give those concepts the respect they are due. Incentives tend to matter (in the right way) when, and to the extent that, managers' commitments matter.

6

Paying Above-Market Wages

Key Insight: Paying workers more than their market wage can increase their productivity. A mandatory retirement policy is necessary when firms overpay older workers. The abolition of mandatory retirement can lower worker wages.

HENRY FORD IS REMEMBERED for his organizational inventiveness (the assembly line) and for his presumption that he could ignore the wishes of his customers (as in his claim that he was willing to give buyers any color car they wanted so long as it was black!). However, he outdid himself when it came to workers.

In 1914, he stunned his board of directors by proposing to raise his workers' wages to $3 a day, a third higher than the going wage ($2.20 a day) in the Detroit automobile industry at the time. When one of his board members wondered out loud why he was not considering giving workers even more, a wage of $4 or $5 a day, Ford quickly agreed to go to $5, more than twice the prevailing market wage. Why?

An answer to why Ford paid more than the prevailing wage won't be found on the pages of standard economics textbooks.[1] In those texts, wages are determined by market conditions, namely, the forces of supply and demand, and supply and demand (often depicted by intersecting lines on a graph) are locked in place, not affected by how, or how much, workers are paid. The supply of labor is determined by what workers are willing to do, while the demand for labor is determined by the combined forces of worker productivity and the prices that can be charged for what the workers produce. The curves are more or less stationary (at least in the way they are presented), certainly not subject to manipulation by how, or how much, employers pay their workers.

In the competitive framework, the "market wage" will settle where the market clears, or where the number of workers who are demanded by employers exactly equals the number of workers who are willing to work. And, once more, no profit-hungry employer (at least in the textbook discussions) would ever pay above (or below) market. For that matter, in standard textbooks, employers in competitive markets are *unable* to pay anything other than the market wage, given the competition for workers. If employers ever tried to pay more, they could be underpriced by other producers who paid the market wage. If employers paid below market, they would not be able to hire employees and would be left without product to sell.

There are two problems with that perspective from the point of view of this book. First, we don't wish to assume away the problem of policy choices. On the contrary, we want to discuss how policies might affect worker productivity, or how employers might achieve maximum productivity from workers. We seek a rationale for Ford's dramatic wage move, if there is one to be found. In doing so, we don't deny that productivity affects worker wages, which is a well-established theoretical proposition in economics. What we insist on is that the reverse is also true—worker wages affect productivity—for very good economic reasons.

Second, a problem with standard market theory is that there is a lot of real-world experience that does not seem to fit the simple supply-and-demand model. The standard model is highly useful for discussing how wages might change with movements in the forces of supply and demand. From that framework, we can appreciate, for example, why wages move up when the labor demand increases (which can be attributable to productivity and/or price increases). At the same time, many employers have followed Ford's lead and paid more than market wages. All one has to do to check out that claim is to watch how many workers put in applications when a plant announces that it is hiring. Sometimes, the lines stretch for blocks from the plant door. When the departments of history or English in our universities have an open professorship, the departments can expect a hundred or more qualified applicants. The U.S. Postal Service regularly receives far more applications for its carrier jobs than it has jobs available. When Boeing came to Los Angeles in late 1996 to hire workers, the line at the work fair stretched for blocks down the street; the end, in fact, could not be seen from the door. These queues cannot be explained by market-clearing wages.

Consider the persistence of unemployment. The traditional view of labor markets predicts that the wage should be expected to fall until the market clears and the only evident unemployment should be transitory, encompassing people who are not working because they are between jobs or are looking for jobs. But "involuntary unemployment" abounds and persists, which must be attributable, albeit partially, to workers' having been paid "too much" (or above the market-clearing wage rate).

We don't pretend to provide a complete explanation for "overpaying" workers here. It may be that employers overpay their workers for some psychological reasons. Overpaying workers may make the employers feel good about themselves and their employees, which can show up in greater worker loyalty, longer job tenure, and harder and more dedicated work. The above-market wages may also remove workers' financial strains, leaving them with fewer problems at home and more energy to devote themselves to their jobs. While we think these can be important considerations, we prefer to look for another reason. We suggest that above-market salaries may be a means of improving incentives for workers to do as the employer wants.

As it turns out, Henry Ford was not offering his workers something extra for nothing in return. He wanted to "overpay" his workers primarily because he could then demand more of them. He could work them harder and longer—and he did. He could also be more selective in the people he hired, which could be a boon to all Ford workers. Workers could reason that they would be working with more highly qualified cohorts, all of whom would be forced to devote themselves to their jobs more energetically and productively. Some, if not all, of the wage would be returned in the form of greater production and sales and even greater job security for workers. But there were other benefits for Ford.

When workers are paid exactly the market wage, there is little cost in quitting. A worker making his market (or opportunity) wage can simply drop his job and move on to the next job with no loss in income. In Ford's case, workers had been quitting with great frequency. In 1913, Ford had an employee turnover rate of 370 percent! That year, the company had to hire 52,000 workers to maintain a workforce of 13,600 workers.

The company estimated that hiring a worker cost from \$35 to \$70, and even then they were hard to control. For example, before the pay raise, the absentee rate at Ford was 10 percent. Workers could stay home from work, more or less when they wanted, with virtually no threat of penalty. Since they were being paid market wage, the cost of their absenteeism was low to the workers. In effect, workers were buying a lot of absent days from work. It was a bargain. They could reason that if they were receiving only the "market wage rate," then that wage rate could be replaced elsewhere if they were ever fired for misbehaving on the job.

At any one time, most workers were new at their jobs. Shirking was rampant. Ford complained that "the undirected worker spends more time walking about for tools and material than he does working; he gets small pay because pedestrianism is not a highly paid line." In order to control workers, the company figured that the firm had to create some buffer between itself and the fluidity of a "perfectly" functioning labor market.

The nearly \$3 above the market that Ford paid was, in effect, a premium he had to pay in order to enforce the strict rules for employment eligibility he imposed. Ford's so-called Sociology Department was staffed by investigators who, after the pay hike, made frequent home visits and checked into workers' savings plan, marital happiness, alcohol use, and moral conduct, as well as their work habits on the job. He was effectively paying for the right to make those checks, and he made the checks in part because he thought they were the right thing to do, but also because the checks would lead to more productive workers.

Ford was also paying for obedience. He is quoted as saying, after the pay hike, "I have a thousand men who if I say 'Be at the northeast corner of the building at 4 A.M.' will be there at 4 A.M. That's what we want—obedience."[2] Whether he got obedience or allegiance may be disputed. What is not disputable is that he got dramatic results. In 1915, the turnover rate was 16 percent—down from 370 percent—and productivity increased about 50 percent.

It should be pointed out that control over workers is only part of the problem. Even if a boss has total control, there must be some way of knowing what employees should be doing to maximize their contribution to the firm. That wasn't a difficult problem for Ford. On the assembly line, it was obvious what Ford wanted his workers to do, and it was relatively easy to spot shirkers. According to David Halberstam in his book *The Reckoning*, there was small chance for the shirker to prosper in the Ford plant. After the plant was mechanized and the $5-a-day policy was implemented, foremen were chosen largely for their physical strength. According to Halberstam, "If a worker seemed to be loitering, the foreman simply knocked him down."[3] Since the high wage attracted many applicants, Ford's workers had to put up with the abuse and threat of abuse or be replaced. The line outside the employment office was a strong signal to workers.

Of course, this type of heavy-handed control doesn't work in every work environment. When productivity requires that workers possess a lot of specialized knowledge that they must exercise creatively or in response to changing situations, heavy-handed enforcement tactics may not work effectively. Indeed, the threat can undermine creativity and productivity. How is a manager to know whether a research chemist, a creator of software, or a manager is behaving in ways that make the best use of his talents in promoting the objectives of the firm? Do you knock him down if he gazes out the window? Managers typically provide a more subtle incentive program than a high daily salary and a tough foreman. The big problem is controlling employees who have expertise you lack.

One way to inspire effort from those who can't be monitored directly on a daily basis is to "overpay" workers and to ensure that they suffer a cost in the event that their performance, as measured over time, is not adequate. The "overpayment" gives workers a reason to avoid being fired or demoted for such reasons as lack of performance and excessive shirking. Even when shirking is hard to detect, the threat of losing a well-paying job can be sufficient to motivate diligent effort.[4]

Many workers are in positions of responsibility, meaning that they have control over firm resources (real and financial) that they typically use with discretion—and can also misuse, or appropriate for their own uses. Their actions are also difficult to monitor. Misuse of funds may only infrequently be discovered. How should such employees be paid? More than likely, they should be "overpaid." That is, they should be paid more than their market wage as a way of imposing a cost on them if their misuse of funds— especially, their dishonesty—is ever uncovered. The expected lost "excess wages" must exceed the potential value of the misused funds. The less likely the employees are to be found out, the greater the overpayment must be in order for the cost to be controlling.

For example, assume a person receives a wage premium of $100 because she is in a position of trust and has control over firm resources. If the person can expect to be discovered one out of every ten times she steals firm property, at which point she will lose her job and her wage premium, the employee will assess the expected cost of theft at $10 per instance. The person who expected to be caught much less frequently, say, one out of every 100 times, will assess the expected cost at $1. To balance the expected cost in the two instances, the wage premium will have to be higher in the second case, or $1,000. Of course, it naturally follows that, given the probability of being caught, the more a person can steal from the firm (or the more firm resources the employee can misuse or misdirect), the greater must the wage premium be to have the same deterrent effect.

Why do managers of branch banks make more than bank tellers? One reason is that the managers' talents are scarcer than tellers' are. That is a point frequently drawn from standard labor-market theorizing. We add here two additional factors: First, the manager is very likely in a position to misuse, or just steal, more firm resources than is each individual teller. Second, the manager's actions are less likely to be discovered than the teller's. The manager usually has more discretion than each teller does, and the manager has one less level of supervision.

Why does pay escalate with rank within organizations? There are myriad reasons, several of which are covered in chapter 10. We suggest here that as managers move up the corporate ladder, they typically acquire more and more responsibility, gain more discretion over more firm resources, and have more opportunities to misuse firm resources. In order to deter the misuse of firm resources, the firm needs to increase the threat of penalty for any misuse, which implies a higher and higher wage premium for each step on the corporate ladder.

Workers in the bowels of their corporations often feel that the people in the executive suite are drastically "overpaid" and that their pay appears to be out of line with what they do. To a degree, the workers are right. People in the executive suite are often paid a premium simply to deter them from misusing the powers of the executive suite. The workers should not necessarily resent the overpayments. The overpayments may be the most efficient way available for making sure that firm resources are used efficiently. To the extent that the overpayments work, the jobs of people at the bottom of the corporate ladder can be more productive, better paying, and more secure.

We have not covered all the possible reasons workers are not paid strictly as suggested by simple supply-and-demand curve analysis. Nevertheless, the Ford case permits us to make two general points. First, moving decisions away from the impersonal forces of the market place and into the more personal forces inside a firm, with long-term relational contracts, can increase efficiency by reducing transaction costs. Second, the decisions made on how the firm organizes its "overpayments" can have important consequences for the efficiency of production, because workers can have a greater incentive to invest "sweat equity" in their firms and to become more productive. The firm that gets the "overpayment" right (and exactly what it should be cannot be settled in theory) can gain a competitive advantage over rivals. Apparently, Ford secured an important advantage by going, in a sense, "off market."

Should workers accept "overpayment"? Better yet, is a greater overpayment always better for workers? The natural tendency is to answer with a firm "Yes!" Well, we think a more cautious answer is in order: "Maybe," or, again, "It depends." Workers would be well advised to carefully assess what is expected of them, immediately and down the road. High pay means employers can make greater demands—in terms of the scope and intensity of work assignments—on their employees, because of the cost the employees will bear if they do not consent to the demands.

Clearly, workers should expect that their employers will demand value equal to, if not above, the wage payments, and workers should consider whether they contribute as much to their firms' coffers as they take. Otherwise, their job tenure may be tenuous. The value of a job is ultimately equal to how much the workers can expect to earn over time, appropriately adjusted for the fact that future payments are not worth as much to workers as current ones are and for the fact that uncertain payments are not worth as much as certain payments. A high-paying job that is lost almost immediately for inadequate performance may be a poor deal for an employee.

To make this point with focus in our classes, we have often told our MBA students that they are unlikely to be offered upon graduation salaries at the high end of the executive level. However, if by some chance they were offered such a salary—say, $250,000 a year—they should seriously consider turning it down. We suggest that most should probably consider jobs with annual salaries more in the range of $50,000 to $70,000, or whatever is the going market wage for their graduate school cohorts. Our students are generally startled by our brazen suggestion.

Why should any sane person turn down such a lucrative offer, if a sane employer tenders it? An answer is not all that mysterious. Unless a new graduate is able and willing to return $250,000 a year in value, he or she will be unlikely to retain such a high-paying job for very long. The person who quickly fails at a high salary can end up doing far worse than the person who begins her career by succeeding at a more modest salary.

It is important to remember that the actual extent of the "overpayment" is not determined solely by employers, as was true with Ford in 1913. Employees also have a say. They have an interest in limiting the overpayment in order to limit the demands placed on them and to increase their job security. That is to say, the extent of the "overpayment" is, itself, determined by negotiation, if not by market forces, with the wage pressures not always in the way expected. Workers may press for a lower overpayment while the employer presses for the opposite.

Along this line, we have seriously suggested in another book (but with little hope of being taken seriously by political operatives) that members of Congress should not have control over their own pay.[5] By restricting their overpayment, they thwart the competition for their jobs and increase their job security—and the current value of being in Congress. Rather than cutting their pay in order to reduce the net value of being in Congress, we suggest, it might be wiser to increase members' pay rather dramatically to, say, half a million a year. That could increase the competition in congressional races, increase the quality of candidates who run, and undercut the job security for members of Congress. At the same time, the higher pay could make members far more responsive to voter interests than the current pay does by imposing formula-driven reductions in their pay if deficits or inflation exceed specified levels.

Firms might also "overpay" their workers because they have "underpaid" their workers early in their careers. The "overpayments" are not so much "excess payments" as they are "repayments" of wages forgone early in the workers' careers. Of course, the workers would not likely forgo wages unless they expected their delayed overpayments to include interest on the wages forgone. So the delayed overpayments must exceed underpayments by the applicable market interest rate. In such cases, the firms are effectively using their workers as sources of capital. The workers themselves become venture capitalist of an important kind.

Why would firms do that? Some new firms must do it just to get started. They don't have access to all the capital they need in their early years, since their product or service has not been proven. They must ask their workers to invest "sweat equity," which is equal to the difference between what the workers could make in their respective labor markets and what they are paid by their firms. The underpayments not only extend the sources of capital to the firm but also give the workers a strong stake in the future of the firm, which can make the workers work all the harder to make the firm's future a prosperous one. The up-front underpayments can make the firm more profitable and increase its odds of survival, which can be a benefit to the workers as well as owners. Of course, this is one reason many young workers are willing to accept employment in firms that are just starting out. Young workers often have a limited financial base from which to make investments; they do, however, have their time and energy to invest.

Underpayments to workers coupled with later overpayments can also be seen as a means by which managers can enhance the incentives workers have to become more productive. If workers are underpaid when they start, their rewards can be hiked later by more than they would otherwise be to account for productivity improvements. These hikes can continue—and must continue—until the workers are effectively overpaid later in their careers (or else the workers would not have accepted the underpayments earlier in their careers). However, managers must understand that they must be able to *commit* themselves to the overpayments and that there must be some end to the overpayments.

Not too many years ago, firms regularly required their workers to retire at age sixty-five. Retirement was ritualistic for managers. Shortly after a manager had his or her sixty-fifth birthday, someone would organize a dinner at which the manager would be given a gold watch and a plaque for venerable service and then be shown to the door with one last pleasant goodbye.

Why would a firm impose a mandatory retirement age on its workers? Such a policy seems truly bizarre, given that most companies are intent on making as much money as they can. Often the workers forced to retire are some of the most productive in the firm, simply because they have more experience with the firm and its customer and supplier networks.

While we acknowledge that mandatory retirement may appear mistaken, particularly in the case of highly productive employees, we think that for many companies a mandatory retirement policy makes good business sense—when they have been "overpaying" their workers for some time. (Otherwise, we would be hard pressed to explain why such policies would survive and would need to be outlawed.) To lay out that logic, we must take a detour into an analysis of the way workers who come under mandatory retirement policies are paid throughout their careers.

Paying market wages, or exactly what workers are worth at every stage in their careers, does not always maximize worker incomes. That has been a central point of the discussion in this chapter to this point. We extend that discussion here by showing how the manipulation of a worker's *career* wage structure, or earnings path over time, can actually raise worker productivity and lifetime income. However, as we also show, when worker wages diverge from their value over the course of their careers, mandatory retirement is a necessary component of the labor contract.[6]

Suppose that a worker goes to work for Apex, Inc., and is paid exactly

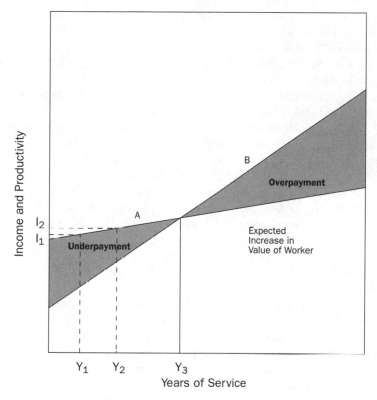

Figure 6.1 Twisted Pay Scale

what she is worth at every point in time. Assume she can expect to have a modest productivity improvement over the course of a thirty-year career, described by the slightly upward sloping line A in Figure 6.1. If her income follows her productivity, her salaries will rise in line with the slope of line A. In year Y_1, the worker's annual income will be I_1; in year Y_2, it will be I_2, and so forth.

Is there a way by which management can restructure the worker's income path and, at the same, enable both the workers and the firm to gain? No matter what else is done, management must clearly pay the worker an amount equal at least to what he or she is worth *over the course of her career*. Otherwise, the worker would not stay with the company. The worker would exit the firm, moving to secure the available higher career income. However, management need not pay each year an amount equal to the income points represented on line A. Management could pay the worker less than she is worth for a while so long as management is willing to compensate by overpaying her later.

For example, suppose that management charts a career pay path given by line B, which implies that up until year Y_3, the workers are paid less than they are worth, with the extent of the underpayment equaling the shaded area between the origin and Y_3. However, the workers would be compensated for what amounts to an investment in the firm by an over-payment after year Y_3, with the extent of the overpayment equal to the shaded area above line A after Y_3.

Are the firm and worker likely to be better off? Notice that the actual proposed pay line B is much steeper than line A, which, again, represents the worker's income path in the absence of management's intentional twisting of the pay structure. The greatest angle of line B means that the worker's income rises by more than warranted by the year-to-year increas-es in her productivity. This implies that the worker has a greater incentive to actually do what management wants done, which is to increase produc-tivity. This is the case because the worker gets a disproportionately greater reward for any given productivity improvement. Also, the cost of being fired from slacking off as retirement approaches is much greater when older workers are "overpaid." The increase in productivity can translate into greater firm revenue, which can be shared among the workers, man-agement, and owners.

Would workers ever want to work for a firm that intentionally under-pays its workers when they are young or just starting out with the compa-ny? You bet. The workers can reason that everyone in the firm will have a greater incentive to work harder and smarter. Hence, they can all enjoy higher prospective incomes over the course of their careers. Normally, commentaries on worker pay implicitly assume that the pay structure is what management imposes on workers. Seen from the perspective of the economic realities of what is available for distribution to all workers in a firm, we could just as easily reason that the kind of pay structure represent-ed by line B is what the workers would encourage management to adopt. Actually, the twisting of the pay structure is nothing more than an innova-tive way for managers to increase the money they make off their workers while also increasing the money workers are able to make off their firms. In short, it is a mutually beneficial deal, something of a "free good," in the sense that more is available for everyone.

If twisting the pay structure is such a good idea, why isn't it observed more often than it is in industry? Perhaps some variant of twisted pay schedules is more widely used than is commonly thought, primarily because they are not identified as such. Public and private universities are notorious for making their assistant professors work harder than full pro-fessors who have tenure and far more pay. Some large private firms, like General Motors and IBM, appear to have pay structures that are more like line B than line A. However, millions of firms appear to be unwilling or unable to move away from a pay structure like line A.

One of the problems with line B is that young workers must accept a cut in pay for a promise of greater pay in the future—and the pay later on must exceed what the workers can get elsewhere *and*, crucial to workers, more than what their firm would have to pay if it simply hired replacement workers at the going market wage. Obviously, the workers take a considerable risk; there is no guarantee that their firm will live up to its promise by raising their pay later to points above their market wage or, worse, that it will not fire them.

Needless to say, the firm must be able to make a *credible commitment* to its workers that it will live up to its part of the bargain, the quo in the quid pro quo. Truly *credible commitments* require that the firm be able to demonstrate a capacity and inclination to do what it says it will do. The firm's promises must be believable to those who make the early wage concessions. Many firms are not going to be able to twist their pay structures and gain the productivity improvements because they are new, maybe small, with a shaky financial base and an uncertain future. New firms have little history for workers to use to assess the value of the firms' commitments. Small firms are often short-lived firms. Financially shaky firms, especially those that suffer from problems of insolvency or illiquidity, are unlikely to be able to garner the trust of their workers. Firms that are in highly fluid, ever-changing and competitive markets, are also unlikely to be able to twist their pay structures. All of these tend to have to pay workers their market worth, or even a premium, to accommodate the risks the workers must accept when the company's existence is in doubt.

What firms are most likely to twist their pay structures? Ones that have been established for some time, have a degree of financial and market stability, have some monopoly power—and have proven by their actions that their word is their bond. To prove this, firms cannot simply go about willy-nilly dismissing workers or cutting their pay when they find cheaper replacements. To do so would undermine their credibility with their workers.

We can't be too precise in identifying the types of firms that can twist their pay structures for the simple reason that there can be extenuating circumstances. For example, we can imagine some unproved up-start companies would be able to pay their workers below market wages. Indeed, they might have to do so simply because they do not have the requisite cash flow early in their development. New firms often ask, or demand, that their workers provide "sweat equity" in their firms through the acceptance of below-market wages, but always with the expectation that their investment will pay off. Which new firms are likely to be able to do this? We suspect that firms with new products that represent a substantial improvement over established products would be good candidates. The likely success of the new product gives a form of base-line credibility to the firm owners' commitments that they intend to—and can—repay the "sweat equity" later. Indeed, the greater the improvement the new product represents, the more likely the firm can make the repayment, and do so in an expeditious manner, and the more likely the workers will accept below-market wages to start. The very fact that the product is a substantial improvement increases the likelihood of the firm's eventual success for two reasons. The first reason is widely recognized: a product that represents a substantial improvement will likely attract considerable consumer attention. The second reason is less obvious: the firm can delay its wage payments, using its scarce cash flow in its initial stages of production for other things, such as quality control, distribution, and promotion. The firm gets capital—sweat equity—from an unheralded source, its workers. The workers' investment of their sweat equity can enhance the firm's survival chances and even lower the interests that the firm must pay of debt (because the debt is more secure).

Of course, there are times when firms must break with their past commitments. For example, if a firm that was once insulated from foreign competition must all of a sudden confront more cost-effective foreign competitors in domestic markets (because, say, transportation costs have been lowered), then the firm may have to break with its commitments to overpay workers late in their careers. If it doesn't, the competition will simply pay people the going market wage and erode the markets of those firms that continue to overpay their older workers. Without question, many older American workers, for example, middle managers in the automobile industry, have hard feelings about the advent of the "global marketplace." They may have suffered through years of hard work at below-market wages in the belief that they would be able, later in their careers, to slack off and still see their wages rise further and further above market. The advent of global competition, however, has undercut the capacity of many American firms to fulfill their part of an implied bargain with their workers.

Even though they may have hard feelings, it does not follow that the workers would want their firms to try to hold to their prior agreements. Many workers understand that their wages can be higher *than they would be* if their firms tried to keep their prior agreement. Without the reneging, the firm might fold. In a sense, the workers made an investment in the firm through their lower wages, and the investment didn't pay off as much as expected. However, we hasten to add that some Americans workers have probably been burned by firms that have used changing market conditions as an *excuse* to break with their commitments or that have been sold to buyers who felt no compulsion to hold to the original owners' prior commitments.[7]

The answer to the question central to this section, "Why does mandatory retirement exist?," can now be provided, at least partially. Mandatory retirement at, say, age sixty-five or seventy may be instituted for any number of plausible reasons. It might be introduced simply to move out workers who have become mentally or physically impaired. Perhaps, in some ideal world, the policy should not be applied to everyone. After all, many older workers are in the midst of their most productive years, because of their accumulated experience and wisdom, when they are in their sixties and seventies. However, it may still be a reasonable *rule* because its application to *all* workers may mean that *on average*, by applying the policy without exception, the firm is made more efficient and profitable.

However, the *expected* fitness of workers at the time of retirement is not the only likely issue at stake. We see mandatory retirement as we see all employment rules, as a part of what is presumed to be a mutually beneficial employment contract, one that helps both the firms that adopt it and the workers who must abide by it. Parts of the contract can make the mandatory retirement rule economically sound.

We have spent much of this chapter exploring the logic of twisting workers' career income paths. If such a twist is productive and profitable and if workers must be overpaid late in their career to make the twist doable, then it follows that firms will want, at some point, to cut the overpayments off. What is mandatory retirement? *It is a means of cutting off at some definite point the stream of overpayments.* It is a means of making it possible, and economically practical, for a firm to use a twisted pay scale and to improve incentives to add to the firm's productivity and profitability. To continue overpayments until workers—even the most productive ones—collapse on the job is a policy that courts financial disaster.

Having said that, suppose Congress decides that mandatory retirement is simply an inane employment policy, as it has done? After all, members of Congress might reason, many of the workers who are forced to retire are still quite productive. What are the consequences?

Clearly, the older workers who are approaching the prior retirement age, who suffered through years of underpayment early in their careers but who are at the time of the abolition of mandatory retirement policy being overpaid, will gain from the passage of the law. They can continue to collect their overpayments until they drop dead or decide that work is something they would prefer not to do. They gain more in overpayments than they could have anticipated (and they get more back from their firms than they paid for in terms of their early underpayments). These employees will, because of the actions of Congress, experience an unexpected wealth gain.

There are, however, clear losers. The owners will suffer a wealth loss; they will have to continue with the overpayments. Knowing that, the owners will likely try to minimize their losses. Assuming that the owners can't lower their older workers' wages to market levels and eliminate the overpayment (because of laws against age discrimination), the owners will simply seek to capitalize the expected stream of losses from keeping the older workers on and buy them out.

To buy the workers out, the owners would not have to pay their workers an amount equal to the current value of the workers' expected future wages. The reason is that the worker should be able to collect some lower wage in some other job or enjoy the leisure of retirement if he or she is bought out.

In order for the buyout to work, of course, both the owners and workers must be no worse off and, preferably, should gain as a result of any deal that is struck. How can that be? Owners and workers can easily make a deal that leaves both sides no worse off. The owners simply pay the workers the current value of the overpayments (adjusted for the timing and uncertainty of the future payments).

But, can both sides *gain* by a buyout deal? That may not always be so easy. The owners would have to be willing to pay workers more than they, the workers, are willing to accept. There are several reasons such a deal may be possible in many, but not necessarily all, cases. First, the workers could have a higher discount rate than the owners. This may be the case because the owners are more diversified than their workers in their investments. Workers tend to concentrate their capital, a main component of which is *human capital*, in their jobs. By agreeing to a buyout and receiving some form of lump-sum payment in cash (or even in a stream of future cash payments), the workers can diversify their portfolios by scattering the cash among a variety of real and financial assets. Hence, workers might accept less than the current (discounted) value of their overpayments just to gain the greater security of a more diversified investment portfolio. Also, the workers cannot be sure how long they will be around to collect the overpayments. By taking the payments in lump-sum form, they reduce the risk of collection and increase the security of their heirs.

Second, sometimes retirement systems are overfunded, that is, they have greater expected income streams from their investments than are needed for meeting the expected future outflow of retirement payments. This is true, for example, of the California State Employee Retirement System. Therefore, if the company can tap the retirement funds, as the State of California did in the mid-1990s, it can pay workers more in the buyout than they would receive in overpayments by continuing to work. In so doing, they can move those salaries "off budget," which is what California has done in order to match its budgeted expenditures with declining funding levels for higher education.

Third, some workers may take the buyout because they expect their companies to be in financial difficulty down the road because of competition. The higher the probability the company will fail in the future (especially the near future), the more likely workers will be willing to accept a buyout that is less than the current value of the stream of overpayments.

Fourth, some workers might take the buyout simply because they have tired of working for the company or want to walk away from built-up hostilities. To that extent, the buyout can be less than the (discounted) value of the overpayments.

Fifth, of course, older workers have to fear that the employer will not continue to pay workers more than they are worth indefinitely. The workers' fears arise from a combination of two factors: the owners can shuck their overpayments with a buyout, and they still enjoy a great deal of discretion, in spite of any law that abolishes mandatory retirement rules. The owners can, if they choose to do so, lower the amount of the buyout payment simply by making life more difficult for older workers in ways that are not necessarily subject to legal challenge (for example, by changing work and office assignments, secretarial assistance, discretionary budgeted items, flexibility in scheduling).[8] The owners may never actually have to take such actions to lower the buyout payments. All that is necessary is for the *threat* to be a real consideration. Workers might rightfully expect that the greater their projected overpayments, the more they must fear their owners will use their remaining discretion to make a buyout doable.

We should also expect that workers' fears will vary across firms and will be related to a host of factors, not the least of which is the size of the firm. Workers who work for large firms may not be as fearful as workers at small firms, mainly because large firms are more likely to be sued for any retaliatory use of their discretionary employment practices (and efforts to adjust the work of older workers in response to any law that abolishes mandatory retirement rules). Large firms simply have more to take as a penalty for what are judged to be illegal acts. Moreover, it appears that juries impose much larger penalties on large firms, with lots of equity, than on their smaller counterparts. This unequal treatment before the courts, however, suggests that laws that abolish mandatory retirement rules give small firms a competitive advantage over their larger market rivals.

All we have done is to discuss the transitory adjustments that firms make with their older workers who are near the previous retirement age. We should expect other adjustments for younger workers, not the least of which is a change in their wage structures. Not being able to overpay their older workers in their later years probably means that the owners will have to raise the pay of their younger workers. After all, the only reason the younger workers would accept underpayment for years is the prospect of overpayments later on.

There are four general observations from this line of inquiry that are interesting:

1. The abolition of mandatory retirement tends to help those who are about to retire.

2. Abolition might help some older workers who are years from retirement, who work for large firms, and who can hang on to their overpayments. It can hurt other older workers who are fired, demoted, or not given raises or who have their pay actually cut.

3. It can increase the wages of younger workers by lowering the amount by which they will be underpaid. However, their increased wages while they are young will come at the expense of smaller overpayments later in their careers. Many, if not all, of

these younger workers will not be any better off because of the abolition of mandatory retirement than they would have been were a retirement rule permitted.

4. Overall, productivity might be expected to suffer, given that owners can no longer twist their career pay structures for their workers. As a consequence, workers will not have as strong an incentive to improve their productivity. They simply cannot gain as much by doing so. This means that the abolition of mandatory retirement rules can lower worker wages from what they otherwise would have been.

The simple point that emerges from this line of discussion is that the level and structure of pay counts for reasons that are not always so obvious. But our point about "overpayment" is fairly general, applying to the purchase of any number of resources other than labor. You may want to "overpay" suppliers at times just to ensure that they provide the agreed-upon level of quality, to ensure that they will not take opportunities to shirk because they can lose, on balance, if they do so.[9]

The moral of the analysis is that most firms have good economic reasons for doing what they do. There are certainly solid economic grounds for overpaying workers, just as there are good reasons for mandatory retirement. We like to think that members of Congress were well intended when they abolished mandatory retirement rules back in 1978. Unfortunately, they simply did not think through these complex matters very carefully. (Perhaps the politics of the moment did not allow them to do so.) If they had considered the full complexity of firms' retirement policies, many older workers would not now be suffering through the impaired earnings and employment opportunities that members of Congress are now decrying.

7

Fringes, Incentives, and Profits

Key Insight: Firms provide their workers with fringe benefits for the same reason they sell products: they make money doing it. Workers should be thankful for employers who look for ways to reduce salaries and wages by offering fringe benefits.

WORKERS TEND TO THINK and talk about their fringe benefits in terms remarkably different from those they use to discuss their wages. Workers who profess that they "earn" their wages will describe their fringes with reference to what their employers "give" them. "Gee, our bosses *give* us three weeks of vacation, thirty minutes of coffee breaks a day, the right to flexible schedules, and discounts on purchases from company goods. They also provide us with medical and dental insurance and cover 80 percent of the cost. Would you believe we only have to pay 20 percent!"

Wages are the result of hard work, but fringes, it seems, are a matter of employer generosity. Fringes are assumed to come from a substantially different source, such as out of the pockets of the stockholders, than wages, which come out of the revenues workers add to the bottom line.

Employers use some of the same language, and their answers to any question of why fringes are provided are equally misleading, though probably more gratuitous. The main difference is that employers inevitably talk in terms of the cost of their fringes. "Would you believe that the cost of health insurance to our firm is $4,486 *per employee*? That means that we spend millions, if not tens of millions, each year on all of our employees' health insurance. Our total fringe-benefit package costs us an amount equal to 36.4 percent of our total wage bill!" The point that is intended, though often left unstated, is, "Aren't we nice?"

This chapter is a challenge to many readers, since it will develop a radically different way of thinking about fringe benefits. It requires readers to set aside any preconceived view that fringes are a gift. We don't want to be overly crass in our view of business (although that may appear to be our intention from the words we have to use within the limited space we have to develop our arguments). We want only to be realistic when we surmise that from our economic perspective (the one that is likely to dominate in competitive business environments), the overwhelming majority of firms that provide their workers with fringes do so for the very same reason that they hire their workers in the first place: to add more to their profits than they could if they did something else. *Like it or not, most firms are in the business of making money off their employees—in all kinds of ways.*

The reason many firms don't provide their workers with fringe benefits—with health insurance being the most common missing fringe in small businesses especially—is that they can't make any money by doing so. The critical difference between those employers that do provide fringes and those that don't is not likely to have anything to do with how nice each group wants to be to its employees. We suspect that both groups are equally nice, or equally crass. There is really no reason to believe that people who do not provide some form of fringes (or provide less of some forms) are, on average, any more derelict in their duty to serve humanity than are the people who do.

When making decisions on fringe benefits, employers face two unavoidable *economic* considerations. First, fringes are costly, and some fringes, like health and dental insurance, are extraordinarily costly. Second, there are limits to the value workers place on fringes. The reason is simply that workers value a lot of things, and what they *buy*, directly from vendors or indirectly via their employers, is largely dependent on who is the lowest-cost provider.

Yes, workers *buy* fringe benefits from employers. They do so when the value the workers place on the fringes exceeds the cost of the fringes to the firms. When that condition holds, firms can make money by, effectively, "selling" fringes—for example, health insurance—to their workers. How? Most firms don't send salespeople around the office and plant selling health insurance or weeks of vacation to their employees like they sell fruit in the company cafeteria, but they nevertheless make the sales. They do it somewhat on the sly, indirectly, by offering the fringes and letting their particular labor market conditions adjust. If workers truly value a particular fringe, then the firms that provide the fringe will see an increase in the supply of labor available to them. They will be able to hire more workers at a lower wage and/or be able to increase the "quality" (productivity) of the workers that they do hire.

Firms are paid for the cost of providing fringe benefits primarily in two ways. First, their real wage bill goes down because of the increased competition for the available jobs that results from the greater number of job seekers who are attracted by the fringe. This reflects the willingness of workers to *pay* employers for the fringe benefits. Two, employers gain by being more discriminating in whom they hire, employing more productive workers for the wages paid and thus increasing sales.

No matter what happens in particular markets, we know several things about the pattern that emerges in the fringe-benefit market:

- Many firms (but not all) can make money by "selling" fringes to their workers.

- Firms won't provide the fringes if the combined gains from lower wages and better workers are not greater than the cost of the fringes.

- Workers who suffer a decline in their wages because of their fringes will still be better off because of the fringes that they buy. Otherwise, the fringes would not be made available by the firm or the number of job seekers would not increase, and the firms could not justify providing the fringe.

- If providing a given fringe is profitable for firms, there will be competitive pressures to provide it. Otherwise, firms that do not provide the fringe will have a higher cost structure (because their total wage bill will be higher by more than the cost of the fringe) and will be in a less competitive position.

To see these points with greater clarity, we must do what we try to do as little as possible in this book: look to a graph. However, in this case the graph is a simple one—supply and demand—and the analysis is straightforward. We have drawn in Figure 7.1 normal labor supply and demand curves. The downward sloping labor demand curve, D_1, shows that more workers will be demanded by firms at lower wage rates than at higher wage rates and reflects the circumstance in which no fringe benefit is provided. The upward sloping line, S_1, shows that more workers will come on the markets at higher wage rates than at lower ones and reflects an initial circumstance in which a given fringe benefit (such as health insurance) is not provided. These embedded assumptions regarding the slopes of the lines are totally reasonable and widely accepted as reflecting market conditions. At any rate, without the fringe the workers will receive a wage rate of W_1, where the market clears.

Consider the simplest of cases, one in which the firm's cost in providing a fringe benefit is a uniform amount for each worker and in which the provision of the fringe has no impact on worker productivity but increases the value of work and increases the supply of workers. The demand curve in Figure 7.1 drops down vertically by the per-worker cost of the fringe, from D_1 to D_2. This happens because the firms are simply not willing to pay as

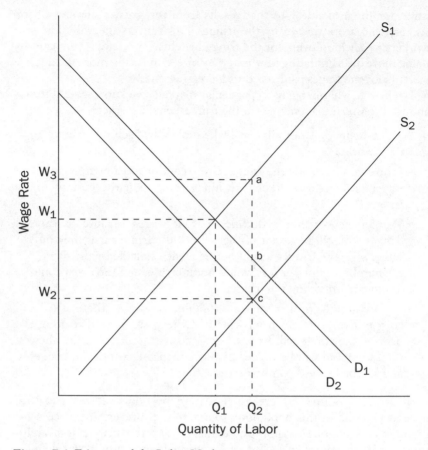

Figure 7.1 Fringes and the Labor Market

high a wage to their workers if they have to cover the cost of the fringe. On the other hand, the supply of workers shifts outward, from S_1 to S_2, because work is now more attractive because of the fringe, leading more workers to apply for jobs. Workers are willing to work for a lower money wage *when the fringe is provided* (and, again, for simplicity we assume that each worker values the fringe by the same amount). The vertical difference between S_1 and S_2 represents how much each worker values the fringe and is willing to give up in wage rate for the fringe; this vertical difference is a money measure of the value of the fringe to workers.

What happens, given these shifts in supply and demand? As can be seen in the figure, the market-clearing wage falls from W_1 to W_2. Are workers and firms better off? A close examination of the figure reveals that more workers are employed (Q_2 instead of Q_1), which suggests that something good must have happened. Otherwise, we must wonder why firms would want to hire more workers and more workers would be willing to be employed. It just doesn't make much sense to argue that firms and/or workers aren't better off when both sides agree to more work (and when the fringe is provided voluntarily).

Notice that the total cost of the fringe, the vertical distance between the two demand lines, or bc, is less than the reductions in the wage, $W_1 - W_2$, from which we can draw two implications. First, the firm is clearly making money off its original employees ($W_2 + bc$ is less than W_1). Second, the firm's total cost per worker ($W_2 + bc$) falls, which explains why it is willing to expand its hires.

Notice, also, that while the workers accept a lower wage rate, W_2, instead of W_1, they gain the value of the fringe, which in the graph is the vertical distance ac. The sum of the new lower wage, W_2, plus the value of the fringe, ac, is W_3, which is higher than the wage without the fringe ($W_2 + ac = W_3 > W_1$). Thus, both sides gain.

How much of the fringe benefit should be provided? It would be nice if we could tell each person reading this book exactly what to do. It would be silly to try, given the variation of business and market circumstances. What we can do is look to rules that are generally applicable. The rule the firms should follow is no different from the rule they should follow in any other productive market circumstance: *firms should continue to expand the fringe so long as the added cost from the fringe is less than the reduction in their wage bills, which can be no greater than the workers' evaluation of the fringe.*

For example, the number of days of paid vacation should be extended so long as the value workers place on additional vacation days is greater than the cost to the employer of providing the additional day. Since workers' evaluation of each additional day will fall (at least after some number of days) and the cost of the additional day will rise after some number of days off, a point will be reached beyond which the additional cost of the next vacation day will exceed its value (or the possible reduction in the wage bill). At that point, employers have maximized their profit from "selling" the fringe to their workers.

Of course, tax rules will affect the exact amount of the fringe, as well as the combination. Certainly, if fringe benefits—for example, health insurance—are not subject to taxation, then employers should, naturally, provide more of them than otherwise, simply because part of the cost of the benefit is covered by a reduction in worker taxes. The result might be that workers actually get more of the benefit than they would buy, *if they were covering all of the cost themselves*. Still, the employers must provide the benefit; otherwise, they will not keep their compensation costs competitive with those of rival employers.

We expect employers and workers to treat fringes like they do everything else, seeking some *optimum* combination of fringes and money wages. Again, this means that employers and workers should be expected to weigh their additional (or marginal) value against their additional (or marginal) cost. An employer will add to a fringe like health insurance so long as the marginal value (measured in money wage concessions wages or increased production from workers) is greater than the marginal cost of the added fringe. Similarly, workers will "buy" more of any fringe from their employer so long as its marginal value (in terms of improved health or reduction in the cost of private purchase) is greater than its marginal cost (wage concessions).

While we can't give specifics, we do know that managers are well advised to search earnestly for the "optimum" combination (which means some experimentation will likely be in order), even though the process of finding the optimum is beset with imprecisions. The firms that come closest to the optimum will be the ones that can make the most money from their employees. They will also be the ones that provide their employees the most valuable compensation for the money spent—and so will have the lowest cost structure and be the most competitive. By trying to make as much money as possible from their employees, firms not only stay more competitive; they also benefit their workers as well.

So far, we have considered only fringes in which the added cost of the fringe to the firm is less than the value of the fringe to the workers. What if that were not the case? Returning attention to Figure 7.1, suppose that the cost of the fringe to firms were greater than the value of the fringe to workers (in the graph, the distance *bc* is greater than the distance *ac*). What would happen? The straight answer: nothing. The fringe would not be provided. The reason is obvious. Both sides, workers and owners, would lose. The resulting drop in the wage would be smaller than the cost of the fringe to the employers, and the resulting drop in the wage would be greater than the value of the fringe to the workers. (To see this point, just try drawing a graph with the vertical drop in the demand greater than the outward shift of the supply.) *Such a fringe would not—and should not—be provided because it would be a loser to both sides.*

Firms that persist in providing such a fringe will have difficulty competing, simply because their cost structure will be higher than that of other producers. Such firms are subject to takeovers. The takeover will very likely be friendly, because those bidding for the firm in the takeover will be able to pay a higher price for the stock than the going market price, which will be depressed by the fact that one or more fringes provided to workers is not profitable. Those involved in the takeover may, after acquiring control, eliminate the excessively costly fringe(s) (or reduce it to profitable levels), enhance the firm's profitability and competitive position, and then sell the firm's stock at a price higher than the purchase price.[1]

Workers will support such a takeover—and may be the ones managing the takeover—because they can see a couple of advantages. They can have a fringe eliminated that is not worth the cost they have to pay for it through lower wages. They can also gain some employment security, as a result of the improved competitive position of their firm. The workers may even take over the firm for the same reason anyone else might do so: to improve the firm's profitability and stock price (but, as we see in chapter 12, an employee buyout can be problematic).

We can now understand why firms typically provide their employees with health insurance and so many small firms do not. At the most general level, it simply pays large firms more to provide the insurance than it pays small firms to do so. Large firms can sell a large number of health insurance policies, achieving economies associated with scale and spreading the risks. That's a widely recognized answer.

At another level, the answer is more complicated and obscure. Small and large firms do not generally hire from the same labor markets. Small firms tend to provide lower-paying jobs. The workers in lower-paying jobs within small firms simply don't have the means to buy a lot of things that workers in larger firms have, and one of the things workers in small firms don't seem to buy in great quantities is insurance. Given their limited income, workers simply don't think that insurance is a good deal, and they would prefer to buy other things with higher monetary compensation. One of the reasons low-income workers may gravitate to small firms is that they shy away from large firms where they would have to give up wages to buy the insurance, because of company policies that apply to all workers.

Of course, the analysis gets even trickier when it is realized that lower-income workers, many of whom work for small firms, tend to be younger workers, who also tend to be healthier and in need of a different combination of fringes compared to older workers. The young can appreciate that the price they would have to pay for health insurance through their firms is inflated by a number of factors related to supply and demand. First, the price of health insurance has been inflated by a host of cost factors, not the least of which is the increased liability doctors face for virtually anything that goes wrong with patients when they are under the doctors' care. The radical application of expensive medical technologies to care for older dying patients has also jacked up the cost of insurance and care for the young.

Second, older workers, many of whom are in large firms and tend to have a strong demand for health insurance, have increased the demand for insurance (and health care). The exemption of health insurance from taxable income (which helps higher-income workers more than lower-income workers) has also artificially inflated the demand for health insurance (and health care). The net result of the cost and demand effects has been to increase health insurance costs, making the insurance an unattractive deal for many young and low-income workers, many of whom work for small firms.

We know the objections to our line of analysis. Critics might say that we have overlooked the human factor. Fringe benefits are important to workers, and they should have fringe benefits even when they aren't profitable. We see a couple of problems with that claim. If the fringe were as important as claimed, then surely workers would be willing to give up a lot for it. The problem is that the cost may be greater than the benefit. If workers are forced to take a fringe because it is "important," then they could be forced to pay more for something than it is worth to them. We can't quite understand the logic of forcing people to "buy" something that they do not believe is worth the cost. There are lots of things that people think are important for other people to have. But typically it is best to let individuals decide for themselves how much of these important things they buy with their own money. Individuals have information on their own preferences and circumstances that others do not know, and cannot know.

Critics might like to think that employers would pay for any given benefit. If the analysis of this chapter has led to any clear conclusion, it is that the workers pay for what they get. They may not hand over a check for the benefits, but they give up the money nonetheless, through a reduction in their pay. If workers didn't give up much for the fringe, we probably have a benefit that is not worth anything to the workers; the supply curve would not move out. Even here the workers would see wages drop some because the cost of the fringe would lower the demand curve. This would mean both employers and workers would be incurring a cost without getting anything in return.

But critics might argue that managers don't know that certain fringes are "good" for business and their workers. That is often the case, and the history of business is strewn with the corpses of firms that failed to serve the interests of their workers and customers and who were forced into bankruptcy by other firms that were better at finding the best combination of fringes. We see the market as a powerful, though imperfect, educational system. If the critics know better than the managers of existing firms, they can make lots of money by pointing out to those firms why they are wrong and how they could make money from their employees by providing (selling) fringes not now being provided, or adjusting the combination of existing fringes in marginal ways.

We also don't believe that managers are the only ones who should search for the right combination of fringes. Workers should have an interest in joining the search, because they can gain in spite of the fact that their efforts will include a search for how their firms can make more money off them. If workers want more of one benefit, it would seem that all they would have to do is tell their bosses and show them how additional profits can be made *from the workers*. Workers, however, who want benefits without paying for them shouldn't waste their bosses' time. Managers hear from a lot of people who want something for nothing.

We think that workers and owners should talk as frankly about fringe benefits as they do about their wages. Workers earn their wages. The same is true for fringes. There's no gift involved. Both wages and fringes represent mutually beneficial exchanges between workers and their firms.

What is more obvious than the desire of workers for higher salaries and wages? Certainly no sane person would deny that all workers would rather be paid more money rather than less, everything else being equal. But everything else is seldom equal. For example, while workers may prefer to take home bigger paychecks with the work being held constant, they do not necessarily want a higher wage if it entails less pleasant or more diffi- cult responsibilities.[2] But even for the same work, workers may prefer to be paid less money. Indeed, workers are better off because employers are constantly looking for, and succeeding in finding, ways to pay them less. This is a point you very likely haven't seen covered in your human resource studies.

In the analysis that follows, always keep in mind a key point in our above examples: workers can be better off even when they experience a cut in their monetary pay. Workers are better off with the lower pay than they were before because the only way the employer can reduce their pay (with- out reducing their ability to hire competent workers) is by substituting a fringe benefit that is worth even more than the lost pay. Even though monetary pay has been cut, total compensation has been increased. We advance the argument by showing that workers benefit more from a fringe the larger the reduction in their wage.

Our demonstration in this section is subject to one qualification. We assume that all workers have much the same preferences for fringe bene- fits. Even if workers in general are made better off when a fringe benefit is substituted for monetary compensation, it is possible that the fringe bene- fit is one that some workers do not value at all, or do not value as much as they do the loss of money income. This is a problem, however, that both workers and employers have a strong motivation to overcome. Workers will be more attracted to firms that offer the combination of fringe bene- fits and money wages that best conforms to their preferences. For exam- ple, many young workers who seek part-time employment to help pay for college want most of their compensation in money wages and little in the way of tax-free fringe benefits. They need cash, and most face low (or no) tax rates. In general, older workers in higher income tax brackets and with greater demand for medical care will want more of their compensation in the form of untaxed fringe benefits such as health insurance. Therefore, we can expect employers who hire a lot of young part-time workers to offer fewer fringe benefits than employers who most of the time hire adult full-time workers. Also, employers will find it to their advantage in com-

peting for workers to offer a menu of fringe benefits from which workers
can choose. The closer an employer can adjust the fringe benefit package
to the preferences of the workers, the more the employer can save by paying lower money wages.[3]

But even if we assume that all workers benefit equally from the fringe
benefits provided, can we really show that workers receive the greatest
benefit when their wages are cut the most? What is to keep the employer
from receiving all the advantage from fringe benefits that are worth more
than they cost? Sure, an employer will provide fringe benefits that cost
only $50 per worker if they are worth $100 to each worker. But if the
employer then reduces each worker's money income by the full $100,
which she could presumably do without losing any workers, where is the
gain to workers? The answer is that if some way is found to save on the
cost of hiring workers, competition will force employers to share some—
but not all—of those savings with workers.

For example, if one firm discovers a fringe benefit that lowers the cost
of workers, other firms will find advantage in providing that benefit, also.
As workers become less costly to firms in general, they will be more
aggressively sought out, and the competition between firms will prevent
any one firm from lowering the wages of workers by the full value of the
new fringe benefit. Also, even if the fringe benefit could be provided by
only the one firm, so that workers did not become more valuable to other
firms, competition would still prevent the one firm providing the benefit
from cutting the money wage by the full value of the benefit. Assume that
the firm did initially attempt to capture all the value of a fringe benefit by
lowering the wage by its full value. The result would be that workers now
cost the firm a lot less than before, and this cost advantage would make it
profitable to hire more workers. But the only way to hire more workers is
to bid them away from other activities, which means bidding at least some
away from other firms. This can be done only by moving the wage back
up—not to the point where it was before the fringe benefit was added, but
high enough so that the total compensation is higher with the fringe benefit than it was before, even though the money wage is lower than before.

You are excused, however, if you are not yet convinced that when a
fringe benefit is provided, the gain to workers is greater the larger the
reduction in their money wage. Our discussion of the effect of fringe benefits is not sufficiently precise to convincingly establish the connections
between those benefits, the money wage, and the gain to workers. The
best way to get at these connections is by returning to the demand and
supply curves used earlier. We have already seen that if the fringe benefit is
worth providing (its value is greater than its cost), then the wages of workers will fall by more than the cost of the fringe benefit (the employer gains)
but by less than its value to workers (the workers gain). Illustrating this
important point again will set the stage for understanding why the bigger
the wage cut the better for workers.

In Figure 7.2 the initial demand for workers (without the fringe) is given by D_1 and the initial supply of workers (without the fringe) is given by S_1.[4] Given these lines, the market-clearing wage is given by W1 and the number of workers hired is given by Q_1. Now assume that the employer adds a fringe benefit (say another week of paid vacation each year) that costs exactly the same amount per worker as it is worth to each worker. The demand curve for workers will shift down by an amount equal to the cost per worker of the fringe benefit, or D_2. And the workers supply curve will shift down by the same amount to S_2.

These shifts reflect the fact that (assuming workers are worth the same as before and are just as willing to work as before), once the additional vacation is provided: (1) the employer is willing to hire the same number of workers as before if the cost for each remains the same, that is, if the wage drops by the same amount as the additional vacation cost per worker; and (2) the same number of workers is willing to work if the value of compensation remains the same, that is, if the money wage drops by the same

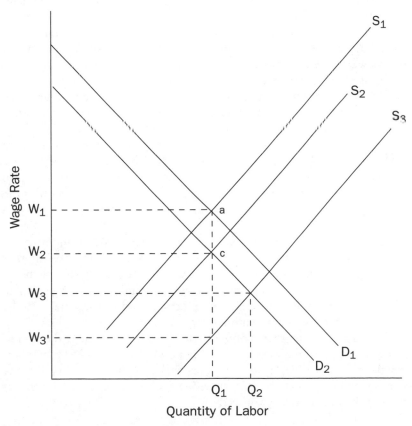

Figure 7.2 Fringes and the Labor Market

amount as the value each worker receives from the additional vacation. With both the demand and supply curves shifting down by the same amount, they will intersect (as shown in Figure 7.2) at the same number of workers, Q_1, but at a wage, W_2, that is less than W_1 by exactly the cost (and value) of the fringe benefit. In essence, nothing has really changed. Workers are receiving compensation that is worth exactly the same as before ($W_2 + ac = W_1$), and the cost of that compensation to the employer is exactly the same.

In the case just examined, it really makes no difference to the workers or to the employer whether the additional vacation is provided or not. So let's forget about additional vacation time and consider a different fringe benefit, say membership in the neighborhood health club, one that costs the employer the same amount to provide, but which is more valuable to the workers. In this case the employer's demand curve for labor remains at D_2. But because of the greater value the workers receive from the health club membership, the supply curve shifts down below S_2, say to S_3, indicating that now people can be enticed into working for the firm at a lower money wage. As seen in Figure 7.2, with the new supply and demand curves, the money wage will decline to W_3 from W_2, and the number of workers hired will increase to Q_2 from Q_1. But the most important thing to notice is that the workers have gained as the money wage is cut. The Q_1 workers who were employed by the firm before receiving the health club membership value that membership enough that they would continue working even if the money wage fell to $W_{3'}$. Even though the money wage is reduced because of the health club membership, each worker is better off by an amount equal to the difference between W_3 and $W_{3'}$, which we can think of as a bonus. And obviously the $Q_2 - Q_1$ newly hired workers are better off, since the wage of W_3 and the health club membership are enough for them to voluntarily leave their previous activities. (You can also see that workers are better off by noting that the wage rate of W_3 plus the value of the fringe, the vertical distance between S_1 and S_3, adds to more than W_1.)

It should be clear that the workers would be even better off if, instead of a health club membership, the firm found another fringe benefit that would drive their wages down even more. It can be easily shown that if another fringe benefit (for example, flexible scheduling) is more valuable to the workers than the health club membership and if that benefit can be provided at the same cost, the money wage will be driven down below W_3. However, again, the workers will be better off (simply because the sum of the lower wage plus the value of the benefit will lead to higher total compensation). The working rule employers should keep in mind is this: the more valuable the fringe benefit provided for a given cost, the lower the wage but the better off the workers.

It should be clear that employers have a strong motivation to provide fringe benefits that cost less than they are worth to workers. Both employers and employees win when such benefits are provided. Yet many people believe that private businesses are not sufficiently motivated to provide fringe benefits to their workers and that the government should mandate certain employment-related benefits. An explanation for this belief may be the widespread view, discussed at the beginning of the chapter, that workers earn their wages but are given fringe benefits by their employers. This perspective is reflected in the common assumption by advocates of mandated benefits that the cost of those benefits will not result in lower wages for workers.[5] If this were true, then employers would have little motivation to provide fringe benefits even if they were worth more than they cost.

But clearly employers do provide fringe benefits without being required to, for reasons that should be obvious by now. It pays employers to provide fringe benefits that are worth more than they cost because workers are willing to pay for more than the costs of those benefits in lower wages. If a fringe benefit, if provided, is not paid for by workers, then it is a fringe benefit that will make both employers and employees worse off.

To see the problem with a fringe benefit that doesn't reduce wages, consider Figure 7.3. Again we start off with demand and supply lines for labor, given by D_1 and S_1, respectively. As before, the initial market-clearing wage is W_1 and Q_1 workers are hired. Now assume that the government mandates a benefit that costs the employer something to provide but that has no value at all to the workers. Such a mandate will shift the demand curve for labor down to D_2, where the vertical distance between D_1 and D_2 is the cost per worker of the benefit, while leaving the supply line unaffected. As seen in Figure 7.3, the result is a decline in the market-clearing wage to W_2 from W_1 and the layoff of Q_1 - Q_2 workers. Even the workers who keep their jobs are clearly worse off, since they end up paying part of the cost of a worthless benefit with lower wages.

But what about a mandated benefit that has no effect on wages, one that is paid for entirely by the employer? Such a benefit would be one that had a negative value to workers; it is one that they would be willing to pay to keep from being provided. For example, assume the government mandated that all employers provide a smokefree work environment. For some employers a smokefree environment makes sense, and many firms had such a policy before they were required. But consider an employer whose workers all smoke. Providing a smokefree work place will shift the demand curve down from D_1 to D_2 to reflect the employer cost of workers spending less time working and more time outside smoking. Also, the employer will see the firm's labor supply curve shift back, since the workers will find the new working conditions less pleasant than the former ones. If the supply curve shifts back from S_1 to S_2, which is the same amount the demand

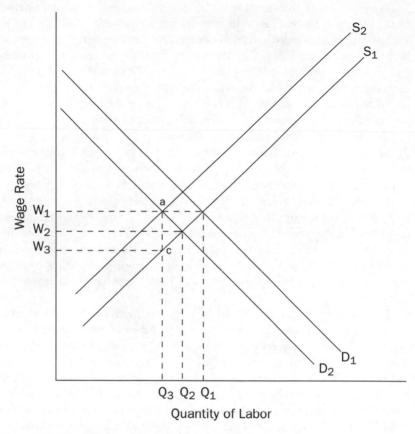

Figure 7.3 Mandated Benefit and the Labor Market

curve shifts down, then the market-clearing wage remains at W_1 but now Q_1 - Q_3 workers are laid off. Even though the wage doesn't fall, the workers are worse off in this case than in any of the previous cases considered—all of which saw the wage fall. Indeed, the workers are obviously worse off in terms of total compensation: they receive a wage of W_1, but they have to endure the cost of *ac* from the smoking ban (which means that they receive *net* compensation of W_3 (W_1 - *ac*).

There are at least three important points that follow from the discussion in this chapter. First, workers benefit from the desire of their employers to cut their wages by providing fringe benefits in much the same way that consumers benefit from suppliers who desire to profit by selling them products. Second, employers have a strong motivation to provide fringe benefits only when those benefits are worth more to workers than they cost. Third, if those who advocate mandated government benefits are correct when they argue that the benefit will be paid for entirely by the employer (will not lower wages), then the benefit isn't worth providing, and mandating it will make workers worse off.

8

Cutting Health Insurance Costs

Key Insight: Health insurance costs can be contained by giving workers a greater incentive to demand less health care through what have been called "medical savings accounts." With such accounts in place, workers' real wages can be lowered.

THE INFAMOUS "HEALTH CARE CRISIS" in the United States amounts to nothing more than costs for a particular service, health care, responding to the market forces of supply and demand. Unfortunately, the forces have been distorted by legal and political factors that have gotten the incentives wrong. In our view, the "crisis" is more a matter of political rhetoric than economics. Political grandstanding alone will hardly solve whatever health care problem exists. Careful reflection by policymakers and managers on the exact sources of the problem might. The current distortion present a possibility for managers to benefit both their firms and its workers by policies that get the incentives right.

If private firms and Washington-based politicians want to reform the system and temper cost increases, they can do so by working with the forces of supply and demand, which means, fundamentally, changing people's incentives to provide and consume health care services.

Health care costs, and the insurance premiums that finance a major share of health care expenditures, have risen faster than the prices of other goods over the past couple of decades.[1] Indeed, the cost of health insurance provided by firms was escalating at double-digit rates in the late 1980s and the very early 1990s when increases in the consumer price index, a broad measure of the cost of living, were falling.[2] In the mid-1990s, health care cost increases slowed, but they were, at this writing, still increasing at a rate that was more than 50 percent higher than the rate of increase in the general cost of living.

In order to understand the problem of insurance cost increases, we need first to consider the market forces that have been at work driving up health care costs. Consider the following list of factors that affect the supply and demand of health care:

1. Doctors have been subject to a growing amount of litigation. They have been sued with growing frequency, partly because they have made mistakes but also because they are now being held responsible for problems over which they may have no control. Patients have found that they can make money by blaming doctors for almost any problem that emerges when they are being treated. Fearful that they will be sued for delivering incomplete or misguided care, doctors have been covering their financial and professional backsides by ordering tests that may be only marginally valuable from a medical perspective but that can help them defend themselves in the event they are sued when problems emerge. They have also been trying to acquire legal protection and to spread the risk of lawsuits by increasing referrals to specialists.

2. Federal expenditures on Medicare for older patients and Medicaid for low-income patients have increased the demand for health care services since the late 1960s, which has tended to boost prices and forced many younger and lower-income patients out of the health insurance market.

3. Medical care has become technologically more sophisticated, and doctors have applied the new technology for offensive reasons (to keep patients alive longer) and for defensive reasons (they don't want to be accused of negligence for failing to employ the latest life-saving technology). The extensive use of the latest and best technology may have saved and prolonged lives, but medical care costs have been driven up in the process.

4. The health care industry has always been plagued by the problem of "asymmetric information," or the doctors knowing more about many patients' medical conditions and what will remedy their problems than do the patients themselves. As a consequence, doctors have always been in a position to induce patients to buy more medical care than the patients might really buy if they had the information and knowledge that is at the disposal of the doctors.

5. Medical technology has drastically lowered the cost of many medical procedures and has, as a consequence, lowered the cost of extending the lives of patients by some varying and uncertain number of months and years. For example, less than four decades ago, heart and kidney transplants and heart bypass operations were impossible. No one knew how to do them. Then, the costs of those procedures were infinite. Their prices may now remain high

in absolute dollar terms, running into the tens, if not hundreds, of thousands of dollars. However, those high prices also are *lower* prices. And the lower prices for those procedures have, no doubt, increased the number of patients who have been willing and able to pay for the procedures (as well as the number of insurers who have helped with the payments). Although the issue has not been statistically evaluated to date, the lower prices for many medical procedures have probably increased total medical expenditures in absolute dollar terms and as a percentage of national income. Hence, some of the so-called health care "crisis" probably mirrors, to a degree, the success of the health care industry in lowering the cost of prolonging life.

6. The cost of employer-provided medical insurance is tax deductible, which means that its price has been artificially lowered, causing more consumers to buy more complete insurance coverage and to demand more medical services than they otherwise would. The greater demand has enabled medical professionals to boost their prices. As tax rates rose in the 1960s and 1970s, workers naturally had growing incentive to take more of their income in tax-deductible fringe benefits and less of an incentive to take their income in taxable money wages. The higher tax rates spurred demand for health insurance and health care—and added to pressure on health care costs.

7. Employers have typically bought insurance policies with very low deductibles, for example, $200 a year. This means that after the first $200 of medical care expenditures in any one year, the cost of additional medical services to the insured patient is often close to zero. This feature of insurance policies has encouraged excessive use of health care services, which, in turn, has driven up employees' insurance premiums and caused some workers to forgo health insurance altogether.[3]

8. The growth in social problems—crimes involving bodily injury, the use of street drugs, and teenage pregnancy—has also contributed to the demand for medical services, which has driven up their prices as well as the price of insurance. The unwillingness or inability of medical professionals to deny services to people who cannot pay for the services has also increased the number of people seeking services. Social attitudes favoring universal medical care coverage have reduced the cost of irresponsible behavior, increasing the demand on the health care industry and inflating costs.

Without question, if the grocery industry were to operate the way the health care industry operates, we would likely have a "crisis" in the grocery business. The reason is simple: people would pay a fixed sum each month (their grocery premium) through their employer that would entitle them to virtually unlimited access to the grocery store shelves (after they have covered the $200 annual deductible) at zero, or very low, cost. Under such an arrangement, we should not be surprised if people consumed significantly more and better food, some of which would have limited nutritional value. We should also not be surprised if the shoppers' grocery premiums went through the roof as people allowed their tastes to run wild, with many low-income shoppers forced out of the markets for grocery policies by the inflated premiums.

How can the so-called "crisis" be solved, at least partially? We don't intend to offer a detailed set of public policy solutions here. Other specialists in the field have done that.[4] We only point out here that many of the supply-and-demand forces we have listed are beyond the control of individual businesses. There is simply not much most individual businesses can do to affect the broad sweep of social attitudes and government tax and expenditure policies. We note, however, that the demand for health care services can be lowered by reducing, at least marginally, government subsidies for the health care of many Americans. This can be accomplished by lowering Medicare and Medicaid expenditures and by eliminating all or part of the tax deductibility of health insurance. The cost of health care can also be lowered by reducing the rewards from suing doctors or by giving patients the right (to a greater or lesser degree) to absolve doctors of liability for problems that may arise while the patients are in the doctors' care.

Frankly, making those recommendations is much easier than getting them passed. They are too politically painful for voters (although we suggest that voters should also consider the gains to everyone from getting health care costs under control).

Barring changes in public policies, what can businesses themselves do to ameliorate their own health care costs? Many businesses have done what has come naturally: they have tried to select workers who are not likely to have medical problems and, therefore, drive up the firms' insurance costs. This is, we remind you, a solution that can benefit both owners *and* many workers, given that healthier workers can mean lower labor costs for firms and lower health insurance premiums. While people might object to this solution on fairness grounds, we stress that it is the type of discriminatory hiring policy that is likely to emerge when health insurance costs have been distorted by political factors, such as the ones we have discussed.

Another private policy solution can emerge if employers and employees recognize that low deductibles on health insurance policies are very expensive because they encourage workers to spend someone else's money, which motivates excessive demand for health care and leads to high insurance premiums. With a deductible of $5,000, the price of an additional dollar of insurance coverage for a forty-year-old male is measured as a tiny fraction of a cent (actually, .06 of a cent). However, when the deductible is $500, the price escalates to 55 cents. When the deductible is as low as $100, the price of an additional dollar of coverage rises to $2.14, a poor bargain for owners and their employees.[5]

There is an obvious solution to the health insurance problem that has the potential of not only introducing greater efficiency into the health care business but also improving the fairness of the system, without any policy change in Washington. This solution seeks to lower the private demand for health care by changing the incentives a firm's workers have to consume health care services.

As we indicated earlier, most firms that offer their workers health insurance provide "Cadillac policies," ones with small deductibles and broad coverage for just about everything that can go wrong, regardless of whether the person is responsible, through destructive behaviors, for the problems encountered. Each worker has little incentive not to use health care services for the slightest problem. Each worker has less incentive to incur the costs that might be required to eliminate or reduce their destructive behaviors.

Each worker can reason that if he or she were to cut back on personal usage of this or that health care service, the company's health insurance costs would not be materially affected. Certainly, the individual's health insurance premiums would not fall by the full value of the health care services not utilized. The savings from nonuse by any one individual, if the savings were detectable at all, would be spread over the entire group of workers through slightly lower premiums for everyone. In short, the individual would gain precious little from personal restraint in consumption of health care services.[6] Hence, the individual has little incentive to curb consumption.

If everyone in a firm were to cut back on health care usage, everyone could possibly gain in terms of reduced insurance premiums. The amount of savings could be substantial, and everyone would share in the savings of everyone else. However, as is so often true in business and, for that matter, all group settings, getting people to do what is in their best collective interest comes up against the prisoners' dilemma we have already discussed. If everyone else cuts back, there is still no necessary and compelling reason for any one person to cut back. The one person's reduction is, again, inconsequential, regardless of what all others do. And, we must add, as we have throughout the book, the larger the group, the more difficult it is to achieve collective cohesiveness of purpose.[7]

The basic problem for the firm should be seen as one of finding a means of giving all workers an incentive to cut their consumption. This can be done by raising the price of health care usage. But how can the price of health care be raised by the firm?

The economist John Goodman, head of the National Center for Policy

Analysis, recommends what appears to us to be a ingenious and practical solution, one that firms can, as some already have, institute on their own— to the benefit of the workers *and* the firm.

To see how Goodman's proposal might work, let us start with a few observations and assumptions. Many firms spend upwards of $4,500 annually per worker on health insurance, partly because, with the small deductible, workers have an incentive to consume a lot of health care. Let us assume that a basic *catastrophic* health insurance policy, one with a very large deductible of about $3,000 (meaning the insurance covers only major medical problems) can be purchased for each employee for a premium of $1,200 per year (which is, we are told, in the ballpark of the actual cost for a group policy).

Suppose also that the employer agrees to provide this catastrophic insurance policy and, at the same time, agrees to place in a bank reserve account (what Goodman prefers to call a "medical savings account" or "MSA") a sum of $3,000 each year per employee. The employer tells the employees that they can draw on that account for any medical "need" (with "need" being defined broadly). The workers can use the account, for example, to pay for visits to doctors, to cover the cost of hospital stays not covered by insurance, or to pay for a membership in a fitness center (reasoning that exercise can prevent the need for some medical care). Finally, suppose that the workers are also told that any balance remaining in the account at the end of the year can be applied to their individual retirement accounts, or even withdrawn at the end of the year to be used for any purpose that the workers choose.[8]

This proposal has a chance of lowering the employees' health care consumption because it requires that people pay for most routine medical care with their own money. Under common insurance arrangements, the additional cost of medical procedures (other than the patients' time) approximates zero (after the low deductible is met). Under the MSA proposal, the cost to the employee of the first $3,000 of medical care is exactly equal to the cost of the service. This is because the employee is made the *residual claimant* on the balance at the end of the year. Hence, we should expect that workers will more carefully evaluate their usage of medical services and cut back. After all, under the old system, the workers were probably consuming "too much," since the cost of doing so was close to zero.

We would expect that the gains from this new MSA system could be shared by both workers and their firms. We have already developed the example in a way that obviously benefits the firm. The firm was paying $4,500 a year for the insurance of each worker. Now, it must pay $1,200 for the insurance and $3,000 for the MSA, for a total of $4,200. The firm saves $300 per worker.

The workers, however, can also gain. Under the old arrangement, the workers were getting "paid" with insurance, not money. Under the MSA system, they are given a pot of money, $3,000, that they can use, if they choose, to buy insurance that will cover the first $3,000 of care. But many would not likely do that. They can self-insure just by holding onto the money and paying the first $3,000 in medical bills. However, they can, conceivably, also buy a variety of other things, from new televisions to education programs to additional days of vacation.[9] Accordingly, the additional money should enable workers to be better off by allocating the sum to higher valued uses.

Both workers and their employers can also gain because the new insurance arrangement can be expected to lower the worker's demand for use of the health insurance provided by their employers. Many workers will want to be careful not to use up their $3,000 account, as they become more careful shoppers of medical care. Workers will make use of the catastrophic insurance only in those situations when they have serious problems and little choice but to make use of medical care, which explains why the premiums for catastrophic insurance are so low.

By providing catastrophic health insurance coupled with a medical savings account, a firm can attract better workers by providing them with a more valuable compensation package at lower cost. Overall, we would expect the firms that adopt this type of insurance system to be more productive and competitive.

We hasten to add that our simple example does not reflect the full complexity of employment conditions most firms face. The problem managers will have in developing acceptance of the MSA is the cross-subsidies that are embedded in current insurance programs. Low-risk workers typically subsidize high-risk workers. Hence, we doubt that the firm's deposit into workers' MSA accounts would equal the insurance deductible, as we have assumed in our example. The reason is that many healthy (typically younger) workers are fortunate in that they often don't go to the doctor or hospital in any given year, and other workers have only modest medical expenditures in most years. They are subsidizing the unhealthy (typically older) workers who make extensive use of medical care. If the MSA deposit were to equal the deductible, this cross-subsidy would be wiped out, and the insurance company would very likely be hit with high bills from the high-risk workers while forgoing the payments from the low-risk workers. To make the MSA system work, the deposit would have to be limited, with the workers themselves sharing in some of the gains in the event they have limited expenses but also sharing in some of the risks if their expenses exceed their MSA deposits. Therein lies the rub, which will keep many firms from instituting the deal. However, some firms will still be able to find a reasonable compromise.

Managers must also be mindful of the possibility that MSAs can set up perverse incentives for some workers for some types of health care. Knowing that they will have to draw down their MSA account in order to cover annual physical examinations (and other preventive health care measures), workers can reason that MSAs increase the immediate cost of physical examinations. But that doesn't mean that the "cost" of physicals goes up for all workers. For some, the cost will rise; for others the cost will fall. Some employees, no doubt, will be more inclined to get physicals, since physicals can be paying propositions (or will have a lower *net* cost to them). That is to say, the employees can reason that the current outlay from their MSA for a physical can be more than offset by the reduction in MSA outlays in the future, since current physicals can catch health problems when they are minor. Thus, current physicals can lower the workers' health care expenditures from their MSA account over the long run.

However, we suspect that it's also a safe bet that some employees will not be able, or will not be willing, to make the required careful calculations or to properly assess the current and future benefits of physicals. Other workers may reason that most of their later health care expenditures for "major" problems that go undetected will be covered as the catastrophic health insurance kicks in. To accommodate these potential problems, employers can consider covering a portion of the current cost of physicals and other preventive measures. The employers can cover the added cost of subsidizing the physicals and preventive care with any reduction in their insurance premiums they get from encouraging physicals and preventive care. If there are no insurance savings from the subsidy, then it seems reasonable to conclude that either the problem of employees skipping preventive cares is not a problem or it is such a minor problem that the insurance companies see no need to reduce the insurance premiums of firms that encourage preventive care.

The main point is that managers must tread carefully in trying to accommodate problems with "preventive care." "Preventive care" can include not only physicals but an array of tests that have little useful medical value. If "preventive care" is defined too broadly and the subsidies are high, managers can be back in the prisoner's dilemma trap and face excessive health care and health care insurance expenditures, the net effect of which is health care benefits that are not worth the costs to the workers.

Has the MSA concept been tried, and has it worked? Yes, on both counts, although the trials to date do not correspond exactly with our example. One of the problems is that medical savings accounts are not tax deductible, which means that a part of the added cost that must be overridden with benefits is the greater tax payments workers and firms must pay. Nevertheless, several firms have already tried the system with beneficial effects:

- After Quaker Oats put $300 in each worker's medical saving account, the company's health care costs grew 6.3 percent a year. However, this was during a period when the health care costs of the rest of the country were growing at double digit rates.
- *Forbes* magazine encourages its employees to curb medical care

expenditures with a variation of the MSA, by paying workers $2 for every $1 of medical costs not incurred up to $1,000. This means that if a *Forbes* employee incurs medical costs of only $300 in a given year, the employee is rewarded with a check of $1,400 at the end of the year [2 x ($1,000 - $300)]. The magazine's health care costs fell 17 percent in 1992 and 12 percent in 1993, years during which other firms' insurance costs were rising.

• The utility holding company Dominion Resources gives each worker who chooses a $3,000 deductible on the company's health insurance policy a deposit of $1,650 a year. Since 1989, its insurance premiums have not risen, while the insurance premiums of other companies have risen by an average of 13 percent a year.

• Golden Rule Insurance Company gives each worker who selects a deductible of $3,000 a $2,000 MSA. In 1993, its health insurance costs were 40 percent lower than they would have otherwise been.[10]

We don't propose to tell firms what to do in their own particular circumstances for a very good reason: we obviously don't know the details of the individual circumstances of what we hope will be a multitude of business readers of this book. We can use our incentive-based approach to explore the *types* of business policies managers should consider and then adjust to fit the particulars of their circumstances. Moreover, our focus on health insurance is illustrative of insights that are relevant across a firm's entire fringe benefit package.

The important point of this chapter is by now an old one for this book: incentives matter. One of the several important reasons many workers pay high health insurance premiums is that they don't have much of an incentive to carefully evaluate their health care purchases. The best way to ensure that workers get the most out of their health care benefits is one that is as old as business itself: make the buyer pay a price that reflects the true cost of his or her decision.

Medical savings accounts are simply a means (perhaps one of many that have not yet been devised) of making workers potentially better off by making all employees pay a price for what they consume. This solution may not work for all businesses. Some worker groups may not want to be bothered with considering the costs of their behaviors. However, it appears that many firms and their workers have not considered policies like medical savings accounts because they have not realized that these plans have the potential to make everyone better off. These are the types of policies all managers should examine. Such policies can raise workers' welfare, the firm's stock prices, and the compensation of managers. Again, we return to what is by now an old point of the book: firms can make money not only by selling more of their product or service but also by creatively restructuring incentives in mutually beneficial ways.

9

Paying Workers' Education and Relocation Costs

Key Insight: 1) Firms generally pay for worker training when the market for the provided skills is highly restricted. Workers pay for their own training when there is a market for the acquired skills. 2) If housing is the only important cost difference between two company locations, then workers' income differences in the two locations should be less than the housing cost difference.

FIRMS PAY FOR SOME THINGS for their workers but not for other things. We consider in this chapter two employee expenses—education and relocation expenditures—that are sometimes covered and sometimes not covered by firms. Our examination of these issues will help us draw out underlying principles and the incentives that go with employer coverage of work-related expenditures.

We suspect that many readers have a personal interest in this chapter, since they may be contemplating getting an MBA or some other advanced business degree and hope their employers will cover the cost. Why would any firm train its workers at firm expense? The most general answer to that question is the same as the one given to explain why firms provide any fringe benefit: firms make available some forms of training because, by doing so, they can make money off their workers. Training enables employers to increase worker productivity, to expand the supply of labor—and to lower their wage bills. Employers sometimes offer training because their training cost is lower than the price the workers would pay have to pay if they got the training on their own. In such cases, employees gain by "buying" their training from their firm, "paying" through reduced wages. An important theme of this chapter is that employer-financed training is no gift; it is a mutually beneficial trade between employers and employees. Of course, there are more details to be added to those generalities.

Firms cannot usually avoid providing some training for their workers, since all workers must understand what is expected of them in their particular work environments. Workers must learn their companies' "cultures," lines of communication, and the division of decision-making authority. However, such observations on training hide the full complexity of the decision relating to whom—the firm or worker—should be expected to pay for it. In almost all work environments, the costs of the training are usually divided, which raises an interesting question: *Along what conceptual lines should we expect the training costs to be divided?*[1] To the student-reader, the relevant question is "When can I expect my boss to cover the cost of my education?" The employer-reader sees the issue differently: "When should I cover the cost of my workers' education and how can I at the same time avoid wasting money and sending the wrong incentive signals to my workers?"

Many workers—including many skilled craftsmen (plumbers and carpenters, for example)—pay for their own training.[2] Just about all undergraduate students and many, if not most, MBAs cover their own educational expenses. Many readers of this book know, through personal experience, that MBA students often pay for their graduate educations while they are still employed by their firms. At the same time, some firms pay the tuition and fees of their managers who go back to college for MBAs. Again, what divides the two groups, those workers who train themselves and those who don't?

We suggest that the division is, to an important degree, based on the nature of the human capital that is acquired. If the acquired human capital is "specific"—that is, the acquired skills are related to the particular needs of the worker's firm, which means that a worker with the acquired skills is not more attractive to other firms than any other worker—then the training is likely to be paid by the employer. The only reason the worker might cover the cost of such training for the development of specific human capital is that he or she might be promised a higher future income stream with the firm, and the present value of the additional income must be at least equal to the cost of the training.

However, the worker will rightfully fear that once he or she has incurred the training cost, the firm will renege on its part of the bargain. The fear can be especially relevant when the firm is financially unsound. Hence, the trained worker will be left without compensation for the cost incurred. The source of the basic problem is one that we have encountered before: *credibility*. Employers tend to pay for the training involving specific human capital when their promise to compensate workers in the future for the costs the workers incur is not always credible, or believable.

Of course, when the employer's promise is tolerably credible, workers may cover the costs for their own firm-specific education (for example, they may study the personnel manual or product manuals on their own time). Workers are most likely to cover such costs when they have been with their firms for a significant period of time and when the managers have a reputation for keeping their word.

Workers might also cover the costs of firm-specific training when workers can retaliate (at little expected cost) against their employers in the event that the employers renege on their agreements. For example, workers who use highly fragile pieces of test equipment might pay for their specific human capital in the knowledge that they can, with a low probability of detection, misuse or abuse the equipment under their control. In this case, the equipment can be viewed as the employer's bond. By putting workers in charge of equipment, the employer says, "If I ever fail to hold to my word, you can impose a substantial cost on me, perhaps more cost than I can impose on you." In such cases, employers should have no trouble getting their workers to do double time learning their jobs.

However, even in such cases, the problem of credibility does not evaporate. The workers' implied threat of destroying equipment must be believable. The more believable the threat, the more likely that the costs of firm-specific training can be incurred by the workers.[3] And in order for the threat to be believable, workers must be able to impose costs on the employer without being caught, fired, and prosecuted. This leads to the interesting conclusion that if workers in charge of fragile equipment can be "caught" misusing and abusing that equipment, it is more likely that the employers will have to cover the cost of their training. The worker's threat of retaliation will not be as forceful.

Nevertheless, we might expect employers to pay for specific human capital when they have a reputation for fair and honest dealing. As we have argued before, employers are likely to be less risk averse than their employees, since they may know more than their workers about how the workers' human capital will be utilized in the future. Employers can also spread the risk of the human capital investment over a large number of workers. By paying for their workers' specific human capital, employers can also reduce the employment risks of their workers. The training can be a way of saying to the workers: "We intend to keep you around for a while. Otherwise, we would not be investing in your skills. Once we give you the firm-specific training, you will be more valuable to us."

As a consequence, if the worker pays for the specific human capital, the greater income stream that the employer would have to provide the worker as compensation will have to include a risk premium, a cost that can be totally avoided by the employers who cover the training costs. Moreover, with the employers' heightened commitment to their workers' future employment, the workers should be expected to work for less than otherwise.

If the human capital is "general"—that is, the acquired education is wanted by a number of firms—then the workers will tend to pay for the training themselves. The reasoning is much the same as in the earlier case, aside from the fact that the positions of the employers and employees are reversed. Employers are, understandably, reluctant to pay for this type of training because the worker can then take the training and run. After training, the workers will be in greater demand by the market, which means that they can be hired elsewhere at a higher wage, a reflection of the market value of the acquired general human capital. Firms will, consequently, hold back on training their workers, since they can hire the trained workers from other firms without incurring the training costs. The firms that provide the training can see their market share erode as they are underpriced by their more savvy competitors.

Hence, when all firms resist providing the training but pay higher prevailing market wages for those workers with the training (for example, graduate degrees in business), workers will voluntarily secure the training. Their higher expected lifetime earnings will cover their training costs.

Again, the basic problem in the covering of the costs is one of credibility, but this time it is the workers' credibility that is at stake. If workers can, in some way, assure their employers that they will remain with the firms after receiving the general human capital, then the firm will most likely cover the training costs. The costs can, in effect, be repaid by the workers through the acceptance of a lower-than-market wage for some time into the future.

Workers can enhance the credibility of their commitments in a number of ways. They can, through years of service to the firm, develop a reputation with their employers that their word is their bond. Workers can also, as a part of their pay packages, have some of their compensation deferred until, for example, retirement. The workers can also agree to lose some or all of the deferred income if they decide to leave the company. The deferred income becomes, in effect, their bond, which is cashed in by their employer if the worker succumbs to the temptation of higher market wages and reneges on the training agreement. Here, naturally, the present discounted value of the deferred income that is subject to being lost by the workers must be greater than the cost of the general human capital they develop at the employer's expense.

Workers can also make formal contracts with their employers, including a requirement that the worker stay with the firm for some specified number of years or else have to repay the entire cost of the training and that the employee will not go into competition with his or her employer for some specified number of years.

One of the authors of this book got his Ph.D. funded in part by his first university employer (to the tune of half of his previous year's annual salary). However, he had to agree to stay with the university for two years for each year of graduate support. H&R Block, the tax preparation service, provides extensive training on the tax laws for its tax preparers, but it also requires them to agree not to go into the tax business outside H&R Block for several years.

Many MBA students who are reading this book as a part of a course assignment are probably having their graduate educations paid for by their employers. That may seem odd, given that most MBA degrees increase the marketability and pay of graduates, which might be a problem for employers who are paying the bills. Our logic leads us to believe that those students will tend to have the following characteristics:

1. The students whose employers are paying their educational tabs are probably older students who have been with their companies for a number of years. They have achieved some credibility with their employers, meaning that their promise to stay with the firm carries weight.

2. It may also be that those students have won what is, in effect, a "prize" in an ongoing "tournament" organized by their employers. The educational prize has been designed to increase all worker productivity in the firm. In cases in which employer-paid general human capital is the result of a tournament, the employer will not necessarily be upset if the new MBAs leave the firm. The education can still have been a paying proposition because the firm has already been compensated for the cost of the MBAs by greater overall worker productivity.

3. A number of MBA students have probably signed a document with their firm that carries the weight of a contract and that binds them to their firms for several years or requires them to repay the cost of their MBAs. Those students may have also agreed to repay the cost of those courses in which their performance does not meet some predetermined standard (for example, the students must receive a grade higher than a B). After all, the employer will want to make sure that the worker/students are no more predisposed to shirk in the classroom than they are on the job. By having the grade restrictions, the employer will ensure that the education has the potential of paying off.

4. The students are in managerial positions in which the benefits of having an MBA are likely to show up fairly rapidly in greater firm returns. The shorter the recovery period, the more likely the firm will cover the cost of managers' MBAs.

5. Some of the students will have permitted a portion of their past compensation to be deferred to some point in the future, which can act like a bond. In general, the employer will tend to select those workers for general education, like an MBA, who will incur a cost if they leave the firm.

6. The students will tend to come from the ranks of those who are on the executive "fast track" or seem likely to move up the corporate ladder within the firm. Employers have a natural interest in making sure that such fast-moving executives are well educated for

their future posts. However, there is another, complementary reason for their selection for MBA programs. If the "fast-track" students leave their firms upon graduation, they will give up their expected higher status and income streams within the firm.

7. Students are also likely to come from companies that promise to be around for a number of years. Financially shaky firms in highly unstable markets are going to be reluctant to pay for the cost of their workers' MBAs. Credit will, for them, be hard to come by. They will want their employees to use their own credit for their education, thereby freeing up the company's credit to finance company-specific investments that the workers would not invest in. Financially shaky companies will also not be able to count on being around to collect on the benefits of their workers' training. And the workers in such companies are not likely to have accepted much of their income in deferred forms or to strong expectations of long careers with their companies, factors that reinforce the tendency of workers to pay for their own MBAs.

All in all, as a rule, we would expect most of the students whose education costs are covered by their employers to be weighted toward heavily experienced managers who work for established, stable, and generally large firms.

However, we hasten to add that it is only a manner of speaking when we say that employers cover the cost of their workers' general human capital. In one way or another, we would expect workers to cover the cost, directly or indirectly. Firms that offer to fund the general education of their workers can expect to see, as a consequence, a greater supply of more qualified workers and a total wage bill that is lower than it would otherwise be.

Much training is, admittedly, a mix of firm-specific and general human capital components. The cost tends to be divided according to who—the employer or employee—benefits. The more firm-specific the training, the greater the share of the cost that will be borne by the employers. Nothing is free in business, especially education. No matter what the form, someone will pay the piper.

Major corporations are constantly hiring workers from one part of the country only to ask them to move to another, often more expensive part. They also often ask their employees to relocate, moving them from one location with a low cost of living to another location with a higher cost of living. Few question whether the firms ordering the movement should pay the cost of the moving van and travel. The trickier issue is whether companies need to fully cover the difference in the cost of living.

Well, you can imagine, our best answer is that "it depends." But we can do better than that. We can show that if the cost-of-living difference is spread across all goods bought by the relocating workers, the living cost difference will likely have to be covered. However, if the cost difference is concentrated in any one good, for example, housing, the firm can get by with increasing the relocating workers' salaries by less than the cost-of-living difference.

To see these points, which allow us to deduce general principles, suppose that your company's headquarters is in La Jolla, California, where the cost of housing is much higher than in many other parts of the country. Suppose, also, that you want to hire an engineer from Six Mile, South Carolina, where the cost of housing is relatively low. In fact, suppose you learn that the cost of housing in La Jolla is exactly five times the cost of housing in Six Mile. A modestly equipped 2,000-square-foot house in La Jolla on one-tenth of an acre, for example, sells for about $500,000. Approximately the same house can be bought in Six Mile (with much more land) for $100,000.

The engineer you are interested in hiring is earning $100,000 a year in Six Mile. In your interviews with the engineer, she tells you, quite honestly, that she likes the job you have for her. However, she also informs you that, after comparing La Jolla with her hometown, she has found that housing is the only major cost difference. There are minor cost differences for things like food, clothing, and medical care, but those differences wash out, especially after considering quality differences. The two areas are substantially different, she admits, but she values the amenities in the two locations more or less the same. La Jolla has the ocean close by, but Six Mile has the mountains just a short distance to the west.

However, the engineer stresses that at an interest rate of 8.5 percent, the $400,000 additional mortgage she will have to take out to buy a house in La Jolla that is comparable to the one she has back in Six Mile means an added annual housing expenditure for her of $34,000. Therefore, she wants you to compensate her for the difference in the cost of housing, which implies an annual salary of $134,000 (she also expects all moving and adjustment costs to be covered by your firm).

Do you have to accede to her demands? Many managers do. But, assuming that she is being truthful when she says that the amenities of the areas and the other costs of living balance out, the answer is emphatically no. You should be able to get by with paying her something less than $134,000 a year. There are two ways of explaining the no answer. First, you should recognize that the engineer is getting a lot of purchasing power back in Six Mile in one item, housing. If you gave her the demanded $34,000 in additional salary, she would be able to replace her Six Mile house in La Jolla. However, the money payment you provide is fungible, which means that she could buy any number of other things with the added income, including more time at the beach (than she spent in the mountains back in Six Mile) or more meals out (and there are far more restaurants in La Jolla).

The engineer would actually prefer the $134,000 annual income in La

Jolla to the $100,000 income in Six Mile, which goes a long way toward explaining why she is pressing the issue. If that is the case, she could also be happier in La Jolla with something less than $134,000 in salary than she is in Six Mile. To get her to take your job, all you need to do is make her slightly better off at your company's location than she is in Six Mile. Doing that does not require full compensation in the housing cost.

Another way of making the same point, but with greater clarity, is through the use of Figure 9.1, which contains a representation of the engineer's income constraints (or "budget lines," for those who remember their formal economics training) in the two locations. To make the analysis as simple as possible and to stay within the constraints of the two-dimensional graph, we consider two categories of goods: housing, which is on the horizontal axis, and a representative bundle of all other goods on the vertical axis.

The figure shows that with her $100,000 salary in Six Mile, the engineer can buy H_1 units of housing, if she spends all of her income on housing (which, admittedly, would never be practical), or she can buy A_1 bundles of all other goods, if she buys no housing (which is also not practical).

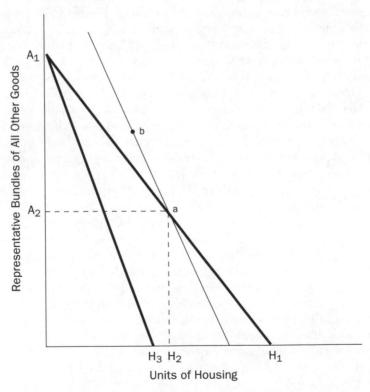

Figure 9.1 Choosing between Housing and Bundles of Other Goods

More than likely, the engineer will buy some combination of housing and all other goods, say, combination *a*, H_2 of housing and A_2 of all other goods.

If the engineer were to get only the same $100,000 in income in La Jolla, she would have to choose from the combinations along the inside curve, which extends from A_1 (meaning she could still buy, at the limit, the same number of bundles of all other goods) to H_3 (much less housing if only housing were bought). Clearly, the engineer would be unlikely to take an offer of $100,000, simply because there is no combination along A_1H_3 that is superior to combination *a* in Six Mile.

If you accede to her demand of $134,000 in annual income, her income constraint will be the thin line that is parallel to A_1H_3 and goes through *a*.[4] Clearly, she could be as well off in La Jolla at such a salary because she could still take combination *a*, but is she likely to do that?

The answer is not likely, because of the changes in relative prices. The price of housing in La Jolla is much higher than the price of housing in Six Mile, which is why her thin line income constraint is much steeper than her old income constraint (A_1H_1). The "law of demand" (the economist's analytical pride and joy), which says that price and quantity of goods and services are inversely related, can be expected to apply to housing in our example. Hence, the engineer will likely buy less housing and more of other goods, which implies a movement toward the vertical axis. She very likely will choose a combination like *b*. She will obviously be better off there because were she not, she would have remained with consumption bundle *a*. If she is better off, then you can cut her income below $134,000, taking part of the gains she would otherwise get.

We can't say, theoretically, exactly how little you can pay the engineer. All we can say is that, given the conditions of this problem, you don't have to pay her what she asks, $134,000. You might be able to pay her $130,000 or $125,000—something between $100,000 and $134,000. That's not much help, but it is some help, especially given that many of our previous students, when given the problem, think that the engineer's demands would have to be met.

The only time her demands would have to be met is if the added cost of living in La Jolla were distributed more or less evenly among all goods, not just concentrated in housing (which, for those who know both areas of the country, is where a sizable share of the cost differential actually is). This leads us to the conclusion that the more concentrated the cost differential between two areas, the less of the overall cost differential must be made up in the form of salary, or money income.

This leads to another useful insight. If you are looking for an employee who is living in an area where the cost of living is lower than yours, you can save on salary by looking where the lower cost of living is concentrated in a single good, such as housing. Conversely, if you are thinking about moving your plant to a "low-cost area" like Six Mile, don't expect to save in salaries an amount that is equal to the difference in the cost of living. You will be able to lower your salaries, but not by the entire cost-of-living differential.

Our problem has been relatively simple, given that we have assumed away many of the differences between the two locations. Candidates appraise locations differently. Some people like urban life and the Pacific coastal areas, and other people like rural areas and the mountains of the Appalachian region. Those comparative likes will ultimately go into determining the salary that you will have to pay. You may want someone who is competent to do the job you have, but that is not all that you will be concerned about. You might take someone who is less competent than someone else simply because that person appreciates the amenities of your area more than other more competent candidates, which means that you can get the targeted less-competent person for less money. That person may not produce as much, but he or she can still be more cost-effective.

When talking about their hiring processes, businesspeople almost always talk about getting the "best" person. We think there is some truth in what they say, but we also know that businesspeople are not always *completely* accurate. What business people should really want is the most *cost-effective* person, and that person is not necessarily, or even often, the most competent.

Our way of looking at the complicated process of business hiring is obviously not fully descriptive of what actually goes on. We can't deal with all the complications here and would not want to waste your time if we could. We are suggesting, perhaps, some new thoughts, drawn from the economic way of thinking. Our way of looking at the problem also provides guidance in the search for job candidates.

Consider a somewhat different problem. Suppose that you have located two engineers who are candidates for your job, and both live in places like Six Mile that have much lower housing costs than La Jolla. Which one do you choose in order to minimize the cost of the new hire to your firm? Of course, you would look at their credentials, but everyone knows to do that. You want the most productive person, but you also want to get the new hire for as little as possible.

Suppose that both candidates are equally productive. What do you do then? If housing is the biggest cost differential, you look at (or ask about) the sizes of their houses, and you should then choose to focus your recruiting efforts on the candidate with the smallest house. Why? You can get that candidate for a lower salary, everything else equal. He or she has a low preference for housing, as revealed by the choice of housing in Six Mile. The person who has a $100,000 house in Six Mile needs a salary of something less than $134,000 in La Jolla (to compensate for the additional $400,000 mortgage). The candidate who has a $300,000 house in Six Mile (which is likely to be the largest house for miles around) will need a salary of something less than $202,000 (to compensate for the $1.2 million in additional mortgage).

This point can also be made graphically. Consider Figure 9.2, in which lines A_1H_1 and A_1H_3 of Figure 9.1 are replicated. A person who buys combination *b*, including a relatively small house in Six Mile, would require an additional income of something less than the horizontal distance *ab* (which is the additional income that the person needs to duplicate in La Jolla his or her Six Mile house). A person who buys combination *d*, which includes a much larger house in Six Mile, would require an additional income of something less than *cd*. In the graph, *cd* is about twice the size of *ab*.

You might—just might—be able to find someone with a large house in a place like Six Mile who might take the lower offer. We are only using comparative house sizes as a useful guide for narrowing the search or, in other ways, lowering the cost of your search. The person with a mansion in Six Mile is, in short, likely to be a hard sell.

What you really want to find is someone who has a small house in a place like Six Mile and who is crazy about the beach and the moderate climate near the coast in southern California. Indeed, one of the often over-

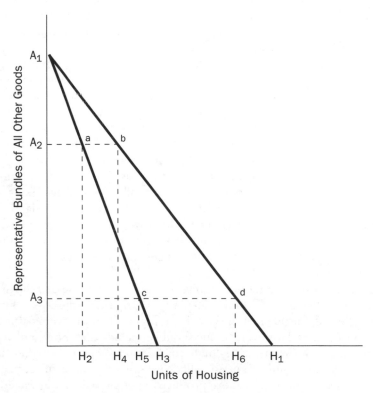

Figure 9.2 Choosing Employees Based on the Sizes of Their Houses

looked reasons for interview trips is not only to assess the person's likely ability on the job but also to assess how much he or she likes the new location relative to his or her established location. People who like your location relatively more can simply be had for less.

We need to return to the question we started with: Should relocating workers be compensated for housing cost differences? The answer is a qualified no. If housing makes up the main cost difference, then workers moving to a higher housing cost location would be too well compensated if the full cost of living difference were paid. He or she would take less. How much less is a problem that can be solved only through interviews and negotiations.

We caution, however, that our analysis flows from an unstated but important assumption—that the housing cost difference in the two locations reflects actual *cost* differences that are not offset by benefit differences. That is, many times, a questionable assumption. Property near the coast in southern California is much more expensive than housing in many (but not all) other parts of the country. It is also much more expensive than similar property fifty or a hundred miles inland but still in California. We must ask why property is so expensive and why so much of the cost difference is in the land the house sits on. An acre of land in Six Mile may cost no more than a few thousand dollars. On the other hand, an acre in La Jolla (at this writing) can cost upwards of a cool $1 million (a fact that explains why lots are measured in square feet)!

Why the difference? Obviously, the demand for property is much higher in La Jolla than in Six Mile, which implies that a lot of people must see some added benefits to being in La Jolla. This implies that, for a lot of people, the full difference in housing cost between the two areas need not be covered by added monetary income. A part of the difference in living cost is covered by the "nonmoney income" associated with the additional amenities in La Jolla that are not available in Six Mile.

The first rule of management (and other disciplines) has sometimes been stated as "Different strokes for different folks." In our discussion, we do not mean to suggest that everyone would want to live in La Jolla. If that were the case, the price of land in La Jolla would be far higher than it already is. We mean only to point out that "cost of living" differences cited by businesspeople are not always relevant cost differences because of benefit differences.

To make our point in more concrete terms, it may be true that the measured "cost of living" in La Jolla is 30 percent higher than the cost of living in Six Mile and, for that matter, 30 percent higher than the average for the rest of the country. However, no one should conclude that the cost of *doing business* in La Jolla (or any other "high-cost" area) is 30 percent higher than other parts of the country. The so-called cost of living can be offset in part by amenities and in part by more productive people who are attracted to the high-cost area. Many people with limited productivity will simply not be able to compete with their more productive counterparts in their search for property.[5] In making their employment decisions, firms need to keep these considerations in focus. They need to look carefully at what is implied by "cost of living."

III

EXECUTIVE INCENTIVES

10

Executive "Overpayments"

Key Insight: The higher up in an organization, the more executives are "overpaid," and that is intended and to be expected.

MANY WORKERS at the bottom of the typical large corporate pyramid grumble that their companies' executives are living off the fat of the workers' efforts and that the executives could not possibly be worth their overblown annual salaries (often running into the tens of millions). On the surface, those who grumble seem to have a point.

The CEO of Time Warner, for example, made more than $137 million during the last five years of the 1980s, more than half of which, $78 million, was received in one year alone (and $75 million of that year's compensation was in the form of a bonus provided as a reward for the merger of Time, Inc., and Warner Communications, which he helped orchestrate). However, a number of other CEOs made several tens of millions during the same period that the Time Warner CEO was pocketing his fortune.[1] The astronomical levels of executives' reported compensation prompt many workers and stockholders to argue that their companies would be better served if much of the executives' compensation and perks were used to pad the pay of lower-echelon workers.

At the same time, there is a less publicized trend in executive compensation packages—CEOs who risk all, taking no salary, with their reward tied totally to the prices of their companies' stock through grants of stock options. When he was appointed CEO of Ingram Micro, Inc., a California-based computer distributor, in 1996, Jerre Stead took a wage of zero in spite of the fact that Ingram was reportedly ready to pay him $1.5 million in salary and bonus.[2] Stead insisted on having the right to buy up to 3.6 million shares of Ingram (or 2.8 percent of the company) over five years. Since the company, at the time of Stead's appointment, was preparing to go public, Stead could end up a wealthy man in spite of having received no wage. One compensation expert estimated at the time that if Stead could triple the price of Ingram's stock over five years, his wealth could rise by a hefty $100 million—nothing to sneeze at, to say the least.[3]

No one should forget that compensation tied to stock prices can translate into no gain and all losses (measured in forgone salary opportunities). When Nelson Peltz became CEO of Triarc Companies, a conglomerate in food, chemicals, and energy, in 1993, he accepted an annual salary of $1 along with a bundle of stock options. As of 1996, Peltz had worked for nothing; he had been unable to exercise his stock options, since the price of Triarc stock had fallen by as much as 40 percent since the start of 1994.[4]

You can bet that some CEOs fiercely defend their high incomes, especially when their pay is dependent on their firms' performance. Former Scott Paper CEO Al Dunlap, renowned for revitalizing dying companies with ruthless cuts in jobs, wages, and perks, exudes pride for the $6.5 billion in additional wealth he made for Scott shareholders by radically downsizing and restructuring Scott: "My $100 million [in compensation, attributable in large measure to stock options he received and to additional stock he bought when he took over the head of the company] was less than 2 percent of the wealth I created for all Scott shareholders. Did I earn that? Damn right I did. I'm a superstar in my field, much like Michael Jordan in basketball and Bruce Springsteen in rock 'n' roll."[5] He adds that if there is criticism, it should be leveled against his predecessors at Scott, who were running the company into the ground. His central admonition, all too easily forgotten, is, "You cannot overpay a good CEO and you can't underpay a bad one. ... If his compensation is not tied to the shareholders' returns, then everyone's playing a fool's game."[6]

We agree that some workers have a complaint worthy of serious reflection. Many corporate leaders in this country are extraordinarily well paid, and, we agree, some are probably "overpaid" (in a particular sense to be defined later), but not always for the reasons lower-level workers give. Even Dunlap acknowledges that "only a handful of chief executives are worth the big bucks they are paid. Many are grossly overpaid and should be fired and then replaced by CEOs whose pay is strictly performance-based."[7] Kenneth Mason, former president of Quaker Oats, has much the same low opinion of the compensation packages received by many corporate heads: "It is a sad commentary on the intellectual vigor and financial discipline of the U.S. business community that so many corporate executives are receiving entrepreneurs' rewards for doing bureaucrats' jobs."[8] Moreover, it appears to be the case that the extent of executive "overpayment" is related to how much members of the board of directors have invested in the companies they are asked to monitor: the greater the board members' financial stake in their companies, the less likely the executives will be "overpaid," with the converse equally true.[9]

However, it remains a safe bet that in many companies the higher up the corporate ladder the executive is, the greater the gap between his or her individual worth to the company and the pay received. However, it does not follow that the overpayments serve no useful purpose for the company or that any intentional policy of overpayment should be abandoned in favor of higher salaries for nonexecutives. Such a change in pay policy can have hidden perverse consequences for the company and its lower-level workers.

In making those points, and in showing the underlying logic, we do not mean to suggest that companies do not make mistakes in executive compensation that should be rectified. That would be a silly position to take. Business in all of its dimensions is filled with mistakes. We only mean to argue that there are good reasons for many corporate pay policies that result in executive pay that exceeds the individual's marginal contributions to company income and profits.

Some of the high pay of executives is a reflection of intentional incentives included as a part of executives' pay contracts. Their pay is sometimes directly tied to corporate profits or to their companies' stock prices. Clearly, there have been some cases in which executives' pay has risen as firm profits have sunk and losses emerged. However, research shows a positive tie between company performance and executive pay. Indeed, the finance professor Sherwin Rosen found that top executive pay rises between 1 and 1.25 percent when the company's rate of return (as identified on the company's accounting statements) rises by 1 percent, not a bad deal for stockholders, given that most top executives' pay represents a minor fraction of company income.[10]

Much of the very high level of compensation is related to the fact that top executives are often given stock options, or the right to buy stock at a specified price, which means if the stock price goes up, the executive can do what everyone in the market wants to do, buy low and sell high. The executives' pay is as high as it is simply because their companies did well.

Critics of executive pay contend that a firm's performance over time is dependent upon the actions of a number of people who are not always in the executive suite. However, we should expect executives to evaluate how much they contribute to the company, and their assessments should work into the pay deals that they demand. Executives who are considering the top position in a company and who believe a company will do well regardless of their contribution should be eager to work for that company, and the competition among the potential executive recruits should check the extent of the stock options and the price the executives will have to pay for the stock in the event the options are exercised. Competition will constrain the deals that are made. Many executives are extraordinarily well paid simply because their companies did far better than anyone could have expected when their pay deals were negotiated.

There is a good reason for concentrating pay incentives (especially those related to stock prices) on top-level managers: they are the ones who control the most resources, whose decisions can have the greatest impact with firms, and who can be motivated by tying their pay to firm performance. Workers at the bottom of the corporate pyramid typically control few firm resources, and their *individual* actions (because each person is one of many similarly situated workers) are often immaterial to the performance of the entire firm. As a consequence, although we do not wish to be caught saying never, we stress that ties between pay of lower-level workers and firm performance may have little to no effect on the overall performance of the firm. This means that as pay incentives are extended down the corporate ladder, we should expect to see the extensions have progressively less impact on the performance of the company and, hence, the stock price, predictions that have been supported, albeit weakly, by empirical work.[11]

Many firms do have profit-sharing plans in which all workers share in the earnings of their companies. For example, Levi Strauss announced in 1996 a new incentive plan for all of its 37,500 employees that would, at the end of six years, reward workers with a bonus of as much as a year's pay if the company's profit goals were achieved. The plan could cost the company as much as $750 million in shared profits, but the company must be betting that the incentive plan will increase profits by at least $750 million over what they would otherwise be in 2002.[12]

The fact that profit-sharing plans are available for many workers, along with our logic outlined earlier, suggests that we should revise our conclusion to the following: the lower down the corporate pyramid the worker, the more tenuous or limited the connection between compensation and overall firm performance. The Levi Strauss incentive proposal may sound like a lot, but much less is at stake than might be initially thought, since the workers will not receive the bonuses for six years and, even then, the bonuses may not match a full year's pay. If a full year's pay is paid at the end of six years, the annual bonus in present value terms can average less than 10 percent of a worker's annual pay over the next six years.[13] If the bonus is further discounted by the probability that not all of it will be received (due to employee resignation or firing), the expected value of the bonus can easily be a minor fraction of the salary.

Providing workers with stock options or even shares of stock is a way of giving them a stake in their companies and an incentive to do what the owners want them to do: work hard to increase firm profits and, thus, the price of the stock. If the firm's stock price goes up, the workers can gain by exercising their stock options (buying at the stipulated price of, say, $10, and selling at the going market price of, say, $22) or just selling the stock (which they may have earlier been granted instead of a wage increase of $10) for $22. However, while the practice of giving workers some stake in their firms through shares of stock appears to have been growing in the 1990s, it is still not widespread among major U.S. companies. Only about 3 percent of the top 1,000 U.S. corporations granted *all* workers some stock stake, either in the form of options or outright shares. Between 8.5 percent and 13 percent provided a stock stake to more than 60 percent of their employees.[14]

Executive income can be far more dependent on built-in incentives. However, it does seem reasonable to conclude that if strong incentive pay for executives has its intended effect, lower-level workers can also be better off than they would have been otherwise, since their incomes and job security are enhanced by executive decisions that lead to higher profits and stock prices. Lower-level workers, in other words, can have an interest in seeing their bosses' incomes, but not necessarily their own, strongly tied to firm performance. And the evidence does suggest that when the pay (salary plus bonuses) is evaluated across firms with varying rates of return on common stock through time, a positive relationship is evident: the higher the rates of return, the higher the executive pay. In addition, executive *total* compensation (including salary, bonuses, and benefits from stock options and stock grants) appears to be strongly related to firm performance. The greater the firm performance, the greater the total compensation of executives.[15]

The economics professor Kevin Murphy found that for executives who worked for companies that in the 1974—1979 period had *negative* rates of return greater than 20 percent, the average annual change in executive pay was a mere half percent.[16] Murphy also found that pay increased with greater rates of return, reaching a nearly 11 percent for those executives whose companies had positive rates of return greater than 40 percent. In the period from 1981 through 1984, the pay of the executives working for companies with rates of return greater than 40 percent increased by 17 percent.[17]

Furthermore, Murphy found that the changes in the prices of the executives' stock holdings could dwarf the changes in their compensation (or even their absolute levels). Executives who worked for companies with greater than *negative* 20 percent stock price returns suffered an annual average decline in the value of their stock holdings of nearly $3 million (at the same time that their pay averaged $506,700). Those who worked for companies with a greater than positive 40 percent stock return realized an increase in the value of their stock holdings of $3.7 million (at the same time that their average pay was $494,300).[18]

Professors Michael Jensen and Kevin Murphy found that every $1,000 increase in stockholder wealth corresponds to just over two cents more in CEO median annual cash pay but a $3.25 increase in median executive wealth,[19] a finding that caused one of the authors to conclude in the

Harvard Business Review that "top executives are worth every nickel they get."[20] Critics, however, may rightfully charge that top executive pay is not sufficiently dependent on firm performance and should be dramatically raised, as Kenneth Mason has argued.[21] The relatively weak connection between the fortunes of executives and those of stockholders may be explained by the fact that CEOs can be easily monitored, evaluated, and dismissed by their board members, but firings appear to be used very sparingly as a means of discipline.[22]

Jensen and Murphy suggest that the weak connection between CEO compensation and firm performance and the very limited use of firings may be attributable to the fact that public disapproval of high salaries (and the attendant political considerations) may impose artificially low upper bounds on CEO compensation. Hence, in order to attract CEOs (by ensuring that the expected value of the compensation package is maintained), the boards have to limit pay cuts and, for that matter, firings.[23] Still, the market appears to believe in the future value of current announcements of executive pay plans that tie the executives' long-term compensation to the long-term performance of firms through outright stock grants, stock options, and bonuses. According to one team of researchers, firms that install incentive plans for their executives can expect to see their stock prices jump by 2.4 percent within two months over and above what they would otherwise have been.[24]

Surely, however, direct incentives for executives do not explain all of the sometimes exorbitant levels and growth of some executives' pay.[25] Stockholders and their boards must be concerned with incentives for lower-level workers as well when they set executive compensation levels. As noted, executive compensation can be used to give aspiring executives within the firm an incentive to work hard.

The high pay of executives can be *partially* explained by the fact that the people who become executives generally get their positions because they have demonstrated that they are more capable than other workers. Moreover, a move to a higher-ranking position can actually increase the productivity of the manager. As Rosen has observed, "Scarce talents of the most capable managers are economized by assigning them to positions at or near the top of the largest firms, where their ability is magnified to greater effect by spreading it over longer chains-of-command and larger scales of operations. This is what sustains high average earnings of top level executives in large firms and also implies that firm size and executive pay should be positively related," which has been shown to be a pervasive feature of executive pay.[26] Hence, they not only deserve higher salaries; they must be paid higher salaries because, if they are not, other firms will hire them away.

Once someone is promoted to the executive ranks, his or her pay must also go up significantly at the time of the promotion simply because the executive becomes more visible to the rest of the relevant business community. Before the promotion, other firms may be unaware of the executive's abilities. After all, he or she may be toiling away with a team of other workers where his or her abilities can be difficult to evaluate, especially by outsiders. By promoting a person, a company announces to other firms that it has found someone in its midst who is unusually productive and might even be on a fast track to the top office in the firm. Outsiders no longer have to incur the costs associated with searching through a large group of some other firm's workers to find productive managerial talent. They can "cherry pick," limiting their picking to the "cherries" identified by others.

The gap between the pay of those who are promoted and that of those under them, which can be substantial, can be partially explained not so much by actual productivity differences as by the fact that the more productive workers at the bottom of the corporate ladder have not yet been "discovered," and, just as in the case of aspiring actors, managers understand—or should understand—that being "discovered" can be as important in rising through the ranks as actually acquiring the skills to undertake higher level jobs. Not all people with the acquired skills (many of whom may be reading this book) will make it onto the upper rungs of the corporate ladder.

Hence, outsiders can be expected to target those who are promoted elsewhere, competing with the newfound executive's own firm. Put another way, a firm must make promotions count in terms of added pay and all the trappings that can go with higher office as a defense against "executive raiders" intent on minimizing their search costs for managerial talent.

Rising through the ranks probably requires a dose of luck and political acumen, with both considerations having little to do with actual productivity, as many people would measure it. Many workers no doubt grumble about executive pay with cause. They, the grumblers left behind, may in fact be more productive than some of the people above them; they just haven't met with the requisite measure of luck. Also, being discovered often requires work at getting oneself noticed through, for example, self-promotion, and the time devoted to such activities can be time taken away from improving one's managerial skills. Moving up the ladder on the fast track requires not just managerial skills per se; it requires some *optimum* combination of skills and self-promotion and schmoozing. There are no doubt many workers left behind who are indeed more productive than those who are promoted; they just never found the right use for their time. In effect, they have acquired too much in the way of basic skills and not enough of, say, political savvy.

Just because pay differences between the ranks may be partially based on luck, it does not follow that the differentials should be eliminated, even if they could given competitive forces. All corporations can be expected to do is establish promotion and pay policies that will enable them to achieve a reasonable measure of success—not perfection—in picking the "best" people for higher-level jobs. If they sought perfection in the selection process, companies would surely fail, simply because mistakes are usually unavoidable in most complex business/employment environments. In their quest for perfection, companies would also incur excessive search costs, making them uncompetitive vis-à-vis other companies that were willing to accept occasional mistakes.

The pay of executives may also be "excessive" for another reason involving the difficulties of selecting managers. When people are hired at the bottom of the corporate ladder, upper-level managers may have only a rough idea as to whom among the large group at the bottom are worthy of higher ranks. They can, for example, check references and look at their workers' educational records—what schools they attended and what grades they made—but such factors are not always highly correlated with a willingness to work hard and smart in given corporate environments.

How can upper-level managers motivate lower-level workers to reveal how hard and smart they are, willing and able to work? Piece-rate pay and two-part pay contracts, which we have covered, can help. So can bonuses. Another incentive system used is an executive "tournament," which is held among lower-level workers, with the "prize" being a promotion to the next rung on the corporate ladder.

Any overt or covert announcement of a tournament can have two effects. First, it can cause the workers to compete among themselves for the prize. All workers can work harder for the prize with the added value being claimed by upper managers and owners who announce the competition.[27] Second, aware of the competition among employees, workers who might be hired at the lower levels in the firm with the tournament will self-select. Those who think that they will not "win" and who will therefore suffer the cost of the competition but will not receive a "prize" will self-select out of employment with the firm.

Participation in the tournament is therefore likely to be concentrated among those who have a degree of confidence in their abilities. Workers who self-select into the competition can then compete in the knowledge that their cohorts at work will, on average, be more productive than they would have been had the tournament not been held. Their *expected* lifetime pay with the firm should, accordingly, mirror the higher expected productivity of the workers hired.

In order for the tournament to have the intended effect, the pay upon promotion (or winning) must be attractive to all who compete at the lower levels—after the higher pay is discounted by the probability that any one person will receive it. In group settings, most reasonable worker/competitors will likely assume that the probability of their being selected for the promotion is significantly below 1.0 (or certainty). After all, when they start the contest, the competitors will have only limited information on just how hard and smart their cohorts will apply themselves. And pay and the probability of promotion do appear to be inversely related. According to one study, pay increments with promotions increase substantially between managers at adjacent levels within corporations, and the pay increments when promoted vary inversely with the prospects of being promoted, which should be expected: the stiffer the competition (and the lower the prospects of being promoted), the greater the pay increase must be in order to maintain the drive among managers to be promoted.

Those participating in tournaments should demand a higher expected pay because tournaments are by nature "games," meaning that the outcome is dependent upon how the other participants play, or seek the prize. This aspect of tournaments necessarily introduces some variance in the outcomes, which implies unavoidable uncertainty into how individual participants should "play" (or compete). The pay should be expected to compensate the participants for the problems associated with the inherent risk and uncertainty (vis-à-vis other pay systems—for example, piece rate—that simply require the workers to maximize their output without consideration to what other workers do).[28]

The value of the prize (which includes an "overpayment") must therefore be some multiple of the total costs each worker can be expected to expend in seeking the promotion. The lower the probability of any one worker receiving the prize, the greater must be the value of the prize—the overpayment, or the gap between the promoted person's actual worth to the company and the pay (plus fringes and perks). If the gap were nonexistent, then the prospects of promotion would not have the intended impact a tournament is supposed to have on all workers' productivity.[29]

Put another way, promoted workers usually get substantial pay increases with larger offices and more perks not because they necessarily "deserve" all that they get but because the firm may want to validate the tournament and to hold other tournaments in the future. The executive's "overpayment" is covered by the firm not so much by what the chosen executive actually does (although, as noted, that can be an important factor) as by the added output generated by the competition among all those who seek promotion.

Why is it that pay rises so fast as people are promoted through the ranks? Again, there is, no doubt, some correlation between rank and abilities, although it is by no means perfect. The higher up the ladder, the greater the abilities of executives—as a rule. However, we suspect that pay differences have a lot to do with probabilities. Someone at the bottom looking up the ladder can figure that the probability of his or her actually making it through the rungs falls the further up the ladder he or she looks. A worker at the bottom might give him or herself a probability of 20 percent of making it to the first rung, given the few people in the immediate work group, but the worker might give himself or herself a probability of .001 percent of making it to the top rung (and even that probability might be overstating the prospects of success), since he or she might be competing with everyone in the organization and those who may join the organization in the future. And the worker is likely to reason that the greater the number of workers at the bottom and the greater the number of rungs in the corporate ladder, the smaller the probability of reaching the top rung.

Executive pay, in other words, must rise disproportionately to productivity just to account for the declining probability of any one person making it through the rungs. The purpose of the progressively larger "overpayments" as one moves up the ladder is not necessarily so much to promote social justice among workers, although such considerations are rarely totally overlooked either, as it is to properly motivate all workers who are contemplating moving through the corporation.

Again, why is it that the pay gap between top executives and workers at the bottom has been growing over the past decade or so? Popular wisdom has it that the growing gap can be attributable to insane corporate policies that are stacked in favor of executives by board members who were appointed to their positions to do what they have done, that is, to raise the income of the executives at the expense of owners and lower-order workers. According to Graef Crystal, a prominent critic of corporate pay, boards of directors not only raised their CEO pay by an average of 21 percent in 1995 (several times the rate of inflation), but they raised pay for reasons that are hard to identify. Ten percent of the variation of pay among top executives can be explained by company performance: better performing companies tend to pay their CEOs better. Twice that much (21 percent) of the variation can be explained by company size: larger firms tend to pay their CEOs better. That leaves 69 percent of the variation unexplained.[30]

There is always a hint of truth in such claims, but we aren't willing to concede that none of the unexplained variation (just because it isn't picked up in regression analysis) in corporate pay has a rational basis. Corporate boards do some pretty stupid things from time to time (which market pressures force them to correct or suffer the consequences). However, we suspect the growing gap has something to do with the actual impact of executives on corporate earnings, since their decisions can be more important in a rapidly changing global economy, and with the declining probability that workers will make it to the executive suite, given the "flattening" of corporate command-and-control organizational structures. The probability that a particular person will become a chief executive officer has simply gone down at the same time that the risks associated with being an executive has gone up.

We should also not overlook the prospect that the high pay of top executives may be a means of driving down the pay of the workers at the bottom. Indeed, that can be the purpose of the overpayment of the people at the top. By raising the pay of executives, the directors can attract more people to the firm who hope that they will eventually make it to the top and receive the overpayments. In this sense, there is not only a gap between higher-level and lower-level worker pay; there is also a gap between what the lower-level workers are paid and their expected pay, and the gap between the actual and expected pay of lower-level workers can expand as the gap between the actual pay of the lower-level and higher-level workers increases.

All of this means that workers may indeed be right when they complain that their chief executive could not possibly be worth the zillions that he or she makes. "Worth" is not necessarily the point of the pay. Properly aligning the incentives of workers throughout the organization is the point that should not be overlooked.[31]

The overpayments provided executives can, of course, be fortified by market competition for executive talent. All firms interested in maintaining proper incentives can compete with each other for executive talent, but their competition can be constrained by the fact that they cannot wipe out their overpayments. If they did, then incentives, and production, throughout their firms could be impaired.

Executives can also be "overpaid" because, as we argued earlier, they are in positions of trust, and they have command over large amounts of firm resources. Typically, the higher up the executive, the greater the resources that the executives can direct. Firms want to make sure that the executives do not violate their fiduciary responsibilities. One method of discouraging violations is to ensure that the executives incur a significant cost if they are ever fired, and that objective can be accomplished partially by paying executives more than they are "worth" in the market. Hence, we can conclude that the overpayment will be related to the probability of executives' misdeeds being detected as well as the damage that the executive can do to the company if he or she ever succumbs to the temptation to violate his or her responsibilities. In general, the lower the probability of detection, the greater the need for a penalty and pay premium; the greater the damage that the executive can do, the greater the pay premium.

Overall, what the stockholders want to do is align the private interests of their chief agents—the executives—with their own interests, which is maximizing the value of their investment portfolios, and stockholder portfolios can include shares in a variety of companies. As we have noted before, stockholders may naturally be less risk averse than their executives, who can have a high percentage of their own personal portfolios—including their human (managerial) capital—tied up in the firms they manage. Executives may understandably worry about the failures of their particular companies, which can undercut the market value of their human capital. Therefore, shareholders are better off when executives face incentives that reduce their reluctance to take risks.

Stock options are a means of eliminating some of the downside risks managers face. The executives gain only if the stock price rises and do not lose if it falls. Often, the high levels of executive compensation reflect the exercise of stock options, which were made a part of their contracts simply as a means of encouraging them to take calculated market risks that their bosses, the stockholders, want them to take.

That is to say, executives may be the highest-paid workers in a firm because more of their pay tends to be at risk; they need extra compensation for accepting the extra risk. And stockholders want it to be that way, given the considerable discretion top executives have and the influence they can have over firm performance. Lower-ranking managers will not have as much discretion, nor will they likely have as much influence over firm performance. Their bosses will largely check their actions. Hence, lower-ranking managers can be expected to have a smaller share of their pay at risk, leading to a smaller risk premium than the top executive receives.

We don't want to overlook the fact that executives, like lower-level workers, can shirk their responsibilities and engage in opportunism, one form of which is using the powers of their office to appoint board members who are willing to go along with pay increases for the executives. This form of overpayment can be disparaged for many reasons, but it remains a reflection of the principle/agency problem that has been at the heart of most topics in this book. Such "overpayments" may, in some sense, be "wrong," but we are not so sure that anything can or should be done about *all* such overpayments. Eliminating all such forms of opportunism is simply impossible, and the best stockholders and boards can be expected to do is to minimize this source of overpayment. All we can say is that we should expect that the more difficult it is to monitor executives, the more likely they will be overpaid, or the greater the overpayment.

Executive compensation as a *process* is far more complicated than simply setting a compensation package for executives that is, for example, heavily weighted toward rewarding executives for their companies' performance, whether measured by the bottom line or by stock prices. It may be a great idea, for example, to tie compensation to stock prices. Executives will like that—so long as they expect the price of the stock to rise. The problem is not the concept, but the application of the concept in practice. Any compensation scheme that is installed can be uninstalled, and executives can be expected to work for a change in their pay-for-long-term-performance scheme if their stock prices start going down. To the extent that the compensation scheme is changed (or can be changed), it can lose much of is potential incentive benefits. Executives can figure that they need not press for performance because they can, at some future point, shift their compensation from stock to salary. (The problem of adjustments in executive pay is hardly trivial; one study in the 1970s and 1980s found that the compensation incentive plans in the country's 200 largest industrial companies had an average life of 18 months.[32]) Moreover, stockholders may not want to *always* hold firmly to their pay-for-long-term-performance pay scheme, since they may begin to lose valuable executive talent when the price of their stock nosedives. This is especially true if stock prices fall because of economic conditions beyond the control of the executives.

Therein lies an applicable principle: compensation schemes should have some rigidity and should be changed only when firm performance cannot be attributed to management. It goes without saying that the more control executives have over their own compensation, the less effective will be any set of incentive plans. Then again, any rule that allows payment adjustments attributable to forces external to the firm leaves open the prospects for executive opportunism; executives can claim that firm performance is "someone else's fault." Therein lies an even more basic principle: boards of directors and their appointed compensation committees must be willing to stand tough. There's simply no escaping the need for tough judgments in business. Otherwise, the firm risks being a takeover target.

There is an emerging trend in executive compensation that often rankles even some of the more staunch defenders of high executive pay: the growing tendency of firms to provide their executives with huge payoffs when their firms fail and/or the executives are fired. John Walters, whom AT&T employed as president with an eye toward later making him CEO, was granted a payoff of nearly $26 million after the board reneged on its agreement to promote him. The board members concluded that he was not up to the job he was hired to do. Michael Ovitz walked out Disney's door after only fourteen months on the job with a $90 million payoff, while Gilbert Amelio left Apple Computers after only seventeen months with a $7 million payoff.[33]

How can such payoffs be justified, if at all? Maybe the payoffs are a form of board graft, which is often implied when the payoffs are mentioned in the media. If that were all there was to it, it would appear to us that the firm that systematically did such things would increase its risk of becoming a takeover target.

We suspect that there is more to the matter than greed and graft, although we don't want to totally dismiss such concerns. People and firms are imperfect, which has been a major theme of this book. We simply note that the payoffs can provide benefits for the company, mainly in the form of avoiding costly suits from fired executives. The payoffs may be high, but still lower than the realistic options. The payoffs also enable the company to move swiftly —that is, to move failed executives out the door with a view toward replacing them with talented people who can do a better job. The firms can avoid the considerable damage an executive can do— through action or inaction—to the firm if the payments are not made and the executive lingers in the job for months while the board attempts to negotiate a more modest payoff.

But, often the payoffs are nothing more than payments that fulfill the terms of the executive's contract with the firm. Knowing that they can be fired in short order at the will of the board, smart executives have negotiated the dismissal payoffs. The payoffs are simply the "tit" in "tit-for-tat" deals. In making their employment deals, firms must realize that they will invariably be seeking to pull an executive away from a known employment circumstance, which may carry with it substantial security because of the record the executives has established, and place the executives in a less well knowm and, therefore, more insecure employment circumstances. The firms can expect to pay, in one way or another, for the added insecurity the firm effectively asks the executives to assume (and the greater the insecurity or risk of being fired, the greater the added payment, a force that will cause firms pause in its willingness to act recklessly). Also, in agreeing to the new employment deals with dismissal rewards, the executives have, in effect, possibly given up something in the way of the level of their compensation, if they are able to stay with the firm, for the security that comes with the dismissal payoffs. The firm also benefits in such deal, since it knows what the limits of the payoff will be in the event the firm elects to fire the executive. Presumably, the bargain is expected to be mutually beneficial to both the executive and firm.

Firms often make mistakes; they end up agreeing to pay deals for executives who prove to be "losers," but firms are in the business of taking such risks. The contract with any given executive can be seen as nothing more than a risky investment (or business venture) among an array of similarly risky investments (or ventures). This means that executive payoffs must be judged not by how they work in individual cases of miserable failures involving outlandish payoffs but in terms of how the "portfolio" of such deals payoff in the aggregate. This is to say that AT&T and Disney, and their stockholders, may have lost handsomely in the cases of the fired executives already cited. However, the *approach* the companies have taken may be working very profitably, a fact that is often not mentioned in news reports of the lavish payoffs firms provide their failed executives.

There is another justification for the executive payoffs that seeks to overcome the different circumstances of the executives and stockholders. Members of the board can understand that executives might be more reluctant to pursue risky ventures that offer the prospects of high returns than are the stockholders. After all, the stockholders can have highly diversified investment portfolios, with shares owned in a number of companies (or mutual funds). The stockholders also do not have their human capital invested in the firms they own. The executives are indeed different. By taking the jobs that they do, they invest their human capital in a given firm, and they put their human capital at risk. Because of the extent to which their compensation package may be heavily weighted toward stock and stock options in their firm, the executives can easily have a portfolio that is less diversified than the firm's stockholders. The lack of diversification can be a important pressure on the executive to "play it safe." The executives can lose their careers with risky investments; as we have seen, they may not gain nearly as much as their stockholders/residual claimants in the event that risky investments actually pay.

The dismissal payoffs for executives can simply be a means by which firms can encourage executives to take more risk and thereby more closely align executive interests with stockholder interests. With the guaranteed payoffs, the firms are saying to their executives, "If you fail, some of your loss will be covered. Hence, we encourage you to take risks." The payoffs can also send a message to executives who are contemplating taking the top jobs: "If you fail, you will also be covered, at least in part." Accordingly, firms that do not make the payoffs on dismissal may be hiking their costs of recruiting executives and/or may have to settle for less qualified executives.

Research shows that executive pay rises with the size of the firm. The larger the firm, the greater the executive pay. According to one study of executive pay at seventy-three large corporations in the United States between 1969 and 1981, when a firm's sales rise by 10 percent its executives will, on average, receive 2 to 2.5 percent more in annual salary plus bonus, an estimate remarkably close to the sales-pay relationship found by the researcher for the 1937—1939 and 1967—1971 periods.[34] Other studies on executive pay in the United States and Great Britain have found similar ties of executive pay to firm assets; when firm assets grow by 10 percent, executive compensation grows by 2.5 percent to 3.2 percent (which may explain why executives often seek to expand into areas that have nothing to do with their core line of business, which may dampen profits but raise executives' pay).[35]

We don't know whether these findings are good or bad for the firms involved. On the one hand, the rise in pay may reflect the rise in the ability of executives to engage in opportunism, but it may also reflect a growth in the actual productivity of executives as they move up the corporate ladder. The more productive managers are, the more likely they are to be promoted, and any move up the ladder necessarily increases the manager's productivity simply because his or her actions radiate down the corporate hierarchy through more people.[36] On the other hand, the rise in pay may reflect an intentional policy to encourage lower-level workers to work harder and smarter. As firms grow, they need higher pay for executives in order to enhance incentives and to get more production from workers down the hierarchy (or to offset the tendency of workers down the hierarchy to shirk as the firm expands).

All we can say in closing is that high executive compensation often makes more economic sense than commentaries in the popular press would lead readers to believe. Stockholders, board members, and upper management need at least to think about how they can manipulate their executive pay structure, up and down the hierarchy, as a means of making money for their firms. Higher executive pay can mean more work and output from people who have not yet been chosen for the executive suite, and from others most of whom will never be chosen (although many will make every effort to be chosen).

At the same time, the executives themselves must be mindful of the fact that market forces are also afoot that can ultimately check what they can do and how much they are paid. Executives whose companies do poorly because of their misguided decisions and opportunism can anticipate that their personal market value will suffer. Their firms may also be subject to takeover; bright investors can buy the firm, replace the existing management team with a more competent team, and then sell the firm at a higher price. The poor performance of one management team can represent a profitable opportunity for its competitors in the market for firms and management talent.

11

How Debt and Equity Affect
Executive Incentives

Key Insight: Debt encourages risky investments, which explains why firms must generally pay higher interest rates as they increase their debt-to-equity ratio.

THE FIRM WITH A SINGLE OWNER totally avoids agency costs, or those costs that are associated with shirking of duties and the misuse, abuse, and overuse of firm resources for the personal benefit of the managers and workers who have control of firm resources. Agency costs show up in lost output and a smaller bottom line for the firm. However, in the real world, firms often need more funds for investment than one person can generate from his or her own savings or would want to commit to a single enterprise. Any single owner, if the business is even moderately successful, typically has to find ways of encouraging others to join the firm as owners or lenders (including bondholders, banks, and trade creditors).

Therein lies the source of many firm problems, not the least of which is that a firm's expansion can give rise to the agency costs that a single-person firm would avoid. Managers and workers can use the expanding size of the firm as a screen for their shirking. The addition of equity owners (partners or stockholders) can dilute the incentive of any one owner to monitor what the agents do. Hence, as the firm expands, the agency costs of doing business can erode, if not totally negate, any economies of scale achieved through firm expansion.

One of the more important questions any single owner of a growing firm must face is, "How will the method of financing growth—debt or equity—affect the extent of the agency cost?" Given that agency costs will always occur with expanding firms, how can the combination of debt and equity be varied to minimize the costs from shirking and opportunism?

That question is really one dimension of a more fundamental one: "How can the financial structure affect the firm's costs and competitiveness?"

In this short chapter, our focus is on debt, but that is only a matter of convenience of exposition, given that any discussion of debt must be juxtaposed with some discussion of equity as a matter of comparison, if nothing else. We could just as easily draw initial attention to equity as a means of financing growth. In fact, debt and equity are simply two alternative categories of finance (subject to much greater variation in form than we are able to consider here) available to owners. Owners need to search for an "optimum combination."

By debt, of course, we mean funds, or the principal, that must be repaid fully at some agreed-upon point in the future and on which regular interest payments must be made in the interim. The interest rate is simply the annual interest payment divided by the principal. Also, we must note that in the event the firm gets into financial problems, the lenders have first claim on the firm's remaining assets.

By equity, or stock, we mean funds drawn from people who have ultimate control over the disposition of firm resources and who accept the status of residual claimants, which means that a return on investment (which is subject to variation) will be paid only after all other claims on the firm have been satisfied. That is to say, the owners (stockholders) will not receive dividends until after all required interest payments have been met; the owners are guaranteed nothing in the form of repayment of their initial investments. Obviously, owners (stockholders) accept more risk on their investment than do lenders (or bondholders).[1]

Does it matter whether a firm finances its investments by debt or equity?[2] You bet it does (otherwise, we must wonder why the two broad categories of finance would ever exist). The most important feature of debt is that the payments, both the payoff sum and the interest payments, are fixed. This is important for two reasons. One reason is the obvious one—it enables firms to attract funds from people who want security and certainty in their investments. The modern aphorism "Different strokes for different folks," if followed in the structuring of financial instruments, can mean lower costs of investment funds, growth, and competitiveness. Debt attracts funds from people who get their "strokes" from added security.

Fixed payments on debt are more important for our purposes for another reason: if the firm earns more than the required interest payments on any given investment project, the residual goes to the equity owners. If the company fails because of investments gone sour, then the firm is limited in its liability to lenders to the amount of their loans. If the firm is forced to liquidate its assets and the sale is insufficient to cover the debt, then it's simply going to be a sad day for the lenders (as well as the stockholders, who will get nothing). The lenders can claim only what is left from the sale. That's it. Any profit remaining after all expenses have been covered doesn't have to be shared with the lenders. The remaining profits go to the equity owners.

Clearly, the nature of debt biases, to a degree (depending on the exact features), the decision making of the owners, or their agent-managers, toward seeking risky investments, ones that will likely carry high rates of return. These high rates will, no doubt, incorporate a premium for risk taking, but they can also provide equity owners with an opportunity for a premium residual, given that they get what is left after the interest payments are deducted from high returns. If a firm borrows funds at a 10 percent interest rate, for example, and invests those funds in projects that have an expected rate of return of 12 percent, the residual left for the equity owners will be the difference, 2 percent. If, on the other hand, the funds are invested in a much riskier project that has a rate of return of 18 percent, then the residual that can be claimed by the equity owners is 8 percent, four times as great as in the first case.

The project with the higher rate has a risk premium built into it (or else everyone investing in the 12 percent projects would direct their funds to the 18 percent projects, causing the rate of returns in the latter to fall and in the former to rise). However, much of that additional risk is imposed on the lenders. They are the ones who must fear that the incurred risk will translate into failed investments (which is what risk implies). But they are not the ones who will be compensated for the assumed risk they bear. Indeed, once a lender has made a loan, the managers can extend their indebtedness with more venturesome investments, increasing the risk imposed on the original lenders.

As a general rule, the greater the indebtedness, the greater incentive managers have to engage in risky investments. Again, this occurs because much of the risk is imposed on the lenders, and the benefits, if they materialize, are garnered by the equity owners.

It should surprise no one that as a firm takes on more debt, lenders will become progressively more concerned that they will lose some or all of their investments. As a consequence, they will demand compensation in the form of higher interest payments, which reflect a risk premium. Those lenders who fear that the firm will continue to expand its indebtedness after they make the initial loans will also seek compensation prior to the rise in indebtedness by way of a higher interest rate. To keep interest costs under control, firm managers will want to find ways of making commitments as to how much indebtedness the firm will incur, and they must make the commitments believable, or else higher interest rates will be in the making. Again, we return to a reoccurring theme in this book: managers' reputations for credibility have an economic value. In this case, the value emerges in lower interest payments.

Lenders, of course, will seek to protect themselves from risky managerial decisions in other ways. They may seek, as they often do, to obtain rights to monitor and even constrain the indebtedness of the firms to whom they make loans. Managers also have an interest in making such concessions because, although their freedom of action is restricted in one sense, they can be compensated for the accepted restrictions in the form of interest rates that are lower than they otherwise would be. Firm managers are granted greater freedom of action in another respect; they are given a greater residual with which they can work (to add to their salary and perks [if they have the discretion to do so]), extend the investments of the firm, or increase the dividends for stockholders).

Lenders may also specify the collateral the firm must commit. Lenders will not be interested in just any form of collateral. They will be most interested in having the firm pledge "general capital," or assets that are resalable, which means that the lenders may be able to recover their invested funds. Lenders will not be interested in having "specific capital," or assets that are designed only for their given use inside a given firm. Such assets have little, if any, resale market.

Firm assets are often more or less "general" or "specific," which means they can be better or worse forms of collateral. A firm can pledge assets with "specific capital" attributes. However, managers must understand that the more specific the asset (the narrower the resale market), the greater the risk premium that will be tacked onto the firm's interest rate, and the lower the potential residual for the equity owners.

Lenders will also have a preference for lending to those firms that have a stable future income stream and that can be easily monitored. The more stable the future income, the lower the risk of nonpayments of interest. The more easily the firm can be monitored, the less likely managers will be able to stick creditors with uncompensated risks. The more willing lenders are to lend to firms, the greater the likely indebtedness.

Electric utility companies have been good candidates for heavy indebtedness, because their markets are protected from entry by government controls and regulations (although this is changing), what they do is relatively easily measured, and their future income stream can be assumed to be relatively stable. Accordingly, their interest rates should be relatively low, which should encourage managers to take on additional debt so that equity owners can claim the residual for themselves. (At this writing, the deregulation of electric power production was about to be a reality in California. When this comes to pass, it will allow open entry into the generation of electricity. We should expect deregulation to lead to a higher risk premium in interest rates, although the price of electricity can be expected to fall for consumers with increased competition for power sales.)

The incentives of indebtedness are dramatically illustrated in the biggest financial debacle of modern times, the dramatic rise in savings and loan bank failures of the 1980s. The S&L industry was established in the 1930s to ensure that the savings of individuals, who effectively loaned their funds to the S&Ls, could be channeled to the housing industry (a concentrated focus of S&L investment portfolios that in itself added an element of risk, especially since housing starts vary radically with the business cycle). The money the S&Ls loaned came mostly (up to 97 percent) from their depositors, only 3 percent came from the owners (in the form of reserve and equity requirements). Such a division, of course, made the S&L owners eager to go after high-risk but high-return projects. They could claim the residual from what was then a fixed interest payment on deposits.

When interest rates began to rise radically with the rising inflation rates of the late 1970s, alternative market-based forms of saving became available, not the least of which were money market certificates and mutual funds, which were unrestricted in the rates of return they could offer savers. As a consequence, savings started flowing out of S&Ls, which greatly increased the pressure on S&Ls to hike, when they were freed to do so, the interest rates on their deposits and to offset the higher interest rates by searching out risky investments that carried high returns of returns.

The S&L's incentive for risky investment was heightened by the fact that depositors' incentives to monitor the loans were severely muted by federal deposit insurance, which effectively assured the overwhelming majority of all depositors that they would lose nothing if all their S&L loans went sour.

To compensate for these perverse incentives, the federal government closely monitored and regulated the investments of the S&Ls through 1982. But that year, S&Ls were given greater freedom to pursue high-risk investments at the same time that the protection to depositors was increased. The result should have been predicted from the simple idea that if you give enough people a large enough temptation, many will succumb. S&Ls went after the high-risk/high-return—and high residual—investments. The S&Ls that made the risky investments were in a position to pay high interest rates, thereby attracting funds from other, more conservative S&Ls. In order to protect their deposit base, conservative S&Ls had to raise their interest rates, which meant that they, too, had to seek riskier investment, all of which led to a shock wave of risky investment that spread through the S&L/development industry.

Unfortunately, many of those investments did what should have been expected by their risky nature: they failed. The government had to absorb the losses and then return to doing what it had done before 1982—closely monitor the industry and more severely restrict the riskiness of its investments (it was unwilling to give depositors greater incentives to monitor their S&Ls).

Clearly, fraud was a part of the S&L debacle. Crooks were attracted to the industry.[3] However, the debacle is a grand illustration of how debt can, and did, affect management decisions. It also enables us to draw out a financial/management principle: if owners want to control the riskiness of their firms' investments, they had better look to how much debt their firms accumulate. Debt can encourage risk taking, which can be good or bad, depending on whether the costs are considered and evaluated against the expected return.

Why, then, would the original equity owners ever be in favor of issuing more shares of stock and bringing in more equity owners with whom the original owners would have to share the residual? Sometimes, of course, the original owners are unable to provide the additional funds in order for the firm to pursue what are known (or expected) to be profitable investment projects. The original owners can figure that while their *share* of firm profits will go down, the *absolute level* of the residual they claim will go up. A 60 percent share of $100,000 in profits beats 100 percent of $50,000 in profits any day.

Another, less obvious reason is that the additional equity investment can reduce the risk that the lenders face with loans to the firm. This means that the equity owners can claim a greater residual due to the fact that firm interest payments can fall with the reduction in the risk premium.

Often investment projects require a combination of specific and general capital to be used together. Consider, for example, the predicament of a remodeling firm that uses specially designed pieces of floor equipment (which may have little or no market value outside the firm), as well as trucks that can easily be sold in well-established used truck markets. The investment projects can be divided according to the interests of the two types of investors. The equity owners can be called upon to take the risk associated with the floor equipment, while the lenders are called upon to provide the funds for the trucks. Indeed, the lender might not even make the loan for the general part of the investment unless equity owners agreed to take the specific part precisely because the general investment would have limited value (or would carry undue risk) without the specific-capital investment. (There may be no reason for the trucks if the firm has no floor equipment to work with.)

The original owners can also have an interest in selling a portion of their ownership share because, by doing so, they can reduce the overall risk of their full portfolio of investments by reinvesting the proceeds elsewhere, spreading their investments among a number of firms. If the original owners held their full investments in the firm and refused to sell off a portion, then they might be too cautious in the choice of investments they would want the firm to pursue—too reluctant to take the risky investments that can be the more rewarding endeavors.

By selling a portion of their interest in the firm, the original owners can actually change the direction of the firm's investment projects and its growth and can make the firm more profitable, which translates into greater wealth for the original owners. The original owners can do this by lowering their (risk) costs by spreading their investments and then by taking on more risky but more profitable investments in the original firm.

Again, the financial structure of the firm is important—and it can matter to management policies and to the bottom line.

Finance Professor Michael Jensen argues there is another reason for indebtedness for some firms: the interest payments on the debt can tie the hands—or reduce the discretionary authority—of managers who might otherwise engage in opportunism with their firms' residual.[4] If a firm has little debt, then the managers may have a great deal of funds, or residual, to do with as they please. They can use the residual to provide themselves with higher salaries and more perks. They can also use the funds to contribute to local charities that may have little impact on their firm's business (they may have a warm heart for the cause they support or they may want to take credit for being charitable with their firms' funds). They may also use the funds to expand (without the usual degree of scrutiny) the scope and scale of their firms, thereby justifying their own higher salaries and improved perks (since size and executive compensation tend to go together).

The investment projects the managers choose may indeed be profitable. The problem is that if the funds had been distributed to the stockholders, the stockholders could have found even more profitable investments (and even more worthy charitable causes).

As industries mature (or reach the limits of profitable expansion), the risk that managers will misuse firm funds can grow. There may be few opportunities for managers to reinvest the earnings in their own industry. They may then be tempted to use the excess residual to fulfill some of their own personal flights of managerial fancy (give to charitable causes or pad their pockets) or to reinvest the funds in other industries that may or may not have a solid connection to the original firm's core activities. Because of the additional costs of centralization and coordination of the investments across industries, the stock prices of mature companies can become depressed.

How can the firm be disgorged of the residual? Jensen suggests through indebtedness: the greater the indebtedness, the smaller the residual and the less waste that can vanish through managerial opportunism. Jensen argues that one of the reasons for the popularity of firm takeovers through "leveraged buyouts," which means heavy indebtedness, is that the firm is forced to give up the residual through higher interest payments, tying the hands of the agent-managers and curbing their ability to misuse firm funds. The value of the firm is enhanced by the indebtedness, mainly because it reduces the discretion of managers who have been misusing the funds. And managers can misuse their discretion in counterproductive ways, not the least of which is by diversifying the array of products and services provided on the grounds that diversity can smooth out the company's cash flows over the various cycles that go with the products and services. As Al Dunlap recognizes, "The flaw in that thinking is that shareholders are quite able to diversify on their own, thank you. Management doesn't have to do that for them."[5] But management does have to pass back the cash flow to the lenders and focus attention on their core business for shareholders.

This all leads us to an interesting proposition. We should expect firm indebtedness to increase with the maturity of its industry. Firms in a mature industry have more stable future income streams. They can be more easily monitored, given people's experience in working with the firms, their knowledge of how such firms operate, and their tendency to misappropriate funds when they do. Also, by taking on more debt, firms in mature industries can alert the market to their intention of ridding themselves of their residual and of eliminating the misuse of managerial discretion, all of which can drive up the price of the firm's stock to a point that it would not otherwise have reached.

Of course, if firms in mature industries don't take on relatively more debt and managers continue to misuse the funds by reinvesting the residual in the mature industry or other industries, then the firm can be ripe for a takeover. Some outside "raider" will see an opportunity to buy the stock, which should be selling at a depressed price, paying for the stock with debt. The increase in indebtedness can, by itself, raise the price of the stock, making the takeover a profitable venture. However, if the takeover target is, because of past management indiscretions in investment, a disparate collection of production units that do not fit well together, the profit potential for the raiders is even greater. The firm should be worth more in pieces than as a single firm. The raiders can buy the stock at a depressed price, take charge, and break the company apart, selling off the parts for more than the purchase price. In the process, the market value of the "core business" should be enhanced.

The moral of this chapter should now be clear: the financial structure of firms matters, and it matters a great deal. The structure can affect managerial actions and determine policies. The structure can also determine whether the firm will be the subject of a takeover. The one great antidote for a takeover should be obvious to managers, but it is not always (as evident by the fact that takeovers are not uncommon): firms should be structured, in terms of both their financial policies and their internal policies, in such a way that the stock price is maximized. In that case, potential raiders will have nothing to gain by taking over the firm, and the jobs of the executives and their boards will be secure. Of course, one of the primary functions of a board of directors is to monitor the executives and the policies that are implemented with an eye toward maximizing stockholder value. As we will see in the following chapters, those executives and boards that do not maximize the price of their stocks do have something to fear from corporate raiders. They have definite reason, as we will see, to denigrate the social value of corporate raiders and to foil the takeover efforts of the raiders.

12

The "Hostile" Takeover as
Managerial Incentive

Key Insight: "Hostile takeovers" are hostile only to executives who misuse firm resources. Hostile takeovers result in losers as well as winners but are generally efficient.

IT IS A COMMON PRACTICE for one firm to take over another firm. IBM recently acquired Lotus. Walt Disney Company acquired Capital Cities/ABC. And Time/Warner took over Turner Broadcasting at about the same time that Turner was looking for financing to buy CBS. During the first eight months of 1995, $270 billion worth of mergers and takeovers had been announced, a fact that caused reporters at *Business Week* to wonder if the U.S. economy had not entered a "new era of bigness."[1]

There are many reasons for such takeovers and different ways for them to occur. There may be complementarities in the production and distribution of the products of two firms that can be best realized by one firm. For example, Disney produces programs that can be aired on ABC's TV network, as well as on company-owned stations. Or, as was commonly the case in earlier manufacturing mergers, two firms may find that they can realize economies of scale by combining their operations. And, as will be discussed in chapter 14, one firm may be supplying another firm with highly specific capital, in which case a merger between the two reduces the threat of opportunistic behavior that can be costly to both.

Most takeovers are what are referred to as "friendly." A friendly takeover occurs when the management of the two firms work out an arrangement that is mutually agreeable. The takeover of ABC by Disney was a friendly one. Indeed, takeovers occur for the same reason all market transactions occur: generally speaking, efficiencies are expected, meaning that both parties can be made better off. So it should not be surprising that most takeovers are friendly.

But there are takeovers that are opposed by the management of the firms being taken over, as was the case, at least initially, in IBM's takeover of Lotus. These takeovers are referred to as "hostile" and are commonly seen as undesirable and inefficient. "Hostile" takeovers are depicted as the work of corporate "raiders" who are interested only in turning a quick profit and who disrupt productivity by forcing the management of the targeted firms to take expensive defensive action and distracting them from long-run concerns.

If managers of target corporations always acted in the interest of their shareholders (the real owners of the corporation), then a strong case could be made that so-called hostile takeovers are inefficient, since managers of the target corporation would then oppose a takeover only if it could not be made in a way that benefited their shareholders, as well as those of the acquiring corporation. But if managers could always be depended upon to act in the interest of their shareholders, then there would be no need for many of the corporate arrangements that have been discussed in this book.

Indeed, the strongest argument in favor of "hostile" takeovers is that they bring the interests of managers more in line with those of shareholders than would otherwise be the case. There is a so-called "market for corporate control" that allows people who believe that they can do a better job managing a company and maximizing shareholder return to oust the existing management by outbidding them for the corporate stock. Although there are not many such takeover attempts, and not all attempts are successful, just the threat of a "hostile" takeover provides a strong disincentive for managers to go as far as they otherwise would like in pursuing personal advantages at the expense of their shareholders. This suggests that there are efficiency advantages from "hostile" takeovers, a proposition that is much debated. The issue of efficiency is not unrelated, however, to the primary concern of this chapter, which is why "hostile" takeovers are less hostile than they are commonly depicted.

A takeover is often considered hostile for the very reason that it promotes efficiency. A management team that is doing a good job managing a firm efficiently has little to fear from being taken over by a rival management team. The stock price of a well-managed firm will generally reflect that fact, and it will not be possible for a corporate raider to profit by buying that firm's stock in the hope of increasing its price through improved management. Only when the existing managers are not running the firm efficiently, because of incompetence, an inability to abandon old ways in response to changing conditions, or a tendency to act in their own best interest rather than that of shareholders, is a takeover likely. But under these circumstances, a takeover that promises to increase efficiency will not be popular with existing managers, since it will put them out of work.

Not surprisingly, managers whose jobs are threatened by a takeover will see it as "hostile."

The fact that pejorative terms such as "hostile takeover" and "corporate raiders" are so widely used is testimony to the advantage existing managers have over shareholders at promoting their interests through public debate. The costs from a "hostile" takeover are concentrated on a relatively small number of people, primarily the management team that loses its pay, perks, and privileges. Each member of this team will lose a great deal if the team is replaced and so has a strong motivation to oppose a takeover. And even a grossly inefficient management team can be organized well enough to respond in unison to a takeover threat and to speak in one voice. That voice will usually characterize a takeover as hostile to the interests of the corporation, the shareholders, the community, and the nation, and we might expect managers to be more vociferous the more inefficient the management.

But if a takeover is actually efficient, what about the voice of those who benefit? Why is the media discussion of takeovers dominated by the managers who lose rather than by the shareholders who win? And there is plenty of evidence that the shareholders of the target company in a hostile takeover do win. For example, it has been estimated that during the takeover wave in the 1980s, stock prices of firms targeted for hostile takeovers increased about 50 percent, which suggests that the managers of the targeted firms may have destroyed a considerable amount of their corporations' value before the companies were targeted for takeover.[2] As we will discuss, this increase in stock values does not necessarily prove that a takeover is efficient. The stock prices of the firm that is taking over the target firm could be depressed, for example.[3] But even if the takeover is not efficient, the shareholders of the target firm should favor it and counter the negative portrayal put forth by their managers. This seldom happens, however, because there is typically a large number of shareholders, with few, if any, having more than a relatively small number of shares. Most shareholders have diversified portfolios and are only marginally affected by changes in the price of any particular corporation's stock. The probability that the actions of a typical individual stockholder will have an impact is very low, approaching zero. So even if the gain to shareholders far exceeds the loss to management, the large number of shareholders and their diverse interests make it extraordinarily difficult for them to speak in unison. Shareholders are not likely to influence the terms of the debate in ways that promote their collective interest.

If shareholders and management were on equal footing at influencing the public perception of hostile takeovers, almost no takeovers would be reported as hostile. Consider a hypothetical situation that is similar to what is commonly seen as a hostile takeover.

Assume that you are the owner of a beautiful house on a high bluff overlooking the Pacific Ocean near Carmel, California. You are extremely busy as a global entrepreneur and are unable to spend much time at this house. Since the house and grounds require full-time professional attention, you have hired a caretaker to manage the property. Assume that you pay the caretaker extremely well (mainly because you want him to bear a cost from being fired for shirking and engaging in opportunism) and give him access to many of the amenities of the property. He's very happy with the job, and you are pleased enough with his performance.

But one day a wealthy CEO who is planning to retire in the Carmel area makes you an offer of $15 million for the house, about 50 percent more than you thought you could sell it for. Although you were not interested in selling at $10 million, you find the $15 million offer very attractive. For whatever reason, the house is worth more to the retiring CEO than to you. It could be that the CEO values the property more than you simply because she will have more time to spend living in and enjoying the house. Or it could be because the CEO believes a profit can be made on the house by bringing in a caretaker who will do a far better job managing the property, thus increasing its value to above $15 million. But it really makes little difference to you why the CEO values the house more than you do, and you are quite happy to sell at the price offered, whatever the reason.

Imagine how surprised you would be if, as the sale of your house was being negotiated, the news media reported that your property was the target of a hostile takeover by a "house raider" interested only in personal advantage. What's so hostile about being offered a higher price for your property than you thought it was worth? And are you somehow worse off because the buyer also sees private benefit in the exchange?

But the media weren't interested in your opinion. Instead, reporters had been talking to your caretaker, who knew he would lose his job if the sale went through. So the caretaker was reporting that the sale of the property was the result of a hostile move by an unsavory character. Obviously, this scenario is silly, and the media are not likely to report this, or any similar sale of a house, as a hostile takeover. But is this any sillier than reporting a corporate takeover as hostile when the owners of the corporation (the shareholders) are being offered a 50 or 100 percent premium to sell their shares? Not much.

The two situations are not exactly the same, but they are similar enough to call into question the hostility of most hostile takeovers. One important difference between the two situations is that if such a report did start to circulate about the sale of your house and somehow threatened that sale, you would have the motivation and the ability to clearly communicate that it was your house, that you found the offer attractive, and that there was nothing at all hostile about the sale. This difference explains why our example should not be taken as a criticism of the press. When there is one owner (or a few), as in the case of a house, the press can easily understand

and report that owner's perspective. But when there are thousands of owners, as in the case of corporations, it is much easier for reporters to obtain information about a corporation from its top managers.

The fact that there is a multitude of owners in the case of corporations is the basis for other differences between the sale of a house and the sale of a corporation. Just as reporters find it easier to rely on top management for information on a corporation, so do the owners of a corporation find it easier to rely on management to make most corporate decisions, even major decisions such as those that affect the sale of the corporation. Obviously, the reason for granting a management team the power to act somewhat independent of shareholders is that shareholders are so large in number, so dispersed in location, and so diverse in interests that they cannot make the type of decisions needed to manage a corporation, or much of anything else for that matter. But as we have discussed in detail throughout this book, there are risks associated with letting agents (managers) act on behalf of principals (owners-shareholders). As the owner of the house outside Carmel, would you want your caretaker to negotiate the sale for you? Only if the caretaker were subject to a set of incentives that go a long way in lining up his interests in the sale with yours.

The reason many corporate practices and procedures are what they are can often be explained in terms of motivating corporate agents to behave in ways that serve the interests of their principals. Aligning the interests of managers with those of owners when there are attempts by outsiders to gain control of a corporation from the current management team is particularly difficult. There are corporate arrangements (to be considered later), however, that are best understood as motivating corporate managers to take shareholders' interests into account in the case of takeover offers. These arrangements aren't perfect, as evidenced by the popularity of the terms "hostile takeover" and "corporate raider." It should be emphasized though that both shareholders and managers can benefit from such arrangements.

The benefit to shareholders from arrangements that motivate a management team to promote the stockholders' interests should be obvious. The benefit to managers is more subtle. Managers who accept restrictions that reduce their ability (or incentive) to frustrate attempts by outsiders to take control of the corporation are worth more than managers not subject to such restrictions. How much would you be willing to pay an agent who could gain at your expense with impunity? So while managers can be expected to take advantage of allowable opportunities to protect their jobs against a takeover attempt, they would not want to work for a corporation that didn't go a long way to restrict those opportunities.

The most important way managers can protect themselves against a hostile takeover is by doing a good job managing. Being a good manager requires more than the skills that can be learned in an MBA program and honed with experience. It also requires corporate arrangements that provide strong incentives for managers to work together as a team for the good of the shareholders and that provide them with clear information on how well they are doing. These arrangements take many forms, and they are very attractive to managers quite apart from their ability to improve managerial performance. For example, few managers complain about executive compensation packages that increase in value when the price of the corporate stock increases. A corporate executive who receives a large payoff from exercising a stock option provided by his or her compensation package will tell you that this income is justified because increasing stock prices reflect, at least in part, management's skill at making decisions that benefited the shareholders.

There is a lot of truth in this justification for high incomes for corporate managers. Although it is obviously possible for stock prices to increase or decrease for reasons that have nothing to do with the performance of managers, good management decisions do have positive effects on the price of a corporation's stock. But managers who want to take some of the credit and reward when the corporate stock is going up should also be prepared to accept some of the consequences when the stock is going down. From the perspective of efficient incentives, it is best if managers suffer more loss from declining stock prices when they are to blame for that decline than when they are not. Though not perfect, this is what hostile takeovers tend to do. If a corporation's stock price declines because of a general decline in the stock market or for reasons that have nothing to do with the performance of management, there is little for a "corporate raider" to gain from a takeover. The threat of a takeover, particularly a takeover that existing management sees as hostile, is likely only when those mounting the takeover bid believe that better management can increase the value of the stock.

So far, we have explained why corporate takeovers that enrich the owners are often characterized as hostile in the press. The shareholders typically see nothing hostile about these takeovers, but the corporate managers whose jobs are threatened do. And managers, not shareholders, are the ones reporters turn to when they are looking for a corporate spokesperson. We have also noted that hostile takeovers are efficient for the very reason that managers consider them to be hostile: they force managers to either manage the corporation in the best interests of the shareholders or lose their lucrative jobs. The management team that is incompetent or complacent or that becomes more concerned with its privileges and perks than with running a tight ship reduces the profitability of the corporation and the price of the corporate stock. This creates the opportunity for an individual, or group of individuals, to purchase the corporation's stock at a low price, take a controlling interest in the corporation, and then profit by putting in a management team whose superior performance increases the price of the stock.

But are hostile takeovers efficient? Not everyone believes they are. Hostile takeovers are commonly seen as ways to increase the wealth of people who are already rich at the expense of the corporation's average workers (not just its managers), the corporation's long-run prospects, and the competitiveness of the general economy. For example, responding to a hostile takeover bid for Chrysler Corporation by Kirk Kerkorian, a major newspaper editorialized, "[W]hen Kerkorian was complaining about insufficient return to stockholders, the value of [his] investment in Chrysler had more than tripled, to $1.1 billion. That's not good enough? To satisfy his greed, Kerkorian seems prepared to endanger the jobs of thousands of Americans and the health of a major corporation so important to the economy. . . ."[4]

This editorial comment ignores the efficiency effects of a corporate takeover. But at the same time, the effect of a hostile takeover on economic efficiency is more complicated than has been suggested in this chapter so far. The stockholders of the corporation being taken over do gain. But what about the stockholders and bondholders of the corporation doing the taking over? Don't they lose as their firm runs up lots of debt to pay high prices for the stock of the acquired firm? Also, doesn't the threat of a hostile takeover motivate managers to make decisions that boost profits in the short run but that harm the corporation's long-run profitability? And what about the fact that important parts of an acquired firm are often spun off after a hostile takeover, leaving a much smaller firm, with many of its workers being laid off? Shouldn't these losses be set against any gains that the shareholders of acquired firms receive, and isn't it possible that the losses are larger than the gains?

These are good questions, and they deserve serious consideration. But first, let's consider in more detail the magnitude of the gains to the shareholders of a corporation that is targeted for a takeover. The evidence suggests that they are quite large. For example, a study by the Office of the Chief Economist of the Securities and Exchange Commission looked at 225 successful takeovers from 1981 through 1984 and found that the average premium to shareholders was 53.2 percent. In a follow-up study that covered 1985 and 1986, the premium was found to have dropped to an average of 37 and 33.6 percent, respectively. These averages probably understate the gains because they compare the stock price one month before the announcement of a takeover bid with the takeover price, and often the price begins increasing in response to rumors long before a formal offer is tendered.[5] These percentages represent huge gains in total dollars, amounting to $346 billion over the period 1977—86 (in 1986 dollars), according to one study.[6]

Those who own something that others are bidding for should be expected to see their wealth increase. So it is not really surprising that takeover bids increase the wealth of the corporation's stockholders. But that is not necessarily true for the stockholders of a corporation that mounts a takeover bid. In a competitive bidding process, it is possible to bid too much, and some believe that this is particularly true of the company that makes the winning bid, usually the bidder who is most optimistic about the value of the object of the bidding.[7] This is no problem when bidding for something the bidder wants for its subjective value (say, a piece of antique furniture), since the object probably is worth more to the winning bidder than to others. But a productive asset (such as an offshore oil field) is valued for its ability to generate a return, which is less dependent on who owns it.[8] Therefore, if the average bid is the best estimate of the value of the object, then there is a good chance that the winning bid is too high.

Economists have referred to this possible tendency to overbid as the "winner's curse." But the winner's curse may not be all that prevalent for two reasons. First, people who are prone to fall victim to this curse are not likely to acquire (or retain) control over the wealth necessary to keep bidding on valuable property, certainty not property as valuable as a corporation. Second, in many bidding situations each bidder receives information on how much others are willing to pay as the bidding process takes place and adjusts his evaluation of the property accordingly. This is the case in corporate takeovers, where offers to pay a certain price for a corporation's stock are made publicly.

So, we should expect that the winning bid for the stock of a corporation targeted for a takeover will fairly accurately reflect the value of that corporation to the winner and therefore not greatly affect the wealth of the acquiring corporation's stockholders; the more competitive the bidding process, the closer the bid price to the actual stock value. And that is exactly what the evidence suggests. According to a 1987 study by the economists Gregg Jarrell and Annette Poulsen, stockholders of acquiring corporations realized an average gain of between 1 and 2 percent on 663 successful bids between 1962 and 1985. Interestingly, and not surprisingly, as takeover activity increased, the return to acquiring firms decreased, with the average percentage return being 4.95 in the 1960s, 2.21 in the 1970s, and -0.04 (statistically insignificant) in the 1980s.[9]

What about the possibility that the additional value realized by shareholders of the target corporation is paid for by losses to bondholders? For example, a takeover could increase the risk that either the acquiring or the acquired firm will suffer financial failure, while increasing the possibility that one or both will experience very high profits. Shareholders stand to benefit from the high profits if they occur and so can find the expected value of their stock increasing because of the increased risk. The additional risk cannot generate a similar advantage from bondholders, since the return to bondholders is fixed. They lose if the corporation goes bankrupt but don't share in any increased profits if the corporation does extremely well. According to several studies of takeovers between the 1960s and the 1980s, however, takeovers do not impose losses on bondholders.[10] No doubt some bondholders suffer small losses, while some realize small gains, but the best conclusion is that, under even the worse case, any loss to bondholders does not come close to offsetting the gains to stockholders.

So far we have been talking about the average wealth effect on shareholders and bondholders from takeovers. Just because the average wealth effect of a hostile takeover is positive does not mean that all such takeovers create wealth. People make mistakes in the market for corporate takeovers just as they do in other markets, and in all aspects of life. The question is not whether people make mistakes but whether they are subjected to self- correcting forces when they do. The bidders subject to the winner's curse should themselves be the subject of a takeover. The evidence suggests that in the case of hostile takeovers, they are. In a 1990 study, the economists Mark Mitchell and Kenneth Lehn asked, "Do Bad Bidders Become Good Targets?" Looking at takeovers over the period January 1980–July 1988, they found that firms resulting from takeovers that were wealth reducing (according to the response of stock prices) were more likely to face a subsequent takeover than were those takeovers that were wealth increasing. The market for corporate control does not prevent mistakes from being made, but it creates the information and motivation vital for correcting them when they occur.[11]

If you are a corporate manager, you may be thinking that the threat of a takeover might motivate you to act in ways that increase the value of the corporate stock in the short run but that are harmful to the profitability of the corporation in the long run. Is it true that managers are less likely to be ousted in a hostile takeover if they concentrate on short- run profits at the expense of long-run profits? The answer might be yes if the prices of corporate stock reacted only to short-run profits. But there is plenty of evidence to suggest that stock prices reflect the market's collective estimate of the long-run profitability of corporations.[12]

People's view of the future is always cloudy and uncertain, and no one argues that stock prices are a completely accurate gauge of the present value of a corporation's future prospects. But as soon as new information becomes available on a corporation's future profitability, it is in the interest of investors to interpret this information as accurately as possible and to make decisions on the purchase or sale of stock that quickly cause the price of that stock to reflect the new information. Errors are always being made, but the errors of some create profitable opportunities for others to correct those errors with their buying and selling decisions. And those who consistently make errors soon find themselves lacking the resources (and also the desire) to continue making decisions that affect stock prices.

Consider a decision facing you as a manager about whether to commit to an expensive research and development project that will reduce profits over the near term but that is expected to more than offset this loss with higher profits in the future. Should you be fearful that investing in this project will, because of the reduction in current profits, drive the price of your stock down, making your corporation more vulnerable to a hostile takeover? The answer is probably not, especially if your estimate of the long-run profitability of the R&D project is correct. There are two good reasons for believing this. First, the obvious fact that price-earnings ratios vary widely between different stocks provides compelling evidence that stock prices reflect more than current profits. Second, studies indicate that a corporation's stock price generally increases when the corporation announces increased spending on investment and generally decreases when a reduction in investment spending is announced.[13] A study by Brownyn Hall found that, over the period 1976—1985, firms taken over by other firms did not have a higher R&D-to-sales ratio than did firms in the same industry that were not taken over.[14] There is no reason for managers to become short-sighted because of the threat of a hostile takeover. Indeed, the best protection against a takeover, hostile or otherwise, is to make decisions that increase the long-run profitability of the corporation, even if those decisions temporarily reduce profits.

What about the fact that once a corporation is taken over, it is sometimes broken up as the acquiring firm sells off divisions, often profitable divisions? Isn't this disruptive and inefficient? There is no doubt that takeovers are disruptive, particularly when they result in parts of the acquired firm being spun off. But disruption is not necessarily inefficient. Indeed, any economy that hopes to be efficient has to motivate rapid responses to changing circumstances, and those responses are necessarily disruptive. Making the best use of resources in a world of advancing technologies, improved opportunities, and global competition requires continuous disruption. The alternative is stagnation and relative decline.

Many of the mergers that took place in the 1960s and 1970s created large conglomerate structures that, even if efficient at the time, soon ceased to be efficient. Increased global competition began rewarding smaller firms that had quicker response times to changing market conditions. Technology reduced the synergies that might have existed at one point for firms that produced different products. It became less costly for firms to buy inputs and components from other firms, thus increasing firms' ability to specialize in their core competencies (in the vernacular of earlier chapters, transaction costs fell).

In many cases these changes made the divisions of the corporation worth more as separate firms than as parts of the whole. Many managers, however, prefer to be in charge of a large firm than a small one and are reluctant to divest divisions even if they are worth more by themselves or as part of another organizational structure. This managerial reluctance was partly responsible for the depressed stock prices of the 1960s, 1970s, and early 1980s that allowed corporate raiders to buy controlling interests in conglomerates and then increase the conglomerates' total value by spinning off some of their divisions.[15]

Another complaint about the spinning off of divisions and the downsizing that often accompany takeovers is that workers are laid off. The claim is made that while stockholders may come out ahead, they do so at the expense of workers who lose their jobs. There is evidence that hostile takeovers do result in reductions in the workforce. But the questions we want to consider are the following:

- Is this a valid criticism of takeovers?
- Which workers are most likely to be laid off, and how big is the cost to the workers when compared against the gain to shareholders?

The fact that workers are laid off after hostile takeovers is consistent with the view that these takeovers promote efficiency. The most natural thing in the world for managers to do when sheltered against the full rigors of competition is to let the workforce grow larger than efficiency requires. This is most evident in what are often referred to as "bloated government bureaucracies" (a fact that is partially attributable to the absence of the takeover option). But the same thing can and does happen in private corporations, though generally to a lesser degree.

Economic progress occurs most rapidly when there are strong pressures to produce the same output with less effort, to lay off workers when they are no longer needed. This often causes dislocations in the short run, but in the long run it increases the availability of the most valuable resource (human effort and brainpower) to expand output elsewhere in the economy. So a strong case can be made that one of the advantages of the market for corporate control is that it increases the pressure on managers to keep the size of their workforces under control. If there were an active market for the control of government bureaucracies, where bureaucracy raiders could profit from the savings realized by eliminating redundant government jobs, does anyone doubt that these agencies would be run more efficiently—with far fewer workers?

Some of the efficiencies derived from hostile takeovers (and therefore some of the benefits to corporate shareholders) are the result of workers losing their jobs. But what is the extent of this loss, and which workers are most likely to be laid off? To address this question, sixty-two hostile takeover attempts (fifty of which were successful) between 1984 and 1986 were examined.[16] According to this study, layoffs were common but seldom exceeded 10 percent of the workforce and were typically far less than that. Also, it was estimated that the probability of being laid off was 70 percent higher for white-collar workers than for blue-collar workers. The jobs of managers, not those of workers on the line, were most at risk. In addition, layoffs at targeted firms that were not taken over were greater (as a percentage of the workforce) than those in firms that were taken over. This suggests that the threat of a takeover provides a strong incentive for efficiencies even when no takeover actually occurs.

Even if it is accepted that hostile takeovers are generally efficient, it does-n't follow that there should be no corporate defenses against such takeovers. Ideally, there should be some resistance to takeover offers, but not "too much." Neither efficiency nor the interest of stockholders would be enhanced if the managers of a corporation simply acquiesced to the first takeover bid that offered more for the corporation's stock than the current price. The first bidder is not necessarily the one best able to improve the performance of the target corporation, and therefore the first bidder is not necessarily the one who can make the best offer. By being able to mount some defense against hostile offers, corporate managers can stimulate an aggressive auction that results in a winning bid that more accurately reflects the value of the corporation.

On the other hand, efficiency and the interests of shareholders can be harmed if the defenses against takeover bids are too impenetrable. If a takeover looks impossible, no one will make the effort to acquire control of even the most poorly managed corporation. Also, a significant invest-ment is involved on the part of an outsider to determine the potential for improving the management of a target corporation and the maximum price that can be paid for its stock while still making the takeover pay off. There is little motivation to incur the cost of this investment unless it gives a bidding advantage to those who do so. So takeover defenses that go "too far" in requiring the initial bidder to make his information generally avail-able can discourage takeover efforts to the point of reducing the amount of the winning bid.

No one can know exactly what is the best defense against a hostile takeover from the perspective of efficiency. Obviously the most efficient defense varies from situation to situation. But some types of defenses seem to be more efficient than others.

Interestingly, there is evidence that bringing litigation against bidders increases the amount that is ultimately paid for the stock of the target cor-poration, assuming that the target corporation loses the case.[17] Managers of the target corporation can also offer to repurchase the stock acquired by a raider at a premium, a practice known as *greenmail*. Some studies indicate that greenmail imposes significant negative returns on shareholders of the target (repurchasing) firm, but other studies indicate that greenmail can result in small gains for the repurchasing firm's shareholders.[18] Managers of the target corporation will want to be careful, however, if considering a policy of greenmail, since any gain to shareholders probably comes at the price of encouraging others to attempt a takeover in the hope of similarly extracting greenmail. Paying greenmail on a consistent basis is obviously not a way of promoting the long-run profitability of a firm.

A very effective way for managers of a corporation to defend against a takeover is through what is referred to as poison pills. A poison pill is a rule that allows shareholders of the target corporation to acquire additional shares at attractive prices, which serves to dilute the stock holding of the acquiring corporation. Although there are different types of poison pills, studies indicate that they are in general harmful to the wealth of the target corporation's shareholders.[19]

Managers can also protect themselves against takeovers by lobbying for legislation that reduces the chances that a takeover will be successful. Such legislation imposes a variety of regulations on takeover activity, but the studies that have been done suggest that, in general, they reduce shareholder wealth. The stock price of firms typically declines relative to the overall stock market when the state in which they are incorporated passes antitakeover legislation.[20]

Obviously, the interests of managers and those of shareholders are not in perfect alignment in the case of takeovers. But there are possibilities for overlap that are worth noting. A justification for a controversial severance-pay contract for top managers is based on the desirability of reducing management opposition to takeover bids that benefit shareholders. Top corporate managers are commonly granted what are referred to as *golden parachutes*, which provide them with handsome compensation when they leave the corporation. Such compensation can be particularly useful in cases where top managers have to invest heavily in knowledge that is highly specific to the corporation, and therefore worth little elsewhere. Golden parachutes can also encourage executives to take greater risks, since they know that they will receive significant severance pay packages if the risks they take result in losses and they lose their jobs.[21] The argument is that when these managers are offered generous severance pay, they are less likely to oppose a takeover offer that promotes efficiency and increases shareholder wealth, golden parachutes thus help bring the interests of top managers more in line with those of their shareholders. But, as with all incentives, care has to be exercised. Golden parachutes should not be so lucrative that they make an executive indifferent about keeping his or her job.[22]

Like all arrangements, golden parachutes can be poorly designed and abused. It may make sense to provide golden parachutes to only the CEO of a corporation and a few members of the top-level management team. Typically, a significant number of managers are involved in facilitating a smooth transfer of control. But there is no reason to extend golden parachutes to managers not involved in such a transfer. Also, while golden parachutes can be too stingy to promote the shareholder interests, they can also be too generous from the shareholders' perspective. Ideally, golden parachutes are provided only to those managers whose responsibilities are relevant to a takeover, and the severance compensation provided are tied to premiums in share prices generated by the takeover.

There is at least tentative support for the proposition that golden parachutes promote the interests of shareholders. According to one study of corporations that adopted golden parachutes, corporate stock value increases an average of about 3 percent when the adoption is announced. One interpretation of this result is that the golden parachutes increased the connection between the interests of shareholders and managers. It is possible, of course, that part of the increased stock value results from the belief that the announcement suggests that management expects a takeover bid and wants to protect itself against it.

The primary point of this chapter is that many so-called hostile takeovers are not really hostile, at least not from the perspective of the owners of the corporation being taken over. Throughout the chapter, we have suggested that hostile takeovers promote efficiency by encouraging managers to behave as good agents for their stockholders.

The efficiency of hostile takeovers will surely remain subject to debate. And certainly no serious person would argue that all hostile (or even friendly) takeovers are efficient. Mistakes are made in the market for corporate control that, after the fact, leave all parties worse off. So the debate over hostile takeovers will continue, and so will hostile takeovers. Of course, from the perspective of most managers, the fact that hostile takeovers will continue is more important than the debate over their efficiency. But the best way for managers to protect themselves against unwelcome attention in the takeover market is to do a good job enhancing the long-term profitability of the firm. And this is probably the best argument in support of the efficiency of hostile takeovers. Even if every hostile takeover that is attempted is itself inefficient, the fact that takeovers can and do occur creates a strong incentive for managers to manage firms efficiently on behalf of their shareholders.

13

How Honesty Pays in Business

Key Insight: People are honest to one degree or another because honesty pays, and honesty often pays well in business.

THE POPULAR PERCEPTION is that business is full of dishonest scoundrels—especially high ranking executives—who cheat, lie, steal, and worse to increase their profits. This perception is reflected in and reinforced by the way businesspeople are depicted in the media. According to one study, during the 1980s almost 90 percent of all business characters on television were portrayed as corrupt.[1] No one can deny that people in business have done all kinds of nasty things for a buck. But the impression of pervasive dishonesty among businesspeople is greatly exaggerated. Businesspeople are no more likely to behave dishonestly than are other people. In fact, there are reasons discussed in this chapter why business-people might be more honest than the typical American on the street. Moreover, there are ways businesspeople can commit themselves to incentive arrangements that motivate honest behavior in ways that their customers find convincing.

The case to be made for honesty in business is not based on any claim that businesspeople are particularly virtuous, or ethical to the core of their beings. We can make no claim to keen insights into the virtue of business-people or anyone else. We might even be persuaded that businesspeople have less virtue on average than do those who choose more caring occupations, such as teachers, social workers, missionaries, and nurses. But we do claim to know one simple fact about human behavior, and that is that people respond to incentives in fairly predictable ways. In particular, the lower the personal cost of dishonesty, the greater the extent of dishonesty within most identified groups of people. If businesspeople act honestly to an unusual degree (or different from the way other people behave in other situations), it must be in part because they expect to pay a high price for behaving dishonestly. This is, in fact, the case, because businesspeople have found, somewhat paradoxically, that they can increase profits by accepting institutional and contractual arrangements that impose large losses on them if they are dishonest.

Though seldom mentioned, most business activity requires a high degree of honest behavior. If business is going to be conducted at any but the simplest level, products must be represented honestly, promises must be kept, costly commitments must be made, and businesspeople must cooperate with each other to take the interests of others, particularly consumers, into consideration. Indeed, if the proverbial man from Mars came down and observed business activity, he might very well conclude that businesspeople are extraordinarily honest, trusting, and cooperative. They sell precious gems that really are precious to customers who cannot tell the difference between a diamond and cut glass. They promise not to raise the price of a product once customers make investments that make switching to another product costly, and they typically keep the promise. They make good-faith pledges that the businesses they own, but are about to sell, will continue to give their customers good service. They commit themselves to costly investments to serve customers, knowing that the investments will become worthless if customers shift their business elsewhere.

The way businesspeople behave in the marketplace suggests a level of morality that is at variance with the self-interest that economists, in their theoretical models, assume motivates business activity. Some argue that the economist's assumption of self-interest is extreme, and we recognize that many people, including many businesspeople, behave honestly simply because they feel it is the right thing to do. But few would recommend that we blindly trust in the honesty of others when engaged in business activity. The person who is foolish enough to assume that all businesspeople are honest and trustworthy has only to encounter a few who are not to find himself separated quickly from his wealth.

Is there a contradiction here between the honesty that characterizes most business activity and the fact that businesspeople are not generally assumed to be honest? The answer is no. Indeed, the reason businesspeople generally behave honestly is best explained by the fact that it would be foolish to assume that they are honest. And many businesspeople are honest precisely because others assume they won't be.

It is easy to imagine a situation in which businesspeople can profit at the expense of their customers, workers, and others with whom they deal if they behave deceitfully. For example, the quality of many products (say, used cars or diamonds) is difficult for consumers to easily determine. The seller who takes advantage of this by charging a high-quality price for a low-quality product would capture extra profits from the sale. A business owner who is about to retire can profit by making promises not to be fulfilled until after his retirement and that he does not plan to keep. The monopoly producer of a superior product (but one that requires the consumer to make costly investments in order to use it) can offer the product at a low price and then, once the consumer becomes dependent on it, increase the price significantly. Other examples of the potential profit from dishonest behavior are easily imagined. In fact, such examples are about the only type of behavior some people ever associate with business.

Again, we want to emphasize that dishonest behavior of the types we have described does occur. But such dishonest behavior is the exception, not the rule of much business, despite the story-telling talents of Hollywood writers. The reason is that in addition to being a virtue from a strictly moral perspective, honesty is also important for quite materialistic reasons. An economy in which people deal with each other honestly can produce more wealth than one in which people are chronically dishonest. So there are gains to be realized from honesty, and when there are gains to be captured, there are people who, given the opportunities available in market economies, will devise ways to capture them.

A businessperson who attempts to profit from dishonest dealing faces the fact that few people are naively trusting. It may be possible to profit from dishonesty in the short run, but those who do so find it increasingly difficult to get people to deal with them in the long run. And in some businesses it is extremely difficult to profit from dishonesty even in the short run. How many people, for example, would pay full price for a "genuine" Rolex watch or a diamond necklace from someone selling them out of a Volkswagen van at the curb of a busy street? Without being able to provide some assurance of honesty, the opportunities to profit in business are very limited.

So businesspeople have a strong motivation to put themselves in situations in which dishonest behavior is penalized. Only by doing so can they provide potential customers, workers, and investors with the assurance of honest dealing required if they are to become actual customers, workers, and investors.

The advantage of honesty in business can be illustrated by considering the problem facing Mary, who has a well-maintained 1990 Honda Accord that she is willing to sell for as little as $4,000. If interested buyers knew how well maintained the car is, they would be willing to pay as much as $5,000 for it. Therefore, it looks like it should be possible for a wealth-increasing exchange to take place, since any price between $4,000 and $5,000 will result in the car's being transferred to someone who values it more than the existing owner. But there is a problem. Many owners of 1990 Honda Accords who are selling their cars are doing so because their cars have not been well maintained and are about to experience serious mechanical problems. Assume that 75 percent of the 1990 Honda Accords being sold are in such poor condition that the most a fully informed buyer would be willing to pay for them is $3,000, with the other 25 percent worth $5,000. This means that a buyer with no information on the condition of a car for sale would expect a 1990 Honda Accord to be worth, on average, only $3,500. But if buyers are willing to pay $3,500 for a 1990 Accord, many of the sellers whose cars are in good condition will refuse to sell, as is the case with Mary, who is unwilling to sell for less than $4,000.

So the mix of 1990 Accords for sale will tilt more in the direction of poorly maintained cars, and their expected value will decline, and even fewer well-maintained 1990 Accords will be sold. This situation is often described as a market for "lemons," and it illustrates the value of having sellers who commit themselves to honesty.[2] If Mary could somehow convince potential buyers of her honesty when she claims her Accord is in good condition, she would be better off, and so would those who are looking for a good used car. The advantage of being able to commit to honesty in business extends to any situation where it is difficult for buyers to determine the quality of products they are buying.

The advantages of honesty in business and the problem of trying to provide credible assurances of that honesty can also be illustrated as a game. In Figure 13.1, we present a payoff matrix for a buyer and a seller, giving the consequences from different choice combinations. The first number in the brackets gives the payoff to the seller, and the second number gives the payoff to the buyer. If the seller is honest (the quality of the product is as high as he claims) and the buyer trusts the seller (she pays the high-quality price), then both realize a payoff of 100. On the other hand, if the seller is honest but the buyer does not trust him, then no exchange takes place and both receive a payoff of zero. If the seller is dishonest while the buyer is trusting, then the seller captures a payoff of 150, while the buyer gets the sucker's payoff of -50. Finally, if the seller is dishonest and the buyer does not trust him, then an exchange takes place in which the buyer pays a low-quality price but gets a lower-quality product than she would be willing to pay for, and both the seller and buyer receive a payoff of 25. From a joint perspective, honesty and trust are the best choices, since this combination results in more wealth for the two to share. But this will not be the outcome, given the incentives created by the payoffs in Figure 13.1. The buyer will not trust the seller. The buyer knows that if her trust of the seller is taken for granted by the seller, then he will attempt to capture the largest possible payoff from acting dishonestly. On the other hand, if he believes she does not trust him, his highest payoff is still realized by acting dishonestly. So she will reasonably expect the seller to act dishonestly. This is a self-fulfilling expectation, since when the seller doesn't expect to be trusted, his best response is to act dishonestly.

		BUYER	
		Trust	Doesn't Trust
	Honest	(100, 100)	(0, 0)
SELLER			
	Dishonest	(150, -50)	(25, 25)

Figure 13.1

The seller would clearly be better off in this situation (and so would the buyer) if he could somehow create an arrangement that reduced the payoff he could realize from acting dishonestly. If, for example, the seller arranged it so that he received a payoff of only 50 from acting dishonestly when the buyer trusted him, as is shown in Figure 13.2, then the buyer (assuming she knows of the arrangement) could trust the seller to respond honestly to her commitment to buy. The seller's commitment to honesty would allow both seller and buyer to realize a payoff of 100 each, rather than the 25 they each receive without the commitment.

But how can a seller commit himself to honesty in a way that is convincing to buyers? What kind of arrangements can sellers establish that penalize them if they attempt to profit through dishonesty at the expense of customers?

There are many business arrangements and practices that can act as a means of committing sellers to honest dealings. We briefly consider some of them here. The arrangements are varied, as one would expect, since the ways a seller could otherwise profit from dishonest activity are also varied.

Notice that our discussion of the situation described in Figure 13.1 implicitly assumes that the buyer and seller deal with each other only one time. This is clearly a situation in which the temptation for the seller to cheat the buyer is the strongest, since the immediate gain from dishonesty will not be offset by a loss of future business from a mistreated buyer. If a significant amount of repeat business is possible, then the temptation to cheat decreases and may disappear. What the seller gains from dishonest dealing on the first sale can be more than offset by the loss of repeat sales. So, one way sellers can attempt to move from the situation described in Figure 13.1 to the one described in Figure 13.2 is by demonstrating that they are in business for the long run. For example, selling out of a permanent building with the seller's name or logo on it, rather than from a Volkswagen van, informs potential customers that the seller has been (or plans on being) around for a long time. Sellers commonly advertise how long they have been in business (for example, "Since 1942" is added under the business name) to inform people that they have a history of honest dealing (otherwise they would have been out of business long ago) and plan on remaining in business.

As we will see, however, in chapter 15, the advantages motivated by

		BUYER	
		Trust	Doesn't Trust
SELLER	Honest	(100, 100)	(0, 0)
	Dishonest	(50, -50)	(25, 25)

Figure 13.2

repeated encounters tend to break down if it is known that the encounters will come to an end at a specified date. For this reason firms attempt to maintain continuity beyond what would seem to be a natural end-period. Single proprietorships, for example, seem to be less trustworthy when the owner is about to retire, or sell. A common way of reducing this problem is for the owner's offspring to join the business ("Samson and Sons" or "Delilah and Daughters"), ensuring continuity after their parent's retirement. Indeed, even though large corporations have lives that extend far beyond that of any of their managers, they often depend on single proprietorships to represent and sell their products. As discussed later, it is common for such corporations to have programs to encourage the sons and daughters of these single proprietors to follow in their parents' footsteps.

The advantage of letting people know that you have been, and are planning to be, in business a long time is that it informs them that you have something to lose—potential future business—if you engage in dishonest dealing. In effect, you are providing potential customers with a *hostage*, something of value that the customers can destroy if the seller does not keep her promises. There are numerous other ways that businesses provide hostages to make their commitments to honest dealing credible. Before examining some of these arrangements, however, it is important to consider an important feature that hostages should have.

The use of hostages has a long history and is traditionally thought of as a way to reduce the likelihood of hostilities between two countries or kingdoms. For example, if King A intended to wage war on Kingdom C and wanted to keep Kingdom B neutral, he could assure King B of his good faith by yielding up his beloved daughter to King B as a hostage. Assuming King A really did love his daughter, he would then be very reluctant to break his promise and invade Kingdom B after conquering Kingdom C. But even if King A does have a compelling incentive not to wage war against King B as long as his daughter is King B's hostage, a potential problem remains. King B may find the daughter so attractive that he values her more than her father's promise not to invade. Therefore, King B may decide to join with Kingdom C against King A and keep the daughter for himself. This suggests that an ugly daughter (one only a father could love!) makes a better hostage than a daughter who is more appealing.

The general proposition that comes from this example is that the best hostage is one that is highly valued by the person giving it and that is valued not at all by the person receiving it. The example also suggests that sometimes it is best, particularly if the hostage is valuable to the person holding it, for the parties to exchange hostages. For example, if King A has only beautiful daughters, then the best arrangement may be for him to exchange a beautiful daughter for one of King B's handsome sons (presumably for Queen A's keeping). Of course, it is now important that King B value his son more than he does King A's daughter and that Queen A value her daughter more than she does King B's son.

A firm's reputation can be thought of as a hostage that the firm puts in the hands of its customers as assurance that it is committed to honest dealing. A firm's reputation is an ideal hostage because it is valuable to the firm but has no value to customers apart from its ability to ensure honesty. A firm has a motivation to remain honest in order to prevent its reputation from being destroyed by customer dissatisfaction, but customers cannot capture the value of the reputation for themselves. The more a firm can show that it values its reputation, the better hostage it makes.

Consider the value of a logo to a firm. Companies commonly spend what seems an enormous amount of money for logos to identify themselves to the public. Well-known artists are paid handsomely to produce designs that do not seem any more attractive than those that could be rendered by lesser-known artists (many of whose artistic efforts have never gone beyond bathroom walls). Furthermore, companies are seldom shy about publicizing the high costs of their logos.

It may seem wasteful for a company to spend so much for a logo, and silly to let consumers know about the waste (the cost of which ends up in the price of its products). But expensive logos make sense when we recognize that much of the value of a company logo depends on its cost. The more expensive a company's logo, the more that company has to lose if it engages in business practices that harm its reputation with consumers, a reputation embodied in the company logo. The company that spends a lot on its logo is effectively giving consumers a hostage that is very valuable to the company. Consumers have no interest in the logo except as an indication of the company's commitment to honest dealing but will not hesitate to destroy the value of the logo (hostage) if the company fails to live up to that commitment.

Expensive logos are an example of how businesses make nonsalvageable investments to penalize themselves if they engage in dishonest dealing. Such investments are particularly common when the quality of the product is difficult for consumers to determine. The value of the products sold in jewelry stores, for example, can vary tremendously, and few consumers can judge that value themselves. Those jewelry stores that carry the more expensive products want to be convincing when they tell customers that their products are worth the prices being charged. One way of doing this is by selling jewelry in stores with expensive fixtures that would be difficult to use in other locations: ornate chandeliers, unusually shaped display cases, expensive countertops, and generous floor space. What could the store do with this stuff if it went out of business? Not much, and this tells the customers that the store has a lot to lose by misrepresenting its merchandise to capture short-run profits. Nonsalvageable investments serve as hostages that sellers put into the hands of customers.

Another rather subtle way that sellers use "hostages" to provide assurances of honesty is by letting consumers know that they (the sellers) are making lots of money. If it is known that a business is making a lot more profit from its existing activity than it could make in alternative activities, consumers will have more confidence that the business won't risk that profit with misleading claims. The extra profits of the business are a hostage that will be destroyed by consumers' choices if the business begins employing dishonest practices. Expensive logos and nonsalvageable capital are not only hostages in themselves; they also inform consumers that the firm is making enough money to afford such extravagances. Expensive advertising campaigns, often using well-known celebrities, also serve the same purpose. Through expensive advertising, a company is doing more than informing potential customers about the availability of the product; it is letting them know that it has a lot of profits to lose by misrepresenting the quality of the product.[3]

The importance businesspeople attach to committing themselves to honesty sometimes leads them to put their profits at risk of being lost through competition with other firms. Consider a situation in which a firm has a patent on a high-quality product that consumers would like to purchase at the advertised price but a product that would be difficult to stop using because its use requires costly commitments. The potential buyers fear that the seller will exploit the long-term patent monopoly on the product by raising the price after the buyer commits to it at the attractive initial price. The seller may promise not to raise the price, but the buyer will be taking an expensive risk to trust the honesty of the promise. A long-term contract is possible, but it is difficult to specify all the contingencies under which a price increase (or decrease) would be justified. Also, such a contract can reduce the flexibility of the buyer as well as the seller, and legal action to enforce the contract is expensive.

Another possibility is for the seller to give up her monopoly position by licensing another firm to sell the product. By doing so, the seller makes her promise to charge a reasonable price in the future credible, since if the seller breaks the promise the buyer can turn to an alternative seller. Giving up a monopoly position is a costly move, of course, but it is exactly what semiconductor firms that have developed patented chips have done. To make credible their promise of a reliable and competitively priced supply of a new proprietary chip (the use of which requires costly commitments by the user), semiconductor firms have licensed such chips to competitive firms. Such a licensing arrangement is another example of making profits via a hostage intended to encourage honesty.[4]

The more difficult it is for consumers to determine the quality of a product or service, the more advantage there is in committing to honesty with hostage arrangements. Consider the case of repair work. When a person purchases repair work on his car, for example, he can generally tell if the work has eliminated the problem. The car is running again, the rattle is gone, the front wheels now turn in the same direction as the steering wheel, and so on. But few people know if the repair shop charged them for only the repairs necessary, or if it charged them for lots of parts and hours of labor when all it really did was tighten a screw. One way repair shops can reduce the payoff for dishonest repair charges is through joint ownership with the dealership selling the cars being repaired. In this way the owner of the dealership makes future car sales a hostage to honest repair work. Dealerships depend on repeat sales from satisfied customers, and an important factor in how satisfied people are with their cars is the cost of upkeep and repairs. The gains a dealership could realize from overcharging for repair work would be quickly offset by reductions in both repair business and car sales.

Automobiles are not the only products in which it is common to find repairs and sales tied together in ways that provide incentives for honest dealing. Many products come with guarantees entitling the buyer to repairs and replacement of defective parts for a specified period of time. These guarantees also serve as hostages against poor quality and high repair costs. Of course, guarantees not only provide assurance of quality; they provide protection against the failure of that assurance. Sellers often offer extra assurance, and the opportunity to reduce risk, by selling buyers a warranty that extends the time, and often the coverage, of the standard product guarantee.

While guarantees and warranties reduce the incentive of sellers to act dishonestly, they create opportunities for buyers to benefit from less than totally honest behavior. These opportunities are present to one degree or another in all forms of insurance and come as two separate problems, one known as *moral hazard* and the other known as *adverse selection*. Consider first the problem of moral hazard.

Knowing that a product is under guarantee or warranty can tempt buyers to use the product improperly and carelessly and then blame the seller for the consequences. With this moral hazard in mind, sellers put restrictions on guarantees and warranties that leave buyers responsible for problems they are in the best position to prevent. For example, refrigerator manufacturers ensure against defects in the motor but not against damage to the shelves or finish. Similarly, automobile manufacturers ensure against problems in the engine and drive train (if the car has been properly serviced) but not against damage to the body and the seat covers. While such restrictions obviously serve the interests of sellers, they also serve the interests of buyers. When a buyer takes advantage of a guarantee by mis-representing the cause of a difficulty with a product, all future consumers pay because they must make up for the higher costs to the seller. Buyers are in a prisoners' dilemma in which they are better off collectively using the product with care and not exploiting a guarantee for problems they could have avoided. But without restrictions on the guarantee, each indi-vidual is tempted to shift the cost of careless behavior to others.

Adverse selection is a problem associated with distortions arising from the fact that buyers and sellers often have different information that is rel-evant to a transaction. Most of this chapter has been concerned with the ways sellers commit themselves to honestly revealing the quality of prod-ucts when they have more information about that quality than do buyers. But in the case of warranties it is the buyer who has crucial information that is difficult for the seller to obtain. Some buyers are harder on the product than average, and others are easier on the product than average. The use of automobiles is the most obvious example. Some people drive in ways that greatly increase the probability that their cars will need expen-sive repair work, while others drive in ways that reduce that probability. If a car manufacturer offers an extended warranty at a price equal to the aver-age cost of repairs, only those who know that their driving causes greater than average repair costs will purchase the warranty, which is therefore being sold at a loss. If the car manufacturer attempts to increase the price of the warranty to cover the higher than expected repair costs, then more people will drop out of the market, leaving only the worst drivers buying the warranty.[5]

Even though people would like to be able to reduce their risks by pur-chasing warranties at prices that accurately reflect their expected repair bills, the market for these warranties can obviously collapse unless sellers can somehow obtain information on the driving behavior of different dri-vers. If all buyers were honest in revealing this information, they would be better off collectively. But because individual buyers have a strong motiva-tion to claim they are easier on their cars than they actually are, sellers of warranties try to find indirect ways of securing honest information on the driving behavior of customers. For example, warranties on "muscle" cars that appeal to young men are either more expensive or provide less cover-age than warranties on station wagons.

This chapter has focused primarily on business arrangements that moti-vate firms to deal honestly with customers, and our discussion of these arrangements is far from exhaustive. Honesty is also important in the interaction between shareholders and managers, employers and workers, and creditors and debtors, and many different types of arrangements exist that motivate trustworthy behavior in these relationships. Such business arrangements serve a variety of purposes, such as marketing products, financing capital investment, and securing productive workers, but understanding any of them requires recognizing the importance businesspeople attach to being able to commit themselves credibly to honesty in their dealings with others.

IV

FIRM INCENTIVES

14

What Firms Should Do

Key Insight: The firm's decision on whether to make or buy is determined by the tradeoff between the efficiencies of market specialization and the costs of transactions.

PEOPLE WOULD NOT BOTHER organizing themselves into "firms" if there were not gains to be had by doing so. But therein lies a fundamental dilemma for managers: How can managers ensure that the gains that could be had are actually realized and are shared in some mutually agreed upon way by all of the stakeholders in the firm? The problem is especially difficult since every group associated with the firm—owners, managers, line workers, buyers, and suppliers—probably wants to take a greater share of the gains than it is getting and contribute less in the way of work and investment than it is contributing. Managers have to find ways of overcoming the stakeholders' inclination to "give little but take a lot." One of the jobs of incentives is to overcome that inclination by tying how much people receive to what they give to the firm.

One of the most important lessons businesspeople learn is that efficiencies can be realized from specialization and exchange. Anyone who attempted to produce even a small fraction of what he or she consumed would be a very poor person indeed.

The late economist Leonard Reed wrote a famous article in which he pointed out that no one person could make something even as simple as a lead pencil.[1] It takes literally thousands of people specializing in such things as the production of paint, graphite, wood products, metal, machine tools, and transportation to manufacture a pencil and make it conveniently available to consumers. No one knows enough—or can know enough—to do everything required in pencil production. Prosperity depends on our ability to become very efficient in a specialized activity and then to exchange in the marketplace the value we produce for a wide range of products that have been efficiently produced by other specialists. Our ability to exchange in the marketplace not only allows us to produce more value through specialization but also allows us to obtain the greatest return for our specialized effort by imposing the discipline of competition on those from whom we buy.

In this chapter, we extend our discussion of how transactions costs in markets can cause firms to extend the scope and scale of their operations. We are concerned with a special form of transactions cost resulting from "opportunistic behavior" that can cause firms to make things themselves even though outside suppliers could produce those things more efficiently.

Firms derive much the same advantage from specialization and exchange that individuals do. But that comment begs an important question: Exactly what should firms make inside their organizations, and what should they buy from some outside vendor? Business commentators have a habit of coming up with rules that don't add very much to the answer. For example, one CEO deduced, "You should only do, in-house, what gives you a competitive advantage."[2] Okay, but why would anyone get a competitive advantage by doing anything inside, given that such a move reduces, to one degree or another, the advantage of buying from the cheapest outside competitor? Answers have varied over time (although the one we intend to stress relates to incentives).

At one time, the answer to the make-or-buy problem would have focused on technological considerations: firms often produce more than one product because of what economists call "economies of scope," a situation in which the skills developed in the production of one product lower the cost of producing other products.[3] But even firms with diverse product lines are actually quite specialized, they purchase most of the inputs they use in the market rather than produce them in-house. General Motors, for example, does not produce its own steel, tires, plastic, or carpeting. Instead, it is cheaper for General Motors, and other automobile manufacturers, to purchase these products from firms that specialize in them and to concentrate on the assembly of automobiles.[4] Neither do restaurants typically grow their own vegetables, raise their own beef, catch their own fish, or produce their own toothpicks.

Given the advantages of specializing in productive activities and buying most of the needed inputs in the marketplace, it is reasonable to ask why firms do as much as they do. Why don't they buy almost all the inputs they need, as they need them, from others and use them to add value in very specialized ways? Instead of having employees in the typical sense, for example, a firm could hire workers on an hourly or daily basis at a market-determined wage reflecting their alternative value at the time. Instead of owning and maintaining a fleet of trucks, a transport company could rent trucks, paying only for the time they are in use. Loading and unloading the trucks could be contracted out to firms that specialize in loading and unloading trucks. The transport firm would specialize in actually transporting products. Similarly, the paperwork required for such financial activities as internal control, payroll, and tax reporting could be contracted out to those who specialize in providing these services.

Indeed, as discussed in chapter 2, taken to the limit, there would cease to be firms as we typically think of them. Rather, there would be only individual resource owners all operating as independent contractors, buying (or renting) everything they needed to add value in a very specialized way and then, after the value was added, selling to another individual who would add more value until a good or service was finally sold to the consumer.

This extreme form of specialization and reliance on market exchange is clearly not what we observe in the economy. There are limits to the efficiency to be realized from further specialization, and it is useful for man agers to understand the cause of these limits and what it implies about the advantages of producing in-house rather than buying in the market.

The problem with total reliance on the market should now be familiar: there are significant costs—transactions costs—associated with making market exchanges. As explained earlier, you have to identify those who are able and willing to enter into a transaction, negotiate the specific terms to the transaction and how those terms might change under changing circumstances, draw up a contract that reflects as accurately as possible the agreed-upon terms, arrange to monitor the performance of the other party to make sure the terms of the agreement are kept, and be prepared to resolve conflicts that arise between the agreement and the performance. Because of these transactions costs, it is often better for some individual or some group of individuals to directly manage the use of a variety of resources in a productive enterprise that we call a firm.

Transactions costs are lower, for example, when owners of labor become employees of the firm by entering into long-run agreements to perform tasks, which are not always spelled out clearly in advance, under the direction of managers in return for a fixed wage or salary. A market transaction is not needed every time it is desirable to alter what a worker does. Employment contracts typically allow manager wide discretionary authority to redeploy workers as circumstances change without having to incur further transactions costs. Furthermore, with a uniform employment contract with a large number of workers, a manager can direct productive interactions between these workers that might otherwise require negotiated agreements between each pair of workers. As an example, ten workers could be hired with ten transactions, each negotiated through a relatively simple and uniform employment agreement. If those ten workers were independent contractors who had to interact with each other in ways that employees of a firm often do, they might well have to negotiate the terms of that interaction in forty-five separate agreements.[5]

In general, the higher the cost of transacting through markets, the more goods a firm will make in-house. The reason restaurants don't make their own toothpicks is that the cost of transactions is extremely low in the case of toothpicks. It is hard to imagine the transactions costs of acquiring toothpicks getting so high that restaurants would make their own. But one might have thought the same about beef until McDonald's opened an outlet in Moscow, before the collapse of the Soviet Union. Because of the primitive nature of markets in Russia at that time, relying on outside suppliers for beef of a specified quality was highly risky. Because of the high transactions costs, McDonald's raised its own cattle to supply much of its beef requirements for its Moscow restaurant.

Negotiating an agreement between two parties can be costly, but the most costly part of a transaction often involves attempts to avoid opportunistic behavior by the parties after the agreement has been reached. Agreements commonly call for one or both parties to make investments in expensive plant and equipment that are highly specific to a particular productive activity. Once the investment is made, it has little, if any, value in alternative activities. Investments in highly specific capital are often very risky and therefore unattractive, even though the cost of the capital is less than it is worth. The problem is that once someone commits to an investment in specific capital to provide a service to another party, it is very tempting for that other party to take advantage of the investor's inflexibility by paying less than the original agreement called for.[6] There are so-called "quasi-rents" that are appropriable, or that can be taken by another party through unscrupulous, opportunistic dealing.[7] The desire to avoid this risk of opportunistic behavior can be a major factor in a firm's decision to make rather than buy what it needs.

Consider an example of a pipeline to transport natural gas to an electric generating plant. Such a pipeline is very expensive to construct, but we will assume that it lowers the cost of producing electricity by more than enough to provide an attractive return on the investment. To be more specific, assume that the cost of constructing the pipeline is $1 billion. Assuming an interest rate of 10 percent, the annual capital cost of the pipeline is $100 million.[8] Further assume that the annual cost of maintaining and operating the pipeline is $25 million. Obviously, it would not pay investors to build the pipeline for less than a $125 million annual payment, but it would be attractive to build it for any annual payment greater than that.[9] Finally, assume that if the pipeline is constructed, it will lower the cost of producing electricity by $150 million dollars a year. The pipeline costs less than it saves and is clearly a good investment for the economy. But would you invest your money to build it?

Any price between $125 and $150 million a year would be attractive to both investors in the pipeline and the electric generating plant that would use it. If, for example, the generating plant agrees to pay investors \$137.5 million each year to build and operate the pipeline, both parties would realize annual profits of \$12.5 million from the project. But the investors would be taking a serious risk because of the lack of flexibility after the pipeline is built. The main problem is that a pipeline is a *dedicated* investment, meaning there is a big difference in the return needed to make the pipeline worth building and the return needed to make it worth operating after it is built. While it takes at least \$125 million per year to justify building the pipeline, once it has been built, it will pay to maintain and operate it for anything more than \$25 million. Why? Because that is all it takes to operate the line. The pipeline investment itself is a *sunk cost*, literally and figuratively, not to be recaptured once it has been made. So, after investors have made the commitment to construct the pipeline, the generating plant would be in a position to capture almost the entire value of the initial pipeline investment by repudiating the original agreement and offering to pay only slightly more than \$25 million per year.[10]

Of course, our example is much too extreme. The generating plant is not likely to risk its reputation by blatantly repudiating a contract. And even if it did, the pipeline investors would have legal recourse, with a good chance of recovering much, if not all, of their loss. Furthermore, as the example is constructed, the generating plant has more to lose from opportunistic behavior by the pipeline owners than vice versa. If the pipeline refuses service to the plant, the cost of producing electricity increases by \$150 million per year. So the pipeline owners could act opportunistically by threatening to cut off the supply of natural gas unless they receive an annual payment of almost \$150 million per year.

But our main point should be taken seriously by cost-minimizing and profit-maximizing businesspeople: *anytime a transaction requires a large investment in dedicated capital, there is the potential for costly problems in negotiating and enforcing agreements.* Opportunistic behavior is seldom as blatant as in the example, where it is clear that a lower price is a violation of the contract. But in actual contracts involving long-term capital commitments, unforeseen changes in circumstances (e.g., higher costs, interrupted supplies, stricter government regulations) can justify changes in prices, or other terms of the contract. Typically, contracts attempt to anticipate some of these changes and incorporate them into the agreed-upon terms, but it is impossible to anticipate and specify appropriate responses to all possible changes in relevant conditions. Therefore, there are usually ambiguities in long-term contractual arrangements that open the door for opportunistic behavior of the type just discussed and that can be resolved only through protracted and expensive legal action.

Committing to investments in dedicated capital thus carries great risk from opportunistic behavior unless there is some assurance that such behavior will not pay. One way to obtain this assurance is for the investment to be made by the same firm that will be using the output it produces. Alternatively, the firm that makes the investment in the specific capital can merge with the firm that depends on the output from that investment.

The early history of the automobile industry provides an example of a merger between two companies that can be explained by the advantages of producing rather than buying when dedicated capital investment is involved.[11] In 1919, General Motors entered into a long-term contract with Fisher Body for the purchase of closed metal car bodies. This contract required that Fisher Body invest in expensive stamping machines and dies specifically designed to produce the bodies demanded by GM. This put Fisher Body in a vulnerable position, since, once the investment was made, GM could have threatened to buy from someone else unless Fisher Body reduced prices substantially. This problem was anticipated, which explains why the contract required that GM buy all of the closed metal bodies from Fisher and specified the price as equal to Fisher's variable cost plus 17.6 percent.

However, while these contractual terms protected Fisher against opportunistic behavior on the part of GM, they created an unanticipated opportunity for Fisher to take advantage of GM. The demand for closed metal bodies increased rapidly during the early 1920s (in part because of increased auto sales, but also because of a dramatic shift from open wooden bodies to closed metal bodies). The increased production lowered Fisher's production costs and, indeed, made it possible for Fisher to lower its costs significantly more than it did. Evidence suggests that Fisher took advantage of the 17.6 percent "price add-on" by keeping its variable costs (particularly labor costs) and, therefore, the price charged GM higher than necessary.

General Motors was aware of this "overcharge" and requested that Fisher build a new auto body plant next to GM's assembly plant. This would have eliminated the costs of transporting the auto bodies (a variable cost that came with the 17.6 percent add-on) and reduced GM's price. Fisher refused to make the move, however, possibly because of concerns that such a dedicated investment to GM requirements would be exploited by GM. As a result of the potential haggling, threats, and counterthreats, GM bought Fisher Body in 1926, and the two companies merged. GM could buy Fisher because the companies' tenuous dealings, with their accompanying transactions costs, were depressing both companies' market value. GM could pay a premium for Fisher simply because of the anticipated transactions cost savings.

In an ideal world without transactions costs, General Motors would have bought auto bodies from specialists subject to the constant discipline of market competition. In the real world of transactions costs, GM was better off making the auto bodies itself.

The construction of electric generating plants next to coal mines provides another example of the potential benefits to a firm of producing an input rather than buying it when highly specific capital is involved. There is an obvious advantage in "mine-mouth" arrangements from reducing the cost of transporting coal to the generating plant. But if the mine and the generating plant are separately owned, the potential for opportunistic behavior exists after the costly investments are made. The mine owner, for example, could take advantage of the fact that the generating plant is far removed from a rail line connecting it to other coal supplies by increasing the price of coal. To avoid such risks, common ownership of both the mine and the generating plant is much more likely in the case of "mine-mouth" generating plants than in the case of generating plants that can rely on alternative sources of coal. And, when ownership is separate in a "mine-mouth" arrangement, the terms of exchange between the generating plant and the mine are typically spelled out in very detailed and long-term contracts that cover a wide range of future contingencies.[12]

There are other ways a firm can benefit from the advantages of buying an input rather than producing it while reducing the transactions cost when specialized equipment is involved. It can make sense for the firm to buy the specialized equipment and then rent it to the supplier. If the supplier attempts to take advantage of the crucial nature of the input, the firm can move the specialized equipment to another supplier rather than pay a higher-than-expected price for the input. This is exactly the arrangement that automobile companies have with some of their suppliers. Ford, for example, buys components from many small, specialized companies, but it commonly owns the specialized equipment needed and rents it to the contracting firms.[13]

Firms are also aware that those who supply them with services are reluctant to commit themselves to costly capital investments that, once made, leave them vulnerable to opportunism. In such cases, the firm that provides the capital equipment and rents it to the supplier can benefit from the fact that less threatened suppliers will charge lower prices. This consideration may also be a motivation for auto manufacturers to own the equipment that some of their suppliers use. It also provides a very good incentive-based explanation, and justification, for a business arrangement that has been widely criticized.

An arrangement that reduced the threat of opportunistic behavior on the part of firms against workers was the much-criticized company town. In the nineteenth century it was common for companies (typically mining companies) to set up operations in what were at the time very remote locations. In the company towns, the company owned the stores where employees shopped and the houses where they lived. The popular view of these company stores and houses is that they allowed the companies to exploit their workers with outrageous prices and rents, often charging them more for basic necessities than they earned from backbreaking work in the mines. The late Tennessee Ernie Ford captured this popular view in his famous song "Sixteen Tons."[14]

Without denying that the lives of nineteenth-century miners were tough, company stores and houses can be seen as a way for the companies to reduce (but not totally eliminate) their ability to exploit their workers by behaving opportunistically. Certainly workers would be reluctant to purchase a house in a remote location where there was only one employer. The worker who committed to such an investment would be far more vulnerable to opportunistic wage reductions by the employer than would the worker who rented company housing. Similarly, few merchants would be willing to establish a store in such a location, knowing that once the investment was made they would be vulnerable to opportunistic demands for price reductions that enabled them to cover their variable costs but left them with no return on their capital cost. Again, in an ideal world without transactions costs—and without opportunistic behavior—mining companies would have specialized in extracting ore and would have let suppliers of labor buy their housing and other provisions through other specialists. But in the real world of transactions costs, it was better for mining companies to also provide basic services for their employees. This is not to say that there was no exploitation. But the exploitation was surely less under the company town arrangement than if, for example, workers had bought their own houses.[15]

The threat to one party of a transaction from opportunistic behavior on the part of the other party explains other business and social practices. Consider the fact that despite valiant efforts, the vast majority of farm workers have never been able to effectively unionize in the United States. No doubt many reasons explain this failure, but one reason is that a union of farm workers would be in a position to harm farmers through opportunistic behavior. A crop is a highly specialized and, before harvested, immobile investment, one whose value is easy to expropriate at harvest time. In most cases, if a crop is not harvested within a short window of opportunity, its value perishes. Therefore, a labor union could use its control over the supply of farm workers to capture most of a crop's value in higher wages by threatening to strike right before the harvest. While this threat would not necessarily be carried out in every case, it would be too serious for those who had made large commitments of capital to agricultural crops to ignore. Not surprisingly, farm owners have strongly resisted the unionization of farm workers.

The threat of opportunistic behavior is surely an important consideration in another important exchange relationship, that of marriage. Although there clearly are exceptions, rich people seldom marry poor people. The story of the wealthy prince who marries poor but beautiful Cinderella is, after all, a fairy tale. Rich people generally marry other rich people. As with all activities, there are many explanations for marital sorting, including the obvious fact that the rich tend to hang around others who are rich. But an important explanation is that marriage is effectively a specialized investment that, once made, commits and creates value not easily shifted to another enterprise, or object of affection. The rich person who marries a poor person is making an investment that is subject to hold-up. This possibility is not ignored, as evidenced by the fact that prenuptial agreements are common when large differences in wealth exist between the two parties to a marriage. But because of the difficulty of anticipating all possible contingencies relevant to the distribution of wealth upon the termination of a marriage, such agreements still leave lots of room for opportunistic behavior. Marriage between people of roughly equal wealth reduces, though it hardly eliminates, the ability of one party to capture most of the value committed by the other party.

A good general rule for a manager is to buy the productive inputs the firm needs rather than make them. When inputs are produced in-house, some of the efficiency advantages of specialization provided through market exchange are lost. But, as with most general rules, there are lots of exceptions to this one. In many cases, the loss from making rather than buying will be more than offset by the savings in transactions costs. Typically, firms should favor making those things that require capital that will be used for specific purposes and, therefore, will not have a ready resale market.

The decision a firm faces over whether to expand through additional outlets that are owned by the firm or that are franchised to outside investors has many of the features of decisions to make or buy inputs. Franchising is simply a type of firm expansion—with special contractual features and with all the attendant problems. Franchise contracts between the "franchiser" (franchise seller) and the "franchisee" (franchise buyer) typically have several key features:

- The franchisee generally makes some up-front payment and also pays a royalty that is a percentage of monthly sales for the right to use a brand name and/or trademark—for example, the name "McDonald's" along with the "golden arches."

- The franchisee also agrees to conduct business along the lines specified by the franchiser, including the nature and quality of the good or service, operating hours, sources of purchases of key resources in the production process, and the prices that will be charged.

- The franchiser agrees to provide managerial advice and to undertake advertising, to provide training, and to ensure that quality standards are maintained across all franchisees.

- The franchiser typically retains the right to terminate a franchise agreement for specified reasons, if not at will.

The own-or-franchise decision is similar to the make-or-buy decision, because both types of decisions involve problems of monitoring, risk sharing, and opportunistic behavior. At one time, scholars believed that firms expanded by way of franchising only as a means of raising additional capital by tapping the franchisee's credit worthiness. If the firm owned the additional outlet, it would have to bring in more investors or lenders at higher capital costs. Supposedly, franchisees could raise the money more cheaply than the franchiser.[16]

However, the Emory University economist Paul Rubin has argued with force that franchising per se doesn't, and can't, reduce the overall cost of capital—at least not as directly as previously argued.[17] A firm in the restaurant business, for example, can contemplate expanding through franchising only if it has a successful anchor store. It can establish another outlet through the sale of its own securities, equities or bonds, in which case the investors will have an interest in both the successful anchor restaurant and the new one. That investment in a combination of the proven and the new restaurants is likely to be less risky than any single investment in just the new restaurant, which, because it has the same menu as the anchor restaurant, has a good chance of success but is still unproved. Hence, the cost of capital for the franchisee, everything else held constant, is likely to be higher than for the original restaurant owner.

Why franchise? Rubin believes the reason for franchising is that the agency cost is lowered (but not totally eliminated) by expanding through franchising. The manager of the company-owned restaurant is probably paid a salary plus some commission on (or a bonus related to) the amount of business the restaurant generates. The manager's incentive is weakly related to the interests of the owners; therefore, the manager must be closely monitored. The franchisee, on the other hand, becomes the residual claimant on the new restaurant business and, accordingly, has a stronger incentive to reduce shirking and other forms of opportunistic behavior than do typical employees.

We noted that monitoring costs are *not eliminated* through franchising. This is the case because franchisees can still benefit from shirking. Customers often go to franchised outlets because they have high confidence in the nature and quality of the goods and services offered. McDonald's customers know that they may not get the best burger in town when they go to a McDonald's, but they do have strong expectations about the size and taste of the burgers and the cleanliness of the restaurant. McDonald's has a strong incentive to build and maintain a desired *reputation* for its stores, and therein lies the monitoring catch. Each franchisee, especially those that have limited repeat business, can "cheat" (or free ride on McDonald's overall reputation) by cutting the size of the burgers or letting their restaurants deteriorate. The cost savings for the individual cheating store is captured by the franchisee, but it reduces demand for other McDonald's restaurants. This is a prisoner's dilemma in which all stores can be worse off if noncooperative behavior becomes a widespread problem. So, McDonald's must set (and has strong incentives to do so) production and cleanliness standards and then back up the standards with inspections and fines, if not outright termination of the franchise contract.

McDonald's (and any other franchiser) also controls quality by requiring the individual restaurants to buy their ingredients—for example, burger patties and buns —from McDonald's itself or from approved suppliers. McDonald's has good reason to want its franchisees to buy the ingredients from McDonald's, not because (contrary to legal opinion) it gives McDonald's some sort of monopoly control but because McDonald's has a problem in monitoring outside suppliers.[18] Outside suppliers have an incentive to cut corners on the quality standards with the consent of the franchisees that, individually, have an interest in cutting their individual costs. Moreover, by selling key ingredients, the franchiser has an indirect way of determining if its royalties are being accurately computed. So-called tie-in sales are simply a means of reducing monitoring costs. Of course, the franchisees also have an interest in their franchiser having the lowest possible monitoring cost: it minimizes the chances of free riding by the franchisees and maintains the value of the franchise. Similarly, a franchiser like McDonald's (like its franchisees) has an interest in holding all franchisees to uniform prices that are higher than individual McDonald's might want to choose. By maintaining uniform retail prices, McDonald's encourages its franchisees to incur the costs that are necessary to maintain desired quality standards.

These points help explain up-front payment and royalty provisions in franchise contracts. The value of the franchise to the franchisee—and what the franchisee will pay, at a maximum, for the franchise—is equal to the present value of the difference between two income streams, the income that could be earned with and without the franchise. The greater the difference, the greater the up-front payment the franchisee is willing to make. However, the franchisee is not likely to want to pay the full difference up-front, because the franchiser would then have little incentive to live up to the contract (to maintain the flow of business and to police all franchisees). The franchiser could run off with all the gains and no costs. As a consequence, both the franchiser and the franchisee will likely agree to an up-front payment that is less than the difference in the two income streams plus a royalty payment. The royalty payment is something the franchisee, not just the franchiser, will want to include in the contract simply because the franchiser will then have a stake in maintaining the franchisee's business. A combination of some up-front payment and royalty is likely to maximize the gains to both franchisee and franchiser.

Franchising also has risk problems no matter how carefully the contract is drawn. Typically, franchisees invest heavily in their franchise, which means the franchisee's investment portfolio is risky because it is not highly diversified. This, in turn, can mean that the franchisee will be reluctant to engage in additional capital investment that could be viewed as risky because of the lack of diversity in his or her investment. As a consequence, franchisers tend to favor franchisees that own multiple outlets. A franchisee with multiple outlets can spread the investment risk of its investments and can more likely internalize the benefits of its investments in maintaining store quality (customers are more likely to patronize, or to fail to patronize, another of the owner's outlets).

Obviously, both ownership and franchise methods of expansion have costs and benefits for investors. We can't settle here the issue of whether a firm like McDonald's should expand by owning additional outlets or by franchising them. All we can do is point out that franchising should not be as important when markets are "local." It should not, therefore, be a surprise that franchising grew rapidly in the 1950s, with the spread of television, who greatly expanded the market potential for many goods and services, and a rapid decline in transportation costs, which allowed people to move among local markets.[19] *Franchising tends to be favored when there is a low investment risk for the franchisee and when there are few incentives for free riding by both franchisee and franchisers.* We should expect that franchises should be favored as monitoring costs increase (implying that farther the store location is from the franchiser's base, the more likely it is that the expansion will be through franchising, a conclusion that has been supported by empirical studies[20]). Also, we would expect that the fewer the repeat customers in a given location, the greater the likelihood that the store will be company-owned. When a store has few repeat customers, the incentive to cheat is strong, which means that a franchiser would have to monitor the franchisee closely to suppress the incentive for the franchisee to cheat or free ride—which implies there might be fewer cost advantages to franchising the location.[21] If monitoring costs go down, we should expect firms to increase their ownership of their outlets.

Much of what we have written in this chapter is based on the presumption that people behave opportunistically. We see this presumption as well grounded, given the extent to which people do behave that way in their daily dealings (and most managers have no trouble identifying instances of opportunistic behavior in workers, suppliers, and investors). We may, however, have given the impression that we believe that *all* people are *always* willing to behave opportunistically, which is simply contradicted by everyday experience. The business world is full of saints and sinners, and most people are some combination of both. We base our discussion on a presumption that people behave opportunistically not because such an assumption is fully descriptive of everyone in business but because that is the threat managers want to protect themselves against. Businesspeople don't have to worry about the Mother Teresas of the world. They do have to worry about less-than-perfect people. (And they do have to worry about people who pretend to be like Mother Teresa before the deal is consummated.) They need to understand the consequences of opportunistic behavior in order that they can appropriately structure contracts and embedded incentives.

In this chapter, we have shown how opportunistic behavior can arise in the most basic of management decisions, whether to "make or buy." An important task of a good manager is to constantly attentive to the trade-off between the advantages of buying and those of making, and one of the major worries is the extent of opportunistic behavior in that decision. In assessing this trade-off, managers need to be aware that the decision is dependent on the nature of what is to be bought or produced and that bureaucratic tendencies within a firm can distort decisions in favor of producing in-house even though buying would be more efficient. The firm that loses sight of this distortion may soon be outcompeted by smaller firms that rely less on internal allocation and more on specialization and market transactions to produce at lower cost.

This suggests that the size and specialization of firms will change over time in response to technological advances that alter the relationship between the costs of market transactions and the costs (as well as the efficiency) of managerial control. In chapter 2 we discussed the effects that improvements in communication, transportation, and management information systems are having on the size and focus of firms. The trend for firms to downsize and to refocus on their "core competencies" can be explained, at least in part, by the lowered costs enjoyed by smaller, more specialized firms that deal with each other through market exchange in collaborative productive efforts. But no matter how specialized firms become, resources will continue to be allocated differently within firms than they are across markets. The reason firms will continue to exist is that, over some range of productive activity, it is more efficient for resources to be directed by managerial control than by market exchange.[22]

15

The Last-Period Problem

Key Insight: An established end to a business relationship will speed up the end to the relationship.

MUCH OF THIS BOOK has been concerned with how different parties to business deals can take advantage of other parties and how managers can structure their organizational and pay policies to minimize what we call "opportunistic behavior." This chapter discusses how an announced end to a business relationship can inspire opportunistic behavior. Its goal is, however, constructive—to present ways to structure business deals, and the embedded incentives, in order to maximize the durability and profitability of the deals. To do that, business relationships must be ongoing, with no fixed end, to the extent possible. Having a fixed termination date can encourage opportunistic behavior, which can reduce firm revenues and profits. That is to say, a reputation for continuing in business has economic value, which explains why managers work hard to create such a reputation.

A terrific *advantage* of dealing with outside suppliers is that the relationship is constantly up for renewal and can easily be terminated if it is not satisfactory to both parties. But therein lies an important *disadvantage* of dealing with outside suppliers: the relationship lacks permanence, and there is no confidence that the buyer-supplier relationship will be renewed. The supplier must consider the probability that the end of the contract will be the end of the relationship, since he or she might not be the low bidder the next time around, a possibility that can have a profound effect on the relationship. Without much question, firms have begun to develop relationships with suppliers that approximate partnerships because of the "last-period" problems inherent in relationships that are totally grounded in the low-bidder status of the suppliers.

The basic problem is that during the last period of any business relationship, there is less penalty for cheating, so there is a major incentive to cheat. As a consequence, cheating on deals in the last period is more likely than at any other time in the relationship.

Consider a simple business deal. Suppose that you want a thousand widgets of a given quality delivered every month, starting with January and continuing through December, and that you have agreed to make a fixed payment to the supplier when the delivery is made. If you discover after you have made payment that your supplier has sent fewer than a thousand units or that the units are of inferior quality, you can simply withhold future checks until the supplier makes good on his or her end of the bargain. Indeed, you can terminate the year-long contract, which can impose a substantial penalty for any cheating early in the contract. Knowing that, the supplier will tend to have a strong incentive early on in the contract period to do what he or she has agreed to do.

However, the supplier's incentive to uphold his or her end of the bargain begins to fade as the year unfolds, for the simple reason that there is less of a penalty, in terms of what is lost from your ending the working relationship, that you can impose. The supplier might go so far as to reason that during the last period (December), the penalty for cheating is very low, if not zero. The supplier can cut the quantity or quality of the widgets delivered during December and then take the check before you know what has been done. The biggest fear the supplier has is that you might inspect the shipment before handing over the final check. You may be able to get the supplier to increase the quantity or quality somewhat with inspection, but you should expect him or her to be somewhat more difficult to deal with. And you should not *expect* the same level of performance or quality.

The problem is that you have lost a great deal of your bargaining power during that last month, and that is the source of what we call and mean by the "last-period" (or end-period) problem. It is a problem, however, that can be mitigated in several ways. The simplest and perhaps most common is by maintaining continuing relationships. If you constantly jump from one supplier to another, you might save a few bucks in terms of the quoted prices, but you might also raise your costs in terms of unfulfilled promises by suppliers during the last period of their association with you. "Working relationships," in other words, have an economic value apart from what the relationship actually involves, for example, the delivery of so many widgets. This is one important reason businesses spend so much time cultivating and maintaining their relationships and why they may stick with suppliers and customers through temporary difficulties.

Nothing works to solve the last-period problem, however, like success. The more successful a firm is—the greater the rate of growth for the firm and its industry—the more likely others will recognize that the firm will continue in business for sometime into the future. The opposite is also true; failure can feed on itself as suppliers, buyers, and workers begin to think that the last period is near. Firms understand these facts of business life. As a consequence, executives tend to stress their successes and downplay their failures. Their intent may not be totally unethical, since bad business news can cause the news to get worse. Outsiders understand these tendencies. As a consequence, many investors pay special attention to whether executives are buying or selling their stock in their companies. The executives may have access to (accurate) insider information that is not being distributed to the public.

Another simple way of dealing with the last-period problem in new relationships is to leave open the prospect of future business, in which case the potential penalty is elevated (in a probabilistic sense) in the mind of the supplier. When there is no prospect of future business, the *expected* cost from cheating is what can be lost during the last period. When there is some prospect of future business, the cost is greater, equal to the cost that can be imposed during the last period plus the cost (discounted by the probability that it will be incurred) inherent in the loss of future business.

When dealing with remodeling or advertising firms, for instance, you can devise a contract for a specified period, but you can suggest, or intimate, in a variety of creative ways that if the work is done as promised and there are no problems, you might extend the contract or expand the scope of the relationship. In the case of the remodeling firm, you might point out other repairs in the office that you are thinking of having done. In the case of the advertising firm, you might suggest that there are other ad campaigns for other products and services that you are considering.

By using these strategies, you should be able to secure somewhat better compliance from your supplier during the last period of the contract; how much the compliance is improved can be related to just how well you can convince your supplier that you mean business (and a lot of it) for some time into the future. However, we are not suggesting that you should outright lie about uncertain future business. The problem with lying is that it can, when discovered, undercut the value of your suggestions of further business and bring back to life the last-period problem. In other words, you need to be prepared to extend, from time to time (if not always), working relationships when in fact they work the way you want them to work.

If you are not able to develop that impression, the last period can come sooner than you might think (or sooner than December in our example). The contractual relationship can unravel because of the way you and the supplier begin to *think* about what the other is thinking and how the other might act as a consequence.

If, in our example, both you and your supplier are inclined to cheat on the contract, and you have already figured that your supplier will cheat to the maximum (send nothing) during the last period, then December becomes irrelevant and November becomes the last period. Your incentive then is to cheat on the supplier in November. Well, with November now the last period, you can imagine what your supplier is thinking. He is contemplating cheating in November before you get a chance to cheat. Ah, but you can best the supplier by cheating in October. That thought suggests that when contemplating the contract before it is signed and sealed, you and the supplier can reach the conclusion that January is the (relevant) last period—which means that the deal will never be consummated. In this way, the *last*-period problem becomes a *first*-period problem, one of setting the terms of the contract. This way of thinking about the contract can make the signing problematic, and more costly than it need be, assuming that you find ways around the problem.

This line of argument reminds us of an old joke about a prisoner condemned to death. As it happened, the prisoner was told on Sunday that he would be hung between Monday and Saturday, *but the day of his hanging would be a total surprise.* He reasoned, "They can't hang me on Saturday because it wouldn't be a surprise. So, Friday is the last day of the relevant period." Therefore, he reasoned, "They can't hang me on Friday because if they wait until then, it won't be a surprise." Continuing this line of reasoning, Friday gave way to Thursday, and so forth. He eventually concluded that they couldn't hang him. When they hanged him on Wednesday, *he was really surprised!*

This joke suggests that the last-period problem doesn't always lead to an unraveling in which the last period becomes the first. But the last-period problem is potentially serious and is one reason that firms exist. Firms are collections of departments (and people) who have continuing relationships that are not always up for rebidding, which means that the parties can figure that they will be continued, eliminating a clear-cut last period. The last-period problem is also a significant reason that the corporation is such an important business form. The corporation is a legal entity whose existence is independent of the life of the owner or owners; it typically lives on beyond the death of the owners. Because ownership is in shares, the corporation makes for relatively easy and seamless transfer of ownership, which means that the lifespan of a corporation is usually longer than that of a partnership or proprietorship, two organizational forms that die with the owners. This means that the corporate charter should be prized simply because it adds value to the company by muting (though not always eliminating) the last-period problem.

The last-period problem extends beyond buyer-supplier relationships of the sort we described for the purchase of widgets. There is clearly a last-period problem for military personnel. When officers or enlisted men and women are given their transfer orders, they can sit back and relax, knowing that the penalties that can then be imposed on them have been severely limited by the orders to move on. The problem becomes especially severe when personnel are about to leave the military altogether. Military people have a favorite expression for what we call shirking during the last period. They call it "FIGMO": "F—k you, I've got my orders." We are sure that the military has devised a variety of ways to mute the impact of FIGMO, but it is equally clear that the problem of shirking as military men and women approach the ends of their assignments remains a pressing one. Sometimes you just have to accept some costs of shirking (otherwise, you might end up concluding that people should be fired the moment they enlist, which can be more costly than the shirking).

In chapter 4, we reviewed a laboratory study involving two teams of students whose task was to expend their "work effort" under various reward systems (revenue sharing, profit sharing, enforcing contracts, and tournaments).[1] The tournaments had by far the greatest impact on the students' effort level, especially when they were closely monitored. We noted that when the probability of being caught slacking off was 70 percent, the students had a median effort level of 75 for most of the rounds—until the last round, at which time the students had nothing to lose from shirking (cutting their effort level). Between the twenty-fourth and twenty-fifth rounds, the median effort level of one team fell from 75 to about 40, or about 47 percent.[2] What is remarkable (and what shows the limitations of relying solely on economic reasoning) is that the effort level for this one team did not fall more (and the effort level of the other team did not fall at all between the twenty-fourth and twenty-fifth rounds).

The last-period problem can surface with a vengeance when an employee who has access to easily destroyed records and equipment is fired. The firm doing the firing must worry that the employee will use his or her remaining time in the plant or office to impose costs on the firm to "get back" at it. As a consequence, firings are often done quickly, as a surprise, with the employee given only enough time to collect his or her personal things in the office—all to minimize damage. The firm may even hand the employee a paycheck for hours of work not done, simply to make the break as quickly as possible and discourage fired workers from imposing even greater costs through damage to records and equipment. Indeed, when the potential for serious damage is present and likely, firms may hire a security guard to be with the fired employee until he or she is escorted to the door for the last time.

The last-period problem can also show up in the greater incentives people have to shirk as they approach retirement. To prevent retiring workers from shirking, deferred compensation can be used, with some of the compensation withdrawn if shirking does occur. A variation of this type of solution for executives is to tie their compensation to their firm's stock (through grants of shares or stock options). If executives shirk toward the ends of their careers, causing their companies to do poorly, the executives will lose more than any remaining salary they are due for the duration of their tenure; they will lose depreciation of the value of the stock (or failure of the stock price to rise), which approximates the discounted value of the company's lost earnings attributable to the executives' shirking while still on the job.

Apparently, corporations' executive compensation committees are aware of the last-period problem. The economists Robert Gibbons and Kevin Murphy have found from their econometric studies that as CEOs get closer to retirement age, their compensation tends to become more closely tied to their firm's stock market performance.[3]

Another way of solving the last-period problem is through *performance payments*, which means that payments are made as a project is completed. For example, separate payments can be made to a house builder when the house is framed, when it is under roof, and when wiring is in and the interior walls have been finished. However, a significant portion of the total amount due should be withheld until after the entire project is completed and the results approved. For example, 20 percent of the entire construction cost may not be paid until after the final inspection.

Business critics often decry the extent to which many pension plans are not fully "funded"—that is, the firm has not set aside enough money in investment accounts to meet its retirees' scheduled benefits. The underfunded pension plans can be a way by which firms seek to solve a form of the last-period problem of retired workers, especially unionized workers, whose concern for the financial stability of the firm may stop when they get their gold watch. Unions often negotiate the retirement payments and fringe benefits for unionized retirees at the same time they negotiate the pay packages for current workers. Even when retirement benefits are fixed for retirees' lives, the retirees have an interest in the continuation of the firm, but only when the pension plans are not fully funded. When they are fully funded, the retirees have a smaller stake in the continuation of the firms. They can reason, "Who cares what the workers get paid; we've got ours!" When the retirement plans are not fully funded, the retirees must worry that excessive wage demands by current workers might decrease the ability of the firm to fund retirement benefits in the future and meet the scheduled benefit payments. Hence, underfunded pension plans can be a way of tempering union wage demands by giving retirees a stake in keeping wage rates lower than they otherwise might be.

The very fact that an "old" owner of a business can sell to a "young" owner also enhances the incentive of the old owner to maintain the reputation of the firm. However, once the firm is sold, there is an incentive for the old owner to allow the firm's reputation to decline, a prospect that encourages a speedy transfer of a business when the deal is closed. If the new owner can't take over the business in a timely fashion, then he or she might overcome the last-period problem simply by ensuring that the old owner retains stock in the business.

Of course, the new owner might prefer to have complete control of the business once it is acquired. However, the value of the share he or she controls might be greater if the old owner retains some incentive to keep the reputation and material and human resources of the business intact between the time the sale is completed and the transfer of ownership is finalized. Otherwise, the old owner may have an incentive not only to relax on the job but also to set up a totally new business and then raid the old company of its key employees and customers.

If the old owner retains some interest in the firm, then he or she also has an incentive to work with the new owners, giving them time to develop the required reputation for honest dealing with employees and customers and to take control of one of the more elusive business assets—the network of contacts. The practice of keeping the old owner on after the sale of the business is common among businesses such as medical offices; doctors first establish a firm that looks and operates like a partnership, after which the sale is finalized. In these cases, the old owners work with the new owners to make the transfer as seamless as possible, because the sale price will be higher if the new owner has a good chance to establish a reputation for honest dealing and to take charge of the contacts.

Scott Cook, who in 1983 developed the widely used home-finance software package called "Quicken," the major product of Cook's Intuit, Inc., was courted in 1994 by Microsoft. Cook eventually agreed to sell controlling interest in Intuit to Microsoft for $1.5 billion in Microsoft stock, 40 percent above Intuit's market price at the time. Microsoft agreed to pay a premium price for a couple of reasons. First, Bill Gates, CEO of Microsoft, saw a need to have a dominant personal finance program that could be integrated into his Microsoft Office line and that would allow him to pursue his goal of transforming the way people manage their money. The value of Intuit was greater as an integrated part of Microsoft than by itself. Second, and more important for the purposes of this chapter, Cook agreed to become a vice president of Microsoft and to retain an interest in the future development and use of Quicken. This way, Cook could minimize the impact of the last-period problem, and the sale of Intuit would mean that Quicken might continue to develop. The proposed buyout of Intuit eventually was killed by the Justice Department, which threatened to sue Microsoft for antitrust violation. However, the example is still a good one, not only because it involves prominent business personalities and their successful firms but also because of the moral it illuminates: sometimes, by selling only a part of the company, an owner can increase the value of the part that is sold, enhancing the combined value of the part that is sold and the part that is retained.

The last-period problem also helps to explain why parents are so eager for one of their offspring to go into their business as the parents approach retirement age. This not only extends the life of the business but also increases the amount of business that can be done as the parents near retirement, because the elevation of the son or daughter puts off the last period until some time in the future.

Why do signs on business establishments sometimes read, for example,

"Sampson & Sons" or "Delilah & Daughter"? The usual answer is that the parent is proud to announce that a child has joined the business. That is probably the case, but we also think it has a lot to do with the parent's effort to assure customers and suppliers that the original owner will not soon begin to take advantage of them.

The economists David Laband and Bernard Lentz have found that the rate of occupational following within families with a self-employed proprietor is three times greater than within other families, which suggests that proprietors have good reason—measured in continuing the value of their companies—to bring their children into the business.[4] Caterpillar, the manufacturer of farm equipment and heavy machinery, depends on its dealers to maintain customer trust and goodwill. One way Caterpillar has attempted to enhance customer trust is to set up a school to help children of dealers learn about and pursue careers in Caterpillar dealerships.[5]

Firms commonly complain that goods delivered in the last days of a supplier's operation are of inferior quality. The problem? It may be the incentives, or lack thereof, that people have to deliver goods of waning quality during their last days. Bankruptcy laws can be explained in part as a means of reducing these end-period problems.[6] They extend the potential end of the firm and can give the firm a new lease on life and set back the last-period problem indefinitely.

Japanese firms are renown for organizing themselves into groups of firms called *keiretsu*s. *Keiretsu* members buy from one another, share information, and organize joint ventures to produce goods and services. The largest and best known *keiretsu* is Mitsubishi, which has twenty-eight core member firms and hundreds of other firms that are loosely tied to the core firms. They integrate their activities in a number of ways, including having their headquarters close together, having the CEOs of the various firms meet regularly to exchange information, and organizing social and business clubs that are open to employees of the *keiretsu* member firms. The members often own stock in one another's companies.

In the United States, many of the activities of *keiretsu* would likely worry the antitrust authorities because the organization would be construed as monopolistic. Some *keiretsu* activities may indeed restrain competition in some markets, causing prices of Japanese goods to be higher than they otherwise would be (especially in the domestic market, where competition from other producers around the world may be impaired by import restrictions). The *keiretsu* might also be seen as a highly efficient means by which Japanese firms are able to make use of new technologies, quickly incorporating them into products. The Japanese have demonstrated a knack for bringing new products to market quickly.

However, we mention the *keiretsu* organizational form here only because of one of its more unheralded benefits: it is a form of business organization that seeks to solve the last-period problem. The integration

of the member firm's purchases and sales and strategic plans for the future
is a means by which members can assure one another that their business
relationships will be enduring and that the members' employees have minimum incentive to behave opportunistically in the short run and have maximum incentive to work with their joint future income stream in mind.[7]
Being ousted from the *keiretsu* can inflict substantial costs on opportunistic
firms and their employees. Even the social gatherings of *keiretsu* employees can be construed as a means by which the employees can "bond."
Here, we are not so much concerned with the "warm and fuzzy" feelings
people might have from integrating their lives. Instead, we mean that by
integrating their lives at the social level, employees can provide each other
with mutual assurances that they will live up to expectations in their business dealings, that they will not act opportunistically. The employees who
do not live up to expectations can lose the long-term benefits of their
social and business relationships.[8]

In short, the *keiretsu* is a clever means by which opportunistic behavior
is made more costly. It seeks to reduce some of the shirking and monitoring costs of doing business that exist when business is done at arm's length.

Indeed, one of the more unrecognized benefits of the firm in general is
that it does, under one "roof," what is attempted in a *keiretsu*. The firm
seeks to bring people together and have them associate and work together
on a continuing basis for the purpose of minimizing the last-period problem. As we noted early in the book, it's quite possible for all departments
within a firm and all stages of an assembly line to be operated on a market
basis, with every department and every stage of the assembly line buying
from one another. However, such an organization of economic activity
would give rise to a multitude of last-period problems, especially if there
were no attempt to ensure that everyone worked together as something
approximating a *keiretsu*.

The relatively greater use in Japan of formal and informal long-term
buyer-supplier relationships, sometimes cited as "strategic industrial
sourcing" combined with so-called "relational contracting," may be partially explained by the fact that the Japanese, as commonly argued, have a
business culture grounded in a long-term, future-oriented perspective that
prescribes long-term contracts. The Japanese, to a greater degree than
Americans and Europeans, may have a pervasive sense of duty that ensures
that the parties will abide by any contracts that have been consummated,
and the Japanese may have a greater aversion than others to ongoing con-
tentious bargaining relationships that develop when contracts are always
up for grab by the lowest-cost bidder.[9] The long-term business relationships may also be a consequence of the growing affluence in Japan, which
has elevated the importance of quality over price, which, in turn, has
induced large Japanese firms to work with their suppliers in an effort to
enhance product quality.[10] The long-term contracting can also be
explained partially by the encouragement the Japanese government has

given to the creation of long-term buyer-supplier relationships in the past (especially during World War II) and the existing laws and legal sanctions against abusive treatment of subcontractors by their customers.[11]

But it seems to us altogether reasonable that long-term contracting must be grounded in factors other than culture and affluence. One economic explanation may start with a recognition of the extent to which firms are integrated in Japan. In some industries, Japanese production is far less integrated into identified "firms" than is the case in the United States and other countries. In the United States and Western Europe, for example, 50 to 60 percent of automobile manufacturing costs are incurred in-house. In Japan, in contrast, only 25 to 30 percent of automobile production costs are typically incurred in-house, or inside Japanese firms.[12] Only 20 percent of Honda's production costs are incurred inside, which means it buys 80 percent, or $6 billion, of its inputs from outside suppliers.[13] Because of the lack of integration, Japanese firms may need to develop long-term buyer-supplier relationships to a much greater degree than do more highly integrated firms just to overcome the potential last-period problems.

Put another way, Japanese firms are able to engage in what is called strategic outsourcing, and do so competitively, *because* they are willing and able to develop long-term working relationships. If they didn't, they would have to endure the added costs associated with the ever-present closing of those relationships. It doesn't surprise us that many buyer-supplier relationships in Japan have the "look and feel" of integrated firms as buyers and suppliers help each other and invest in each other's companies (which is what happens, to more or less degree, within unified firms).

When Honda signs a contract with a supplier, it expects the working relationship to continue for twenty-five to fifty years, which effectively means that the last-period problem is set back considerably.[14] The permanence of the buyer-supplier relationship runs both ways, with commitments from both Honda and its suppliers. Honda and its suppliers agree to stay together through ups and downs (at least up to a point). Hence, Honda can justify incurring the costs associated with helping its suppliers increase productivity, even providing the needed technology and specialized equipment. Such expenditures, in addition to investments in the specific assets of the suppliers, have the added advantage of forging a *bond*, the value of which is forgone if Honda does not abide by its agreement. Managers at Honda are basically saying to suppliers, "Look at what we are doing. We are serious in our commitment. If we renege, our up-front investment will be worth very little. We will lose our projected income stream from the investment. Because of those costs, you can count us in for the long run." Such tie-ins aid in making the contracts self-enforcing and durable; they help to make the long run a viable perspective.

Should production be rigidly integrated, as in American firms, or more loosely integrated, as in Japanese business consortiums? We cannot answer that question with the certitude that many readers will want. Japanese firms obviously gain the benefits of keeping their suppliers in a position that is marginally more tenuous and, maybe, more competitive with other potential suppliers, but they have to deal with the marginally more severe last-period problems. Many factors, which are offsetting and subject to change depending on the costs associated with contracting and with principal-agency problems, are involved. We suspect that different organizational forms will suit different situations and eras (as has been the case in Japan, where relational contracting has not always been prevalent[15]).

Answers will come from real-world experimentation in the market-place. We suspect that competition will press firms to adjust their organization forms and their incentive structures, as some variation of organizational form proves relatively more successful for them. Many American firms have had to seriously consider and, to a degree, duplicate the added organizational flexibility of Japanese firms. Why? These structures have obviously worked in some industries, most notably the automobile industry. It takes seventeen hours to assemble a car in Japan and twenty-five to thirty-seven hours to assemble a comparable car in the United States and Europe. Japanese firms can develop a new car model in forty-three months, whereas it takes American and European firms more than sixty months, and Japanese cars come off the production line with 30 percent fewer defects. The worst American-made air conditioning units have a thousand defects for every defect found in the best Japanese-made units.[16]

Firm integration and relational contracting are hardly the only means of moderating last-period problems. Joint ventures, which more often than not require up-front investments by the firms involved, can also be seen as extensions of efforts to reduce last-period problems. They have the potential to enhance the quality of the goods and services produced while lowering production costs. Joint ventures can lower production costs not only because they give rise to economies of scale and scope through the application of technology but because they can lower the potential costs associated with opportunistic behavior and monitoring. They make the future income streams of each party a function of the continuation of the relationship.

The last-period problem is nothing more than what we have tagged it, a problem that businesses must consider and handle. It implies costs. At the same time, firms can make money by coming up with creative ways of making customers and suppliers believe that the last period is some reasonable distance into the future. Failing firms have a tough time doing that, which is one explanation that the pace of failure quickens when the prospects are recognized; customers and suppliers can be expected to withdraw their dealings as the expected date of closing approaches.

Firms that want to continue to exist have an obvious interest in making sure there is a resale market for their firm, not just the assets that might be sold separately. The owners and workers can then capture the long-run value of their efforts to build the firm. By highlighting the last-period problem, we are suggesting that the firm resale market can boost the long-term value of those assets simply by alerting people to the fact that the firm expects to continue for some time into the future. This means that those firms—brokers—who make a market for the sale of firms add value in a way not commonly recognized, by giving firms the prospect of longevity.

The "hollow corporation," in which everything is "outsourced" and nothing is produced directly, is sometimes viewed as the organizational ideal, because the firm owners can rely on competitive forces to keep the prices of what they sell as low as possible. We doubt that the "hollow corporation" will ever dominate the economic landscape of any country for a simple reason that comes out of the analysis of this chapter: the absence of the continuing association of employees under one roof would mean that last-period problems would arise in spades. The direct association of people under one roof has an unappreciated benefit: like the *keiretsu* in Japan, the firm permits the creation of abiding relationships that reduce the incentive to behave opportunistically in the short run and enhance the incentive to work with long-term goals in mind. "Bonding" is something that firms do.

16

Pricing with Incentives in Mind

Key Insight: Profitable pricing strategies involve creative ways of using incentives to segment markets.

INCENTIVES ARE NECESSARILY embedded in a firm's pricing policy. Lowering the price of a product increases the incentive for consumers to purchase. Conversely, increasing the price reduces that incentive. Accordingly, people tend to buy more when the price falls and buy less when the price rises. This inverse relationship between price and quantity is commonly called the "law of demand." For a firm to be successful, it has to choose the "right" price, given the demand (or specifics of the inverse relationship between price and quantity) for its products. The "right" price achieves maximum profit by striking a balance among charging more, selling more, and covering the costs of production.

Saying that the firm must choose the "right" price is easier than actually choosing it. The maxim offers little practical guidance to managers confronting the complex problem of keeping the firm as profitable as possible. For example, managers can never be completely sure what the demand for their company's product is. Moreover, a company's demand is not given from on high; it can be influenced by management decisions. Good managers can increase the demand for their products by improving the quality of those products, increasing the credibility with which those products are advertised and their quality is ensured, and establishing a reputation for honesty and fair dealing. Indeed, much of our previous discussion on different aspects of getting the incentives right can be thought of as aimed at increasing the demand for the goods and services being produced. But demand is also affected by other factors, and many of them are beyond managers' ability to control or predict.

So managers, no matter how good they are, will always have to make guesses about the demands for their products—about how much they can sell of their products at different qualities and prices. There are techniques for estimating product demands (a discussion of which goes beyond the purpose of this book) and, though these techniques are never perfect, they can help managers move from making *mere* guesses to making *educated* guesses about demand.

But even if managers knew all there was to know about the demand for their products, they would still be faced with tough decisions calling for creative pricing strategies. In standard discussions of competitive markets, firms have no choice; they must set the price that competition dictates. Even when the firm has some choice in setting the price, there is no scope for creativity on the part of a firm's managers. Given knowledge of the demand and the cost of production, there is only one profit-maximizing price. Once that price is determined (by the simple rule of charging the price that motivates consumers to purchase the quantity at which marginal revenue equals marginal cost), the only sensible thing for a manager to do is to charge it. Absolutely no creativity is involved.

In the real world, there is plenty of scope for creative pricing. And such creativity can be very profitable. We have discussed throughout this book how firms compete on many margins. It is common to think of firms competing by producing better products and charging lower prices. And certainly the long-run consequence of firms struggling against each other for more consumer dollars is better products at lower prices. But in this chapter we concentrate on how managers can increase the competitiveness of their firms by producing more creative pricing strategies. Managers can often do as much for their firms, and their careers, by coming up with better pricing approaches as by coming up with better products. Of course, as is true of everything else in business, managers must have the proper incentives to be creative in their pricing strategies.

Real-world managers are not limited to charging only one price for a product (although fair trade laws and the penalties that go with their violation do restrict the range of pricing options available to many managers). As those business people who fly frequently know, several different prices are charged for coach seats (or first-class seats) on most flights. For example, passengers who book their flights weeks in advance often pay less (often several hundred dollars less) than passengers who book their flights days before their departure. By charging different prices for the same product, firms are able to earn higher profits than is possible with only one price. Some creativity can be exercised by carefully announcing prices.

There is a joke based on the pricing creativity of an optometrist. When a customer inquires about the price of a pair of glasses, the optometrist answers, "Seventy-five dollars," and then pays close attention to the customer's expression. If he doesn't cringe, the optometrist quickly adds, "For the lenses." If the customer still doesn't cringe, the optometrist adds, "For each one."[1]

There are, of course, better (perhaps less devious) ways of charging different prices. Consider the demand you face for a book you have written. Let us suppose that you can sell 10,000 copies by charging a price of $25 to everyone, thereby realizing total revenues of $250,000. But you could also sell fewer copies at higher prices. The one person most anxious to read your book is willing to pay $50 for it; the next most anxious reader is willing to pay slightly less for it, on down to the 10,000th most anxious reader, who is willing to pay the $25 price at which you could sell all 10,000. You can even sell more copies, of course, but only by charging less than $25.

How should you price your book? If you could somehow charge each reader the maximum amount he or she is willing to pay, then you obviously would not sell each copy for $25. You would charge prices that are higher than $25 on the first 9,999 copies, which would necessarily yield far more in revenues than you would get by charging $25 for each and every copy.[2]

Rarely, if ever, can a seller expect to be able to practice such "perfect" price discrimination (and sellers need to consult their lawyers to ensure that they do not violate laws that prevent charging different prices to different customers within the same identified classes of customers that cannot be justified on cost considerations). Even if the demand is known exactly, so that the seller knows the maximum amount that can be charged for each unit of the product, the seller is unlikely to be able to identify the consumer who is willing to pay the maximum for each. And if such detailed information were known, it could still be difficult for the seller to charge each consumer a different price because of resale possibilities. For example, if resale is easy (meaning cheap), those who are being charged less than $30 for the book could buy extra copies and sell them to the most anxious readers (who would otherwise be charged more than $45) for $35. Such arbitraging reduces the ability of sellers to profit from price discrimination. But it does not prevent creative managers from finding less than perfect, but still profitable, ways of charging different prices for a product.

Let's return to the book example. Book publishers cannot differentiate between every potential buyer of a book and charge each a different price. But they can separate the market into two broad categories of buyers, those who are most impatient to read the latest novel by, say, Tom Clancy and those who want to read it but do not mind waiting a while. If publishers can separate (or segment) these groups, they can charge a different price to each group. But how can they do that? One method: sell hardback and paperback editions of the same book. Hardback books are issued first and are sold at a far higher price than the paperback edition, which will not be made available until six months or a year later. In this way the seller charges those customers who are less sensitive to price (or who have an *inelastic* demand) a higher price than those who are sensitive to price (or who have an *elastic* demand). Those customers with inelastic demands reveal their impatience by their willingness to pay the high hardback price. There is no problem with arbitrage in this case, since those who pay the low price do so long after the high-price customers have made their purchase.

Of course, sellers don't always have to package their products differently, as publishers do, to distinguish between buyers who have inelastic demands and those who have elastic demands. Just after new, more powerful models of computers are introduced, their prices can be quite high, only to fall later. Many chalk up the falling prices on computers to reductions in production costs, which may very well be true. However, we suggest an additional explanation for why computer prices fall with the age of the models: the sellers are using time to segment their markets, charging those who are eager to get the new models a high price and charging those who are less eager and more willing to wait a lower price.

Department stores almost always have storewide sales after Christmas. Commonly, the after-Christmas sales are explained as a way for the stores to get rid of excess inventories. There is a measure of truth to that explanation; stores cannot always judge correctly what will sell in December. However, it is also clear that shoppers have more inelastic demands before Christmas than they have after Christmas. Hence, the stores are often doing nothing more than segmenting their markets. They plan to hold after-Christmas sales and order accordingly. They are not making less money by the sales; they are, in truth, making more money because they can charge different prices in the two time periods, attracting customers they otherwise would have lost.

Grocery stores and the suppliers of the products grocery stores sell have also found a way of getting customers to reveal how sensitive they are to price, which allows those who are less price-sensitive to be charged more than those who are more price-sensitive. In almost every daily newspaper you can find pages of coupons that, if you cut them out and take them to the designated store, allow you to save twenty-five cents, fifty cents, and sometimes a dollar or more, on a host of different products. No coupons, no savings.

Those who go to the trouble of cutting out these coupons and carrying them to the store are revealing themselves as being relatively price-sensitive. So when you fail to present coupons as you go through the checkout line at your local supermarket, you are telling the cashier that you are not very sensitive to price, that your demand is relatively inelastic. The cashier responds by charging you more for the same products than he or she charged the coupon-laden customer ahead of you. The problem of arbitrage is handled by limiting the amount a customer can buy of a product.

Moreover, not many people are tempted by the opportunity to buy one bottle of shampoo for fifty cents off and then trying to sale it for twenty-five cents off to someone in the parking lot who doesn't have a shampoo coupon. The cost of creating the secondary market for something as cheap as shampoo is surely greater than the price differential, especially when only a few units can be bought at the favorable price and sold at a higher price.

Sometimes a firm can profit by charging different prices to different customers without appearing to do so. This can be accomplished by putting the same price on two products that are consumed together by some customers, but not by others. Consider the owner of a theater who realizes that some customers are willing to pay more to go to the movies than others are. Obviously, the owner would like to charge these customers more. But the owner has no way of determining who the price-insensitive customers are when they are paying for their tickets. So how does the manager charge the price-insensitive customers more without losing the remaining customers?

There is a way that we have all observed, but probably didn't think of as an example of price discrimination. Assume that the theater owner believes that those customers who are willing to pay the most to watch a movie are generally the ones who most enjoy snacking while watching. If this assumption is correct (and we will argue in a moment that it probably is), the owner takes advantage of the demand of the enthusiastic movie watchers by charging a moderate price for the tickets to the movie and high prices for the snacks sold in the theater lobby. By keeping the ticket prices moderate, the owner encourages customers with a high demand elasticity for the movie to buy tickets, since they are not going to do much snacking anyway. While the low-elasticity demanders will surely complain about the high prices on all the snacks they eat, they still consider the total cost of their movie experience acceptable, since they were willing to pay more for their ticket than they were charged.

If it were not true that those who are willing to pay the most to watch a movie also enjoy snacking the most, then it is unlikely that we would observe such high prices for snacks at the movies.[3] Assume that the opposite were true, that those who are not willing to pay much to watch a movie are the ones who most enjoy snacking when watching the movie. If this were the case, the owner of the theater would find that charging moderate prices for the tickets and high prices for the snacks was not a very profitable strategy. Since the avid movie watchers are not snacking much, they would be willing to pay more than the moderate price to get into the theater. And since the other customers care more about snacking than seeing the movie, they would see little advantage in paying the moderate price for the movie when the snacks were so expensive. In this case, the most profitable pricing strategy would be high ticket prices and low snack prices. The enthusiastic movie watchers would still come and end up paying more. And the snackers would now be willing to pay the high ticket prices for the opportunity to eat lots of cheap snacks.[4] The fact that we do not see such pricing in theaters suggests that, at least for most consumers, our assumption is correct.

Any time a firm can identify consumers on the basis of their sensitivity to price, it is in a position to vary its price for different groups in ways that increase the incentive for consumers to purchase its product. The advantage of being able to separate customers willing to pay high prices (again, those who have relatively inelastic demands) from those who are more price sensitive (those who have relatively elastic demands) is so great in some cases that it explains why some firms will incur costs to reduce the quality of their products so they can sell them for less.

For example, soon after Intel introduced the 486 microprocessor, it renamed it the 486DX and introduced a modified version, which it named the 486SX. The modification was done by disabling the internal math coprocessor in the original 486, a modification that was costly and reduced the performance of the 486SX. Intel then sold the 486SX for $333, less than the $588 it charged for the 486DX. Why would Intel spend money to damage a microprocessor and then sell it for less?[5] The answer is that this enabled Intel to separate out those customers who were willing to pay a lot for a microprocessor from those whose demand was more sensitive to price. Intel could sell the 486DX to the former at a price that would have driven the latter to its competitors. Yet it managed to keep the business of the more price-sensitive customers by lowering the price to them without worrying that this would drive the price down for the high-end customers. There was no way for the lower-price consumers to buy the lower-price product and sell it to the high-end consumers, since its performance had been reduced.

Similarly, when IBM introduced its LaserPrinter E in May 1990, it set the price lower than the price for its earlier model, the LaserPrinter. The LaserPrinter E was almost exactly the same as the LaserPrinter except that the former printed at a rate of five pages per minute while the latter printed at a rate of ten pages per minute. Why was the LaserPrinter E slower? Because IBM went to the expense of adding chips that had no purpose other than to cause the printer to pause so that it printed slower. Why did IBM go to extra expense to produce a lower-performance printer? Again, to separate consumers with inelastic demands from those with elastic demands so that it could charge for the former a higher price.

One of the authors, Lee, enjoys playing golf (although why he does is a mystery). He buys brand-name golf balls that have been labeled with XXX to indicate that they have some flaw and are sold at a discount. Many good golfers are willing to pay extra for regular brand-name balls, which supposedly travel farther than the XXX balls. Lee, on the other hand, sees no advantage in hitting his balls farther into the woods. And, anyway, he is not convinced that there really is any difference between the regular high-priced balls and the XXX balls, except that the manufacturer went to the extra expense of adding the XXXs. While we have no documentation, we suspect that golf manufacturers simply put XXXs on a certain percentage of their balls so that they can separate their market into two groups—golfers like Lee, who are quite sensitive to price, and golfers who, because they have a reasonable idea where their balls are going, are not very sensitive to price.

Another technique firms can use to separate price-sensitive consumers from those who are less sensitive is to make unadvertised price discounts available, but only to those who search them out and ask for them. Obviously, those who go to the trouble to find out about a discount and then ask for it are more concerned about price than those who do not. This approach to identifying customers for discounts on long-distance calls is (at this writing) being used by AT&T. According to an article in *The Wall Street Journal*, AT&T responded to Sprint Corporation's ten-cents-a-minute rate for calls made during weekends and evening hours by offering a flat rate of fifteen cents anytime, a plan it called One Rate.[6] But AT&T really had two rates, one of which it did not advertise. The unadvertised rate, available only to those who asked for it, allowed AT&T customers to call around the clock for ten cents a minute. As reported in the *Journal*, "AT&T customers can get dime-a-minute calling 24 hours a day, seven days a week—if they know to ask for it. That is the hardest part, for AT&T has been uncharacteristically quiet about the new offer. The company hasn't advertised the 10-cent rate; it hasn't sent out press releases heralding the latest effort to one-up the folks at Sprint."[7] The old adage about oiling only what squeaks certainly applies in this case. (We suspect that AT&T was not all that pleased with *The Wall Street Journal* simply because the publicity reduced AT&T's ability to segment its market by reducing the "search costs" that would otherwise have faced AT&T customers who read *The Wall Street Journal*.)

Sometimes it is possible to charge the same customer more than one price for different units of a product and, by doing so, get the customer to pay more than he or she otherwise would. This pricing strategy often works to the firm's advantage even though it is impossible to separate consumers into different groups and charge each a different price, as in the previous examples. The simplest case, both to put into practice and to analyze, involves charging two prices for the same good. Assume that you are selling AA batteries and the cost of producing each of these batteries is twenty cents. Let us suppose that the best you can do when charging one price is to set the price at sixty cents, which allows you to sell 24,000 units. This pricing policy yields a profit per unit of forty cents (sixty cents - twenty cents), which yields a total profit of $9,600 (forty cents x 24,000). But you can raise your profit above $9,600 if, once your customers buy 24,000 batteries at sixty cents each, you can lower the price on any additional batteries they buy. For example, if you reduce the price to fifty cents on all batteries purchased beyond 24,000, you can increase battery sales to, say, 36,000 and make an extra profit on the additional 12,000 units of thirty cents each (fifty cents minus twenty cents), which means that profits can go up by $3,600 (thirty cents x 12,000).[8]

In fact, firms do use such two-part pricing strategies, but, of course, not exactly in the way just described. For example, if a firm announced that it was going to charge sixty cents for each battery until the first 24,000 were sold each week, and then charge fifty cents per battery for the remainder of the week, it probably would not sell the 24,000, since customers would attempt to postpone their purchases until enough other consumers had made theirs. But a firm can effectively achieve much the same result by making everyone the following offer: buy two batteries at a price of sixty cents and get the third for fifty cents. Such a two-part pricing offer is easy to implement and can increase profits. Not surprisingly, such offers are commonly observed.

The more competition and price rivalry exist in an industry, the smaller the gain a firm in that industry can realize from charging different customers different prices. Even relatively price-insensitive customers will be bid away by rival firms when price competition is intense if one firm tries to charge those customers much more than it does its more price-sensitive customers. Nevertheless, the more the firms in an industry can segment their market so as to buffer the price competition between them, the greater the scope for creative pricing strategies that can increase profits, a point to which we can now turn.

Firms in an industry could simply get together and agree not to lure consumers away from each other by reducing prices. This would allow them to keep prices, and their collective profits, higher than would be possible if all firms made a futile attempt to increase their market shares by charging lower prices. But there are two problems with this approach to reduce price competition. The first problem is that any agreement to restrict competition *can* be illegal, and firms, and their managers, who enter into such an agreement risk harsh antitrust penalties. The second problem is that, even if agreements to restrict price competition were not illegal, they would still be almost impossible to maintain. Members of industry cartels that have agreed to set prices above competitive levels face another prisoners' dilemma. While they are collectively better off when everyone abides by the agreement, each individual sees the advantage in reducing price below the agreed-upon amount. If other firms maintain the high price, then the firm that cheats on the agreement can capture lots of additional business with a relatively small decrease in its price. On the other hand, if the other firms are expected to cheat on the agreement, it would be foolish for a firm to continue with the high price, since that firm would find most of its customers lured away. Only if firms ignore prisoner-dilemma temptations and take the risk of making the cooperative choice can cartel price agreements be maintained. Not surprisingly, such agreements tend to break down.

The Organization of Petroleum Exporting Countries (OPEC) is a classic example of a cartel with all the hopes and dreams of a well-oiled cartel but with rampant cheating. What is amazing is that the cartel held together for as long as it did in the 1970s. Today it pretends to set production restrictions, only to have them violated fragrantly. One unheralded explanation for Saddam Hussein's invasion of Kuwait was that, prior to its invasion of Kuwait, Iraq had been trying to hold to its assigned quota while Kuwait had flagrantly violated its quota, denying Iraq sales and the higher world oil price the cartel sought. By taking over Kuwait and (possibly) then Saudi Arabia, Hussein hoped that he could introduce some needed production discipline into the cartel and raise the world price of oil, a threat that helps to explain why the industrial countries, including the United States, were willing to defend Kuwait militarily. The allied forces were, in effect, trying to maintain the natural competitive instability in the cartel (as well as trying to deny a tyrant greater political clout on the world stage).

Some pricing policies can moderate price competition between rival firms without the need for a cooperative agreement. Indeed, these policies do more to moderate competition when competition results in all firms implementing them.

Consider a pricing policy that would seem to favor your customers with protection against high prices but that is a smart policy because it makes higher prices possible. The strategy is quite simple. It calls for an unqualified pledge: "We will meet or beat any competitor's price." A so-called "meet-the-competition" pricing policy tells your customers that if they are offered a lower price by a competitor, you will match it. This policy is commonly advertised as "guaranteed lowest prices" by retail stores like Circuit City. To implement such a policy, you inform your customers that if they can find a lower price on a product within thirty days of purchasing it from you, they will receive a rebate equal to the difference. Obviously, such price guarantees have value to the customers, but what is not widely appreciated is that the guarantees, especially if they are also made by those you are in competition with, allow you to charge more than otherwise. How can this be?

One straightforward explanation is that the price assurance gives customers some insurance about the price they are paying and therefore increases their demand. The greater demand leads to higher prices.

But there is another explanation, one based on an equally simple proposition: if you want to charge higher prices, there is an obvious advantage in discouraging competitors from reducing their prices to steal your customers away. This is exactly what a meet-the-competition policy does. Your competitors are probably not all that eager to initiate a price-cutting campaign. Attempting to take customers away from another firm through lower prices is always costly. If successful, the new business is likely to be worth less to the pricing-cutting firm than to the firm that loses it because the price the customers are paying is now lower. In addition, existing customers will want to receive the lower price as well, which can cut deeper into any profits that might have otherwise been possible. Of course, if a price-cutting campaign aimed at capturing new customers fails to do so, the campaign is all cost and no benefit. So if your competitors know that you have a meet-the-competition agreement with your customers, they will have less, and likely nothing, to gain from trying to attract those customers by cutting their prices.

A meet-the-competition pricing policy can not only be good for your profits; it can also be good for your competitors. By allowing you to keep your prices higher than otherwise, your meet-the-competition policy gives your competitors more room to keep their prices high. This suggests that, as opposed to most competitive strategies, which become less effective when mimicked by the competition, your meet-the-competition policy becomes more profitable when the same policy is implemented by other firms in the industry. Just as your competitors are better off when you do not have to worry about the competitive consequences of keeping your prices high, so are you better off when your competitors are relieved of the same worry.[9]

A related pricing policy is to offer some of your customers the status of most-favored-customer, which entitles them to the best price offered anyone else. (Again, this policy must be checked with lawyers, since some such policies in some circumstances might be construed as illegal.) If you lower your price to any customer, under this policy you are obligated to lower it for all of your most-favored customers. As with the meet-the-competition policy, what at first glance appears to favor your customers can actually give the advantage to you. A most-favored-customer policy increases the cost of trying to take customers away from rival firms by reducing price. And when one firm has such a policy, its reluctance to engage in price competition makes it easy for other firms to keep their prices high. So, as with meet-the-competition policy, the advantage firms realize from a most-favored-customer policy is greater when all the firms in a industry have such a policy.

If the idea that a policy of being quick to reduce prices for your customers can result in higher prices seems counterintuitive, you are in good company. In their book *Co-opetition*, Harvard business professor Adam Brandenburger and Yale management professor Barry Nalebuff relate how Congress, in an effort to control the cost of campaigning, required television broadcasters to make candidates for Congress most favored customers. In the 1971 Federal Election Campaign Act, Congress made it against the law for TV broadcasters to lower their rates for a TV spot to any commercial customer without also lowering their rates to candidates. The result was that TV broadcasters found it extremely costly to reduce rates for anyone, and the networks made more money than ever before. Politicians had the satisfaction of knowing that they did not pay more for air time than anyone else, but they probably ended up paying more (as commercial advertisers surely did) than they would have had Congress not forced the broadcasters to implement a most-favored-customer pricing policy.

Congress made a similar mistake in 1990 when it attempted to reduce government reimbursements for drugs by stipulating that Medicaid would pay only 88 percent of the average wholesale price for branded drugs, or, if lower, the lowest price granted anyone in the retail trade drug business. Instead of lowering prices, the law actually raised them. By making itself a most-favored customer, the federal government gave the drug companies a strong incentive to raise prices for everyone. And, indeed, that is exactly what happened, according to a study cited by Nalebuff and Brandenburger, which found that prices on branded drugs increased from 5 to 9 percent because of the 1990 rule changes.[10] The advantage the government may have realized by keeping its price at 88 percent of the average wholesale price was probably more than offset (it was often receiving a discount, anyway) by the higher average prices. And certainly non-Medicare patients ended up paying higher drug prices, a disguised form of what NBC News should surely want to cover in its "Fleecing of America" segment.

Another pricing strategy that allows the firms in an industry to reduce price competition has become increasingly common in recent years. This strategy involves a creative way of identifying those customers who are most likely to buy from your firm anyway and then lowering the price they pay. At first glance such a strategy would appear counterproductive. Why would you lower the price for those who are likely to buy from you even if you charge a higher price? The answer is that by making price concessions to your most loyal customers, you can end up charging them higher prices.

A good way of explaining this seemingly paradoxical possibility is by considering the frequent-flyer programs that almost all the airlines now have. These programs are commonly thought of as being motivated by each airline's desire to take business away from other airlines by effectively lowering ticket prices. No doubt this was the primary motivation when, in 1981, American Airlines introduced its AAdvantage program. And the rapidity with which other airlines countered with their own frequent-flyer programs suggests intense competition among the airlines. But intended or not, the proliferation of these programs has had the effect of reducing the direct price competition among airlines and, as a result, may be allowing them to maintain higher prices than would otherwise be possible. An airline's frequent-flyer program reduces the effective, if not the explicit, price it charges its most loyal customers and reinforces their loyalty.[11] By increasing the motivation of an airline's frequent flyers to concentrate their flying on that airline, it decreases the payoff other airlines can expect from trying to lure those customers away with fare reductions. This allows the airline with the frequent-flyer program to keep its explicit fares higher than if other airlines were aggressively reducing theirs.[12] This decreased motivation to engage in price competition becomes mutually reinforcing as more airlines implement frequent-flyer programs.

From the perspective of each airline, it would be nice to be able to steal customers from other airlines with lower fares, but collectively the airlines are better off by reducing this ability. And this is exactly what the spread of frequent-flyer programs has done, to some degree, by segmenting the airline market. There is now less competitive advantage in reducing airfares, and less competitive disadvantage in raising them. The effect has been to reduce the elasticity of demand facing each airline, which allows all airlines to charge higher prices than would otherwise be sustainable.[13]

A pricing strategy similar to frequent-flyer programs has begun to spread in the automobile industry. In 1992 General Motors joined with MasterCard and issued the GM credit card. By using the GM card, consumers earned a credit equal to 5 percent of their charges, which can be applied to the purchase or lease of any new GM vehicle (with a limit of $500 per year up to $3,500 for any one purchase). While not all the major automakers have followed the GM lead, several have. And the more automakers that join in, the better for the car industry in general. Just like frequent-flyer programs, automobile credit cards allow car companies to focus implicit price reductions on their most loyal customers. An individual is not likely to use a GM credit card unless she is planning on buying a GM car or truck. As the number of car companies that issue their own credit cards increases, the auto market will become increasingly segmented and there will be less advantage from price competition. Again, a pricing policy that allows a firm to target its most loyal customers and favors them with price cuts can have the effect of increasing the prices charged.

Saying that firms *should* come up with creative pricing schemes is easier said than done. Managers must have the right incentives to do it. If an organization offers rewards only for developing new product lines or for getting workers to increase production of existing product lines, managers may overlook equally effective alternative ways to increase profits. Firms would be well advised to use profit as a prominent performance measure because it gives managers flexibility to look for profits in all kinds of ways, in the way products are developed and marketed and in the way they are priced.

We cannot exhaust the possibilities for creative pricing policies in this chapter. We have, however, indicated some of the ways that managers can increase the profitability of their firms by taking full advantage of the subtle interactions between incentives and pricing policies.

Lower prices surely increase the incentive a consumer has to buy your product. However, some customers have a stronger incentive to take price into consideration than others, and these different price sensitivities create profitable opportunities to charge different prices for the same product. Such opportunities increase as the danger that your customers can be captured by aggressive price cutting by rival firms decreases. Fortunately, there are pricing policies that can reduce that danger. Such policies as meet-the-competition pricing can reduce the incentive other firms have to engage in price competition. Other policies, such as those represented by frequent-flyer programs, reduce price competition by reducing customer incentives to take price (at least the explicit price) into account. By tailoring such pricing strategies to their particular circumstances, managers can do what good managers are paid to do: use incentives to increase the profitability of their firms.

Managers should be given an incentive to consider the profitability of devoting attention to pricing as well as to other ways of increasing the profitability of their firms. We suspect that the American Airlines manager who came up with the idea of the AAdvantage frequent-flyer program has been handsomely rewarded for his or her creativity. When a pricing innovation is as distinctive and profitable as the AAdvantage program has been, it is easy to recognize and reward those who are responsible. But few pricing innovations have the bottom-line impact that the AAdvantage program has had for American Airlines, making it more difficult to sort out how important a particular contribution is. Rewarding managers for creative pricing strategies is best done in the same way they are rewarded for all the many marginal things they do to improve their firm's profitability—by tying their compensation to that profitability. The closer managerial compensation comes to creating the incentives of a residual claimant, the more alert managers will be to adding value along the entire spectrum of possibilities, from coming up with better products, to developing less costly ways of producing those products, to devising more creative ways to price them.

17

The Value of "Mistreating" Customers

Key Insight: When firms "mistreat" their customers, both the firms and their customers often benefit.

HAVE YOU EVER heard of a business consultant recommending to her clients that they mistreat their customers? Probably not. The standard recommendation is to give customers what they want, pamper them, treat them as individuals, and never attempt to force them to do things they don't want to do. Most of the time, this is surely sound advice. But not always. More often than most business consultants seem to realize, business can provide more value to their customers by mistreating them—by giving them what they individually don't want, by ignoring their individual desires, by requiring that they do things they would not voluntarily do, and by charging them high prices for frills that cost more than they are worth.

If people always consumed services individually, with the value they received from their consumption unaffected by what others do, then mistreating them would seldom be a good business strategy. But many services are consumed either together or in the presence of others. When this is the case, suppliers should always be alert to the possible *collective* benefits that both they and their customers can realize when the customers are mistreated on an *individual* basis.

In many cases, the benefit from mistreating customers is explained by the fact that by mistreating individual customers, a supplier allows the customers to overcome a prisoners' dilemma and be better off collectively. To see why, assume that you are the manager of a shopping mall that is soon to open for business and are eager to attract retailers who will pay as much as possible for the opportunity to locate in your mall. This is a situation in which you should not be too accommodating to each potential customer, or, in this case, tenant. A far better approach is one of creatively "mistreating" potential tenants—requiring that they operate their stores in ways different from the way they would voluntarily choose if given a choice.

Hours of operation are one of the most important requirements you should impose on prospective tenants. It would be unusual if all tenants were to choose the same hours of operation. But you as manager would be smart to require that all tenants keep their stores open similar hours. The most obvious reason is there are significant costs involved in having the mall open, and it often doesn't make sense to incur those costs if only a few stores are open. You wouldn't want to keep a large mall open, for example, to accommodate a convenience store that wanted to stay open all night. This is why you don't find convenience stores in malls.

The most important reason, however, for requiring that all tenants in the mall operate during similar hours is that it has the effect of lengthening the number of hours they are open. When one store is open for business, it attracts consumers that benefit other stores. Indeed, one of the primary reasons stores like to operate in malls is they each receive spillover business from customers who came to the mall to shop at other stores. But this means that when a store is open, it is creating benefits that it is not capturing entirely for itself, benefits that it would ignore in its own decision whether to stay open or to close. This suggests that, if left to decide on its own, each store would likely stay open fewer hours than is best from the point of view of all stores. As manager of the mall, it is your job to consider the spillover business that stores generate for each other. Every store can benefit if it is required to stay open longer hours than it would choose to on its own.

Consider a hypothetical example in which each store owner in the mall would independently choose to keep his or her store open forty hours a week, with the result that each store earns profits of $1,000 per week. Assume also that if any one store increased its hours to more than forty hours a week on its own, with all other stores staying with their forty-hour-per-week schedule, the store that stayed open longer would see its costs increase as a consequence, with very little additional business. Its profits would fall to $900 per week. On the other hand, if all but one of the stores increased their hours to forty-eight hours per week, they would each increase their profits to $1090 per week, as the mall became more convenient for and popular with shoppers. But the one store that remained open only forty hours would be able to free-ride on the additional popularity of the mall and would then earn $1150 profit per week. On the other hand, if all stores operated forty-eight hours per week, all stores would earn $1100 profit each week. Total profits are greater if all stores stay open forty-eight hours, but individually each store would choose to operate only forty hours. As the manager of the mall, you will increase the value the mall provides tenants—and therefore the amount they are willing to pay in rent—by going against the wishes of each tenant and imposing a forty-eight-hour schedule of operation.

By imposing hours on all stores that are longer than any one would unilaterally choose, you have benefited all of the tenants by removing them from a prisoners' dilemma. A good mall manager will be constantly alert to other areas where he or she can require tenants to do things they would not individually choose to do (or prohibit activities they would individually choose to do) but that create a more profitable setting when done by all (or not done by any). For example, individual stores may profit from having clerks stand outside their stores' entrances and aggressively solicit passing shoppers to come in. But if this becomes a common practice, all stores may suffer, with consumers feeling less comfortable shopping at the mall and taking their business elsewhere. So all storeowners are collectively better off if all such solicitations are banned. They can earn more by having a greater number of shoppers and higher sales, so you may earn more in rent from the storeowners. On the other hand, requiring each store in the mall to advertise in the local paper (or on local TV and radio) more than any store would individually choose to do can increase the profits of all stores by increasing the number of shoppers who come to the mall.

The situation at a mall is similar to that in a community of homeowners who are subjected to a covenant that imposes restrictions on such things as the color of the houses, the type and maintenance of the landscaping, and the number of cars that can be parked outside overnight. Almost everyone living in such communities dislikes some of the restrictions. Yet people are willing to pay more to live in communities with covenants because the cost to each family of abiding by the restrictions is less than the benefit realized from having the restrictions imposed on others.

Private schools face serious competition attracting customers. They have to cover their costs of educating students with tuition payments from parents who have the option of sending their children to public schools they have already paid for with taxes. Obviously, private schools have to treat their customers well if they are to survive. But some of the most successful private schools recognize that treating their customers well as a group can require mistreating them individually. In many respects the education of children is a collective enterprise in which the best results require that all customers be required to do things that many would not voluntarily choose to do.

Consider the example of a private school in Nanuet, New York, that has done very well, in part because it has come up with a creative way of mistreating its customers. Love Christian Academy requires that all the parents have monthly meetings with their children's teachers and volunteer to work at the school at least one day a year. If parents miss, or are even late for, a meeting, they are fined $100. Parents who are fined or who give up a favorite TV show to attend a meeting and avoid the fine often feel mistreated. One parent was quoted as saying he was "not pleased" with being fined for violating one of the rules, and some parents have removed their children from the school because of the strict rules. But the school thrives because most parents feel more than compensated by knowing that their children are attending school with other children whose parents are actively involved in their education.[1]

Similarly, few parents want their children spanked at school. But if the choice is between sending their children to a school where none of the students are spanked or to one in which any student who misbehaves is spanked, including their own, many parents prefer the latter. This is recognized by many private schools that advertise the fact that they believe in maintaining discipline in the classroom by subjecting unruly students to an old-fashioned spanking. Dr. Connie Sims, the superintendent of Love Christian Academy, makes it clear that, before students can be accepted, their parents must accept the school's disciplinary policy.[2]

While no one feels good when his or her children receive poor grades, many parents prefer a school in which that is a possibility to one in which it is not. The school that holds its students to a high standard of academic achievement and gives good grades only to those who achieve that standard will have a better reputation than a school that doesn't. So while the students, and their parents, may feel mistreated if they receive poor grades, they prefer a school with a policy of giving low grades because of the additional educational value created by that policy.

Manufacturers that sell their products through independent dealers often impose restrictions on the price the dealers can charge for the products and on the number of dealers who can sell them in a given area. These restrictions are referred to as *resale price maintenance* agreements and *exclusive dealing* arrangements, respectively. The effect of these restrictions is to increase the prices consumers pay, and for a long time the conventional view of policy critics was that the price maintenance agreements and exclusive dealerships allowed sellers to profit at the consumers' expense. But, as in the previous examples, a policy that at first glance appears to be mistreating customers may actually be in the customers' best interest by allowing them to overcome a prisoners' dilemma.

In certain cases, requiring retailers to charge higher prices (price maintenance) or allowing them to charge higher prices (exclusive territory) makes it possible for a manufacturer to benefit customers because without these restrictions each customer would find it individually rational to behave in ways that are collectively harmful. Consider a product on which customers are able to make a more informed choice when it is properly displayed. One example is furniture, which is best examined in a well-appointed setting containing other pieces of complementary furniture.

Another example is sound equipment that consumers would like to evaluate in sound rooms before purchasing. But unless the manufacturer imposes some restrictions on the retailer, it is unlikely that the consumer will benefit from such helpful displays. The retailer who went to the expense of properly displaying a product or having experts on hand to answer questions for potential customers would be vulnerable to the price competition of retailers who did not provide these services. A retailer with a warehouse and an 800 number could (and many have) run advertisements suggesting that customers visit retailers with showrooms and experts to decide what they want to buy and then call in their order to the warehouse for a discount price.

The problem is that while it makes sense for each customer to take advantage of such offers, if many customers do so they will end up collectively worse off as the retailers with showrooms go out of business. This is clearly an example of a prisoners' dilemma. So retail price maintenance agreements and exclusive-dealing arrangements can be thought of as ways of protecting consumers against their own prisoners' dilemma temptations. By not selling their products through a retailer who refuses to maintain some minimum price, a manufacturer can prevent some retailers from free-riding on the showrooms and expert sales staffs of others. If price competition is not permitted, retailers must compete through the display, service, and sales expertise that make the product more valuable to consumers. Similarly, by providing one retailer the exclusive right to sell its product in a market area, a manufacturer prevents, or at least reduces the ability of, some retailers to free-ride on that retailer's efforts. A retailer with the exclusive right to sell a product in an area has a strong motivation to provide the combination of display and service that consumers find most attractive. And with each consumer able to secure the advantages of good displays and service only by paying for it, the prisoners' dilemma no longer eixsts.

There is no guarantee, of course, that a manufacturer will choose a price (in a resale price agreement) or a market area (in an exclusive dealing arrangement) that makes consumers better off than they would be without such restrictions on retailers. For example, the resale price agreement may require a price that costs the consumer far more than the extra sales and service are worth. Or the exclusive market area may be so large that many customers are inconvenienced by the lack of a nearby store that carries the product. But a manufacturer that makes such mistakes will find itself penalized by competitors who make better use of these restrictions on retailers. Those manufacturers who strike the best balance between "mistreating" their customers with higher prices and restrictions on the number of retailers and protecting their customers against the collectively harmful temptations of the prisoners' dilemma will expand their market share at the expense of those who do not.

Manufacturer restrictions on retailers do not make sense for all products. And manufacturers should be aware that the use of these restrictions might activate overzealous antitrust enforcers even when they do make sense. But such restrictions do provide another example of how you can attract more business with policies that may appear to harm customers but that actually benefit them by helping them escape a prisoners' dilemma.

One of the oldest sayings in business is "The customer is always right." This seems like good advice to a firm that wants to succeed in the marketplace. Even if you believe your customers are wrong, don't disagree with them. Give them what they want, or they will take their business to someone who will agree. There are situations, however, when the only way to succeed is by being willing to tell your customers that they are wrong and to give them exactly what they don't want.

Consider the situation faced by firms that are in the business of rating the bonds of corporations. Corporations that want to issue bonds pay firms such as Standard and Poors, Moody's, Duff and Phelps, and Fitch to evaluate the safety of those bonds and rate them accordingly. A rating of AAA indicates that the bonds are very safe, while a rating of CC indicates that the bonds are in the category of junk bonds and therefore are highly risky. A corporation does not want to misrepresent the safety of its bonds, since doing so would, in the long run, reduce its ability to borrow money. But there is a natural tendency for a corporation to give itself the benefit of the doubt and believe that its bonds are safer than they actually are. Therefore, the rating service that followed the advice "The customer is always right" would seriously jeopardize its usefulness and its profitability. The rating service that developed a reputation for yielding to client pressure for higher ratings would cease to have the credibility that its clients are paying for. So, in the bond rating business, corporations commonly give good money for bad ratings.

Similarly, corporations hire independent accounting firms to audit their financial statements and to report on the degree to which those statements conform to acceptable accounting practices and accurately convey relevant financial information. The managers of the corporations who pay for an audit have objectives (rapid promotions, nicer perks, and higher salaries) that differ from those of the stockholders, bondholders, and others who use corporate financial statements (and who want the highest return on their investments). So managers can have an incentive to bias the financial statements in ways that make them look better but are misleading to investors. But the accounting firm that does the audit has a strong incentive to ignore any desire managers may have for a favorable but undeserved report by being as impartial and accurate in its evaluation as possible. Only by maintaining a reputation for impartiality and accuracy is an accounting firm able to provide a valuable service to all of its clients.

One of the best-documented rules of business is that the lower the price charged for a product, the more of that product consumers will buy. Everything else being equal, consumers prefer low prices to high prices, and it would seem that intentionally charging higher prices for products than they are worth would be a better way of driving away customers than of attracting their business. But everything is not always equal, and there are situations in which a business is well advised to charge its customers high prices to cover the costs of products they don't value that highly.

The benefits a person receives from consuming a good or service are sometimes significantly influenced by who the other consumers are. Consider a rather extreme example. There are two hotels in the town you are visiting that are identical except for their customers. One is patronized by nonaffluent and poorly behaved rowdies who create loud disturbances all night, while the other is patronized by affluent, well-behaved folks who are careful not to disturb their neighbors. Which hotel would you prefer? Preferences differ, and no doubt some would prefer the "action" that is more likely to be available at the first hotel. But it is a safe bet that most affluent, well-behaved people would prefer and be willing to pay more for the second.

This situation suggests what looks like a profit opportunity for one of the hotel owners: establish a reputation for catering to affluent and well-behaved guests by refusing to rent to anyone else, and then charge premium prices. Unfortunately, things aren't so simple. First, it is not easy to tell if a prospective guest is either affluent or well behaved, particularly those who make telephone reservations. Second, even if you could identify those who are "unacceptable," refusing to rent to them would probably be a violation of public accommodation laws in your state.

But there is another way to filter out less desirable customers that, though imperfect, has the advantage of not being illegal and of getting immediately to your primary objective. Just charge higher prices than the other hotel, even though the two are physically identical. The less desirable customers will tend to take their business to the other hotel, which will make your hotel more valuable to those who can afford to pay extra to avoid the less affluent and/or unruly guests. This strategy won't work perfectly. It does not, for example, screen out rock bands that may be affluent but very unruly. But though an imperfect strategy, high prices do have the virtue of generally doing a good job of screening out less desirable guests, and this is clearly a case where virtue is its own reward.

Things are more difficult, however, than we have indicated so far. All hotel owners would like to increase their profits by simply increasing their prices and catering to the well-to-do. Obviously, not everyone can be suc-

cessful with this strategy. Because of competition, those who want to attract
the well-to-do to their hotels with higher prices will find that they also have
to provide nicer facilities and more services than are available at lower-
priced hotels. So construction and operating costs will increase at high-
priced hotels until the rate of return on investment in these hotels is about
the same as the return on investment in low-priced hotels, as well as in most
other investments. But because one of the big benefits to guests at expensive
hotels is being in the company of other guests who can afford to pay high
rates, the frills at those hotels don't have to be worth what they cost.

Indeed, it is widely believed that people pay more for extras than they
are objectively worth at expensive hotels. One of the cut-rate hotel chains
recently took advantage of this belief in an advertisement in which a hotel
guest is shown holding up a small bottle of fancy shampoo and asking
whether it was worth the extra $20 room charge. If not, the listener was
urged to stay at the cut-rate hotel rather than at an expensive hotel. A
clever advertisement, but it ignores the fact that people are getting more
for the extra $20 than the shampoo. They are getting a place to stay that
screens out those who aren't willing or able to pay an extra $20 for a small
bottle of shampoo.[3]

We have confined our discussion to hotels so far, but there are other
businesses where the client effect is important in determining how much
value consumers realize from the service. The client effect is certainly
important for many people when they go out for a leisurely dining experience. People pay a lot of money for a meal in a fine restaurant, and though
the food and service are typically quite good, it seems reasonable to wonder if many people actually value the attention of hovering captains, wine
stewards, and waiters as much as they pay for them. Surely some of the
benefits customers receive from the high prices at fine restaurants come
from the screening performed by those prices. The client effect is hardly a
consideration when you grab your food in a paper bag at a drive-through
window. At McDonald's or Burger King, the price you pay reflects the
value you place on the food, not the value you place on screening out
undesirable customers.

The business of education is another example of the importance of the
client effect. Students who attend a college with other students who are
capable and enthusiastic will typically get a far better education than those
who attend a college with students who are poorly prepared and uninter-
ested, even though the colleges are of similar quality in terms of faculty
and facilities. Students learn not only from their classroom experiences
but also from their after-class interaction with other students. This suggests that the high tuition charges at many small private colleges can be
explained, at least in part, by the value they create as screening devices.

We should point out that the screening explanation for high tuition is
one that we find attractive. Both of the authors have spent their careers
teaching in public universities where the students pay relatively low

tuition. We have often wondered why so many small private colleges can charge such high tuition fees when, generally, most of the professors at these colleges, at least in the academic fields with which we are familiar, have published less and are less well known than our colleagues. Why would students, or their parents, pay so much more to attend the lectures of these professors when they could be attending lectures at our universities for far less? We certainly don't want to believe that our colleagues are not as good at teaching as professors at expensive private colleges. Generally speaking, our colleagues are good teachers.

In our more serious moments we recognize, of course, that private colleges typically put more emphasis on teaching than do large public colleges and universities. Competition drives private colleges to provide more services to their customers for the extra price they pay. But it is hard to believe that the value created by the extra emphasis on teaching at these private colleges is nearly enough to justify the extra tuition charged. Surely much of the extra value is created by using the higher tuition as a screening device.

When bosses repeat the refrain "The customer is always right," workers may be led to believe that the unspoken rule is that they should take whatever the customers throw at them in the way of abuse. As we have seen, the bosses' advice might be a reasonable working rule, but it is also likely to be advice that the boss doesn't want employees to take with complete seriousness. The rule overlooks the fact that abusive customers can make work a form of hell for the workers. If forced to take excessive abuse, the workers would, no doubt, demand higher wages to compensate them for this abuse. At some point, as more and more abuse is encountered, it is altogether reasonable to expect that the higher wages the workers require will exceed the value received by the firm from accommodating abusive customers. Any tolerably reasonable boss will, at some point, ask workers to stand their ground and return the fire of their customers. Otherwise, firm profits can be impaired.

The president of Southwest Airlines understands the (economic) principles at stake. He has been known to write letters to customers who have been abusive to his workers, telling those customers that they should take their business elsewhere. Southwest may lose some business, but it can also gain a total wage bill that will be lower than otherwise, and that can more than compensate the company for the lost business. Also, the policy may screen out unruly passengers, thus making Southwest more attractive to well-behaved passengers.

Indeed, if customers are given too much consideration, they may abuse it at the expense of not just the business but customers in general. Consider refund policies. Most retail stores allow customers to return merchandise that they feel doesn't suit their needs as well as they anticipated. Within reasonable limits, such policies benefit all customers and build goodwill and profitability for the business. Some retailers have pushed those limits, however, and impose almost no restrictions on refunds. Apparently, some of these retailers are now having second thoughts as more and more customers are taking advantage of generous refund policies.

For example, Best Buy has stopped giving refunds on certain products unless the customer has a sales receipt, and even then the customer has to pay a "restocking fee" of 15 percent of the purchase price if the package in which the product came has been opened.[4] Before the change in policy, one Best Buy customer received a refund on a video camera that he claimed was defective. Indeed, it was defective—for a reason the Best Buy repair technicians discovered when they played back the tape inside and saw the splash of water as the camera fell into a swimming pool and sank to the bottom. It was at the bottom when the recording stopped. Wal-Mart has also moved away from its open-ended return policy by imposing on most items a ninety-day maximum beyond which no refund will be made. Before this restriction went into effect, one customer got a refund for a beat-up thermos that Wal-Mart later learned from the manufacturer had been purchased in the 1950s, long before there was a Wal-Mart. Another retailer that has decided to halt its no-questions-asked policy on returns is the catalog store L.L. Bean. According to a spokeswoman for the firm, some customers were returning clothes that had been purchased at garage sales or found in the closets and attics of deceased relatives.[5]

Most customers are honest, and a largely unrestricted return policy would be appropriate for them. But honest people will be the most supportive and appreciative of restrictions when a liberal return policy begins to be abused. And there is a tendency for the number who take advantage of a generous return opportunity to grow over time as some of those who do not initially return items that shouldn't be returned see others doing so. The cost of paying people for fraudulent, or at least highly questionable, returns is soon reflected in the price that everyone has to pay. Imposing strict limits on all customer returns will seem like mistreatment to some customers, but it is really little different from imposing restrictions on the hours of stores in a mall or fines on parents who are late for meetings with the children's teachers. Without such restrictions, each consumer will have an opportunity to gain by engaging in behavior that is collectively harmful.

Treating customers as if they are always right, giving them what they want, and giving it to them at the lowest possible price is standard business advice, and it is generally sound advice. But not always. We have examined several situations in this chapter in which good business calls for "mistreating" customers. Once the situations have been explained, of course, the recommended treatment of customers isn't mistreatment at all. Business owners and managers are well advised to be constantly on the alert for creative ways of "mistreating" their customers. There are many more circumstances in which such creative "mistreatment" can allow a business to better serve its customers than can be known by any one person or discussed in one short chapter. "Mistreatment" often is in the customers' interest and translates into economic improvement for customers and a higher value for the firm.

18

Profits vs. Corporate Social Responsibility

Key Insight: If managers exploit the discretion they have as agents, their shareholders, under certain conditions, will be better off than would be the case if managers always, under all circumstances, sought to maximize their firms' profits.

FORMER SCOTT PAPER CEO Al Dunlap, known for revitalizing dying companies by aggressively cutting jobs, perks, and corporate charity, argues that corporate executives should "mean business" in a book by that title.[1] He minces few words in denouncing his predecessors at the companies he has revitalized for sloppy management practices that ignore this maxim: Executives should singlemindedly focus their corporations' efforts on making money for their shareholders.

Dunlap exudes pride over the $6.5 billion in additional wealth he made for Scott shareholders (as well as the $100 million he added to his personal wealth) in just eighteen months by dramatically downsizing and focusing the firm. Although he never cites him, Dunlap obviously agrees with the free-market economist Milton Friedman, who argued that the only social responsibility of business is to make as much profit as possible—while obeying prevailing laws of honesty and fair dealing.[2]

According to Friedman, management's preeminent responsibility is limited to what it was hired to do—manage the company with the shareholders' objectives in mind, presumably wealth maximization. Dunlap has infused action into Friedman's admonition and justifies that action with a position that Friedman would surely endorse: "The mission of a company is to protect the interests of the investors. They stand front and center for the gravy train, not at the rear of the line."[3] He then adds: "Executives who run their businesses to support social causes . . . would never get my investment dollars. They funnel a portion of profits into things like saving the whales or Greenpeace. That is not the essence of business. If you want to support a social cause, if you have these other agendas, join Rotary International."[4]

By way of sharp contrast, former Secretary of Labor Robert Reich has condemned corporate CEOs for making tens of millions of dollars by "abandoning their workers and communities—indeed, precisely because they have abandoned their employees and communities."[5] He quotes approvingly Frank Abrams, who in 1951, as chairman of Standard Oil of New Jersey, maintained, "The job of management is to maintain an equitable and working balance among the claims of various directly interested groups . . . stockholders, employees, customers and the public at large."[6] In a bygone era, corporations shared their success with their workers and communities. Now, according to Reich, profitable companies shed their workers at will and skip town. The corporation, according to Reich, has been transformed into "the agent of the shareholder alone."[7]

Reich, with the support of President Bill Clinton, took to the media to remind American businesses of their social responsibilities, which he argues should consider the interests of the broader communities within which corporations operate. Reich and Clinton are typical of critics of the Friedman-Dunlap view of corporate responsibility in asserting a fiduciary responsibility of corporate managers that extends beyond the interests of their shareholders to a variety of stakeholders, not the least of which are the people who live in communities where the corporation has facilities.

While our purpose in this chapter is also to challenge the Friedman-Dunlap position, we do so on their terms. Unlike other critics of Friedman and Dunlap, we accept their proposition that the overriding responsibility of corporate executives is to their shareholders. We have little problem with downsizing payrolls and reducing managerial perks when doing so benefits shareholders by making business more efficient. Efficiency improvements can benefit everyone by adding to corporate profits, ensuring the long-run viability of productive jobs, and expanding community tax bases.

However, we also recognize that the interests of shareholders extend beyond the goal of making money. Indeed, we contend that being faithful to the interests of shareholders requires making corporate contributions to charities and communities beyond the level that maximizes shareholder profits. Investors can view business firms as vehicles for social improvements that they, the investors, cannot individually achieve. Many investors are motivated, at least in part, to "join" companies for the same reason that they join civic clubs, as Dunlap suggests—to mount a collective response to an observed social need. Furthermore, we argue that the growing importance of mutual funds (in terms of both their number and their financial clout) as an investment vehicle is allowing shareholders to more effectively communicate their willingness to embrace corporate responsibility at the sacrifice of some personal financial return.

In the debate over the "social responsibility of business," the issue is not whether one is for or against charitable contributions. Both Friedman and Dunlap recognize that most shareholders, as individuals, possess a sense of civic virtue that motivates contributions to worthy causes. Friedman and Dunlap also have no problem with corporate contributions that increase shareholders' returns by, for example, creating consumer and community goodwill.[8] But they reject the idea that corporate executives should be concerned with trying to promote worthy goals by making corporate contributions in excess of profit maximizing levels.

Friedman's and Dunlap's dictum can be recapped: CEOs should concentrate on profit maximization, which is what they were hired to do and what they are most competent at. By doing this job well (and by not having to assess the claims of a multitude of "stakeholders"), CEOs utilize scarce resources to produce the most wealth possible and increase the number of desirable things that can be done. CEOs may have social responsibilities as individuals, and they surely know what charitable projects they feel are most deserving of support. They are free to contribute as much as they want to whatever cause they want with their own money. But even the most talented CEOs have no special ability to choose those charities that their shareholders believe are most worthy. When they make corporate contributions at the expense of corporate profits, they are usurping the responsibility of shareholders to use their money as they see fit.

Shareholders want corporate managers to make them as much money as possible so that they—the shareholders—can make their own decisions on how their earnings, received by way of dividends, are spent, and for most shareholders that involves making contributions to the charitable activities and civic projects they see as most deserving. As Dunlap writes, "Whether the United Way or the Red Cross should be supported is a decision that should be made by individuals."[9] But the Friedman-Dunlap position ignores an important problem that individuals face in making charitable donations. This oversight is especially surprising in the case of Friedman since, as we shall see, the basic problem—which we have frequently cited as the prisoners' dilemma—is one he has discussed in other contexts as the "free-rider problem." Once this problem is recognized, the ground begins to crumple under the argument that shareholder interests are best served *only* by the single-minded pursuit of maximum corporate profits so that shareholders can make their own charitable contributions.

In most situations, people make more responsible decisions with their own money than with other people's money, a point we concede to Friedman and Dunlap. The logic is straightforward: when people use their own money, they bear the full cost of their mistakes and unnecessary expenditures. Corporate executives who own a tiny minority interest in their firms can transfer most of the cost of their spending to other shareholders. Clearly, some executives take advantage of this situation to live lavishly at shareholder expense, a practice that Dunlap finds contemptible.[10] But much of what Dunlap and others see as extravagant spending by undisciplined corporate executives through corporate donations are contributions to the creation and maintenance of "community goods," or goods that provide general benefits to the community (beautification programs, pollution abatement efforts, programs for troubled youth, and poverty relief). These are the types of contributions that individuals prefer to make through an organization, such as a corporation.

Making contributions to community goods through a corporation helps individuals overcome the free-rider problem that plagues the provision of community goods. Friedman himself has recognized this free-rider problem, the existence of which calls into question his and Dunlap's narrow view of corporate responsibility, even as an ideal. Although community goods can generate benefits that are worth more than they cost, because those benefits are generally available once provided individuals have little motivation to contribute to them. The basic reason should be familiar to readers: once the community goods are provided, each individual in the community benefits independent of whether, or how much, the individual contributed. So the temptation for each is to attempt to "free ride" off the contributions of others, with the result that, left to individual action, valuable community goods go unfunded, or grossly underfunded.

We can return to our example of a community good, pollution abatement. The benefits from pollution reduction may be far greater than the cost, with everyone willing to contribute to a cleaner environment in return for reciprocal contributions by others in the community. But when each knows that what others contribute is unaffected by his or her contribution, the free-rider option dominates individual calculations and little, if any, funds may be contributed to pollution reduction—*unless concerted action by members of the community can be mounted collectively.*

Friedman explained several decades ago why another community good, relief of poverty, is underfunded when left to individual contributions. According to Friedman:

> It can be argued that private charity is insufficient because the benefits from it accrue to people other than those who make the gifts—. I am distressed by the sight of poverty; I am benefited by its alleviation; but I am benefited equally whether I or someone else pays for its alleviation; the benefits of other people's charity therefore partly accrue to me. . . . [W]e might all be willing to contribute to the relief of poverty, *provided* everyone else did. We might not be willing to contribute the same amount without such assurance. (emphasis in original)[11]

Friedman acknowledges in this statement that individuals are not in the best position to make charitable contributions in amounts that best advance their own interests. This leaves wide open the possibility that shareholders would be losers if their corporate managers adhered strictly to the Friedman-Dunlap position on businesses' social responsibility. Given the inability of individuals, on their own, to make contributions to charities and community goods in amounts that best serve their collective interest, they could be worse off with increased corporate profits if the additional profits came at the expense of social benefits the corporate contributions could provide.

Corporate CEOs use the mantra of "corporate responsibility" as justification for contributions that bring them recognition and acclaim but that come mostly out of the pockets of others. But their share of the general benefits created by community goods funded by their corporation's contributions is small, the personal accolades they receive for their civic virtue notwithstanding. To claim, as Dunlap does, that "corporate charity exists so that CEO's can collect awards, plaques, and honors, so they can sit on a dais and be adored" ignores completely the satisfaction and benefits that shareholders receive from corporate contributions, much of which would not be realized if the earnings were distributed as dividends and individual shareholders were left to make charitable contributions from their dividends.[12]

We do not claim that the contributions made by corporate executives are always of the type and amount that more than compensate shareholders for the cost of those contributions in reduced profits. But we do claim two things. First, shareholders receive compensation from contributions that reduce corporate profits. And, second, if the sole responsibility of corporate CEOs is to their shareholders, as argued by Friedman and Dunlap, then corporate responsibility should go beyond that of maximizing shareholder profits.

Clearly, many investors care only about their own private welfare, narrowly defined. However, just as clearly, many investors care to some extent about remedying social problems and improving the conditions of others. Such investors can see some corporations—for example, The Body Shop, Tom's of Maine, and Ben and Jerry's Ice Cream—as agents for social change that can, in some areas, be more effective than government. The fact that investments in such companies might yield a lower-than-maximum rate of return is not evidence that they are working against the interests of shareholders. Indeed, given Friedman's more general position that "free markets" efficiently allocate resources, including investment funds, we should let the market—not Friedman or Dunlap—decide how socially responsible firms should be. The easiest case for illustrating the critical flaw in the Friedman-Dunlap view of social responsibility is a corporation that operates in one community, with all of its shareholders living in, and making up most of the population of, that community.

Shareholders may have no motivation to make contributions to community goods as individuals, but that doesn't mean that they cannot see personal gains from making such contributions collectively through the corporation. In this situation, the shareholders receive most of the benefits from their corporations' contributions (assuming, as we do in this example, that the contributions are confined to the local community). If the shareholders could convert the corporate managers into perfect agents, they (the shareholders) would require those managers to violate the Friedman-Dunlap standard for corporate social responsibility by contributing more to the community than that which maximizes profits. Friedman and Dunlap confuse making money with the more general interests of shareholders.

A more realistic case involves a corporation that operates in more than one community and whose shareholders are even more widely dispersed. Most shareholders of such a corporation will realize little advantage from the corporation's contributions, since few will live in the communities that receive those contributions. But most shareholders will live in communities that would benefit from the contributions of similar corporations, even if not those in which they own shares. In this case, being able to assert complete control over the corporation's managers might not be in the best interest of the shareholders. The shareholders of each corporation would understandably instruct their managers to eliminate contributions that reduce their profits (possibly hiring someone like Dunlap to carry out their instructions), while hoping to free ride off the contributions that reduce the profits of other corporations' shareholders. While this free-rider hope may be rational for the shareholders of individual corporations, it leads to smaller overall corporate contributions for community goods than is desirable from the perspective of all shareholders.

Much management theory presumes that it is always in the interest of owners (principals) to have greater control over their managers (agents). In this more realistic case, however, shareholders can actually be better off without complete control over their corporate agents because that control would be used to ensure that corporations followed the Friedman-Dunlap advice of maximizing shareholder profits. We acknowledge that we do not know what the ideal degree of control over corporate managers should be, but our argument does imply that it is less than complete control. We now consider the most realistic case discussed so far and argue that the relationship between shareholders and corporations is increasingly one in which shareholders would benefit from having more control over corporate decisions because they would use that control to demand more corporate responsibility than is favored by Friedman and Dunlap.

While the shareholders of many corporations are widely dispersed, most shareholders have diversified portfolios, with shares in a number of corporations that are also widely dispersed. With the growing popularity of mutual funds, the number of corporations owned by the typical shareholder has increased, as has the number of communities benefiting from the contributions of the corporations represented in each shareholder's portfolio. So even if each corporation confines its contributions to one community, the contributions made by the corporations owned by the typical shareholder will be spread over a large number of different communities.

A large percentage of shareholders now have an ownership interest in some corporations whose contributions go to the communities in which they live. With the widespread ownership of mutual funds, the calculus of shareholders as contributors to community goods becomes similar to that discussed in the first case considered—a corporation operating in the community where its shareholders live. In that case, each shareholder can reduce the free-rider problem he or she faces as a contributor to community goods by having the corporation do some of the contributing, thereby ensuring that one's own contribution in terms of reduced profits is reciprocated by the contributions of others in the same community. In the case of widespread ownership of mutual funds, the free-rider problem shareholders face as contributors is reduced by having all the corporations in their portfolio do the giving. Each owner of a mutual fund can come out ahead by accepting a somewhat lower return to support corporate contributions in other communities because his or her community is benefiting from similar contributions by fund owners in those other communities.

The growth in the number and size of mutual funds creates a situation analogous to that described in the first case of a corporation in one community of shareholders, except now the community is the entire country and beyond. With the growing popularity of mutual funds, shareholders increasingly find themselves in a position to benefit from corporate contributions that spread contributions over many communities, such as some types of pollution control activities. And we can expect increasing support for corporate action that provides no direct benefit to shareholders other than the knowledge that they are contributing to a noble objective, because each knows that his or her contribution is being supplemented by the contribution of many others. With wide ownership of mutual funds, shareholders would, if they had more control over corporate managers, use that control to pressure corporations to make contributions in excess of profit maximizing amounts, thus violating the limited prescription of corporate responsibility put forth by Friedman and Dunlap. And when large blocks of corporate shares are owned through mutual funds or huge pension funds, shareholders are in a better position to exert control over corporate managers through their fund managers. According to a recent article in *The Economist,* "Companies have no choice but to listen to the institutions [such as pension funds], because they own half the shares in the United States. But the institutions have a strong incentive to act in the long-term interest of society as a whole. They represent more than 100 million Americans, so they can reasonably be taken as a proxy for the common good."[13] This helps explain why managers of huge retirement funds (for example, the fund that controls the pensions for California State employees) have a broader view of social responsibility than that recommended by Friedman and Dunlap.

How successful fund managers who apply social responsibility criteria to investment will be at attracting shareholders remains to be seen. We doubt that they will be "successful," at least not by the standard measure of funds, the financial rates of returns achieved for shareholders. There is no free lunch, and neither is there free social responsibility. Our view is that taking social responsibility seriously does cost something, but it is a cost many shareholders are willing to pay if the free-rider problem they face as individuals is mitigated. And this problem is being mitigated by large mutual funds and retirement funds. These funds may be providing investors a service that rivals that of allowing a more diversified portfolio. But it has to be acknowledged that contributors to community goods will always face a free-rider problem and that attempts by mutual funds to reduce this problem are limited by the temptation faced by individual investors to realize a somewhat higher return by choosing a fund that does not apply a social responsibility screen on its investments. Of course, this temptation is less relevant in the case of retirement funds where the individual investor's choices are more limited, and so we would predict that it is through these funds that investors and their representatives will be able to most effectively communicate their collective desire for more corporate social responsibility.

We agree with Friedman and Dunlap that the primary responsibility of corporate managers is to their shareholders. But, unlike Friedman and Dunlap, we believe that being faithful to this responsibility requires sacrificing some shareholder profits to make charitable and social contributions that shareholders would make as individuals except for the free-rider problem.

19

Why Professors Have Tenure and Businesspeople Don't

Key Insight: Tenure is a means by which universities encourage professors to be honest in selecting colleagues and protect them from the slings and arrows of internal politics.

TENURE IS NOTHING SHORT of a holy grail for newly employed assistant professors in the country's colleges and universities. If they do not receive tenure, faculty members must, as a general rule, be dismissed after seven years of service, which means they must seek other academic employment or retreat from academic life. With tenure, professors have the equivalent of lifetime employment. Rarely are they fired by their academies, even if they become incompetent at teaching and/or researching.

Business people rarely, if ever, have the type of tenure protection that professors do. Why the different treatment? Is it that universities are stupid, bureaucratic organizations in which professors are able to obtain special treatment? Maybe so, but we would like to think not. (Indeed, we think our universities have shown great wisdom in granting us both tenure in our current positions, from which we could not be dislodged by anything short of a direct nuclear hit!) We suggest that our explanation for why professors have tenure will help us understand why some form of tenure will gradually find its way into businesses that have begun to rely progressively more on "participatory management" (with low-ranking managers and line workers having a greater say in how the business is conducted).

Professors do not, of course, have complete protection from dismissal, and the potential for being fired is surely greater than that reflected in the number of actual firings. However, when professors are fired it is generally for causes unrelated to their professional competence. The most likely reasons for dismissal are "moral turpitude" (which is academic code for sexual indiscretions with students) and financial exigencies (in which case, typically, whole departments are eliminated).

Most proponents and opponents of academic tenure like to think of it in emotional terms: "Tenure is stupid" or "Tenure ensures our constitutional rights." We would like to suggest that tenure be treated as a part of the employment relationship. It amounts to an employment contract provision that specifies, in effect, that the holder cannot easily be fired. To that extent, tenure provides some employment security, but by no means perfect security. A university may not be able to fire a faculty member quickly, but it can repeatedly deny salary increases and gradually increase teaching loads until the faculty member "chooses" to leave.[1]

Clearly, tenure has costs that must be suffered by the various constituencies of universities. Professors sometimes do exploit tenure by shirking their duties in the classroom, in their research, and in their service to their universities. However, tenure is not the only contract provision that has costs. Health insurance (as well as a host of other fringe benefits) for professors imposes costs directly on colleges or universities and indirectly on students. Nonetheless, health insurance costs continue to be covered by universities because the benefits matter, too, not just the costs. Health insurance survives as a fringe benefit because it represents, on balance, a mutually beneficial trade for the various constituencies of universities. Universities (which can buy group insurance policies more cheaply than individual faculty members) are able to lower their wage bills by more than enough to cover the insurance costs because they provide health insurance. By the same token, professors pay for tenure just as they do other fringe benefits; presumably tenure is worth more to them than the value of the forgone wages.

Why tenure? Any reasonable answer must start with the recognition that academic labor markets are tolerably, if not highly, competitive, with thousands of employers and hundreds of thousands of professors, and wages and fringe benefits respond fairly well to market conditions. If, in fact, tenure were not a mutually beneficial trade between employers and employees, universities—which are constantly in search of more highly qualified students, faculty at lower costs, and higher recognition for their programs—would be expected to alter the employment contract, modify the tenure provision, increase other forms of payment, and lower overall university costs.[2]

The analysis continues with the recognition that jobs vary in difficulty, in time and skills required, and in satisfaction. "Bosses" can define many jobs, and they are generally quite capable of evaluating the performance of those they hire for these jobs. In response to sales, for example, supervisors in fast-food restaurants can determine not only how many hamburgers to cook but how many employees are needed to flip those hamburgers (and

assemble the different types of hamburgers). Where work is relatively simple and routine, we would expect it to be defined by and evaluated within
an authoritarian/hierarchical governance structure of firms, as is generally
true in the fast-food industry.

Academic work is substantially different, partially because many forms
of the work are highly sophisticated, its pursuit cannot be observed directly and easily (since it relies on thinking skills), and it involves a search for
new knowledge that, when found, is transmitted to professional and student audiences. (Academic work is not the only form of work that is heavily weighted with these attributes, a point that is reconsidered later.)
Academic supervisors may know in broad terms what a "degree" should be
and how "majors" should be constituted at any given time. However, they
must rely ultimately and extensively (but not necessarily completely) on
their workers/professors to define their own specific research and classroom curriculums and to change the content of degrees and majors as
knowledge in each field evolves. Academic administrators employ people
to conduct research and to explore uncharted avenues of knowledge that
the administrators themselves cannot conduct or explore because they lack
knowledge of the field.

Fast-food restaurants can be governed extensively (but not exclusively)
by commands from supervisors, and there is an obvious reason why this is
possible. The goods and services produced are easily valued and sold, with
little delay between the time they are produced and the time the value is
realized, as well as easily evaluated. Workers in such market environments
are inclined to see supervisors as people who increase the income of stockholders *and* workers mainly by reducing the extent to which workers shirk
their agreed-upon duties.

Academe, however, is a type of business that tends to be worker managed and controlled, at least in many significant ways. As we will see, this
aspect of the academic marketplace solves many decision-making problems, but it introduces other serious problems—unstable and even volatile
and uncertain decisions made collectively by professors over time and circumstances. Understandably, professors seek contractual protection from
the vagaries of collective decision making. Professors are called upon to
determine what their firms (universities) produce (what research will be
done, what courses are required, and what will be the contents of the various courses, even who will be taught). In addition, they help to determine
who is hired to teach identified courses and undertake related research,
how workers are evaluated, and when they are fired.

Our argument can be stated without using the examples of fast food and
academe, but those examples enable us to deduce a managerial principle of
sorts: the simpler it is to accomplish a job, the more likely it is that managerial control will be delegated to a supervisor. The more sophisticated,
esoteric, and varied the job to be done, the more likely managerial control

will be relegated to the workers themselves and the more democratic the decision making will be.[3]

Again, why academic tenure? We think the forces of supply and demand for tenure are at work. Economists have argued that universities have reason to "supply" tenure.[4] The reason: professors are called on to select new members, which stands in sharp contrast to the way hiring decisions are made in business and in sports. In baseball, the owners, through their agents, determine who plays what position on the team. Baseball is, in this sense, "owner managed." In academe, the incumbent professors select the team members and determine which positions they play. Academe is, in this sense, "labor managed."

In baseball, the owners' positions are improved when they select "better players." In contrast, in academe, if tenure did not exist, the position of the incumbent decision makers could be undermined by their selection of "better professors," those who could teach better and undertake more and higher-quality research for publication in higher-ranking journals.[5] Weaker department members would fear that their future livelihoods (as well as their prestige) would be undermined by their honest evaluations of candidates who were better qualified than themselves.

Thus, tenure can be construed as a means employed by university administrators and board members—who must delegate decision-making authority to the faculty but who want to elevate the quality of what is done at their universities—to induce faculty members to judge honestly the potential of new recruits. In effect, university officials and board members strike a bargain (with varying degrees of credibility) with their professor—decision makers: if you select new recruits who are better than you are, you will not be fired.

Universities have reason to *supply* tenure, but what reason do professors have to *demand* it? We don't buy the argument that most faculty members want to be protected from the broader political forces outside the ivy-covered walls of their universities. Too few faculty members ever go public with their work or say anything controversial in their classes for them to want to give up very much for such protection. Rather, we believe tenure is designed to protect professors from their colleagues, acting alone or in political coalitions, in a labor-managed work environment operating under the rules of academic democracy. That is, faculty members demand tenure so that there will be little or no incentive for other faculty members to run them out of the decision-making unit.

Academic work is often full of strife, and the reasons are embedded in the nature of the work and the way work is evaluated and rewarded, a point one of the authors has discussed in detail elsewhere.[6] Suffice it to say here that tenure is a means of putting some minimal limits on political infighting. It increases the costs predatory faculty members must incur to be successful in having more productive colleagues dismissed. More important, academic decisions about the worth of colleagues and their work are often made by the rules of consensus or democracy among existing incumbents.

Certainly, most professors understand both the esoteric nature of their work and the problems of short-term evaluations. At the same time, they understand that in an academic democracy, ever-changing groups of colleagues have a say in how the work of each professor is evaluated. They recognize implicitly, if not explicitly, that how their work is evaluated by a changing group of colleagues can depend, at the time, on what their work is being compared with. A microeconomics scholar can appreciate the fact that the relative ranking of his or her research depends on whether it is being judged relative to the work of macro or public policy scholars.

In addition, professors understand that the relative standing of their positions and the ranking of their research can change over time with changes in the cast of decision makers, who are likely to adjust their assessments from time to time. The ranking of their research can also change with shifts in the relative merit department members assign to different types and forms of academic work. For example, a macro person understands that even though his or her publications may now be (relatively) highly valued within the department, the ranking can easily change as a result of changes in the way evaluations are made, changes in the value placed on different types of work, and changes in the cast of decision makers. When the decision-making unit is multidisciplinary, shifts in the relative assessments of the worth of individual professors' work in the different disciplines can fluctuate even more dramatically, since each professor is likely to have allegiance first to his or her own discipline and then to other closely related disciplines. Within schools of business, for example, accounting faculty members may have, on the margin, an incentive to depreciate the work of marketing professors, because such depreciation may shift positions to accounting—and vice versa. Even more fundamental, organizational theorists steeped in behavioral psychology may have an incentive to depreciate the work of professors in finance—which may be grounded not in psychology but in economics—since negative shifts in the relative evaluation of economic-based work can marginally improve the chances that positions will be shifted to, say, organizational theory. Like-minded faculty members can be expected to coalesce to increase their political effectiveness in shaping decisions that can, in turn, inspire the formation of other coalitions, thus motivating all coalitions to increase their own efforts. The inherent instability of coalitions can, of course, jeopardize anyone's job security and long-term gains.

Professors have understandable reasons for demanding tenure. One is that the esoteric nature of their work (which they may undertake at the behest of their universities) may diminish the market value of their skills because the narrow focus of their work *might* not translate into alternative future job opportunities in the marketplace. Another reason is that there are political problems inherent within all democratic processes, and professors want, in effect, to be protected from the process and from their colleagues. If their work is intensely specialized, they want some assurance of job security to protect against the changing assessments by ever-changing majorities. Universities can be seen as willing to provide tenure because they must delegate decision-making power to those who have the requisite knowledge and information of different disciplines if they want faculty members to specialize their efforts. Universities also realize, given the nature of academic democracy and the threat it poses, that faculty members have inherent reasons for demanding tenure, and these make it possible to recoup the cost of tenure by reducing professorial wages to less than what they would have to be if the professors did not share a need for job security.

This line of analysis leads to a number of deductions:

- If the work of professors were less specialized, professors would be less inclined to demand tenure. For example, in colleges in which the emphasis is on teaching rather than research, tenure would be less prevalent, or less protective.

- As a group of decision makers or a discipline becomes more stable, we would expect faculty to consider tenure less important and to be less willing to forgo wages and other fringe benefits to obtain tenure.

- If there is close to an even split on democratic decisions related to employment, merit raises, and even tenure, faculty members will assign more value to tenure, because a more or less evenly split vote may change with slight shifts in the composition of the decision makers.

- The further below market the wages of faculty during the probation period and the further above market the wages after tenure, the more valuable tenure will be to faculty members.

- As the diversity within a decision-making unit increases (more disciplines included, with more divergent views on how analyses should be organized and pursued), the demand for tenure will increase.

- Should universities become more constrained in their capacities to fund established faculty positions, tenure may be perceived as even more valuable. Financial exigencies can translate into the loss of faculty positions (with nontenured positions becoming prime targets), so it should not be surprising that faculty will seek with greater diligence to redistribute the remaining positions and rents. Such a situation will also mean that universities will probably have to spend considerable resources seeking to instill academic values, not the least of which will be the pursuit of honest dealings and academic excellence. This emphasis may cause faculty members to

shun an important incentive inherent in the political process (especially in large group settings), the tendency to pursue strictly private objectives at the expense of larger university goals.[7]

If professors have tenure, why don't businesspeople have provision for
the same kind of job security? The quick answer to that question is that
businesses, unlike universities, typically are not labor managed. (Those
that are like universities should be expected to use some form of tenure.)
As noted, in business, goals are usually well defined. Perhaps more important, success can usually be identified with relative ease by using an
agreed-upon measure, that is, profit (or the expected profit stream captured in the market prices of traded securities). The owners, who are
residual claimants, have an interest in maintaining the firm's focus on profits. Moreover, people who work for businesses tend to have a stake in honest evaluations of potential employees, since an honest decision on who is
a "better" recruit can increase the firm's profits and therefore the incomes
and job security of all parties.

Real-world businesses do not always adhere to the process as described.
They use, to a greater or lesser degree, participatory forms of management, and, for some businesses, profit is not always the sole or highest pri-
ority goal. "Office politics" is a nontrivial concern in many firms. The
point is, however, that in business there is not as great a need for tenure as
exists within academe; employees in businesses do not have the incentive
to demand tenure that professors have, primarily because these employees
do not experience the problems inherent in democratic management that
derive from imprecise and shifting goals and from esoteric and ill-defined
research projects. Tenure is seldom found in firms for the simple reason
that in business employers and employees cannot make mutually beneficial trades similar to those made in tenure arrangements.

Let's suppose that political institutions and problems were as well
entrenched in firms as they are in academe, to the point of significantly
undercutting firm profits. What would happen? Clearly, some smart coali-
tion of managers or outside investors would see a potential for increasing
their wealth. They would buy the firm's stock at a low price brought about
by the political encumbrances and reform management practices and then
move to suppress the power of destructive politics and to refocus the managers' and workers' attention on the bottom line. They would clarify the
extent to which the workers' long-run gains would be a function of their
contributions to profits. The price of the stock could then rise. Voila! The
takeover investors would have a wealth increase, and the workers would
have less need for tenure, as professors know that form of job protection.

We suggest that the granting of tenure can be seen as another form of the
tournament we have discussed earlier in other contexts. Tenure decisions
are a way of allowing faculty members to reveal their skills. An employer

cannot depend on a potential employee to be fully objective or honest in presenting his or her qualifications. The graduate school records of new doctorates provide useful information on which to base judgments about new recruits' potential for success as university teachers and researchers. However, such records are of limited worth when a professor's research is at the frontier of knowledge in his or her discipline. The correlation between a person's performance as a student, as a prospective professor, as a teacher, and as a researcher is, at best, imperfect.

In order to induce promising faculty members to accurately assess their abilities and to confess their limits, the competitors (new assistant professors) are effectively told that only some among them will be promoted and retained. Since standards for tenure differ from one university to another, universities offer prospective faculty members an opportunity to, in effect, self-select and go to a university where they think they are likely to make the tenure grade. The prospects of being denied tenure will cause many (but certainly not all) weak candidates to avoid universities with tough tenure standards, especially given the probability that they would have to accept wages well below market during the probation period. The lost wages amount to an investment that probably will not be repaid with interest (in terms of wages above the market after the probation period when tenure is acquired). Thus, the tenure tournaments can reduce, to some extent, the costs universities incur in gathering information and making decisions, because they force recruits to be somewhat more honest in their claims.

Competition for the limited number of prized positions often drives new faculty members to a level of effort and output that exceeds the value of their current compensation. To induce prospective faculty to exert that amount of effort, universities must offer a "prize" that potential recruits consider worth the effort. That is, the recruits must expect the future (discounted) reward to compensate them for the extra effort they expend in the tournament and for the risk associated with not "winning." One approach universities can use to encourage recruits to exert a reasonable level of effort in the competition is to offer those who win the prospect of substantially greater compensation in the future (at least enough to repay the costs of assumed risk and of interest lost on delayed compensation). Another approach that offers future compensation as an incentive is to increase the security of continued employment and compensation once the tournament has ended and the winners have been determined. That is, tenure can be offered as the "prize."

In the absence of tenure (or some similar device), universities would find it difficult to make a credible commitment that prospective recruits who make the necessary competitive investment during the probationary period by accepting below-market wages for above-market effort will receive an income stream that compensates them for all costs, including the required risks. We have stressed the instability inherent in academic democracies, which, by its nature, reduces the credibility of virtually every commitment universities might want to make at employment time. Tenure is a practical means that universities use to provide a reasonable level of job security—to make a credible commitment—that is, to overcome institutional instabilities and pick the "best" professors for continued employment. At the same time, tenure is part of a mutually beneficial trade between new professors and their universities, primarily because it is a feature of the employment contract that new self-selected faculty members will demand before they agree to participate actively and honestly (in the sense that they will reveal the limits of their true abilities) in what amounts to a risky and underpaid employment tournament.[8]

After all is said and done, tenure is nothing more than another contract provision that faculty members prize, universities provide—and just about everyone else criticizes. Businesspeople could also have tenure. All they would have to do is "pay" for it in terms of lost wages. However, businesspeople typically don't have the same strong reasons for wanting tenure as do professors. Tenure survives in the academies of the country mainly because faculty members aggressively demand it (even those who believe strongly in the value of markets) and because universities voluntarily negotiate it. Tenure's long-term survival and the competitiveness of university labor markets suggest that the trade is mutually beneficial.

V

FINAL WORDS

20

The Case Against the
Case Against Incentives

Key Insight: Even if those who see incentives as more likely to de-motivate than motivate are correct, incentives would still be necessary, and it would still be important to get them right.

HAVING WRITTEN A BOOK on the importance of incentives, and on getting those incentives right, it is easy for us to leave the impression that everyone believes that incentives are important. But we would be wrong if we did. There are analysts who have reached conclusions very different from ours on the basis of their studies of the effects of incentives on behavior. Our view is that people respond in predictable ways to incentives. If you want people to do more of something, you increase the payoff they receive from doing it. The payoff can take many different forms, but money is a common and extremely effective one.

Of course, attempts to motivate people by adjusting incentives can lead to perverse outcomes unless those incentives are in proper balance with others. To us, these perverse possibilities are illustrative of the importance of incentives, and of their power to motivate productive behavior. Our discussion would not be complete, however, without considering the arguments made by those who are convinced that attempts to motivate people to be more productive through incentives are not only useless but invariably counterproductive.

Critics of incentives abound in academe and business, but one of the most widely read and seriously considered is Alfie Kohn. Citing the work of dozens of other critics, mainly respected psychologists, in his book *Punished by Rewards*, Kohn presents a well-documented case against the use of incentives to motivate people to become more productive.[1] We focus on Kohn's critique of incentives for one very good reason: he has crystallized the criticisms of incentives, which we will try to present even-handedly, in ways that others have not.[2]

According to Kohn, "*Any* approach that offers a reward for better performance is destined to be ineffective" (emphasis in original).[3] Indeed, "compensations systems often act as barriers to achieving productivity, quality, and intrinsic motivation, but they do not—they cannot—help us reach these goals."[4] These are strong statements, and, if they are true, writing (and reading) a book titled *Managing Through Incentives* has been a futile exercise. Kohn's statement implies that all the money and time that businesses spend on efforts to tie employee compensation to productivity are being wasted, or worse. Although Kohn is clear about how workers should not be paid and motivated, his suggestions for how they should be are less precise. His "basic principles" for compensating employees are "pay people generously and equitably. Do your best to make sure they don't feel exploited. Then *do everything in your power to help them put money out of their minds*" (emphasis in original).[5] We are also informed that "If you want people motivated to do a good job, give them a good job to do."[6]

While we disagree with Kohn's conclusion that incentives (or rewards) for productive behavior don't (indeed, can't) work, and are probably counterproductive, his reasons for reaching that conclusion are interesting, and worthy of consideration. We do not have the professional training to dismiss much of the evidence, drawn mainly from experimental studies done in laboratory settings, that Kohn cites in support of his position. So, after considering Kohn's reasons for objecting to the use of incentives, we critique his conclusion on the grounds that his evidence ignores problems that, while of no importance in the laboratory experiments of psychologists, are of crucial importance in running a business.

While we are primarily concerned with Kohn's arguments that incentives are ineffective, it should be pointed out that his criticisms go beyond instrumental consideration. Even if Kohn believed that incentives worked, he would still object to them as "manipulative" and "dehumanizing," with their use amounting to "treating people like pets," to use some of his descriptive phraseology. According to Kohn, "anyone who is troubled by a model of human relationships founded principally on the idea of one person controlling another must ponder whether rewards are as innocuous as they are sometimes made out to be."[7] We would certainly agree with Kohn that not many people would approve of a world in which a few had the power to manipulate the behavior of everyone else in a robot-like manner. This is not a power that the few could be expected to exercise responsibly. But, as we shall argue, this is not the type of power that incentives allow anyone to exercise in the marketplace.

Our awareness (and belief) that incentives can be, and indeed are, used effectively to influence people's behavior is widely shared among managers but not so widely accepted within the ranks of management writers. Even we, however, do not believe that incentives have the power to turn people into puppets. The surprise is that Kohn expresses this concern, *given his strong conviction that incentives are largely ineffective at controlling behavior*. This supposed inability of incentives to motivate people to do what the incentives are supposed to get them to do makes up the heart of Kohn's (and other critics') case against the use of incentives.

Kohn does not deny that incentives can alter behavior. But he doesn't believe that they can cause behavior to change in a desirable way (even from the perspective of those controlling the incentives) in the long run. Kohn evaluates the effectiveness of incentives (rewards) "on the basis of whether they produce lasting change [in behavior, and] the research suggests they fail miserably."[8] Kohn then cites research indicating that, once the rewards cease, the behavior goes back to what it was before the rewards were given. Even when the reward is continued, the behavior tends to return to the pre-reward pattern as people become satiated, and "the reward eventually stops being rewarding."[9] Kohn recognizes that "people usually continue to get paid for what they do."[10] But then he suggests that even money loses its ability to motivate with the comment "If the goal is to help people change their behavior—for example, by improving the quality of their work—a continued dependence on rewards can create a range of practical problems, including an increase in demands (for money), as managers trying to implement incentive programs on a permanent basis have discovered."[11]

But even if Kohn did not believe that incentives have a decaying effect on behavior, he would oppose them on the grounds that that effect is generally perverse. On the basis of a series of experiments dating back to 1961, Kohn concludes that "rewards killed creativity, and this was true regardless of the type of task, the type of reward, the timing of the reward, or the age of the people involved."[12] The experiments Kohn relies on all involved two groups of subjects (almost always students) performing some task, with one group being rewarded (usually with money) on the basis of how well they performed and the other group receiving no reward. In every experiment cited, the group that received no rewards did better at the task than the group that did. Despite his sweeping comment, Kohn does acknowledge that rewards can sometimes improve performance, but they do so "*only at extremely simple—indeed, mindless—tasks, and even then they improve only quantitative performance*" (emphasis in original).[13]

This is a surprising conclusion, and Kohn devotes considerable space to providing reasons for why it is plausible. His most devastating reason is that rewarding a person for performing a task reduces his interest in the task. Kohn cites several experiments in which two groups (sometimes the groups consist of just one person) were asked to perform a task, such as working on a puzzle, with one group receiving compensation and the other receiving none. After some period of time the subjects were interrupted and told to wait in the room for a few minutes until the next part of the experiment began. They were then observed secretly to see if they would continue working at the previously assigned task now that they had a choice. Those who were being paid were observed to spend less time on the task during this break than those who were not being paid. In other words, being paid to do something seems to reduce one's interest in doing it.[14]

Kohn offers two explanations for this result. One explanation is that the reward for doing something sends a signal that the task must be uninteresting, or that it is not worth doing for its own sake. The second is that the reward makes people feel controlled, *"and we tend to recoil from situations where our autonomy has been diminished"* (emphasis in original).[15] But, for whatever reason, Kohn says that the experimental evidence shows that this negative relationship between reward and interest is independent of the age, sex, race, and social class of the subjects. Trying to get people to engage in an activity by offering them extrinsic rewards has the effect of reducing the intrinsic interest they have in the activity. And this problem cannot be overcome by increasing the value of the reward. Indeed, this makes the problem worse, according to Kohn, since *"the more you like what has been dangled in front of you, the more you may come to dislike whatever you have to do to get it"* (emphasis in original).[16]

While Kohn recognizes that some jobs aren't likely to generate much in the way of intrinsic motivation, he opposes tying reward to performance on any job. Kohn points out that just because some, or even most, people find a particular job uninteresting, it does not mean that everyone does. So why offer rewards that will do little if anything to motivate (or improve the performance of) those who do not find a job interesting at the expense of reducing the interest of those who do? Also, there are creative ways of making almost any task more interesting, and every opportunity should be taken to do so. Not every job can be turned into a thrill-a-minute experience, but the creativity required to make a job more interesting will be snuffed out if we try to bribe people to perform it, according to Kohn.

Kohn supplements his case for making jobs interesting by citing evidence that people actually enjoy working. He writes, "Contrary to the view that an exclusive emphasis on extrinsic rewards is appropriate for certain categories of workers, research has shown that all people who work for a living, regardless of type of occupation or level of education, are 'powerfully affected in their assessment of a job by the level of intrinsic rewards it offers'."[17] And, getting a dig in at economists, Kohn adds, "Economists have it wrong if they think of work as a 'disutility'—something unpleasant that we must do in order to be able to buy what we need, merely a means to an end."[18] Proper management can go a long way to make work even more intrinsically rewarding by "hiring people (and reassigning them) not only on the basis of what their resumes say they are most qualified to do but also on the basis of what they *like* to do" (emphasis in original).[19]

Kohn also faults incentives for rupturing relationships between workers by shifting the emphasis from cooperation to competition. According to Kohn, "the central message that is taught here—the central message of all competition, in fact—is that everyone else is a potential obstacle to one's own success."[20] The competition that is created by incentives not only disrupts workplace cooperation; it also reduces the intrinsic rewards people receive from their jobs and the quality of the work done. As Kohn sees it, "We need to begin by recognizing that cooperation does not just make tasks more pleasant; in many cases it is virtually a prerequisite for quality."[21]

Kohn's arguments are obviously far more extensive that can be adequately covered in a short chapter. But we have made an effort to present his case adequately and fairly. If we have come close to doing Kohn's position justice, you should now be thinking that maybe there is something to the case against incentives, that it cannot be dismissed out of hand as implausible. It should come as no surprise that we are not persuaded by Kohn's arguments. Even if we were to accept the experimental evidence he cites on the effect of tying incentives (rewards) to performance (which we do not, primarily because of contrary evidence from the field of experimental economics and psychology[22]), we believe the case for using incentives in business remains overwhelming.

We begin our critique of Kohn's position by considering his argument that the use of incentives is morally flawed because they involve one person controlling another. No one would deny that incentives are a way of controlling the behavior of people. Indeed, the whole point of this book is that incentives are important, and getting them right is crucially important, because they do exert powerful effects on behavior. But does this mean that the use of incentives to control behavior is necessarily a means by which one person can gain at the expense of others? Emphatically not!

Of course, you can think of one person acquiring all the wealth of another by employing the incentive of torture. But this is not what is going on with the incentives in the business world. Business incentives are not usually thought of as a one-way means of control. Rather, they are arrangements that create general benefits by allowing control to be exerted reciprocally. For example, it is easy to think of employers paying workers more as an incentive to get them to work more productively. But once it is recognized that employers need productive employees to stay in business, it is just as reasonable to think of workers as offering to become more productive as an incentive for employers to pay them more. Typically it is the employer who initiates a performance-pay incentive, but unless workers provide a reciprocal incentive by their willingness to respond productively, the arrangement breaks down and so does the control. So who is controlling whom? The parties are controlling each other's behavior in a mutually advantageous interaction, an interaction that, when not advantageous to some of those involved, leaves them the option to walk away from the deal.

Quite apart from the reciprocal nature of the incentives found in business, incentives are often valuable to those being controlled precisely because they are controlling. This book is full of examples of the advantages of being controlled by others. For example, early in the book we considered the situation of workers involved in team production (a common situation in which the productivity of each worker's effort depends on the effort of other workers). Without some means for rewarding those who work hard (or punishing those who do not), each worker can benefit from shirking even though all are worse off when everyone (or even a significant number) shirks. In these situations, each worker wants to be controlled as long as the control imposed on him is also imposed on other workers; recall the story of the Chinese workers pulling the barge upstream who hired someone to whip them if their rope went slack. Also, being willing to submit yourself to the control of others can increase your opportunity for gain by making your promises of productive performance more credible. Although CEOs might like to spend most of the shareholders' profits on executive perks, they willingly accept controls (incentives) that reduce their ability to profit at shareholder expense because they are more valuable (can earn more) with those controls in place.

As discussed earlier in chapter 13, businesses commonly subject themselves to greater consumer control by making investments in arrangements that allow consumers to impose high costs on them for misrepresenting their products. We have also explained how deferred compensation arrangements can benefit workers by allowing their employer to exert more control over them by increasing the loss they suffer if they leave the firm, either voluntarily or involuntarily.

Of course, a defense against the charge that incentives are controlling would be beside the point if Kohn were correct in his arguments that incentives are largely ineffective. What can we make of these arguments, which form the heart of Kohn's case against incentives? At one level, it is tempting to simply dismiss them and point to an obvious and compelling reason for believing that incentives do work, and extremely effectively. At the level of the most basic economic understanding, consider what happens as the demand for computers increases and the demand for military aircraft decreases. These changes in demand will be communicated through markets in the form of increases in the salaries of electrical engineers relative to the salaries of aeronautical engineers. This shift in relative salaries serves as an incentive for more people to prepare themselves for and to pursue a career in electrical engineering and for fewer people to enter the field of aeronautical engineering. And we can be absolutely sure that this incentive will work very effectively. Examples like this can be multiplied endlessly, establishing without doubt that people respond to market incentives.

We suspect that Kohn would accept this evidence but say that we are missing his point, that he is talking about a different use of incentives. He could claim that he is concerned about the use of incentives, not to attract more people into a given occupation but to get them to work harder at whatever occupation they are in. He might refer to his comment that "the problem is that money is made too salient . . . it is offered contingently—that is, according to the principle 'Do this and you'll get that'."[23] Or Kohn might point to the statement by Morton Deutsch (which he sympathetically quoted) that "there is no evidence to indicate that people work more productively when they are expecting to be rewarded in proportion to their performance than when they are expecting to be rewarded equally or on the basis of need."[24] But this does not allow Kohn to ignore the importance of incentives at attracting people into different occupations, since there is an obvious connection between what a person is working on and how productive he or she is. A worker may exhibit great skill and diligence producing a product, but if no one wants the product (or if consumers value it less than another product that could be made with the same effort), the worker can hardly be considered to be working productively. And it takes differential rewards determined in accordance with the desires of consumers (not equal rewards, or rewards determined in accordance with some measure of need) to attract workers into those jobs where their efforts are valued most. The importance of this point, as obvious as it is, cannot be overemphasized.

When running experiments in a psychology lab, it typically doesn't make any difference what task the subjects are being assigned. This is not the case in business. A firm simply cannot be indifferent to the problem of deciding what people should be working on, not if it wants to stay in business.

We are quite willing to accept, for the sake of argument, that Kohn is correct when arguing that people are more likely to lose interest in, and become less creative at, solving a puzzle in lab experiments when they are paid than when they are not paid. But that situation has limited relevance to the problems that businesses face. A viable business must have employees who are working on a variety of tasks that generate different value and require different levels of skills, effort, risks, pleasantness, and preparation. No firm could get the right mix of employees working in the right mix of jobs without rewarding them for the differential contribution they make to the firm's success—without connecting their compensation to their productivity. If tying rewards to productivity reduces workers' intrinsic interest and performance to some degree, so be it. That is just another cost of doing business. It's better to have someone working with somewhat less enthusiasm in a job that needs to be done than with full enthusiasm at a job that doesn't.

The importance of getting people into the most productive job leads us back to Kohn's criticism that the use of incentives ignores the fact that people enjoy work. We are quite willing to agree with Kohn that most people, most of the time, get a lot of satisfaction and enjoyment from working. We certainly do enjoy, on balance, our jobs. But this is hardly an argument against pay for performance. The person who enjoys working in one job will probably enjoy working in other jobs as well. But what job should the worker be enjoying? We agree with Kohn that a person's preference for the work he or she enjoys most is an important consideration in determining what work he or she does. But so is information on the relative values that consumers place on the output that is produced in different jobs, and consumers communicate this information in the form of differential rewards. Everything else being equal, the person who enjoys working will choose to enjoy it on the job that pays the most. Of course, everything is not always equal, and people may (and often do) turn down a higher salary in one job to work in another they enjoy more. Indeed, since people generally do enjoy some types of jobs more than others, the freedom to turn down higher salaries in the jobs they enjoy least is a significant cause of salary differentials between different jobs. In other words, it is because of the importance of allowing people to choose the jobs they enjoy most that it is so important to tie pay to productivity, where productivity means working in jobs that satisfy the demands of consumers.

But ignore for a moment the problem of getting people in the right job, although we should never forget how important that problem is. Assume that somehow we have everyone in the job where he or she can produce the most wealth, not only enjoying the job but enjoying it more than any other job the person is qualified to do. Furthermore, assume that it did not require differential compensation to achieve this amazing placement of workers. Certainly, even Kohn would admit that this situation is as good as it gets if we want to avoid using incentives that reward people on the basis of their productivity. But even if we started with this ideal confluence of workers and jobs, it would still be necessary to use incentive pay to motivate workers. When talking about the enjoyment of a job, an important distinction needs to be made between *total* enjoyment and *marginal* enjoyment. The *total* enjoyment an individual gets from doing a job may be enormous, but that doesn't mean that the *marginal* enjoyment (the enjoyment from working a little bit more) is very high, or even positive. The marginal enjoyment of anything typically diminishes (beyond some point) as people spend more and more time doing it, and it always diminishes relative to the marginal enjoyment of doing other things that less time is available for. It would be the rare employee who would choose to put in a steady eight hours a day on the job, no matter how much she enjoyed the job in total. Most people make a full-time commitment to their jobs because they are given an incentive to do so, an incentive that compensates for the marginal "dissatisfaction" (or negative satisfaction) from working.

We are not arguing here that it is always a good idea to tie compensation directly to worker output. For reasons discussed much earlier, piece-rate pay can be, and often is, more costly than it is worth since the productivity gains from paying differential amounts on the basis of productivity do not always justify the transactions cost involved in making the necessary distinctions. Also, piece-rate pay can be plagued by the problem that incentives work too well, which means that unless the incentives create a proper motivational balance, say, between quantity and quality, problems can arise. But this is a case for getting incentives *right*, not for dismissing them.

Even in cases where it does not appear practical to pay people on the same job different levels of compensation (with the possible exception of differences for seniority), there are incentives that indirectly connect pay and performance in ways that can motivate more productivity. In many cases the incentive comes in the form of an understanding that if the worker misses too much work, he or she will be fired, which among other things eliminates the differential pay that might have come with seniority. Also, those workers who are more productive are less likely to be laid off in a business downturn, more likely to receive more favorable work schedules and location assignments, and more likely to receive promotions (into more enjoyable and promising jobs).

Despite Kohn's objections, any sensible compensation arrangement will, over some reasonable length of time, connect compensation to productivity. Competitive market pressures will ensure that. Without the incentives created by some connection between compensation and productivity, the temptation will be strong for workers to take a little more time off either by not coming to work or by easing up on the job. There are large numbers of ways that workers can shirk on the job by doing some things (e.g., playing computer games that can be instantly replaced on the computer screen by a spreadsheet) and not doing others (e.g., working on the spreadsheet) that can make an enjoyable job even more enjoyable. Certainly from the perspective of a firm and its customers (and from the collective perspective of its workers), it is desirable to take measures to control shirking, even though it can never be eliminated completely. And rewarding workers on the basis of their productivity is a way of reducing shirking.

Of course, not everyone will take advantage of an opportunity to shirk his or her job responsibilities. Kohn would surely argue that when workers are treated fairly, so few will shirk that any use of incentives to motivate more productivity will do more harm than good. We agree with Kohn when he argues that most workers have an intrinsic desire to do a good job, and that, when satisfied that they are not being taken advantage of, they will not take advantage of their employers by shirking. The problem with Kohn's dismissal of incentives is that without some connection between reward and performance, the most responsible workers will be taken advantage of—which is why workers benefit from having incentives provided by management. Incentives ensure that manager-owners pay up when the workers perform. We have stressed throughout the book that incentives control managers as much as they control workers; they are—or should be, when done right—mutually beneficial deals for manager-owners *and* workers.

Also, there are always a few individuals who will take advantage of opportunities to realize private benefits at the expense of everyone else. If this were not true, what would be the justification for laws to control pollution or forbid littering and for the creation of incentives to obey them? While we might expect most workers to work diligently at their jobs, at least initially, without compensation being tied to productivity, a few will not. And because a few will shirk, we qualified the willingness of the rest to work diligently with the word "initially." Those who are working hard will notice that they are not being rewarded any more than the few who are not working hard. None of the diligent workers will appreciate this, many will feel like they are being treated as suckers, and a few will decide it is better to be a shirker than a sucker. As the number of shirkers increases, those who continue to work hard will notice their workload increasing or becoming more difficult, and the feeling of being a sucker will intensify. So more of the workers will become shirkers. Clearly, this is a situation that can unravel as the workers find themselves in a prisoners' dilemma where shirking is in the best interest of each, although it harms all by threatening the viability of the firm. Tying rewards to performance is an effective way of increasing cooperation by eliminating the destructive prisoners' dilemma that workers would find themselves in otherwise.

So again, even if we accept the validity of Kohn's experimental evidence, we have to conclude that the use of incentives increases the productivity of workers, a conclusion supported by an array of studies cited throughout the book. We agree with Kohn that productivity can be lowered when pay is made contingent on performance in some cases (e.g., in the case of an isolated worker, or that of a worker whose performance and satisfaction are unaffected by the behavior of other workers, as was the case in the experiments Kohn cites to support this conclusion). In most of the experiments, the subjects performed the task in isolation, and there is no indication that those who were not being paid knew that others were. Obviously, this is seldom the situation in the workplace; in real life, the performance of industrious workers is negatively affected by poor performance on the part of associates, and it quickly becomes widely known when some workers are being paid the same for doing less. So even if tying pay to performance does reduce the performance of all below some ideal level, this is a far more productive situation than the productivity meltdown that will occur when, in the absence of some connection between reward and performance, a few shirkers are allowed to egregiously take advantage of their fellow workers.

Properly designed incentives also facilitate the type of worker autonomy that Kohn quite correctly applauds. According to Kohn, "People are most motivated when they are able to participate in making decisions about organizational goals [and that] employees be able to decide on how best to reach them."[25] We agree completely. Not only are workers more motivated when they are given more decision-making authority, they are also more productive, *given the right set of incentives.* No manager or supervisor, regardless of how knowledgeable, knows nearly as much about all the jobs that need to be done within a firm as do the workers themselves. The knowledge that workers have can be used to maximize their output under the existing ways of doing things, and, more important, to improve the way things are done, but only if the workers are given the freedom to use their knowledge as they see fit. The continuous improvement (or *kaisen*, as the Japanese call it) that is such an important part of total quality management seldom comes from the insights of the managers. It comes primarily from the hands-on experience and know-how of those workers who know more about the problems and possibilities of what they do better than anyone else.

But no matter how knowledgeable workers are in their area, they cannot be expected to know how to best coordinate their efforts with those of other specialized workers in other parts of the firm to accomplish the overall goals of the firm. There has to be some means of meshing the efforts of groups of workers who have little information about each other's efforts in ways that realize the best outcome from their collective efforts. There are two ways of achieving this coordination. One is to tell workers what to do and how often to do it. The other is to have a set of incentives in place that conveys information to each group on how to best coordinate its efforts with the efforts of others and rewards the group for doing so. Neither approach is perfect, and there will also be a need for some combination of the two approaches in a viable firm. But the more a firm can rely on incentives, the more information it can productively utilize from more empowered workers interacting with each other in more genuinely cooperative ways.

We are in agreement with Kohn and many other critics in their emphasis on the importance of cooperation and harmony among workers in maintaining a productive setting. But we disagree that incentives are inconsistent with a productive setting because, as Kohn says, "rewards rupture relationships"[26] by setting up a competition in which "everyone else is a rival to one's own success."[27] We do not deny that competition can cause problems between workers. Obviously it can and does. But the mistake that Kohn makes is to assume that we create competition unnecessarily by setting up incentives. While incentives certainly affect the type of competition that occurs, competition will exist no matter what incentives are in place. There is simply no way we could eliminate competition even if we wanted to. As long as our desire for more goods and services exceeds our ability to produce them, people will be in competition with each other for more. Competition is an inevitable fact of life in our world of scarcity. To say that competition can disrupt relations is no more an argument against competition than the observation that gravity can disrupt a safe landing is an argument against gravity. Rather, it is an argument for directing the competition in constructive ways, which means getting the incentives right, just as the potential disruptiveness of gravity is a argument for designing airplanes properly.

We can give no advice on how to design airplanes, but we do believe that in this book we have been able to provide a lot of insight on how to design incentives. No set of incentives, regardless of how well it is designed, can motivate as much cooperation and productivity as we would ideally like. The problem of scarcity is inescapable and imposes trouble-some tradeoffs on everything we do, including designing incentives. But properly designed incentives can help overcome a host of prisoners' dilemma tensions between private interest and collective interest in ways that facilitate far more harmonious and productive interaction than we can ever hope to realize from the natural sociability and goodwill of people.

21

Managerial Lessons in Incentives

INCENTIVES CLEARLY MATTER, especially in business. That message has unified all that we have written. Managers must heed that message, but the task of getting incentives right requires an understanding of the full complexity of the message, as well as an appreciation for what is meant by *incentives*.

We've said it before, but we'll say it again as we draw this book to a close: *the incentives we have in mind include more than money*. Money is only one form of incentive, albeit a very important one, and one that might not be fully appreciated by critics of incentives. Money works, but if it were the only incentive that mattered, managers could sleep more easily at night in the knowledge that all they have to do is dangle a few more bucks before their employees in order to get them to work harder and smarter. And managers would surely be paid less than they are. Good managers are paid premiums because the task of managing through incentives is not at all that simple. The power of incentives is immense and pervasive, which is all the more reason they require careful management.

Management experts often write eloquently about their field of expertise as "management science." There is obviously much *science* to what managers do. After all, there are many predictable connections between managerial actions and outcomes, and we have explored many of those connections. We can only pity the managers who don't understand the science in business—the idea that the *way* workers are paid may affect performance as much as the *amount* they are paid, for example. Top executives, especially, need an understanding of the causal connections between firm policies and the reactions of all stakeholders—managers, workers, suppliers, and customers. Estimates of *how much* people will respond can certainly benefit managerial decision making.

Management, however, is also *art*—maybe more art than science. This is the case because the scope of "incentives" extends far beyond money into an array of nonmoney benefits. We have stressed that managers must be creative in the products and services they design to survive and prosper, but they must be equally creative in the workplace benefits they provide for much the same reasons.

Fringe benefits (in the absence of their tax benefits) would not exist if money were all that mattered to employees. The concepts of "corporate culture," "strategy," and "leadership," which are matters of human design, would likewise be of little concern in management circles if money were all that mattered. But the truth of business is that money, fringes, culture, and leadership all matter—because workers want them. They are an integral part of what the "firm" is, and they are constantly up for redesign and redeployment. Workers need and want money and fringes, but they also need and want some clearly defined direction for what their business is about and where it intends to go. They also need and want leadership, if for no other reason than that leadership can help break the stifling grip of the various prisoner's dilemmas and free-rider problems that workers would otherwise face (and that we have discussed at length throughout this book).

For most workers, a fringe benefit and a good old-fashioned pat on the back can take the place of more than a few dollars, which helps explain why good managers offer their workers fringes as well as encouragement. Different incentives matter in different ways to different degrees to different people. The *art* of management encompasses determining what counts to workers—what motivates and incentivizes them—and then blending what counts—the incentives—in various ways into a productive, cost-effective compensation or incentive package. In many important ways, designing incentive packages is an artistic process, no less creative than the work of the artist who must use a limited number of tubes of colors to blend and create new colors and images to good effect. At the same time, the process must be guided by underlying *principles* of how incentives, whatever they are defined to be, work. This book has sought to provide guidance by identifying the underlying principles and then drawing out a host of lessons.

Any list of lessons developed throughout the book would be lengthy, but surely it would include the following points:

- Price and quantity bought tend to move inversely to one another. That is to say, if the price of a product goes down, people will buy more of it (everything else held constant). They will buy less if the price rises. This means that employers will buy more of any resource—including worker time—if the price they pay for the resource goes down, and less of it if the price goes up.

- Price and the quantity of anything supplied tend to move together. If the price of any product goes up, producers will tend to offer more of that product on the market (everything else held constant). Similarly, if paid more for their labor, more workers will want to work, and the workers will tend to offer more of their time, and vice versa.

- Firms exist because they economize on market-related costs of consummating and enforcing transactions that are external to the firm. However, the very creation of firms gives rise to internal coordination or principal-agency costs that must be controlled if the firm is to remain profitable and to survive.

- The size and scope of firms is affected not only by the internal efficiency of firms but also by the cost-effectiveness of completing markets transactions. For example, firms may "downsize" (reduce employment and the layers of management) because managers and workers have become more productive (due, for example, to a reduction in agency costs) and/or because obtaining production inputs from markets has become less costly.

- All parties to firms—owners, managers, and workers—seek to gain from cooperation. However, to ensure that firms remain profitable, incentives must be found to align the interests of the managers and workers with the interests of the owners. Otherwise, the managers and workers can expect to misappropriate the owners' capital and put the firm at risk.

- Most people have a "moral sense" or "sense of obligation" to do what they should or have contracted to do, at least to some degree. However, they are also beset with temptations to shirk, to fail to live up to obligations, and to be opportunistic—to take advantage of their circumstances for personal gain. These temptations grow with an expansion in the size of the relevant work group.

- Prisoner's dilemmas and free-rider problems abound in business. A large part of business profits (and management pay) come from solving these problems—getting managers and workers to set aside noncooperative solutions and to accept the cooperative solutions in what we have discussed as "business games."

- Competition is pervasive in all aspects of business, and the intensity of competition will continue to grow. To an increasing degree, businesses no longer have the luxury of ignoring the strategic role of incentives in efficient production. Just as they must constantly improve their products to meet world competitive standards, they must improve the effectiveness of their incentive structures to enhance profits or to ward off invasions of their markets by competitors who have found more cost-effective incentives.

• Teams are a means of encouraging cooperation by controlling the size of the relevant group. They reduce the incentive of team members to free ride, to shirk, or to act opportunistically, because they make individual contributions to firm production count and provide for mutual monitoring by team members.

• Problems of manager and worker opportunism escalate as the "last period" of doing business approaches. Efforts that extend the longevity of business tend to mitigate against the costs associated with the last-period problem and, accordingly, help extend the life and profitability of the business.

• Firms protected from market competition by barriers to entry can be expected to extract monopoly profits by restricting output and raising the prices of their products. Similarly, departments within firms that are sole-source suppliers of some input or service within the firm can be expected to behave in much the same manner, extracting some of the firm's profits for the personal gain of the people in the department. Outsourcing (or the threat of outsourcing) is a means by which firms can obtain inputs or services cheaper from suppliers outside the firm. It is also a means of discouraging internal departments from acting like little monopolies.

• Providing workers with work-related or fringe benefits often pays in business simply because the provision of the benefits can increase the supply of workers who are willing to work for the firm. Benefits can (up to a point) be self-financing, because they lead to greater worker productivity and/or lower wage bills.

• Trade-offs abound in business, and all productive activities in firms should be expanded until the value of the last unit of the activities equals its cost. This means that the volume of any good or service produced by a business should be extended until the marginal value equals its marginal cost. It also means that any benefit provided workers should be extended so long as workers are willing to give up more in pay (or some other benefit) than the added cost of extending the benefit.

• Monitoring is not only necessary but often wanted by workers, but monitoring is never perfect. As a consequence, there will always be some "slack" in worker effort, in spite of managers' best efforts to find alternative methods of enlisting worker effort.

• Contracts are a means of overcoming prisoner's dilemmas and free-rider problems (and the "slack" in worker effort), but contracts can never be complete or cover all possible contingencies, which means that they can never be completely effective in containing shirking and opportunistic behavior. Contracts are often expensive to enforce in the courts, which explains why the best contracts are those that are self-enforcing, that is, incorporate incentives for the parties to do that which they have agreed to doing.

- Debt tends to encourage risk taking, which explains why firms may take on debt and why lenders may ask for a progressively higher "risk premium" in the interest rate they charge as a firm becomes more highly leveraged.

- Stockholders tend to have more diversified portfolios than the managers of their firms, which helps explain why managers may be more risk averse than their stockholders. Stockholders want to find methods—incentives—that encourage managers to accept more risk with the prospect of higher rates of return.

- A firm that gets its incentives wrong can be expected to be bought out by entrepreneurs who will buy it at a price depressed by the wrongheaded incentives, correct the incentive system for the purpose of raising the resale price of the firm, and then resell the firm as a unit or in parts.

- The job security of top executives is a function of the extent to which they get their incentive structures right and maximize stockholder value. Takeovers (or the threat of takeovers) can be a powerful force motivating executives to do what they were hired by their boards and stockholders to do.

Some readers might misunderstand what we mean by "managing through incentives." They might worry that we propose that owners and their managers use incentives primarily to get the lower-echelon workers to do what the owners and managers want them to do, regardless of what the workers want to do. Or they might worry that any process of using incentives is inherently "manipulative," meaning contrary to what the workers might really want from their work. They might also worry that incentives are designed to work in one direction, on workers. Such deductions could not be further from our intent.

We recognize that many workers simply don't want to work and won't unless closely monitored and threatened with punishment (withdrawal of rewards). We don't deny such problems of laziness at work, but the problems of managing such workers have been widely recognized. Throughout this book we have stressed another, more important facet of the management problem—that much business is necessarily a *cooperative* endeavor, requiring the cost-effective input of many people, including owners, managers, and workers. The essential problem is that cooperation does not always come naturally for owners, managers, or workers—even when hard work is intended and desired by all. There are inherent incentives, especially within large groups, for people to act noncooperatively, in spite of the fact that such a choice of action or inaction is not in the workers' collective interest. In these cases, which we submit dominate much business activity, the task of managers can be to do what workers want them to do— devising incentives that inspire voluntary and energetic cooperation (or that more than neutralize the inherent tendency of workers to fall down on their jobs).

A central point stressed throughout this book is straightforward: incentives matter because workers want them and are better off because of them. The best incentives are the ones workers would choose if they were managers. Incentives that are put in place because they can somehow benefit managers at the expense of workers are hardly the incentives we have in mind. Such incentives will not likely be lasting, because the firms that try to install such incentives will not be long lasting. The incentive schemes we have always had in mind are those that are mutually beneficial—where the gains of cooperation are shared among all of the various stakeholders in business. We have no doubt that businesses and managers who are successful over the long run will be those who seek resolution of conflicts and cooperation through mutual gain.

Incentives should never be viewed as operating in one direction. Managers do tend to devise incentive packages that are applied to line workers against their will. Because of how the packages are constructed, the incentive packages may appear manipulative. But, as we have stressed, workers have an understandable economic interest in those packages. Is it manipulative for managers to do what their workers want them to do or would do if they, the workers, were the ones constructing the incentive packages? If such packages are "manipulative," who is manipulating whom? We suggest that the best incentive packages are those that the workers would choose to have imposed on themselves, if they understood the competitive constraints facing their firms. At least, we suggest that managers should view incentives this way.

Workers surely want their managers, including the top officers of their companies, to face appropriate incentives. They can also understand that, like themselves, managers respond to incentives, that their own jobs and future incomes are dependent on the incentives their "bosses" face. They can also see that their managers must have the right incentives to get all other incentives within the firm right.

Like it or not, incentives will continue to grow in importance in business because of certain inexorable economic trends. Business will continue to become ever more sophisticated, complex, and global, necessarily relying more and more on the knowledge and creativity of workers further and further down in the corporate hierarchy. Firms will need to use incentives to draw out the contributions of people who have the requisite skills and knowledge to make business work. Like it or not, business will become progressively more participatory, as it has in the past. Command and control management styles will necessarily contract, because people at the "top" of the hierarchy will not know—and cannot know—what to tell the people below to do. The people at the top will be progressively less able to monitor the people in the rest of the organization, who are as likely to be across the globe as across the hallway.

Moreover, the corporate hierarchy will continue to flatten as incentives replace commands and as management and product and market development are seen more and more as participatory endeavors. Top managers of most firms will continue to lose their ability to "micromanage." Design of the broad outlines of a firm's overall business "strategy" will continue to grow in importance for top managers, because that is what they will be able to do. Incentives will rise in importance because they will be part and parcel of the process by which the firm's strategy is implemented.

In a business world in which all activity is close at hand, incentives might be relatively less important than they are. The "boss" could shout out orders and look to see if the orders had been carried out. When business is done over a large geographical area, however, shouting cannot be expected to work very effectively. Memos that give workers directions from on high can get lost in the onslaught of similar messages coming from all directions in the new "information economy." Owners and managers will necessarily look for ways to ensure that the directions that are given are heard with clarity. Incentives will grow in importance because incentives carry messages, and the built-in messages are not sent once, only to be set aside; they are ever present, persistent, relentless. As we wrote at the start of this book, they constantly remind everyone, "This is what the firm is about. And, just as importantly, this is what you can do to help your firm *and* yourself."

Incentives will become progressively more important to managers *because* they will become more important in the competitive stew we call business. Firms will need to use incentives effectively in order to remain competitive, and those firms that become more competitive will force other firms to examine more carefully the incentives they use, with an eye toward restructuring their incentives to meet the competition. Clearly, boards of American firms have dramatically hiked the pay of their executives over the past decade not so much because they want to pad the pockets of the people who have appointed them (if that were the case, executive pay would have been hiked long ago when, as is widely acknowledged, competition in most markets was less intense), but because, generally speaking, board members will be forced by competition to ensure, as best they can, that their executives perform. One economic fact stands out in the global marketplace: capital is footloose. It goes where it is well treated by boards and their executives. Boards that fail to appreciate the growing mobility of capital on a world scale and that try to mistreat capital by not generating competitive rates of return with the incentive systems in place can expect to have a tough time attracting and retaining their needed capital base. The message in this global competitive struggle has made it to Japan where executive salaries are more and more being tied, albeit grudgingly, to firm performance and are being raised to meet world standards. The message will return with added force to American shores as Japanese firms become even more competitive.

The critics can fret all they wish about these trends in the use of incentives, but, we submit, the trends will continue. Those firms that resist the competitive struggle can be expected to be lost to it.

We understand that current management advice emphasizes "objectives." Managers understand the power of establishing clear and measurable objectives for their firms and their employees. "Management by objectives" will remain a clear and guiding theme in business. Firms and their managers and workers cannot operate without knowing what they are supposed to do. At the same time, objectives can lose much of their force if there are no meaningful incentives behind the objectives. The incentives can be explicit or obscure. We've made no secret of our view for giving incentives their rightful due, for making them an explicit part of the process by which objectives are established, implemented, and realized. There is an important measure of truth in the catch phrase "management by objectives," but we insist that the process will be more effective if managers understand that they must manage *through* the power of incentives.

Notes

Chapter 1

1. See Jennifer Reingold, "Executive Pay," *Business Week*, April 21, 1997, pp. 58–102.

2. Al Dunlap and Bob Andelman, *Mean Business: How I Save Bad Companies and Make Good Companies Great* (New York: Times Books, 1996), p. 21.

3. John O'Dell, "Fluor's Top Executives Get Big Pay Raises, Bonuses After Profits Soar 16%," *Los Angeles Times*, February 10, 1997, p. D5.

4. Don Clark, "Intel CEO Grove Made $94.6 million in 1996 by Exercising Stock Options," *Wall Street Journal*, April 9, 1997, p. B8.

5. As reported by Roger Lowenstein, "On the Difficulty of Hiring Good Help," *The Wall Street Journal*, March 27, 1997, p. C1.

6. Gene Koretz, "Truly Tying Pay to Performance," *Business Week*, February 17, 1997, p. 25.

7. As reported in Haig R. Nalbantian and Andrew Schotter, "Productivity Under Group Incentives: An Experimental Study," *American Economic Review*, vol. 87, no. 3 (June 1997), pp. 314–341.

8. Joseph R. Blasi, *Employee Ownership: Revolution or Ripoff?* (Cambridge, Mass.: Ballinger, 1988).

9. As described by Edwin Chadwich, "Opening Address," *Journal of the Royal Statistical Society of London*, vol. 25 (1862), as cited in Robert B. Ekelund and Robert F. Hebert, *A History of Economic Theory and Method*.

10. Mikhail Gorbachev, *Perestroika: New Thinking for Our Country and the World* (New York: Harper & Row, 1987), p. 97.

11. The study covered the pay of 16,000 managers from 250 large corporations during the period 1982–1986. See John M. Abowd, "Does Performance-Based Managerial Compensation Affect Corporate Performance?" *Industrial and Labor Relations Review*, vol. 43 (special issue, February 1990), pp. 52s–73s.

12. See James A. Brickley, Sanjai Bhagat, and Ronald C. Lease, "The Impact of Long-Range Managerial Compensation Plans on Shareholder Wealth," *Journal of Accounting and Economics* vol. 7 (1985), pp. 115–129.

13. Y. Amihud and B. Lev, "Risk Aversion as a Managerial Motive for Conglomerate Mergers," *Bell Journal of Economics*, (Fall 1981), pp. 605–617; B. Holmstron, "Moral Hazard and Observability," *Bell Journal of Economics*, vol. 10 (1979), pp. 74–91; S. Shavell, "Risk Sharing and Incentives in the Principal and Agent Relationship," *Bell Journal of Economics*, vol. 10 (1979), pp. 55–73; and C. Smith and R. Watts, "Incentive and Tax Effects of Executive Compensation Plans," *Australian Journal of Management*, vol. 7 (1982), pp. 139–157.

14. Michael C. Jensen and William H. Meckling, "Property Rights and Production Functions: An Application of Labor-Managed Firms and Codetermination," *Journal of Business*, vol. 52 (1979), pp. 469–506.

15. See N. Fast and N. Berg, "The Lincoln Electric Company," Harvard Business School Case (Cambridge, Mass.: Harvard Business School Press, 1971).

16. S. Adams, "Manager's Journal: The Dilbert Principle," *The Wall Street Journal*, May 22, 1995, p. 14.

17. For criticisms of incentives, see Alfie Kohn, *Punished by Rewards* (Boston: Houghton Mifflin, 1993). Kohn's criticisms are considered in detail in chapter 20. See also Jone L. Pearce, "Why Merit Pay Doesn't Work: Implications for Organization Theory," *New Perspectives on Compensation*, ed. by David B. Balkin and Louis R. Gomez-Mejia (Englewood Cliffs, N.J.: Prentice-Hall, 1987).

18. Indeed, many textile firms have failed because the expanding nontextile economies of their regions have pushed up labor costs, outcompeting some textile firms for the resources they need for continued production.

19. According to econometric research, those firms in the lowest decile of industry performance as measured by profit and stock price increases were about 1.5 times as likely to have a change of top executives as firms in the top decile in profit and stock price performance. See M. Weisback, "Outside Directors and CEO Turnover," *Journal of Financial Economics*, vol. 20 (1988), pp. 431–460; and J. Warner, R. Watts, and K. Wruck, "Stock Prices and Top Management Changes," *Journal of Financial Economics*, vol. 20, pp. 461–492.

20. This perspective on incentives is developed in Harrison C. White, "Agency as Control," *Principals and Agents: The Structure of Business*, ed. John W. Pratt and Richard J. Zeckhauser (Boston, Mass.: Harvard Business School Press, 1991), pp. 187–212; and James A. Robins, "Why and When Does Agency Theory Matter? A Critical Approach to the Role of Agency Theory in the Analysis of Organizational Control" (Irvine: Graduate School of Management, University of California, Irvine, working paper, 1996).

21. Frederick Taylor, *The Principles of Scientific Management* (New York: Harper, 1929).

22. F. A. Hayek, *The Constitution of Liberty* (Chicago: University of Chicago Press, 1960), p. 26.

23. Bruno S. Frey and Heinz Buhofer, "Prisoners and Property Rights," *Journal of Law and Economics*, vol. 31, no. 1 (April 1988), pp. 19–46.

24. Dunlap and Andelman, *Mean Business*, p. 55.

25. As reported by Jeff Bailey, "Garbage Budget: How Can Government Save

Money? Consider the L.A. Motor Pool," *The Wall Street Journal*, July 6, 1995, pp. A1, A4.

26. Brian L. Goff, William F. Shughart, and Robert D. Tollison, "Batter Up! Moral Hazard and the Effects of the Designated Hitter Rule on Hit Batsmen," *Economic Inquiry*, vol. 35 (July 1997), pp. 555–561.

Chapter 2

1. Ronald H. Coase, "The Nature of the Firm," *Economica*, vol. 4 (1937), pp. 386–405, reprinted in R. H. Coase, *The Firm, the Market, and the Law* (Chicago: University of Chicago Press, 1988), pp. 33–55.

2. Ibid., pp. 41–42.

3. Adam Smith, *An Inquiry into the Nature and Causes of the Wealth of Nations* (New York: Modern Library, 1937), pp. 4–12.

4. The late University of Chicago economist Frank Knight speculated that firms arise because of *uncertainty* (*Risk, Uncertainty, and Profit* [Chicago: University of Chicago Press, 1971]). If business were conducted in a totally certain world, there would be no need for firms, according to Knight. Workers would know their pattern of rewards, and there would be no need for anyone to specialize in the acceptance of the costs of dealing with risks and uncertainties that abound in the real world of business.

As it is, according to Knight, some workers are willing to work for firms because of the type of deal that is struck: the workers accept a reduction in their expected pay in order to reduce the variability and outright uncertainty of that pay. Entrepreneurs are willing to make such a bargain with their workers because they are effectively paid to do so by their workers (who accept a reduction in pay) and because the employers can reduce their exposure to risk and uncertainties faced by individual workers by making similar bargains with a host of workers. As Knight put it,

> This fact [the intelligence of one person can be used to direct others] is responsible for the most fundamental change of all in the form of organization, the system under which the confident and adventuresome assume the risk or insure the doubtful and timid by guaranteeing to the latter a specified income in return for the assignment of the actual results. . . . With human nature as we know it, it would be impracticable or very unusual for one man to guarantee to another a definite result of the latter's actions without being given power to direct his work. And on the other hand the second party would not place himself under the direction of the first without such a guarantee. . . . The result of this manifold specialization of function is the enterprise and wage system of industry. Its existence in the world is the direct result of the fact of uncertainty. (ibid., pp. 269–270)

The problem with this explanation for the firm's existence is that the firm is really not needed to accommodate risk and uncertainty. All of the problems of risk transference and risk assumption could be handled through the market. Those who are prepared to assume the risk could simply engage in market transactions. The workers who want a certain income could contract with people who are more confident and venturesome, giving up their varying income for a steady paycheck.

5. Ibid., pp. 41–42. For example, Coase concedes that some people might prefer to be directed in their work. As a consequence, they might accept lower pay just to be told what to do. However, Coase dismisses this explanation as unlikely to be important because "it would rather seem that the opposite tendency is operating if one judges from the stress normally laid on the advantage of 'being one's own master'" (ibid., p. 38). Of course, it might be that some people like to control others, meaning they would give up a portion of their pay to have other people follow their direction. However, again Coase finds such an explanation lacking, mainly because it could not possibly be true "in the majority of the cases" (ibid.). People who direct the work of others are frequently paid a premium for their efforts.

6. Coase recognizes that entrepreneurs could overcome some of the costs of repeatedly negotiating and enforcing short-term contracts by devising one long-term contract. However, as the time period over which a contract is in force is extended, more and more unknowns are covered, which implies that the contract must allow for progressively greater flexibility for the parties to the contract. The firm is, in essence, a substitute for such a long-term contract in that it covers an indefinite future and provides for flexibility. That is to say, the firm as a legal institution permits workers to exit more or less at will and it gives managers the authority, within bounds, to change the directives given to workers.

7. In his classic *The Wealth of Nations*, Adam Smith wrote, "The directors of such companies, however, being the managers rather of other people's money than of their own, it cannot be well expected, that they should watch over it with the same anxious vigilance with which the partners in a private copartnery frequently watch over their own. Like the stewards of a rich man, they are apt to consider attention to small matters as not for their master's honour, and very easily give themselves a dispensation from having it. Negligence and profusion, therefore, must always prevail, more or less, in the management of the affairs of such a company" (*The Wealth of Nations*, p. 700).

8. One of the more important contemporary articles on the "market for corporate control" is by Henry G. Manne, "Mergers and the Market for Corporate Control," *Journal of Political Economy*, vol. 73 (April 1963), pp. 110–120.

9. See Michael C. Jensen, "Eclipse of the Public corporation," *Harvard Business Review* (September–October 1989), pp. 64–65.

10. As reported by A. Furnham, "Wasting Time in the Board Room," *Financial Times*, March 10, 1993, p. xx.

11. See Mancur Olson, T*he Logic of Collective Action: Public Goods and the Theory of Groups* (Cambridge, Mass.: Harvard University Press, 1965). Olson argues that common goals have less force in "large" groups than "small" groups, which explains why cartels don't form in open competitive markets. All competitors might understand that it is in their group interest to cut production and increase

their market price, if all curb production. However, each competitor can reason that its individual curb in output will have no effect on total output and thus cannot be detected. Hence, the "logic of collective action" is for everyone to "cheat" on the cartel, or not curb production, which means that nothing will happen to the market price.

12. The economists Marc Isaac and James Walker found that in an experimental setting, involving computer games in which the research subjects (students) could contribute to their common welfare (or to a "public good"), free riding was prevalent in the initial trials even within groups of four and ten subjects. Anywhere from 30 to 60 percent of the students (depending on the size of the groups and the pay-off for not free riding) initially contributed nothing to the group's common welfare. However, as the experiment continued through ten trials, the extent of free riding rose irregularly in every group. The group that started with 30 percent of the members contributing nothing to the group's common welfare ended the trials with over 60 percent of the group contributing nothing. The group that started with less than 60 percent of the group contributing nothing ended the ten trials with over 90 percent contributing nothing. The researchers also found, as expected, that reducing the private gains to each group member from contributing to the common good led to more free riding (R. Marc Isaac and James M. Walker, "Group Size Effects in Public Goods Provision: The Voluntary Contributions Mechanism," *Quarterly Journal of Economics* [February 1988], pp. 179–199).

13. Workers can also reason that if the residual from their added effort goes to the firm owners, they could possibly garner some of the residual by collusively (by explicit or tacit means) restricting their effort and hiking their rate of pay, which means that the incentive system must seek to undermine such collusive agreement. For a discussion of these points, see Felix R. FitzRoy and Kornelius Kraft, "Cooperation, Productivity, and Profit Sharing," *Quarterly Journal of Economics* (February 1987), pp. 23–35.

14. Oliver E. Williamson, "Hierarchical Control and Optimum Size Firms," *Journal of Political Economy*, vol. 75, no. 2 (1967), pp. 123–138.

15. Vijay Gurbaxani and Seungjin Whang, "The Impact of Information Systems on Organizations and Markets," *Communication of the ACM*, January 1991, pp. 59–73.

16. See Michael C. Jensen and William H. Meckling, "Theory of the Firm: Managerial Behavior, Agency Costs and Ownership Structure," *Journal of Financial Economics*, vol. 3 (October 1976), pp. 325–328.

17. As reported by John A. Byrne, "Has Outsourcing Gone Too Far?" *Business Week*, April 1, 1996, p. 27.

18. "Conditional-sum games" are games in which the value available to the participants is dependent how the game is played.

19. As reported in Peter Passell, "Economic Scene: The Greatest Good for the Greatest Number? Try Lojack," *New York Times*, August 21, 1997, p. C2, citing the research of Ian Ayes and Steven Levitt published by the National Bureau of Economic Research.

20. As reported in Jonathan Dahl, "Many Bypass the New Rules of the Road," *The Wall Street Journal*, September 29, 1994, p. B1.

21. For a discussion of frequent-flier programs as a means of enhancing customer loyalty, see Adam M. Brandenburger and Barry J. Nalebuff, *Co-opetition* (New York: Currency/Doubleday, 1996), pp. 132–158.

22. See Dahl, "Many Bypass the New Rules of the Road," p. B1.

23. As reported by Frederick J. Stephenson and Richard J. Fox, "Corporate Strategies for Frequent-Flier Programs," *Transportation Journal*, vol. 32, no. 1 (Fall 1992), pp. 38–50. The 1991 survey included 506 corporate members of the National Business Travel Association who did not work for airlines.

24. Ibid., p. 41.

25. Ibid., p. 43.

26. James Q. Wilson, *The Moral Sense* (New York: Free Press, 1993).

27. See P. Christopher Earley, "Social Loafing and Collectivism: A Comparison of the United States and the People's Republic of China," *Administrative Science Quarterly*, vol. 34, no. 4 (December 1989), pp. 565–582.

28. Richard Hawkins, *The Selfish Gene* (New York: Oxford University Press, 1989).

29. Olson, *The Logic of Collective Action*, pp. 148–159.

30. See James M. Buchanan, "Ethical Rules, Expected Values, and Large Numbers," *Ethics*, vol. 76 (October 1965), pp. 1–13. From the strictly economic perspective, what is truly amazing in large cities is not how many crimes are committed but how many people respect the property and human rights of their fellow citizens, in spite of the decreased incentives to do so.

31. Wilson, *The Moral Sense*, p. 49.

32. Gary J. Miller, *Managerial Dilemmas: The Political Economy of Hierarchy* (New York: Cambridge University Press, 1992), chap. 9.

33. This game is also referred to as the game of chicken—in which two young drivers speed toward each other head-on, with the winner being the one who refuses to swerve out of the way at the last minute, assuming that the other does.

34. Of course, the problem of each participant's being made worse off by the choice of the other exists regardless of whether each one commits to a decision. But, as will be discussed later in this chapter, a reputation for cooperation can prove beneficial for those in a prisoners' dilemma situation when they anticipate repeated play.

35. For a lucid and informative extended discussion of "games" as applied to business, see Avinash K. Dixit and Barry J. Nalebuff, *Thinking Strategically: The Competitive Edge in Business, Politics, and Everyday Life* (New York: Norton, 1991).

Chapter 3

1. As we will see, even when workers own the firm and could be their own bosses, they invariably hire a boss, typically a tough one at that.

2. It is also true, as we will see in chapter 5, that how wages are paid can be an important factor in determining how productive workers are.

3. This line of analysis has been developed at length by Mancur Olson, *The Logic of Collective Action: Public Goods and the Theory of Groups* (Cambridge, Mass.: Harvard University Press, 1965).

4. The payoff can be in dollars, utility, or any other unit of measure. The only important consideration is that higher numbers represent higher payoffs. This is in contrast to the original prisoners' dilemma example, in which the number in the payoff matrix represented the length of prison sentences, so the higher number represented lower payoffs.

5. Of course, not everyone can receive this payoff.

6. Jane would receive a lower payoff of 25 if she were the only one who did not shirk, but because of her effort the collective payoff would be higher than if she did shirk, as her effort would raise the payoff to the shirkers to something slightly higher than 50.

7. See Dwight Lee, "Why It Pays to Have Tough Profs," *The Margin* (September/October 1990), pp. 28–29.

8. See Gordon E. Moore, "The Accidental Entrepreneur," *Engineering & Science*, vol. 62, no. 4 (Summer 1994): 23–30.

9. For example, in 1992 wage and salary agricultural workers averaged a 40.6-hour week, while self-employed agricultural workers averaged a 47.1-hour week. See United States Bureau of the Census, *Statistical Abstract of the United States: 1993* (113th ed.) (Washington, D.C., 1993): p. 401, table 636.

10. Granted, taxpayers could be viewed as the residual claimants to any efficiency improvement resulting from tough managerial decisions in public enterprises, given that efficiency improvement can result in lower tax bills. However, taxpayers have little incentive to closely monitor the activities of public agencies, and, as a matter of fact, do little of it. The reason is simple: Each taxpayer can reason that there is little direct payoff to anyone incurring the costs of monitoring and enforcing greater efficiency in public agencies. See Gordon Tullock, *The Mathematics of Politics* (Ann Arbor, Mich.: University of Michigan Press, 1972), especially chap. 7.

11. You might expect a manager down in the bowels of a large corporation to urge his workers to "waste" money at the end of the year, but not someone who has a substantial stake in his or her own decisions. The single proprietor–residual claimant is someone who has total claim to the net income stream, which implies maximum incentive to minimize waste.

12. Much of the motivation for privatizing municipal services comes from the cost reductions that take place when residual claimants are in charge of supplying these services. There is plenty of evidence that privatization does significantly lower the cost, often by 50 percent or more, of basic municipal services such as trash pick-up, fire protection, and school buses. See James T. Bennett and Manual H. Johnson, *Better Government at Half the Price* (Ottawa, Ill.: Carolina House, 1983).

13.   The profits received by firms that are too large to be managed by single proprietors also serve to direct resources into their highest valued uses. But this is true because these firms are organized in ways that allow the owners (the residual claimants) to exert some control over those who manage the firm (the hired bosses). The problem that owners of large corporations face in controlling managers is discussed in subsequent chapters.

14.   The prevalence of insurance reflects the risk averseness of most people. Insurance allows people to experience a relatively small loss with 100 percent probability (their insurance premiums) in order to avoid a small chance of a much larger loss, but a loss with an expected value that is less than the insurance premiums. It is interesting to note, however, that the same people who buy fire insurance on their house also buy lottery tickets. Buying a lottery ticket reflects risk-loving behavior since you are taking a small loss with 100 percent probability (the price of the lottery ticket) in order to take a chance on an expected payoff that is less in expected value than the loss. Explanations exist for why rational individuals would buy insurance and gamble. Probably the best known of these explanations was given by M. Friedman and L. J. Savage, "The Utility Analysis of Choices Involving Risk," *Journal of Political Economy*, vol. 56 (August 1948), pp. 279–304. But the fact remains than in situations that would put a significant amount of their wealth or income at risk, most people are risk averse.

15.   In effect, the owners of capital would hold financial assets that would have the look and feel of bonds.

16.   For an extended discussion of points in this section, see Michael C. Jensen and William H. Meckling, "Rights and Production Functions: An Application to Labor-Managed Firms and Codetermination," *Journal of Business*, vol. 52, no. 4 (1979), pp. 469–506.

17.   See the discussion of why workers do not own firms by Benjamin Klein, Robert G. Crawford, and Armen A. Alchian, "Vertical Integration, Appropriable Rents, and the Competitive Contracting Process," *Journal of Law and Economics*, vol. 21 (1978), pp. 297–326. The problem of appropriation by workers is especially acute if the fixed assets are firm specific because they have no alternative use, which implies a limited resell value. As we have seen in other instances, owners of fixed assets with limited resale values open themselves to opportunistic behavior on the part of the buyer, in this case, the workers, who, once the specific investment is made, can appropriate the difference between the purchase and resale price. Workers hired by their capitalist-owners do not generally have the same worry about their work-related investments with their capitalist-owners. The workers' investments in their job-related skills are typically not firm specific. If workers need firm-specific skills, the workers can protect themselves from appropriation by having their firm pay for the investment they might make in firm-specific skills. Put another way, when human capital is relatively important on the job, we would expect the workers to also be the owners, which tends to be the case in accounting and law firms in which the ratio of human to physical capital investments firm tend to be high.

18. Susan, Carey, "ESOP Fables: UAL Worker-Owners May Face Bumpy Ride If the Past Is a Guide," *Wall Street Journal*, December 23, 1993, p. 1.

19. See Susan Chandler, "United We Own." *Business Week*, March 18, 1996, pp. 96–100.

20. Ibid., p. 98.

21. Ibid., p. 99.

22. See the article by Susan Carey, "United Flight Attendants Warn of 'Chaos'," *Wall Street Journal*, June 24, 1997, pp. B-1, B-2.

23. Ibid.

24. As quoted in Lisa Wirthman, "Superior Snooping: New Software Can Catch workers Goofing Off, But Some Say Such Surveillance Goes Too Far," *Orange County (Calif.) Register*, July 20, 1997, p. 1, 10 (connect section).

25. Robert Hessen, *In Defense of the Corporation* (Stanford, Calif.: Hoover Institution Press, 1979), develops this view of the corporation.

26. Noel M. Tichy and Stratford Sherman, "Jack Welch's Lessons for Success," *Fortune*, January 25, 1993, pp. 86–93.

27. Ibid., p. 92.

Chapter 4

1. As reported in Paulette Thomas, "Work Week: Teams Rule," *Wall Street Journal*, May 28, 1996, p. A1.

2. We remind the reader that "cost" is the value of that which is forgone when something is done. Cost can be measured in money, but the real cost is the value of that which is actually given up.

3. Armen Alchian and Harold Demsetz, "Production, Information Costs, and Economic Organization," *American Economic Review*, vol. 62 (1972), pp. 777–795.

4. The role of peer pressure within groups, or teams, or workers has been formally developed by Eugene Kandel and Edward P. Lazear, "Peer Pressure and Partnerships," *Journal of Political Economy*, vol. 100, no. 4, pp. 801–817.

5. Ibid.

6. Researchers have found that on single-play experimental games designed to test the tendency of people to "free ride" on the group's efforts, not everyone contributed to the group's output. However, they also found that the members produced 40 to 60 percent of the "optimal output" of the public good, with the exception of only one notable group, graduate students in economics. These graduate students provided only 20 percent of the optimal output. See Gerald Marwell and Ruth Ames, "Economists Free Ride, Does Anyone Else?" *Journal of Public Economics*, vol. 15 (1981), pp. 295–310.

7. As reported in R. Mitchell, "Managing by Values," *Business Week*, August 1, 1994, p. 50.

8. We should not be surprised if the *pay rates* of the winning and losing teams are closer together than their *incomes*. We doubt, however, a pay system that resulted in the "winners" having a lower rate of pay than the "losers" would long

have the desired incentive impact, given that the higher income must also be discounted by the probability of any team winning. If the winners' pay rate were not
higher than the losers', we would expect the winners to curb their effort.

9. See Felix FitzRoy and Kornelius Kraft, "Profitability and Profit-Sharing,"
Journal of Industrial Economics, vol. 35, no. 2 (December 1986), pp. 113–130; Bion
B. Howard and Peter O. Dietz, *A Study of the Financial Significance of Profit Sharing*
(Chicago: Council of Profit Sharing Industries, 1969); Bertram L. Metzger, *Profit
Sharing in 38 Large Companies, I & II* (Evanston, Ill.: Profit Sharing Research
Foundation, 1975); Bertram L. Metzger and Jerome A. Colletti, *Does Profit Shar-
ing Paying* (Evanston, Ill.: Profit Sharing Research Foundation, 1975); John L.
Wagner, Paul A. Rubin, and Thomas J. Callahan, "Incentive Payment and Non-
Managerial Productivity: An Interrupted Time Series Analysis of Magnitude and
Trend," *Organizational Behavior and Human Decision Processes*, vol. 42, no. 1 (August
1988), pp. 47–74; Martin L. Weisman and Douglas L. Kruse, "Profit Sharing and
Productivity," in Alan S. Blinder, ed., *Paying for Productivity: A Look at the Evidence*
(Washington, D.C.: Brookings Institution, 1990), pp. 95–140: and U.S. Depart-
ment of Labor, *High Performance Work Practices and Firm Performance* (Washing-
ton, D.C.: U.S. Government Printing Office, 1993).

10. John Cable and Nicolas Wilson, "Profit-Sharing and Productivity: An
analysis of UK Engineering Firms," *Economic Journal*, vol. 99 (June 1989), pp.
366–375.

11. See Mark Husled, "The Impact of Human Resource Management Practices
on Turnover, Productivity and Corporate Financial Performance," *Academy of
Management Journal*, vol. 38, no. 2 (June 1995), pp. 635–672; and Casey Ich-
niowski, Kathryn Shaw, and Giovanna Prennushi, *The Effects of Human Resource
Practices on Productivity* (Cambridge, Mass.: National Bureau of Economic
Research, working paper no. 5333, 1996).

12. Haig R. Nalbantian and Andrew Schotter, "Productivity Under Group
Incentives: An Experimental Study," *American Economic Review*, vol. 87, no. 3 (June
1997), pp. 314–341.

13. Ibid., p. 315.

14. Ibid.

Chapter 5

1. See Richard B. McKenzie and Gordon Tullock, *The New World of Economics*
(New York: McGraw-Hill, 1994), chap. 4.

2. Ibid.

3. Edward E. Lawler III, *Strategic Pay: Aligning Organizational Strategies and
Pay Systems* (San Francisco: Jossey-Bass, 1990), p. 58.

4. Frederick W. Taylor, "A Piece Rate System," *American Society of Mechanical
Engineers Transactions*, vol. 16 (1895), pp. 856–893.

5. William G. Lee, "The New Corporate Republics," *Wall Street Journal*, September 26, 1994, p. 12.

6. Howard Banks, "A Sixties Industry in a Nineties Economy," *Forbes*, May 9, 1994, pp. 107–112.

7. FedEx actually tracks its delivery people on their routes, and the workers understand that their pay is tied to how cost-effective they are in their deliveries. Postal workers understand that they are not being so carefully monitored, mainly because there are no stockholders who can claim the profits from a speed-up in their work.

8. Tron Petersen, "Reward Systems and the Distribution of Wages," *Journal of Law, Economics, & Organizations*, vol. 7 (special issue, 1991), pp. 130–158.

9. For a review of arguments offered by psychologists against incentive pay plans, see Alfie Kohn, "Why Incentive Plans Cannot Work," *Harvard Business Review* (September–October 1993), pp. 54–63. Kohn sums up his argument this way: "Do rewards motivate people? Absolutely. They motivate people to get rewards" (p. 62), suggesting that the goals of the firm might not be achieved in the process, given the complexity of the production process and the margins workers can exploit. Kohn's criticisms are reviewed and critiqued in the penultimate chapter of this book.

10. L. Hayes, "All Eyes on Du Pont's Incentive program," *Wall Street Journal*, December 5, 1988, p. B1.

11. R. Koening, "Du Pont Plan Linking Pay to Fibers Profit Unravels," *Wall Street Journal*, October 25, 1990, p. B1.

12. See Benjamin Klein, Robert Crawford, and Armen Alchian, "Vertical Integration, Appropriable Rents, and the Competitive Contracting Process," *Journal of Law and Economics*, vol. 21 (1978), pp. 297–326.

13. As quoted in Gary J. Miller, *Managerial Dilemmas: The Political Economy of Hierarchy* (New York: Cambridge University Press, 1992), p. 117.

14. Ibid.

15. J. H. Pencavel, "Work Effort, On the Job Screening, and Alternative Methods of Remuneration," *Research in Labor Economics* (Greenwich, Conn.: JAI Press, 1977), pp. 225–259.

16. Eric Seiler, "Piece-Rate Vs. Time-Rate: The Effect of Incentives on Earnings," *Review of Economics and Statistics*, vol. 66, no. 3 (1984), pp. 363–375.

17. The study by Pencavel ("Work Effort, On the Job Screening, and Alternative Methods of Remuneration") adjusts the worker data for differences in education, experience, race, and union status. The second study by Seiler ("Piece-Rate Vs. Time-Rate: The Effect of Incentives on Earnings") adjusts for differences in union status, gender, location of employment, occupation, type of product, and method of production, among other variables.

18. Seiler, "Piece-Rate Vs. Time-Rate: The Effect of Incentives on Earnings."

19. See G. L. Mangum. "Are Wage Incentives Becoming Obsolete?" *Industrial Relations*, vol. 2 (October 1962), pp. 73–96.

20. This discussion of offering sales people a menu of contracts is taken from Paul Milgram and John Roberts, *Economics, Organization and Management* (Englewood Cliffs, N.J.: Prentice Hall, 1992), pp. 400–402.

21. We are not privileged to the particulars of the contracts, but the exact dollars involved is irrelevant to our discussion.

Chapter 6

1. Our discussion on the Ford pay increase is heavily dependent on a book by Stephen Meyer, *The Five Dollar Day: Labor, Management, and Social Control in the Ford Motor Company, 1908–1921* (Albany: State University of New York Press, 1981).

2. David Halberstam, *The Reckoning* (New York: Avon Books, 1986), p. 94.

3. Ibid.

4. See J. Bulow and Lawrence Summers, "A Theory of Dual Labor Markets with Applications to Industrial Policy, Discrimination and Keynesian Unemployment," *Journal of Labor Economics*, vol. 4, no. 3 (July 1986), pp. 376–414; and C. Shapiro and Joseph Stiglitz, "Equilibrium Unemployment as a Worker Discipline Device," *American Economic Review*, vol. 74, no. 3 (June 1984), pp. 433–444. So-called "equity theory," based in psychology, suggests that worker overpayment can lead to greater performance because the overpaid workers perceive an inequity in pay among their relevant peers. As a consequence, they seek to redress the over-payment by working longer and harder. Of course, the theory also suggests that underpaid workers will respond by working less diligently and putting in less time. See Edward E. Lawler III, "Equity Theory as a Predictor of Productivity and Work Quality," *Psychological Bulletin*, vol. 70, no. 6 (December 1968), pp. 596–610.

5. Dwight R. Lee and Richard B. McKenzie, *Regulating Government: A Preface to Constitutional Economics* (Lexington, Mass.: Lexington Books, 1987), pp. 157–162.

6. For the analysis presented here, we are indebted to the work of economist Edward Lazear. See Edward Lazear, "Why Is There Mandatory Retirement?" *Journal of Political Economy*, vol. 87 (December 1979), pp. 1261–1284.

7. The analysis can really get sticky and convoluted when it is recognized that *commitments* that firms make are only implicitly made, with no formal contract and often with a host of unstated contingencies. For example, many firms may commit to overpaying their workers *if* the firm is not sold and *if* market conditions do not turn against them. Workers will simply have to consider those contingencies in the wages that they demand early in their careers and later on. All we can say is, the greater the variety and number of contingencies, the less the underpayment workers will accept early in their careers, and the less benefits firms and their workers will achieve from twisting the wage structure.

8. Workers also understand that challenging the actions of owners can get expensive, which means that owners might take actions with regard to their older workers that are subject to legal challenge but only in a probabilistic sense. That is to say, owners might simply demote older workers. Even though employers who take such an actions *could* be taken to court, they might not be taken to court, given the expense the worker might have to incur and the likelihood that the challenge will not be successful.

9. For a fuller discussion of how above-minimal price can give suppliers an incentive to provide above-minimal quality of products, see Benjamin Klein and Keith B. Leffler, "The Role of Market Forces in Assuring Contractual Performance," *Journal of Law and Economics*, vol. 89, no. 4 (1981), pp. 615–641.

Chapter 7

1. Engaging in a takeover can be very expensive, and we recognize that a firm is not likely to be taken over because of the failure of the firm to provide one efficiency-enhancing fringe benefit. But when enough of these types of mistakes are made, the inefficiency mounts, increasing the chance that the firm will be a takeover target.

2. As explained in an earlier chapter, despite what they may say, most young and inexperienced MBA graduates would not want a job paying $200,000 immediately upon graduation. Such an employee would have to contribute at least $200,000 to firm revenues, which he or she, without experience, is not likely to be able to do. The expected value of a job with a much lower salary is likely to be higher, given the much higher probability of the new graduate keeping it.

3. Over half of American companies with 100 or more workers give those workers a chance to tailor their benefits. This means that a worker covered by a spouse's health insurance can opt out of health insurance and have the savings applied to, say, dental insurance or car insurance. The purpose of giving workers the option is, naturally, cost control (*The Economist*, December 21, 1996, p. 91).

4. The remaining discussion draws heavily on an article by one of the authors: Dwight R. Lee, "Why Workers Should Want Mandated Benefits to Lower Their Wages," *Economic Inquiry* (April 1996), pp. 401–407.

5. This assumption is often made explicit. It is commonly argued, for example, that the one-half of the Social Security tax that employers are required by law to pay is really paid by the employer and does not come out of the pocket of the workers.

Chapter 8

1. See Paul J. Feldstein. *Health Policy Issues: A Economic Perspective on Health Reform* (Arlington, Va. : AUPHA Press; Ann Arbor, Mich.: Health Administration Press, 1994); and Paul J. Feldstein, *The Politics of Health Legislation: An Economic Perspective*, 2d ed. (Chicago, Ill.: Health Administration Press, 1996).

2. Put another way, the consumer price index was increasing at decreasing rates, which means that the rate of inflation was gradually but irregularly decreasing for most of the 1980s and 1990s.

3. As many readers will remember from their microeconomics courses, a working rule of consumer maximizing behavior is that the consumer will continue to buy units of any good or service until the point at which the marginal cost of the last unit consumed just equals the marginal value of the last unit. If the person con-

sumes more than that amount, the additional cost of any additional units will exceed their additional value. By "excessive" consumption, we mean that patients are induced to go beyond the point where the marginal value is, while still positive, less than the marginal cost. The reason for this excessive consumption is that the individual consumer isn't paying the entire cost of additional medical care.

4. See John C. Goodman and Gerald L. Musgrave, *Patient Power: Solving America's Health Care Crisis* (Washington, D.C. : Cato Institute, 1992).

5. As reported by Goodman and Musgrave, ibid.

6. Of course, the extent to which the individual's actions can be detected depends on the size of the employment group. In small groups of workers, it would be easier to detect the impact of what one individual does or does not do.

7. One of the more serious problems in having government provide health insurance is that the relevant *group* is really large, extending to the boundaries of the country, which means people may have absolutely no incentives to curb their consumption of health care services. The benefits of doing so are spread ever so thinly over too many people.

8. The particulars of the Medical Savings Accounts are not important here. The important characteristic is broad discretion on the part of the worker, which will likely mean that the worker has a sum of money that is set aside to cover the large deductible under a catastrophic medical insurance policy and that can be used by the employee when it is not spent for medical purposes.

9. Any actual MSA program might for political reasons have restrictions on the range of goods and services that the workers can buy with any MSA balance remaining at the end of the year. For example, one MSA-type proposal would require that the balance go into a worker's retirement account.

10. See "Answering the Critics of Medical Savings Accounts," *Brief Analysis* (Dallas: National Center for Policy Analysis, September 16, 1994), p. 1.

Chapter 9

1. By asking the question as we have, we may cause some readers to forget that education is a "good" that must in part be paid for by the one receiving it. The reason for this is that a major part of the cost of education is the time devoted to study and class attendance. While students might be compensated for their time, they cannot avoid incurring the time cost.

2. Skilled workers often pay for their training indirectly, by taking an apprenticeship with experienced craftsmen, which pays less than the workers could have received in some other job that does not provide training and the promise of a higher future income.

3. The problem is really one of threat and counterthreat, because the employer can also threaten to retaliate against the worker who retaliates for any failure to keep prior agreements.

4. If the engineer is given \$134,000, she can buy the exact combination of goods that she had back in Six Mile, A_2 and H_2. The extra \$34,000 in salary would

go totally to housing, leaving her with the same amount of after-housing income that she had in Six Mile. Her new income constraint line is parallel with A_1H_3 because the prices of the bundles and housing are the same as under A_1H_3, and the relative prices of those goods determine the slope of the income constraint.

5. We should, therefore, expect people in high-cost areas like La Jolla to have relatively high incomes. One reason is obvious: people need a high income to cover the high cost of living. Another reason can go unnoticed: people who live in high-cost-of-living areas get much of their income in nonmoney forms, that is, in the amenities of the area, and these nonmoney forms of income are not subject to the high marginal tax rates that high-income people pay. For example, people who live on the coast in Southern California have to pay high prices for their housing partly because of the climate, which is very temperate (with high temperatures in the 70s) for much of the year. Accordingly, they have modest heating and cooling bills, which increases the demand for and the prices of their houses relative to houses in other parts of California and the Southwest where the climate is more extreme and the heating and/or cooling bills are much higher. Of course, pretty scenery can also increase the demand for houses. People in Boulder have been known to say (or lament) that they have to "eat the mountains," meaning that their food and household budgets are constrained by the high prices of their houses, inflated as they are by the value added by the views of the Rocky Mountains.

Chapter 10

1. See Steve Kichen and Eric Hardy, "Turnover at the Top," *Forbes*, May 27, 1991, pp. 214–218.

2. As reported by Judith H. Dobrzynski, "Top Post at Rock-Bottom Wage: Chief Executive Puts Stock-Only Pay to Ultimate Test," *New York Times*, October 4, 1996, p. C1.

3. Ibid., p. C3.

4. Dobrzynski, "Top Post at Rock-Bottom Wage," p. C1. However, according to the compensation analyst Graef Crystal, Peltz's stock options had an estimated present value of $30 million or more (ibid., p. C3).

5. Al Dunlap and Bob Andelman, *Mean Business: How I Save Bad Companies and Make Good Companies Great* (New York: Times Books, 1996), p. 21.

6. Ibid., p. 177.

7. Dunlap and Andelman, *Mean Business*, p. 23. Dunlap doesn't mince many words when he adds, "In England, where I lived for three years, they have real royalty. In America, we have corporate elitists. Both are self-inflated windbags; they don't believe they're accountable to anyone. They enrich themselves at the expense of hardworking men and women who have actually invested in our companies. It's time they were accountable to someone" (ibid., p. 209). Dunlap apparently had earned his keep as the CEO of Sunbeam, which, when he took charge in July 1996, was a failing business. He quickly cut the payroll from 12,000 to 6,000 workers and the count of factories from 26 to 8 by fall 1997. By fall 1997, revenues

has grown by 25 percent. Net earnings went from a minus $18 million to a positive $35 million. Earnings per share went from minus 22 cents per share to a plus 39 cents a share, and he was looking for a buyer, according to news reports (Jacqueline Bueno, "Sunbeam to Study Takeovers or Own Sale," *Wall Street Journal* [October 24, 1997], p. A3).

8. Kenneth Mason, "Four Ways to Overpay Yourself Enough," *Harvard Business Review* (July–August 1988), p. 72.

9. See Charles M. Elson, "Executive Overcompensation–A Board-Based Solution," *Boston College Law Review*, vol. 34 (September 1993), pp. 937–996.

10. Sherwin Rosen, "Contracts and the Market for Executives," (New York: National Bureau of Economic Research, working paper 3542, 1990). In the 1960s, economists speculated that large oligopolistic firms headed by managers who would be able to pursue their own objectives at the expense of stockholders would tend to base pay on sales, rather than on profits or some other measure of direct stockholder wealth. See William J. Baumol, "On the Theory of Oligopoly," *Economica*, vol. 25 (August 1958), pp. 187–198; and "On the Theory of Expansion of the Firm," *American Economic Review*, vol. 52 (1962), pp. 1078–1087. However, early researchers found that profits, rather than sales, tended to govern executive pay. See Wilbur G. Lewellen and Blaine Huntsman, "Managerial Pay and Corporate Performance, *American Economic Review*, vol. 60, no. 4 (September 1970), pp. 710–720; and Robert Tempest Masson, "Executive Motivations, Earnings, and Consequent Equity Performance," *Journal of Political Economy*, vol. 79 (November 6, 1971), pp. 1278–1292. Both of these studies also found that firms that tied their executives' pay to firm performance got better performance.

11. The research found that announcements of incentive pay schemes (in the form of stock purchase plans) that were available not only to executives had smaller effects on the price of the companies' stocks than did incentive pay schemes that were restricted to only the top or key executives. See Senjai Bhagat, James A. Brickley, and Ronald C. Lease, "Incentive Effects of Stock Purchase Plans," *Journal of Financial Economics*, vol. 14 (1985), pp. 195–215.

12. As reported by Martha Groves and Stuart Silverstein, "Levi Strauss Offers Year's Pay as Incentive Bonus," *Los Angeles Times*, June 13, 1996, p. A1.

13. A worker who this year is paid $25,000 and is expected to be paid $30,000 in six years (assuming a cost of living raise of 3 percent a year) will receive a bonus of $30,000 in 2002, assuming the firm's profit goals are reached. The present value of the $30,000 bonus is, however, only worth slightly more than $15,000 today (assuming an interest rate of 12 percent). The bonus divided by six years will amount to less than 10 percent of the worker's annual income.

14. As reported by Michael A. Hiltzik, "More Firms Giving a Stake to Employees," *Los Angeles Times*, June 15, 1996, p. 32, based on a report from the Executive Compensation Reports.

15. However, bonuses appear to be more strongly related to management performance than are merit increases. See Lawrence M. Kahn and Peter D. Sherer,

"Contingent Pay and Managerial Performance," *Industrial and Labor Relations Review*, vol. 43 (special issue, February 1990), pp. 107s–120s.

16. Kevin J. Murphy, "Top Executives Are Worth Every Nickel They Get," *Harvard Business Review*, March–April 1986, pp. 125–132.

17. Ibid., exhibit I, p. 126.

18. Ibid., exhibit III, p. 129.

19. Michael C. Jensen and Kevin J. Murphy, "Performance Pay and Top-Management Incentives," *Journal of Political Economy* vol. 98, no. 2 (1990), pp. 225–263. The tie between stockholder wealth increase and the increases for the executives varies by the market value of the firms. Executives who headed the firms in the bottom half of the firms studied, measured in terms of firm market value, had a median increase in personal wealth of $8.05 per $1,000 increase in stockholder wealth. Those firms in the top half had a median increase of $1.85 per $1,000 increase in stockholder wealth. Other studies have found stronger ties (perhaps eight times stronger) between executive compensation and firm performance. See Peter F. Kostiuk, "Executive Compensation, Corporate Performance and Managerial Income," Center for Naval Analysis, January 1986, who found that executive compensation rose by 12.5 percent when the accounting rate of return rose by 10 percent, and Andrew Cosh, "The Remuneration of Chief Executives in the United Kingdom," *Economic Journal*, vol. 85 (no. 1, 1975), pp. 75–94, who found that executive compensation rose by 10 percent when the accounting rate of return rose by 10 percent.

20. Murphy, "Top Executives Are Worth Every Nickel They Get."

21. Mason, "Four Ways to Overpay Yourself Enough," p. 73.

22. CEOs whose rates of return match industry standards have only a 4 percent chance of relinquishing their jobs, according to Jensen and Murphy. CEOs whose rates of return are 50 percent below industry averages have a three times greater chance of relinquishing their jobs, but still the probability is only 12 percent and then the turnover may be voluntary, due, for example, to retirement (Jensen and Murphy, "Performance Pay and Top-Management Incentives," p. 20).

23. In contrast to the claims of critics of executive compensation, Jensen and Murphy have found that CEO compensation actually declined in real dollar terms between the 1930s and the 1980s as firm values increased. The incentive executives have to work in their stockholders' interest has also declined, given that the wealth gains to the executives per $1,000 of stockholder gains has declined (ibid., pp. 253–260).

24. See James A. Brickley, Sanjai Bhagat, and Ronald C. Lease, "The Impact of Long-Range Managerial Compensation Plans on Shareholder Wealth," *Journal of Accounting and Economics*, vol. 7 (1985), pp. 115–129.

25. One explanation for the perceived growth in executive compensation in the 1980s is the method of reporting executive pay. Prior to 1978, firms could place executive compensation in the form of stock and stock options at the back of their annual reports, where such pay factors could go unnoticed and unreported in the

media. In 1978, the Securities and Exchange Commission began requiring firms to put all forms of executive compensation in the front of the annual report, where investors and reporters could more easily notice them.

26. Sherwin Rosen, *Contracts and the Market for Executives* (New York: National Bureau of Economic Research, working paper 3542, December 1990), p. 7.

27. The executive tournament can have much the same effect as prizes do in real golf tournament: they improve performance. One study found that when the prize money was raised to a hundred grand or more, the scores of the golfers went down by 1.1 strokes over the course of a 72-hole tournament. Apparently, the prize money had its greatest effect in the later rounds when the players were tired and needed to concentrate on every shot. See Ronald G. Ehrenberg and Michael L. Bognanno, "Do Tournaments Have Incentive effects?" *Journal of Political Economy*, vol. 98 (December 1990), pp. 1307–1324. In addition, bonuses appear to be sensitive to managerial bonuses with the future performance of managers improving with current bonuses. See Lawrence M. Kahn and Peter D. Sherer, "Contingent Pay and Managerial Performance," *Industrial and Labor Relations Review*, vol. 43 (February 1990), pp. 107s–120s.

28. For a discussion of these points and some experimental evidence that suggests that the variance of outcomes in tournaments is greater than the variance in outcomes of piece-rate pay systems, see Clive Bull, Andrew Schotter, and Keith Weigelt, "Tournaments and Piece Rates: An Experimental Study," *Journal of Political Economy*, vol. 95, no. 1 (1987), pp. 1–33.

29. See Jonathan S. Leonard, "Executive Pay and Firm Performance," *Industrial and Labor Relations Review*, vol. 43, no. 3 (1990), pp. 13s–29s. Also, consistent with the Leonard study, another study found that pay increases rapidly with higher ranks, with the CEO earning $100,000 more a year than vice presidents compared to lower-level managers, who earn $10,000 to $30,000 more than their underlings. See Richard A. Lambert, David F. Larcker, and Keith Weigelt, "The Structure of Organizational Incentives," *Administrative Science Quarterly*, vol. 38, no. 3 (September 1993), pp. 438–462. However, another study drew a contradictory conclusion: that the greater the number of vice presidents (which, presumably means a lower probability of being promoted), the greater the pay gap between the CEO and the vice presidents. See C. O'Reilly, Brian Main, and G. Crystal, "CEO Compensation as Tournament and Social Comparison: A Tale of Two Theories," *Administrative Science Quarterly*, vol. 33, no. 3 (1988), pp. 257–274.

30. Graef Crystal, "Average U.S. CEO Boosted Pay 21% in '95, to $4.5 Million," *Los Angeles Times*, May 26, 1996, p. D4.

31. We don't want to be accused of playing to the view that executives are the only group of workers who can be "overpaid." We have presented arguments as to why some workers are "overpaid" (chapter 6). Obviously, in many firms there are also workers who become good at working the pay system to their advantage without their bosses noticing. They can end up overpaid for a very long time. We also are sympathetic to the view that many executives are probably "underpaid," given

how little their rewards go up with their executive actions. At the same time, many workers may be overpaid, in view of how little they can affect their company's revenues for the wages they receive. A contrarian view is developed at length by Robert H. Frank, *Choosing the Right Pond: Human Behavior and the Quest for Status* (New York: Oxford University Press, 1987).

32. The study covered 1975 through 1983 (as reported by Mason, "Four Ways to Overpay Yourself Enough," p. 71).

33. See Judith H. Dobrzynski, "Growing Trend: Giant Payoffs for Executives Who Fail Big," *New York Times,* July 21, 1997, p. A1, A10.

34. Peter F. Kostiuk, "Firm Size and Executive Compensation," *Journal of Human Resources*, vol. 25, no. 1 (1989), pp. 90–105. See also Kevin J. Murphy, "Corporate Performance and Managerial Performance," *Journal of Accounting and Economics*, vol. 7, no. 2 (1985), pp. 11–42.

35. See Cosh, "The Remuneration of Chief Executives in the United Kingdom," *Economic Journal*, vol. 85, no. 1 (1975), pp. 75–94; Jason R. Barro and Robert J. Barro, "Pay, Performance and Turnover of Bank CEOs," *Journal of Labor Economics*, vol. 8, no. 4 (October 1990), pp. 448–481; and Joseph W. McGuire, John S.Y. Chiu, and Alvar O. Elbing, "Executive Incomes, Sales and Profits," *American Economic Review*, vol. 52, no. 4 (1962), pp. 753–761.

36. This theory can explain why one study found that managers located at their corporate headquarters tended to receive greater bonuses for performance than did their counterparts located away from the headquarters. The managers at the headquarters can potentially have a greater impact on more people and, accordingly, are potentially more productive (Kahn and Sherer, "Contingent Pay and Managerial Performance," pp. 107s–120s).

Chapter 11

1. We recognize that debt and equity come in a variety of forms. Common and preferred stock are the two major divisions of equity. Debt can take a form that has the "look and feel" of equity. For example, the much-maligned "junk bonds" often carry with them rights of control over firm decisions and may also be about as risky as common stock. In order to contain the length of this chapter, we consider only the two broad categories, and we encourage readers to consult finance texts for more details on financial instruments. However, readers should recognize that variations in the type of debt and equity could help overcome some of the problems with each that are discussed in this chapter.

2. For a more complete discussion of answers to this question, see Michael C. Jensen and William H. Meckling, "Theory of the Firm: Managerial Behavior, Agency Costs and Ownership Structure," *Journal of Financial Economics*, vol. 3 (October 1976), pp. 305–360.

3. See William K. Black, Kitty Calavita, and Henry N. Pontell, "The Savings and Loan Debacle of the 1980s: White-Collar Crime or Risky Business?" *Law & Policy*, vol. 17, no. 1 (January 1995).

4. Michael C. Jensen, "Eclipse of the Public Corporation," *Harvard Business Review* (September–October 1989), pp. 64–65.

5. Al Dunlap and Bob Andelman, *Mean Business: How I Save Bad Companies and Make Good Companies Great* (New York: Times Books, 1996), p. 81.

Chapter 12

1. Michael J. Mandel, "Land of the Giants," *Business Week*, September 11, 1995, p. 34.

2. See Michael C. Jensen, "Takeovers: Their Causes and Consequences," *Journal of Economic Perspectives*, vol. 2, no. 1 (Winter 1988), pp. 21–48.

3. However, Michael Jensen minces few words on what the data imply: "[T]he fact that takeover and LBO premiums average 50% above market price illustrates how much value public-company managers can destroy before they face a serious threat of disturbance. Takeovers and buyouts both create value and unlock value destroyed by management through misguided policies. I estimate that transactions associated with the market for corporate control unlocked shareholder gains (in target companies alone) of more than $500 billion between 1977 and 1988–more than 50% of the cash dividends paid by the entire corporate sector over this same period" (Michael C. Jensen, "Eclipse of the Public Corporation," *Harvard Business Review* [September–October 1989], pp. 64–65).

4. See "Long-term Risk" (editorial), *Atlanta Journal and Constitution*, April 15, 1995, p. A-10.

5. Unless otherwise noted, the studies cited are discussed in Gregg A. Jarrell, James A. Brickley, and Jeffrey M. Netter, "The Market for Corporate Control: The Empirical Evidence Since 1980," *Journal of Economic Perspectives* (Winter 1988), pp. 49–68.

6. See Jensen, "Takeovers," p. 21. It should be pointed out that this estimate applied to all mergers and acquisitions, not just to "hostile" takeovers. But "hostile" or not, takeovers consistently increase the value of the acquired firm's stock, and probably increase it more when the takeover is opposed by management than otherwise, since offering a higher price is a way around a reluctant management.

7. See Richard H. Thayer, *The Winner's Curse: Paradoxes and Anomalies of Economic Life* (New York: Free Press, 1992).

8. In general, of course, the value of the asset will depend to some degree on who owns it. The highest bidder will likely have good reason to believe that he or she is better able to utilize the asset to create value. In the case of an oil field, the possibilities that one owner will obtain more wealth than another are probably quite limited. In the case of a corporation, the importance of management no doubt provides more opportunity for some owners to run the business more profitably than others.

9. Gregg A. Jarrell and Annette B. Poulsen, "The Returns to Acquiring Firms in Tender Offers: Evidence from Three Decades," *Financial Management*, vol. 18 (Autumn 1989), pp. 12–19.

10. Debra K. Dennis and John J. McConnell, "Corporate Mergers and Security Returns," *Journal of Financial Economics* 16 (1986), pp. 143–187; and Kenneth Lehn and Annette B. Poulsen, "Leveraged Buyouts: Wealth Created or Wealth Redistributed?" in *Public Policy Towards Corporate Takeovers*, ed. by Murray Weidenbaum and Kenneth Chilton (New Brunswick, N.J.: Transaction, 1987), pp. 42–62.

11. See Mark L. Mitchell and Kenneth Lehn, "Do Bad Bidders Become Good Targets?" *Journal of Political Economy*, vol. 98, no. 2 (April 1990), pp. 372–398.

12. More accurately, stock prices tend to reflect the discounted present value of the stream of profits the corporation is expected to generate.

13. John J. McConnell and Chris J. Muscarella, "Capital Expenditure Decisions and Market Value of the Firm," *Journal of Financial Economics*, vol.14 (1985), pp. 399–422.

14. Hall's study is discussed in Jensen, "Eclipse of the Public Corporation."

15. Others have explained the advantages of moving toward smaller and more focused firms in terms of more efficient capital markets, which have made it attractive for firms to substitute reliance on external capital markets for reliance on internal capital markets, which favored multidivision firms. See Amar Bhide,, "Reversing Corporate Diversification," *Journal of Applied Corporate Finance*, vol. 3 (Summer 1990), pp. 70–81.

16. See Sanjai Bhagat, Andrei Shleifer, and Robert W. Vishny, "Hostile Takeovers in the 1980s: The Return to Corporate Specialization," pp. 1–72 in Martin N. Bailey and Clifford Winston (eds.), *Brookings Papers on Economic Activity* (Washington, D.C.: Brookings Institution, 1990).

17. Recall that, unless otherwise indicated, the studies cited are discussed in Jarrell, Brickley, and Netter, "The Market for Corporate Control."

18. Michael C. Jensen and Richard S. Ruback, "The Market for Corporate Control: The Scientific Evidence," *Journal of Financial Economics*, vol. 11 (1983), pp. 5–50; and Wayne H. Mikkelson and Richard S. Ruback, "An Empirical Analysis of the Interfirm Equity Investment Process," *Journal of Financial Economics*, vol. 14 (1985), pp. 523–553.

19. Paul H. Malatesta and Ralph A. Walkling, "Poison Pill Securities: Stockholder Wealth, Profitability, and Ownership Structure," *Journal of Financial Economics*, vol. 20 (1988), pp. 347–376.

20. Michael Ryngaert and Jeffrey Netter, "Shareholder Wealth Effects of the Ohio Antitakeover Law," *Journal of Law, Economics, and Organization*, vol. 4 (1988), pp. 373–383.

21. In the absence of some form of handsome severance pay package, managers may be inclined to take too little risk, or less risk than the stockholders may want them to take. The stockholders can have diversified portfolios of stocks and companies over which they can spread their risks. Managers, on the other hand, can have a fairly narrowly invested portfolio, given that their talent, one of their biggest investments, is typically invested in one firm. Without some incentive to do otherwise, managers may be inclined to protect their investments by investing their firm assets in safe ventures.

22. For a more detailed discussion of golden parachutes, see Jensen, "The Market for Corporate Control."

Chapter 13

1. See Robert Lichter, Linda Lichter, and Stanley Rothman, *Watching America* (New York: Prentice Hall, 1990), p. 146.

2. The general problem of "lemons" is discussed by George A. Akerlof, "The Market for Lemons: Qualitative Uncertainty and the Market Mechanism," *Quarterly Journal of Economics*, Vol. 84 (1970), pp. 488–500.

3. A number of years ago, one of the major pantyhose companies hired the famous football player Joe Namath to advertise its pantyhose by claiming that they were his favorite brand. This was surely not done to convince the public that Joe Namath actually wore a particular brand of pantyhose, or any pantyhose for that matter. A more plausible explanation is that the company wanted an advertisement that would get the public's attention and let people know that they were making enough money in the pantyhose business to hire Joe Namath, who was a very expensive spokesman at the time.

4. When Intel developed its 286 microprocessor in the late 1970s, it gave up its monopoly by licensing other firms to produce it, as discussed by Adam M. Brandenburger and Barry J. Nalebuff, *Co-opetition* (New York: Currency/Doubleday, 1996), pp. 105–106.

5. This warranty problem is similar to the lemon problem discussed earlier in this chapter, but in this case it is the buyers who are supplying the lemons in the form of their behavior.

Chapter 14

1. See Leonard Reed, "I Pencil," *The Freeman*, December 1958, pp. 32–37.

2. Al Dunlap and Bob Andelman, *Mean Business: How I Save Bad Companies and Make Good Companies Great* (New York: Times Books, 1996), p. 55.

3. For example, a firm that has the equipment necessary to produce one type of electrical appliance may find that this equipment can be fully utilized if it is used to produce other types of electrical appliances as well.

4. Historically, automobile manufacturers did produce quite a lot of their parts in-house for reasons that will be explained later in this chapter. But the trend has been to rely more on outside suppliers, with the lowest cost manufacturers leading this trend. For example, Chrysler, the lowest-cost American producer, was producing only 30 percent of its parts in-house in the mid-1990s, versus 50 percent for Ford (the second lowest-cost American producer) and 70 percent for General Motors. Toyota produces only 25 percent of its parts in-house. See John A. Byrne, "Has Outsourcing Gone Too Far?" *Business Week*, April 1, 1996, p. 27.

5. In general, N people can pair off in $[(N-1) \times N]/2$ different ways. So ten people can pair off in $[9 \times 10]/2 = 45$ different ways. The difference between the number of people (number of contracts required in an employment relationship) and

the number of pairs of people (the number of contracts that could be required otherwise) increases as the number of people increases. For example, with 100 people, the number of possible pairs is 4,950. And the number of separate contracts could be larger than the number of pairs of people if they also grouped into teams with different teams having to negotiate with one another.

6. Similarly, a firm that invests in a facility that, because of its location, is dependent on a particular supplier for an important input may find that the supplier demands a higher price than was agreed upon after the facility is built.

7. Quasi-rents are the differences between the return needed for an investment in specialized equipment to be made and the return needed to operate the specialized equipment once the investment in it has been made. The pipeline example in the following discussion will clarify this concept and explain its importance. Also, see Benjamin Klein, Robert Crawford, and Armen Alchian, "Vertical Integration, Appropriable Rents, and the Competitive Contracting Process," *Journal of Law and Economics* (October 1978), pp. 297–326.

8. Technically, this assumes that the pipeline will last forever. While this assumption is obviously wrong, it doesn't alter the cost figure much, if the pipeline lasts a long time. The assumption helps us simplify the example without distorting the main point.

9. The 10 percent interest rate is assumed to be an investor's opportunity cost of capital investment. So any return greater than 10 percent is sufficient to make an investment attractive. It is assumed that the annual $25 million for maintaining and operating the pipeline includes all opportunity costs (if the payments to compensate the investor for maintenance and operation costs are made as these costs are incurred, then the costs for these items are not affected by the interest rate).

10. Economists refer to this as capturing all the quasi-rents from the investment. To elaborate on what we have already said about quasi-rents, rent is any amount in excess of what it takes to motivate the supply of a good or service before any investment has been made. In the case of the pipeline, anything in addition to $125 million a year is rent. On the other hand, a quasi-rent is any amount in excess of what it takes to motivate the supply of a good or service after the required investment is made. In the pipeline example, anything in excess of $25 million a year is quasi-rent. So once the investor has committed to the pipeline, any offer over $25 million a year will motivate the supply of pipeline service and allow the generating plant to capture almost all of the quasi-rent.

11. The following discussion of the relationship between General Motors and Fisher Body is taken from Klein, Crawford, and Alchian, "Vertical Integration, Appropriable Rents, and the Competitive Contracting Process."

12. For a detailed discussion of the mine-mouth arrangements, see Paul Joskow, "Vertical Integration and Long-Term Contracts: The Case of Coal-Burning Electric Generating Plants," *Journal of Law, Economics, and Organization* (Spring 1985), pp. 33–80.

13. The Ford example is discussed on pages 245–246 of Robert Cooter and Thomas Ulen, *Law and Economics* (Glenview, Ill.: Scott, Foresman, 1988). Also, Alex Taylor III ("The Auto Industry Meets the New Economy," *Fortune*, Septem-

ber 5, 1994, pp. 52–60) discusses this strategy by automobile companies as a way of reducing the number of suppliers they depend on (therefore reducing transactions cost) without increasing their vulnerability to hold-up. On p. 54 he states, "Even now some manufacturers pay for the suppliers' equipment so if production falters, they can yank out the machinery and install it in someone else's factory." These arrangements also have advantages from the small contracting companies' perspective, since they provide a signal to the auto companies that the contractors will play straight with them. The advantage of a business's being able to commit itself to honest dealing was discussed in chapter 13.

14. The lyrics of which went, ". . . sixteen tons and what do you get? Another day older and deeper in debt. Saint Peter, don't you call me cause I can't go. I owe my soul to the company store."

15. For a relevant discussion of company towns set up by coal mining firms, see Price V. Fishback, *Soft Coal, Hard Choices: The Economic Welfare of Bituminous Coal Miners, 1890–1930* (New York: Oxford University Press, 1992), esp. chapters 8 and 9.

16. This argument is evident in Donald N. Thompson, *Franchise Operations and Antitrust* (Lexington, Mass.: D. C. Heath, 1971).

17. Paul H. Rubin, "The Theory of the Firm and the Structure of the Franchise Contract," *Journal of Law and Economics*, vol. 21 (1978), pp. 223–233.

18. Rubin, "The Theory of the Firm and the Structure of the Franchise Contract," p. 254. For a review of legal opinion on the so-called tie-in sales of franchise relationships, see Benjamin Klein and Lester F. Saft, "The Law and Economics of Franchise Tying Contracts," *Journal of Law and Economics*, vol. 28 (May 1985), pp. 345–361.

19. G. Frank Mathewson and Ralph A. Winter, "The Economics of Franchise Contracts," *Journal of Law and Economics*, vol. 28 (October 1985), p. 504.

20. See James A. Brickley and Frederick H. Dark, "The Choice of Organizational Forms: The Case of Franchising," *Journal of Financial Economics*, vol. 18 (1987), pp. 401–420.

21. Unfortunately, the only available study on the relationship between the extent of repeat business and the likelihood of franchising (Brickley and Dark, "The Choice of Organizational Forms: The Case of Franchising") does not confirm the theory. These researchers investigated how outlets located near freeways affected the likelihood that they would be franchised. They assumed that locations near freeways would have limited repeat business. Hence, they expected that locations near freeways would tend to be company owned, but they found the exact opposite: outlets near freeways tended to be franchised. The inconsistency between the findings and the prediction could be explained by the fact that the theory is missing something. However, it could also be, as the researchers speculate, that the problem is their measure of repeat business; locations near freeways may get a lot of repeat business.

22. It should be pointed out that even when managers within the firm control resources, this control cannot be exercised independent of market forces, at least

not for long. Unless the firm is using its productive resources to produce goods and services that pass the market test, it will soon be forced into bankruptcy and have to relinquish those resources to more efficient firms.

Chapter 15

1. Haig R. Nalbantian and Andrew Schotter, "Productivity Under Group Incentives: An Experimental Study," *American Economic Review*, vol. 87, no. 3 (June 1997), pp. 314–341.

2. Ibid., p. 335, Fig. 11.

3. Robert Gibbons and Kevin J. Murphy, "Optimal Incentive Contracts in the Presence of Career Concerns: Theory and Evidence," *Journal of Political Economy*, vol. 100, no. 3 (June 1992), pp. 468–506.

4. David N. Laband and Bernard F. Lentz, "Entrepreneurial Success and Occupational Inheritance Among Proprietors," *Canadian Journal of Economics*, vol. 23, no. 3 (August 1990), pp. 101–117.

5. William Davidow and Michael Malone, *The Virtual Corporation*, (New York: HarperCollins, 1992), p. 234.

6. Gibbons and Murphy, "Optimal Incentive Contracts in the Presence of Career Concerns."

7. For an interesting discussion of the *keiretsu*, see Clyde V. Prestowitz Jr., *Trading Places: How We Allowed Japan to Take the Lead* (New York: Basic Books, 1988), pp. 156–166.

8. As Clyde Prestowitz notes, "Thus the *Keiretsu* system reduces risks for the Nippon Electric Company and the other Japanese companies through the accumulation of relationships that can be counted upon to cushion shock in time and trouble" (ibid., p. 164).

9. This explanation for long-term contracting has been argued at length by Ronald P. Dore, *Taking Japan Seriously* (Stanford, Calif.: Stanford University Press, 1987).

10. Ibid., p. 188.

11. Ibid.

12. As reported in Toshihiro Nishiguchi and Masayoshi Ikeda, "Suppliers' Process Innovation: Understated Aspects of Japanese Industrial Sourcing," in *Managing Product Development*, ed. Toshihiro Nishiguchi (New York: Oxford University Press, 1996), pp. 206–230.

13. As reported in Lisa H. Harrington, "Buying Better," *Industry Week*, July 21, 1997, pp. 74–80.

14. Ibid.

15. See Toshihiro Nishiguchi, *Strategic Industrial Sourcing: The Japanese Advantage* (New York: Oxford University Press, 1994), chap. 2.

16. As reported with citations to other sources by Nishiguchi, *Strategic Industrial Sourcing*, pp. 5–6.

Chapter 16

1. As reported by David Friedman, *Hidden Order: The Economics of Everyday Life* (New York: Harper Business, 1996), p. 134.

2. By simply assuming that only 10,000 copies of the book are sold, we are ignoring the fact that the number of copies that maximizes profits generally increases when different prices are being charged for the same product. Here we are interested only in pointing out that such price discrimination increases the total revenue received for any given level of sales.

3. It should be noted that some economists have argued that the high price for snacks at the movie theaters reflect the higher cost of supplying them in movie theaters compared to food stores. Unlike food stores, the snack shop in a movie theater is open for a limited amount of time during the day. So, as the argument goes, the overhead cost is spread over less time and fewer sales. For an elaboration of this argument, see John R. Lott Jr. and Russell D. Roberts, "A Guide to the Pitfalls of Identifying Price Discrimination," *Economic Inquiry*, vol. 29, no. 1 (January 1991), pp. 14–23. We do not quarrel with this reasoning, but we also believe that creative price discrimination provides at least part of the explanation for the high price of movie snacks.

4. Determining the exact combination of prices that maximizes profits depends on the relative differences in demand for the two types of customers. If, for example, the avid movie fans were willing to pay a tremendously high price to see the movie and snackers couldn't care less about the movie but went into frenzies of delight at the mere thought of a Snickers bar, then the best pricing policy would be an extremely high ticket price with extremely low-priced (maybe free) snacks. In this case the theater owner would probably stipulate that snack customers would have to eat the snacks in the theater to prevent them from filling large sacks with popcorn and candy bars. This would be no different from the policy of all-you-can-eat restaurants.

5. It was cheaper to make the 486DX and then reduce its quality than it was to produce the lower quality 486SX directly. This, the following example, and several other examples in which firms intentionally reduced the quality of their products are found in Raymond J. Deneckere and R. Preston McAfee, "Damaged Goods," *Journal of Economics and Management Strategy*, vol. 5, no. 2 (Summer 1996), pp. 149–174.

6. John J. Keller, "Best Phone Discounts Go to Hardest Bargainers," *Wall Street Journal*, February 13, 1997, pp. B-1 and B-12.

7. Ibid., p. B1.

8. As opposed to what many may think, the higher profits from creative pricing do not necessarily come at the expense of consumers. In the situation just described, consumers are also better off to the extent that they value each of the additional 12,000 batteries more than the price they pay for them.

9. Our discussion of meet-the-competition pricing is based on chapter 6 of Barry J. Nalebuff and Adam M. Brandenburger, *Co-opetition* (London: Harper-Collins Business, 1996). Our subsequent discussion of most-favored-customer

policies and preferred customer discounts also draw heavily from Nalebuff and Brandenburger's excellent book.

10. Ibid., pp. 164–165.

11. Even when a person is a member of more than one frequent-flyer program, there is an advantage in concentrating patronage on one airline, since the programs are designed to increase benefits more than proportionally with accumulated mileage.

12. You may be thinking that keeping the explicit fares higher does not mean much if, because of the frequent-flyer programs, the actual fares to customers are lower because of the value of their mileage awards. But one of the big advantages of frequent-flyer programs is that they do not cost the airlines as much as they benefit the customer. Flights are seldom completely sold out, so most of the free flights awarded end up filling seats would have remained unsold. Of course, frequent flyers do use their mileage for flights they would have otherwise paid for. But by allowing frequent flyers to transfer their mileage awards to others, say, a spouse or child, the airlines increase the probability that those who would not have otherwise bought a ticket will use those awards.

13. Another way of seeing the advantage of segmenting the market is by recognizing that reducing the elasticity of demand facing each airline also reduces the marginal revenue of each airline and brings it more in line with the marginal revenue for the industry. The closer each firm's marginal revenue is to the industry's marginal revenue, the closer the independent pricing decisions of each firm in the industry will come to maximizing their collective profits.

Chapter 17

1. See Steve Stecklow, "Evangelical Schools Reinvent Themselves by Stressing Academics," *The Wall Street Journal*, May 12, 1994, p. A1.

2. Ibid. We want to emphasize that our concern here is not whether spanking is the best or even a good way of disciplining children. The point is that many schools can attract business with practices that each of their customers would find objectionable if applied only to their children but that they appreciate when applied to all students.

3. We don't want to overemphasize the difference between the costs of providing a package of extras (or frills) at expensive hotels and the value of those extras to guests. Because of competition, hotels are strongly motivated to provide those extras that, for any given cost, provide as much real value to their guests as possible. But this is consistent with a hotel's being able to realize a competitive advantage by increasing the supply of extras into the range where the extras themselves are worth less to the guests than they are paying for them because of the screening benefit provided by the extra charge.

4. Louis Lee, "Without a Receipt You May Get Stuck with That Ugly Scarf," *Wall Street Journal*, November 18, 1996, p. A-1.

5. Ibid.

Chapter 18

1. Dunlap and Bob Andelman, *Mean Business: How I Save Bad Companies and Make Good Companies Great* (New York: Times Books, 1996).

2. Milton Friedman, "The Social Responsibility of Business Is to Increase Its Profits," *New York Times Magazine*, September 13, 1970.

3. Dunlap and Andelman, *Mean Business*, p. 198.

4. Ibid., p. 199.

5. Robert B. Reich, "Pink Slips, Profits, and Paychecks: Corporate Citizenship in an Era of Smaller Government," talk given at George Washington University School of Business and Public Management (Washington, D.C., February 17, 1996), p. 2.

6. As quoted by Reich, ibid.

7. Ibid.

8. There is clear evidence that, up to some point, corporate giving enhances profits. See K. E. Aupperle, A. B. Carroll, and J. D. Hatfield, "An Empirical Examination of the Relationship Between Corporate Social Responsibility and Profitability," *Academy of Management Journal*, vol. 28, no. 2 (1985), pp. 446–463.

9. Dunlap and Andelman, *Mean Business*, p. 201.

10. Ross Johnson, former CEO of RJR Nabisco, is a commonly used example of a spendthrift corporate manager. Johnson was particularly fond of hosting sporting events featuring celebrity entertainers and athletes and did so at a cost that far exceeded what could be justified as increasing corporate profits. Johnson once expressed admiration for the person in charge of "entertainment and extravaganzas" for being "the only man who can take an unlimited budget and exceed it." See Bryan Burrough and John Helyar, *Barbarians at the Gate: The Fall of RJR Nabisco* (New York: HarperCollins, 1991), p. 25.

11. Milton Friedman, *Capitalism and Freedom* (Chicago: University of Chicago Press, 1962), p. 191.

12. Dunlap and Andelman, *Mean Business*, p. 200.

13. "Investing in Niceness," *The Economist*, August 31, 1996, p. 69.

Chapter 19

1. Accordingly, the degree of protection tenure affords is a function of such variables as the inflation rate. That is, the higher the inflation rate, the more quickly the real value of the professor's salary will erode each time a raise is denied.

2. Granted, tenure may be required by accrediting associations. However, there is no reason that groups of universities could not operate outside accrediting associations or organize their own accrediting associations without the tenure provision–if tenure were, on balance, a significant impairment to academic goals. In many respects, the accrediting association rules can be defended on the same competitive grounds that recruiting rules of the National Collegiate Athletic Association are defended. See Richard B. McKenzie and T. Sullivan, "The NCAA as a

Cartel: An Economic and Legal Reinterpretation," *Antitrust Bulletin*, no. 3 (1987), pp. 373–399.

3. Of course, not all academic environments share the same goals or face the same constraints. Some universities view pushing back the frontiers of knowledge as central to their mission, while others are intent on transmitting the received and accepted wisdom of the times, if not the ages. Some universities are concerned mainly with promoting the pursuit of usable (private goods) knowledge, that which has a reasonable probability of being turned into salable products, while other universities are interested in promoting research the benefits of which are truly public, if any value at all can be ascertained.

4. H. L. Carmichael, "Incentives in Academics: Why Is There Tenure?" *Journal of Political Economy*, vol. 96, no. 2 (1988), pp. 453–472.

5. "Loosely, tenure is necessary," Carmichael concludes, "because without it incumbents would never be willing to hire people who turn out to be better than themselves" (ibid., 1988, p. 454).

6. Richard B. McKenzie, "The Economic Basis of Departmental Discord in Academe," *Social Science Quarterly*, no. 1 (1979), pp. 653–664.

7. As Gary Miller has shown, the benefits of "corporate organization" eventually break down when the parties follow completely rational, individualistic precepts. See Gary J. Miller, *Managerial Dilemmas: The Political Economy of Hierarchy* (New York: Cambridge University Press, 1992).

8. After tenure is awarded, faculty efforts should be expected to decline, while, at the same time, pay rises. In the midst of the tournament, the new faculty members will exert unduly high amounts of effort, because of the prospect of being rewarded in the future by higher pay and greater job security. Also, the rise in compensation and the fall in effort that accompany tenure may correlate with the fact that the added money makes it possible for faculty members to buy more of most things, including great leisure (or leisure-time activities). If we did not expect new faculty members to anticipate relaxing somewhat after attaining tenure and enjoy, being, to a degree, "overpaid," we could not expect the tenure tournament to be effective as a means to an end, which is disclosure of the limits of new faculty members' true abilities.

Chapter 20

1. Alfie Kohn, *Punished by Rewards: The Trouble with Gold Stars, Incentive Plans, A's, Praise, and Other Bribes* (Boston: Houghton Mifflin Co., 1993).

2. However, we stress that Kohn is hardly the only critic, though perhaps the most articulate. For a sample of the way the criticisms have been made in a more academic manner, see Jone L. Pearce,"Why Merit Pay Doesn't Work: Implications for Organization Theory," *New Perspectives on Compensation*, ed. D. B. Balkin and L. R. Gomez-Mejia (Englewood Cliffs, N.J.: Prentice-Hall, 1987), pp. 169–178.

3. Kohn, *Punished by Rewards*, p. 119.

4. Ibid., p. 182.

5. Ibid.

6. Ibid., p. 189. Other critics have been more harsh in their objections to incentives than Kohn. For example, one critic who echos Kohn's view caustically concludes, "One reason these [management] buzzword methodologies [including pay for performance] are attractive is the erroneous belief that human behavior is solely driven by a stimulus-response impulse. . . . The myth of pay for performance or merit pay, a concept that has been around since the turn of the century is that you can use extrinsic rewards to incent employees to change their behavior to achieve outcomes described by management. This is based upon the direct translation of Pavlov's and Skinner's success with animals. What we know is that human motivation is in large part intrinsic. The Hawthorne effect, which essentially revealed that you could improve productivity simply by changing the illumination level in the factory, is a notable example but dispels the common belief about human motivation being based solely on extrinsic 'rewards' " (Steve Barbar, "The Fad Phenomenon" [newsletter] [Granite Bay, Calif.: Barber and Gonzales Consulting Group, August 1, 1997], pp. 2, 3). We would be the last to claim that extrinsic incentives are all that matter, and we have made that point time and again throughout the book.

7. Kohn, *Punished by Rewards*, p. 26.

8. Ibid., p. 37.

9. Ibid.

10. Ibid.

11. Ibid.

12. Ibid., p. 45.

13. Ibid., p. 46.

14. Kohn relies extensively on Edward L. Deci ("Effects of Externally Mediated Rewards on Intrinsic Motivation," *Journal of Personality and Social Psychology*, vol. 18 [1971]:105–15) for his conclusion that paying people to perform a task reduces their intrinsic motivation to perform. But when you read Kohn's footnote (footnote 4, page 298, referring back to his discussion on p. 70), he concedes that Deci's experiment provided only weak support for the conclusion. Indeed, Deci concedes that while a reward *often* decreases intrinsic motivation, it *sometimes* increases it.

15. Kohn, *Punished by Rewards*, p. 78.

16. Ibid., p. 83.

17. Ibid., p. 131.

18. Ibid., p. 131.

19. Ibid., p. 190.

20. Ibid., p. 55.

21. Ibid., p. 54.

22. See, for example, two collections of work in experimental economics, by Vernon L. Smith, *Papers in Experimental Economics* (New York: Cambridge University Press, 1991), and by John H. Kagel and Alvin E. Roth, *Handbook of Experimental Economics* (Princeton, N.J.: Princeton University Press, 1995). See also Vernon Smith, "An Experimental Study of Competitive Market Behavior," *Journal of Polit-*

ical Economy, vol. 70 (April 1962), pp. 111–137; Raymond C. Battalio, "A Test of Consumer Demand Theory Using Observation of Individual Consumer Purchases," *Western Economic Journal*, vol. 11 (December 1973), pp. 411–428; and David G. Tarr, "Experiments in Token Economies: A Review of the Evidence Relating to Assumptions and Implications of Economic Theory," *Southern Economic Journal*, vol. 43 (October 1976), pp. 136–143.

23. Kohn, *Punished by Rewards*, p. 182.
24. Ibid., p. 45.
25. Ibid., p. 193.
26. Ibid., p. 54.
27. Ibid., p. 55.

Index